# Essential
# **Business**
# **Vocabulary**
# **Builder**

Macmillan Education Limited
4 Crinan Street
London N1 9XW

Companies and representatives throughout the world

ISBN 978-0-230-40760-2

First published 2011

Designed by Carolyn Gibson
Cover design by Macmillan

Author's acknowledgements
The author would like to thank Darina Richter for commissioning the book, Karen Spiller for project
management, content editing, and numerous creative contributions on the design side, and
Deborah Manning for proof reading.

Thanks yet again to Marna Warner for transcribing the original interviews on which the listening scripts are
based. Many students at International House, London gave up their time to be interviewed for the listening
material, and I would like to thank in particular Antonella Di Biasi, Bulent Ersoz, Celine Perez, Ilaria Romano,
Massimo Grandi, Miki Hirai, Murat Ozot, Shahrokh Amiri, Shan Shan Liu, Tania Meija, Tomas Leisztinger and
Yasuhisa Takanashi.

In addition I would like to thank Ian McMaster and Bob Dignen for their permission to use some ideas from a
'Business Spotlight' article on conference calls, and Ken Taylor for his permission to use a few ideas from '50
ways to improve your Telephoning and Teleconferencing Skills'.

Printed and bound in Poland by CGS

2025   2024   2023   2022   2021
21   20   19   18   17   16   15   14   13

# Essential

Paul Emmerson

# Business
# Vocabulary
# Builder

## Pre-intermediate to Intermediate

*The words & phrases you need to succeed*

MACMILLAN

# Contents

# 1 Company types and structures

## Types of company

Here is a simplified list of the different types of legal structures for a business.

- *Sole trader* (BrE)/*Sole proprietor* (AmE). This is a one-person business. The person may describe themselves as 'self-employed' (eg the owner of a small shop), or as a 'freelancer' if they are a professional who works for different clients (eg a photographer).
- *Partnership*. A group of people who work together as equals (eg a firm of lawyers or architects). They share the risks and the profits.
- *Private company*. The shares of the company are privately owned, usually by a small number of people. These shareholders typically include the founder of the company, possibly some close family members, and perhaps a few business associates who provided money for the company.
- *Public company* (BrE)/*Corporation* (AmE). These are the large companies that are listed on stock exchanges like Germany's DAX, France's CAC or the UK's FTSE. They are called public because anyone can buy their shares. Note: do not confuse a state-owned enterprise with a public company.

## Departments

The list of departments below is typical for many business – each one corresponds to a business function. Companies also have other departments related to their own particular business activity.

- *Production* might also include *Purchasing* and *Quality Assurance (QA)*.
- *Operations* refers to all the internal processes of a company and might include, for example, *Logistics*.
- *Sales* might also include *Business Development*.
- *Customer Services* might include *Technical Support*.
- *Marketing* might include *Market Research*.
- *Communications* refers to all promotional activities including a strong focus on *Public Relations (PR)*.
- *Finance* has many subdivisions, such as *Financial Control*, *Treasury*, *Accounts* and *Payroll* (= managing salary payments).
- *Human Resources* (HR).
- *Information Technology* (IT).
- *Research and Development* (R&D).
- *Legal*.

As well as departments, an international company may also have divisions organized according to geographical area or major product lines.

## Individuals within the structure

The Chief Executive Officer (CEO) runs the company. The level below CEO is Chief … Officer, for example Chief Financial Officer (CFO).
*The CFO is part of the senior management team.*
*The CFO reports to the CEO* (= has the CEO as their boss).
*The CFO is in charge of* (= responsible for) *all the financial side of the business.*

The next level down might be country level for a large international organization, or departmental level. A job title here might be Sales Director or Head of Sales or VP (= Vice President) Sales.
*The Sales Director for Sweden liaises closely with* (= talks to in order to work better with) *the Chief Marketing Officer at Head Office in the States.*

Below this are people with job titles like *Manager, Officer, Coordinator*, etc. The words *Assistant* or *Deputy* may also occur at any level.
*I'm the Business Development Officer for Sweden.*
*My line manager* (= person directly above me/person who I report to) *is the Sales Director.*
*The Sales Director delegates* (= gives) *a lot of the work to me.*

We say …
*senior people at a higher level*
*junior people at a lower level*

## Company culture

The structure of a company is often closely connected to its culture. In a small company it's easier to be dynamic and innovative, whereas in a large company things are often slow-moving and bureaucratic.

Similarly, if the company is hierarchical (many levels), then people at the bottom aren't allowed to take initiatives without permission from their seniors; decision-making and communication are top-down. If the structure is flat (few levels), then the flow of information can be more bottom-up.

In all cases you hope that the company culture is honest, open and transparent (= not trying to keep things secret).

1 Read the text for general understanding.
2 Read it again and underline the words you don't know. Check their meaning.

3 Highlight words you know passively, but don't use actively. Choose some to write sentences of your own.
4 Check pronunciation at macmillandictionary.com

# Exercises

**1.1 Underline the correct word in italics.**

1 My brother is a plumber. He's *autonomous /* _self-employed_.

2 The people who own a private company might include the founder of the company, some family members, and perhaps a few business *associates / companions*.

3 In a public company anybody can buy the *actions / shares*.

4 A public company is *listed / posted* on a stock exchange.

5 Our railways were recently privatized. I think the service was better before, when they were a *public company / state-owned enterprise*.

6 The Purchasing Department is responsible for *buying parts and raw materials / making the final product*.

7 If you have a complaint, please contact *Consumer Services / Customer Services*.

8 All recruitment and selection is done by our *Human Relations / Human Resources* Department.

9 Innovation is the key to our success and we have recently expanded the *Research and Design / Research and Development* Department.

10 In the Legal Department we have three *lawyers / advocates* trained in commercial law.

11 It's the CEO's job to *control / run* the company.

12 Our Business Development Officer is *responsible for / the responsible for* finding new business opportunities.

13 I can't take that decision. It will have to be referred to *higher people / more senior people*.

14 That decision will have to be taken at *a higher level / a more superior level*.

15 In the department there are six Sales Representatives and their *line director / line manager*.

16 The Sales Department has to *liaise / liaison* closely with Marketing.

17 She *is part of / makes part of* a team of designers.

18 I am the Financial Controller, and I *relate directly / report directly* to the Finance Director.

**1.2 Complete each sentence with a verb from the box.**

| | | |
|---|---|---|
| answers | arranges | ~~checks~~ |
| collects | deals | maintains |

1 The Quality Assurance Section _____*checks*_____ that the products have no defects.

2 The Logistics Department _____ the transport of goods and materials.

3 Technical Support _____ specific questions from customers about how to use the product.

4 The Market Research Section _____ and analyzes information about the needs of consumers.

5 The Accounts Department _____ with invoices and payments.

6 The IT Department _____ the computer network.

**1.3 Complete the text about operations with the words and phrases in the box.**

| | | |
|---|---|---|
| back-office functions | | behind the scenes |
| day-to-day basis | liaise closely | makes a profit |
| meet their needs | recruit | step on anyone's toes |

Everyone knows the functions of company departments such as Marketing and Finance. Marketing is about promoting the company, and making sure that customers can find products that [1]_____. Finance is about controlling the resources of a company to make sure that the business [2]_____ .

But what about Operations? The department name is less well-known, yet many large companies are run on a [3]_____ by Operations Managers. Operations is about the internal processes of a company. In a manufacturing company an Operations Manager will make sure the production process is running smoothly. In a hotel they are responsible for bookings, front desk, maintenance, etc. In a bank they look after the administration of accounts and other [4]_____ .

Operations Managers have to [5]_____ with people from other departments. In the factory, it is with Purchasing Managers who buy the raw materials. In the hotel, it is with Human Resources Managers who [6]_____ new staff. In the bank it is with IT Managers who work [7]_____ to keep everything running. So the Operations Manager has to be careful not to [8]_____ .

**1.4 Read what Pieter says about company culture at his previous company and his current company. The text has eight wrong words. Find them and correct them.**

66 In my last job I worked for a large telecommunications company. It used to be the estate-owned monopoly, but they privatized it in the nineties. Unfortunately, the cultural there hasn't really changed. Decision-making is very slow-moving and bureaucracy – everything has to be agreed all the way up the chain before action can be taken.

I didn't really like working there, and I moved to a smaller competitor two years ago. It's much better now – I have more responsible because my boss trusts me and he relegates a lot of interesting projects to me. Everybody knows what is going on and can make a contribution – communication works well in both directions, both bottom-down and top-up. It's a dynamic, innovation company and we're growing fast. I hope to continue working here for several more years. 99

**See page 146 for some discussion topics.**

# 2 Start-up and growth

## Planning

An entrepreneur sees a gap in the market and wants to found (= start) a new company. First some planning is necessary. The entrepreneur has to:

- Do market research and develop the product.
- Think about pricing, distribution channels, and promotion.
- Raise capital ( = money used to start or invest in a business).

The capital might come from the founder's own funds, loans from the bank, or money invested by other people/business partners.

## Start-up

The founder is now ready to set up (= start) the business. The first steps are to rent premises (= the buildings that a company uses), purchase equipment and supplies, and employ and train staff. The company can now begin its operations.

One thing is certain: the first few years will be difficult. Sometimes a start-up company can get help from venture capital (= money invested in a new business by a specialist company who work in high-growth areas like new technology). VC money is used to run the business, pay salaries, etc in the early years. In exchange the VC company will take part ownership of the company and hope to sell it later for a large profit.

## Growth

In a successful business the number of customers grows, turnover increases, and eventually the company breaks even and then makes a profit. The company employs more staff and divides them into different functions: operations, sales, marketing, accounts, etc. The company develops a network of suppliers. The brand name starts to become well-known among customers.

What happens if the business needs to raise additional capital to expand its operations? There are various options.

- The company can ask the bank for a loan.
- The company can issue new shares and sell them to outside investors.

- The company can attract private equity. Private equity is very similar to venture capital, but it comes at a later stage in the company's growth.

## Maturity

All being well, the company continues to grow. This growth may be organic (through increased sales and developing the product range) or by acquisitions/take-overs (buying other companies).

## Exit strategies

There are various exit strategies available to the owners if they want to sell the company.

- The business can be sold as a going concern (= as an established, profitable business) to other private individuals.
- The business can be sold to a competitor, or to a large foreign company wanting to enter the market. The company that is taken over may or may not keep its brand name.
- The company goes public. This means it is listed on a stock exchange and its shares are sold to individual and institutional investors. The original owners may continue to run the company.

## Risks

The majority of businesses fail (= go out of business). There are many reasons, which include:

- The founder can't get a loan, perhaps because of insufficient collateral (= property you agree to give the bank if you fail to give back the money you borrowed).
- The company can't meet its monthly repayments to the bank.
- The company fails to get enough customers.
- Competition from other companies.
- Changes in the market (demand for the products falls).
- Poor management of cash flow and/or insufficient capital.
- Management problems (eg the founder finds it difficult to delegate work to other people).
- Failure to integrate an acquired business after a take-over.

1 Read the text for general understanding.
2 Read it again and <u>underline</u> the words you don't know. Check their meaning.

3 Highlight words you know passively, but don't use actively. Choose some to write sentences of your own.

4 Check pronunciation at macmillandictionary.com

# Exercises

**2.1 Rearrange the letters to make words. Use the definitions in brackets to help you.**

1 enrtrepeenur ___entrepreneur___
(someone who starts a company and makes business deals)

2 citapal _____
(money used to start or invest in a business)

3 funoder _____
(someone who starts an organization)

4 prmeeiss _____
(the buildings that a company uses)

5 puchrase _____
(*formal* buy something)

6 tunvorer _____
(the money a business makes = revenue)

7 seahrs _____
(the equal parts of a company which people can buy and sell)

8 actisiquion _____
(buying another company; = take-over)

9 cotellaral _____
(property or money that you promise to give the bank if you cannot pay back a debt)

10 damend _____
(the desire or need that customers have for a product)

**2.2 Match an item on the left with an item on the right to make phrases from the text opposite.**

1 start-up          equity
2 exit              name
3 brand             company
4 a going           market
5 private           concern
6 a gap in the      strategy

7 do                a profit
8 employ            capital
9 fail              staff
10 make             some market research
11 raise            to get enough customers
12 rent             premises

**2.3 Complete the sentences with phrases from Exercise 2.2.**

1 The founder of the company is going to retire next year. I think he'll probably sell the business as _____ . But first he needs to _____ to see who might be interested in taking over the business.

2 If the company is going to expand, they will need to _____ . They can either ask the bank, issue new shares, or try to attract _____ .

3 She wants to start her own business and she thinks she can see _____ . She has money of her own, so the first steps are to _____ in a suitable location, purchase equipment and employ staff.

**2.4 Underline the correct word in italics.**

1 The bank *lends you / borrows you* money.
2 You *lend money / borrow money* from the bank.
3 So 'lend' is temporary *giving / taking*.
4 And 'borrow' is temporary *giving / taking*.
5 The bank gives you *a lend / a loan*.

**2.5 Complete the table below.**

| Verb | Noun | |
|---|---|---|
| 1 _____ | development | |
| 2 distribute | _____ | (activity) |
| 3 promote | _____ | (activity) |
| 4 _____ | employment | |
| 5 own | _____ | (activity) |
| 6 grow | | |
| 7 _____ | expansion | |
| 8 compete | _____ | (company) |
| | _____ | (activity) |
| 9 fail | _____ | |
| 10 _____ | acquisition | |

**2.6 Complete sentence b) with one word. The meaning must be the same as sentence a). All the words appear opposite.**

1 a) How are we going to distribute our product?
   b) What distribution ___channels___ are we going to use?

2 a) She was the founder of the business.
   b) She set _____ the business.

3 a) The company is growing strongly.
   b) The company has strong _____ .

4 a) This year the company will make neither a profit nor a loss.
   b) This year the company will break _____ .

5 a) Who supplies them?
   b) Who are their _____ s?

6 a) A lot of people know their brand name.
   b) Their brand name is very well-_____ .

7 a) They're an established business and they make a profit.
   b) They're an established, _____ business.

8 a) The company is going to be listed on the stock exchange.
   b) The company is going to go _____ .

9 a) Why did the business fail?
   b) Why did they go _____ of business?

10 a) Their customers were late in paying them so they couldn't pay their bills.
   b) Their customers were late in paying them so they had cash _____ problems.

**See page 146 for some discussion topics.**

A company profile is a short description of a company. A typical context for a company profile is at the beginning of a presentation.

## Business activity

You usually start a company profile with a general introduction describing your business activity and the sector you operate in (eg financial services, pharmaceuticals). Verbs to describe business activity include: *design, distribute, export, import, make, manufacture, offer, operate, produce, provide, sell, specialize in, supply.*

We **offer** *a wide range of financial services.*
We **provide** *network solutions to the telecom sector.*
We **specialize in** *software for the film industry.*
We **sell** *fashion accessories – our* **main products** *are shoes and bags.*
We're **in the** *hospitality* **business**.

## Location

Here you might talk about your Head Office, the location of your production sites, etc.

We're **based in** *Toulouse. / Our* **Head Office** *is in Toulouse.*
We have **around 20 offices** *all over Europe.*
We have **production sites** *in Romania and Turkey.*
We have **branches** *in Brazil and Mexico.*

## Size / Markets

There are many ways to talk about the size of a company. You can talk about your market, the number of employees, or use a financial indicator such as sales (= turnover/revenue) or profit.

We *only operate in our* **domestic market**.
We're *an international company with* **operations** *in over 40 countries.*
Our **main markets** *are India and the Middle East.*
We're the **market leader**. / We're **second in the market**.
We have a **market share** *of around 25%.*
Our **main competitors** *are AstraZeneca and Pfizer.*
We **employ** *200 people. / We have 200* **employees**.
Our **annual turnover** *is around €40 million.*
Our **operating profit** *last year was €15 million.*
You *can find more information about our* **financial performance** *by looking at* **the Investor relations section** *of our website.*

A company may look small but be part of a larger group with a completely different name.

We're *part of the MediaWorld* **group of companies**.
We *are a* **subsidiary** *of MediaWorld.*
Our **parent company** *is MediaWorld.*
The *company has three* **divisions**.

## History

The history of a company includes its milestones (= events or achievements that mark important stages in its development). Verbs that are typically used to describe a company history include: *be founded, begin, buy, be bought, concentrate on, decide to, develop, diversify, expand, grow, launch, merge, move to, move into, open, purchase, stop, start.*

The company **was set up / established / founded** *in 1998 by my father.*
We **moved** *our Head Office* **to** *Stuttgart.*
We **bought / acquired / took over** *a small local company.*
We **were bought / were acquired / were taken over** *by an American company.*
We **merged** *with a Dutch company two months ago.*
An *important* **milestone** *was when sales passed $3 million.*
We *realized we needed to* **diversify**.
Sales **grew rapidly** *in the Benelux region.*
Sales **suffered badly** *when the law changed.*
We **entered / moved into** *the US market.*
The *publishing division* **was sold off**.
Our *UK subsidiary* **was closed down**.
The *company* **was broken up** *into four parts.*
We **opened** *a new factory / plant / production facility.*
The *company recently* **celebrated** *its 50th anniversary.*
A **key factor** *in our success has been our staff.*

## Future

If you are giving a presentation, this is the part that is likely to be the most interesting.

We**'re going to open** *a new office in Indonesia.*
We**'re going to take on** *an additional 30 staff.*
We**'re going to launch** *a new range of clothes aimed at older women.*
We**'re planning to expand** *into South-East Asia.*
We *hope to* **go public** *(= become listed on the stock market) next year.*
Our *aim is to* **be one of the top three** *biotech companies.*

1 Read the text for general understanding.

2 Read it again and <u>underline</u> the words you don't know. Check their meaning.

3 Highlight words you know passively, but don't use actively. Choose some to write sentences of your own.

4 Check pronunciation at macmillandictionary.com

# Exercises

## 3.1 Match the beginnings of sentences 1–8 with their endings a–h.

1 The company was founded    `c`
2 The company was set    ☐
3 The company merged    ☐
4 The company realized it needed    ☐
5 The company decided to concentrate    ☐
6 The company changed its name    ☐
7 The company moved    ☐
8 The company was taken    ☐

a up by three software engineers from Bangalore.
b over by a larger competitor.
c by three software engineers from Bangalore.
d to Informatica Solutions.
e into the Chinese market.
f to diversify.
g with another Indian software developer.
h on IT services.

## 3.2 Write a sentence number from Exercise 3.1 next to its closest meaning below.

1 Some people started the company. _1c_ and ____
2 The company started selling its products in another country. ____
3 The company decided to focus on one thing. ____
4 One company bought another company. ____
5 Two companies combined to form one company. ____
6 The company knew that it had to develop new products and activities. ____

## 3.3 Fill in the missing letters.

1 An event that marks an important stage in a process is called a m_ _ _ _ _one.
2 A company that is owned or controlled by another company is called a su_ _ _ _ _ary.
3 To sound business-like, say 'a k_ _ fac_ _r' instead of 'one of the important things'.

## 3.4 Complete each sentence 1–3 with the correct adverb a–c. You will make three phrasal verbs.

1 The UK subsidiary was sold    a up
2 The UK subsidiary was closed    b off
3 The UK subsidiary was broken    c down

## 3.5 Write a sentence number from Exercise 3.4 next to the best explanation below.

1 The UK subsidiary was losing money. The parent company decided it would be better if it stopped doing business completely. ____
2 The UK subsidiary was profitable, but it didn't fit the plans of the parent company. Another company was interested in the subsidiary and bought it. ____
3 The UK subsidiary was too large. The parent company divided it into several smaller companies, keeping one and selling the others. ____

## 3.6 Read the profile of clothing company H&M and underline the correct word in italics. Not all the words appear opposite.

H&M is a Swedish clothing company in the 'value fashion' [1]*section/sector*. It has clothes [2]*aimed/pointed* at all age groups and both sexes, but it specializes [3]*in/on* clothes for young women. H&M has more than 1,800 stores in 34 different countries and [4]*employs/employees* over 75,000 people. Its [5]*Head Office/Top Office* is in Stockholm, although the [6]*principal/majority* of its clothing is [7]*manufactured/factoried* in Bangladesh, Indonesia, Romania and Turkey.

The company was [8]*established/found* in 1947 and opened its first store [9]*abroad/outside* in the 1960s. Today it has an [10]*intensive/extensive* network of stores throughout Europe, North America, the Middle East and East Asia.

A key factor in H&M's success has been its [11]*collaborations/collaborators* with 'guest designers', including Karl Lagerfeld, Stella McCartney, Viktor & Rolf and Madonna. A recent guest designer was Jimmy Choo, who designed [12]*a range/an arrangement* of products not normally associated with H&M, like men's shoes. H&M also works with pop stars such as Kylie Minogue to promote the [13]*brand/advertising*.

H&M's main [14]*competitors/concurrents* are US-based Gap and Spain's Inditex (owners of the Zara chain). It's difficult to say which company is the biggest as [15]*sales/sells* differ from year to year and from country to country. At the time of writing Zara had the largest worldwide [16]*balance/revenue* and the largest market [17]*part/share*, and so was the market [18]*leader/winner*. Gap was second [19]*in/on* the market and H&M third.

H&M has slightly [20]*below/lower* prices than its competitors. A recent Annual Report described how this was achieved: having few middlemen; buying large volumes; having a broad, in-depth [21]*knowing/knowledge* of design, fashion and textiles; buying the right [22]*produces/products* from the right market; being cost-conscious at every stage; and having [23]*efficient/proficient* distribution.

Like other clothing retailers, these days H&M has to pay a lot of attention to its social responsibility [24]*policy/politics*. It has to make sure that all [25]*employs/employees* have good working conditions, especially in poorer countries, otherwise it risks negative media coverage and [26]*damage/damages* to its brand.

See page 146 for some discussion topics.

# 4 The manufacturing sector

## Manufacturing

A manufacturing company …
- buys/purchases
- raw materials, parts and components from a supplier

It then uses these to …
- make/produce/manufacture
- products/goods
- in an factory/plant/facility
- using machines/machinery/equipment

The Production Manager …
- controls the whole process, for example by making sure that the correct machine tools are used for each batch (= group of items produced at the same time)
- can speed up or slow down the production process
- tries to reduce or eliminate waste
- tries to minimize inventory in order to reduce storage costs

Note that 'inventory' = raw materials + unfinished work + finished work (stock) in the warehouse.

Inside the factory …
- trucks arrive at the loading bays where they unload
- fork-lift trucks carry parts on wooden pallets from the loading bay to the storage area
- parts are taken from the storage area to the individual workstations on the assembly line

Manufacturing has changed a lot. In the old days a company would make the number of products it thought it could sell, then transfer them to a warehouse, waiting for customer orders. However the goods often remained unsold because customers wanted other products – not the ones in the warehouse. And storage costs were very high.

The modern approach is different. It combines 'just-in-time' with 'lean manufacturing'. 'Just-in-time' means that products are made as a response to a customer order. Everything is done only when it is needed and inventory is kept to a minimum. 'Lean manufacturing' means no waste. Waste is not just useless material lying on the factory floor – it is anything that the customer is not willing to pay for. If something extra might add value for the customer, check first that the customer really wants it.

## Production or assembly?

Another big change is that 'production' nowadays almost never means making a complete product in one place. Take the automobile industry as an example. In the 1950s the factory would have parts and raw materials at one end, an assembly line in the middle, and the finished cars at the factory gate. The whole plant would be in the car maker's own country.

Nowadays things are different. Globalization means that production of car parts, components, and sub-assemblies like engines is outsourced (= subcontracted) to factories all over the world. After production, these parts are then shipped to other countries where they are assembled. After assembly, the finished goods are shipped again to their final markets. The question is: what still happens in the car maker's own country? The answer is often this: no production, no assembly, but coordination of the whole process (the global supply chain).

## Quality control or quality assurance?

The phrase 'quality control' emphasizes the testing of products to uncover defects. The phrase 'quality assurance' (QA) is a more modern term, and it means getting things right first time. In other words, making sure that all the processes in the company work as efficiently as possible so that mistakes do not occur in the first place. If they do, then the process itself needs to be changed to avoid the mistake happening again.

A key idea of QA is that a product should be 'fit for purpose'. This means that it should do the job it was designed to do, and do it well. But there is no point having an unnecessarily high quality that would be expensive and difficult to achieve.

We say …
**inspect/check** a product
**find/detect/uncover** a **defect/fault**
**remove** then **replace** a **faulty part**
And note this common word:
*rework (v)* (do work again because of a defect)
*rework (n)* (the work that you do again)

1  Read the text for general understanding.

2  Read it again and <u>underline</u> the words you don't know. Check their meaning.

3  Highlight words you know passively, but don't use actively. Choose some to write sentences of your own.

4  Check pronunciation at macmillandictionary.com

# Exercises

**4.1 Three items in each group are closely connected. Cross out the one item that is different. Check any unknown words in a dictionary.**

1  manufacturer / producer / ~~supplier~~ / maker
2  plant / warehouse / factory / facility
3  equipment / machines / machinery / inventory
4  buying / purchasing / negotiating / procurement
5  waste / sub-assemblies / parts / components
6  defects / rework / faults / mistakes
7  200 pieces / 200 items / 200 units / 200 batches
8  produce / assemble / build / put together
9  supplies / products / goods / merchandise
10 subcontract / use an outside company / distribute / outsource
11 inspect / examine / check / control
12 find / replace / detect / discover

**4.2 Use an item that you crossed out in Exercise 4.1 to complete the sentences below.**

1  The parts arrived late and the quality is not as good as it used to be. We should look for a new _____*supplier*_____ .
2  We have reduced storage costs by keeping _____ to a minimum.
3  The company is not profitable. We need to try to eliminate _____ in the organization wherever we find it. I'm talking about raw materials, budgets, human resources – everything.
4  The defect rate is 14 in every 1,000 pieces we produce. We can't just throw the whole piece away so it means a lot of _____ .
5  We have our own company magazine that comes out four times a year. We _____ it to employees, customers and all our business partners.
6  We _____ the speed of the assembly line using this panel here.

**4.3 Match an item on the left with an item on the right.**

1  store              value for the customer
2  eliminate          'right first time'
3  unload             production all over the world
4  add                products in a warehouse
5  outsource          fit for purpose
6  coordinate         goods from trucks
7  get things         waste
8  be                 the global supply chain

**4.4 Find a word or phrase from Exercise 4.3 that matches the definitions below.**

1  (three words) good enough to do the job it was designed to do _____
2  unwanted and useless materials _____
3  (two words) the whole series of processes and companies involved in making, storing, transporting and selling a product _____

**4.5 Look at these dialogues between engineers in a factory. Check any unknown words in a dictionary then answer the questions below.**

> Do you know how this new machine works?

> You just press the button and it starts automatically. After that you adjust the settings on the control panel.

> How do you update the software on this device?

> You just connect it to a computer with this lead.

> The machine keeps breaking down.

> Yes, we need to get it fixed. I'll turn it off and put an 'out of order' sign on it.

> Why isn't it working? What's wrong with it?

> Sorry, I unplugged it earlier when I moved it. I'll plug it in again – the socket is right here.

> The machine is making a funny noise.

> Not again. We only had it serviced last month.

> Do you need to connect this sensor to the mains?

> You can do, but it's designed as a handheld device and it runs on batteries.

> I'm trying to set up this machine tool for the next production run but it isn't working properly.

> Yes, one of the pieces doesn't fit.

**Read the dialogues aloud several times, then cover them with a piece of paper.**

**Now fill in the missing letters in the sentences below.**

1  The machine keeps br_ _ ing down and we only had it se_ _ _ _ d last month.
2  I think this is the wr_ _g le_d. It doesn't f_t the socket at the back of this d_ _ce.
3  The machine is making a f_ _ _y noise. We need to get it f_ _ed. I'll un_ _ug it, move it into the corner, and put an 'o_ _-of-o_ _er' sign on it.
4  If you want to connect it to the ma_ _s, there's a so_ _et on the wall over there. But it's not necessary – it r_ _s on ba_ _ _ ies.
5  If you want it to work pr_ _ _ _ ly, you need to adj_ _t the se_ _ngs on the control p_ _l.
6  We need to change the ma_ _ine t_ _ls for the next pro_ _ _ _ion r_n.

**See page 146 for some discussion topics.**

## Service sector industries

The service sector consists of industries such as:

- Banking, financial services and insurance.
- Retailing.
- Hospitality (hotels and restaurants) and tourism.
- Real estate.
- Business services (recruitment, consultancy, legal services, office cleaning, etc).

Manufacturing companies can diversify into services. Of course they change their business model as a result. A good example is companies like IBM and HP. They still make computers, but they now get most of their money from offering services, consultancy and business solutions. So instead of getting a single payment for a piece of equipment, they now receive money for a service on a regular basis. There is a steady income stream every month for an ongoing contract. This is called the subscription pricing model ('subscription' = money that you pay regularly for a service).

## Issues for the service sector

First, in the service sector there is no physical product you can touch, and so it can be difficult for a client to know exactly what they will receive (eg tourism). Even if the client does understand the service offered, it can be difficult to measure its value against the price paid (eg in financial services and consulting).

Second, it is difficult to differentiate yourself from the competition. How does a client choose one investment advisor or hotel or real estate company rather than another? They seem to provide identical services.

Finally, the quality of services depends very much on the quality of the individuals providing the service (a rude waiter can spoil a delicious meal). Employees have to be very customer-oriented. Recruiting, training and retaining staff is very important.

## Describing services

The phrases below can be used when selling a service. They include reference to particular business areas in order to give a context, but they can be adapted to most other areas.

*We provide **customized/cost-effective/innovative solutions** for the telecommunications industry.*

*We can **provide** you with a **comprehensive package** for all your recruitment needs.*

*We **customize** our services to **fit/meet your needs**.*

*We **specialize in** this area. **Outsourcing** the work to us would be cheaper and more efficient than doing it yourselves **in-house**.*

*We **handle** all the details/**all the paperwork** and allow you to **concentrate on what you do best**.*

*We have a **portfolio of clients** that includes the biggest names in the industry.*

*We focus on the **top end of the market**.*

*We offer a **full range of** website development **services**.*

*We offer a **complete** publishing **service**, **from** design and artwork **to** project management and print.*

*We're a **one-stop shop** for all your insurance needs.*

*Our consultants can help you **identify**, **assess** and **implement** the best solutions for your business.*
    ('implement' = make something start to work)

*We're 100% focused on **giving value to our clients**.*

*We're **actively involved** at every stage.*

*We work closely alongside the client to **maximize business opportunities**.*

*This will make a **direct impact on** your **bottom line**.*
    (= this will give you more profits)

*We take a **long-term approach** to **value creation** for our clients.*

*You can choose whether to **lease or buy**.*

*You pay a **subscription** every month to access our site.*

*We **charge** a monthly **fee**.*

*We work **on a commission basis**. We charge a commission of 10%.*

*The **service charge** is €3,000 per year.*

*The **service contract** includes **routine maintenance** and **emergency call-outs** but it doesn't include **spare parts**.*

*You can have **immediate access to your account** online.*

*Our website is secure and easy to use.*

*We give you access to a valuable **online resource**.*

1 Read the text for general understanding.

2 Read it again and <u>underline</u> the words you don't know. Check their meaning.

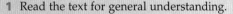

3 Highlight words you know passively, but don't use actively. Choose some to write sentences of your own.

4 Check pronunciation at macmillandictionary.com

# Exercises

**5.1 Find one wrong word in each sentence. Write the correct word at the end.**

1 Our business ~~modal~~ is to get a steady stream of revenue from clients every month. _____model_____

2 We customerize our services to fit the client's needs. _____

3 Should we do all our recruitment in-the-house? It might be better to outsource recruitment to a specialist company. _____

4 We offer a complete service for all your business needings. _____

5 In our investments we focus mainly in companies with a high growth potential. _____

6 We charge a month fee of €600 for our services. _____

7 We work on a commission basic – 10% of the value of any transactions we handle. _____

8 They gave us a good service – they were very customer-orientationed. _____

**5.2 Match the beginnings of sentences 1–8 with their endings a–h.**

1 We offer a full                    [d]
2 We're a one-stop                   [ ]
3 We provide cost-effective          [ ]
4 We're 100% focused                 [ ]
5 We're actively involved            [ ]
6 This will make a direct            [ ]
7 We take a long-term                [ ]
8 We handle all the paperwork and    [ ]

a on giving value to our clients.
b shop for all your business needs.
c allow you to concentrate on what you do best.
d range of banking services.
e at every stage.
f solutions for the hotel and restaurant sector.
g approach to value creation for our clients.
h impact on your bottom line.

**5.3 Fill in the missing letters. The words are all prepositions.**

1 We work with the biggest names _in_ the industry.
2 We offer a full range _ _ services.
3 We offer a complete publishing service, _ _ _ _ design and artwork _ _ project management and print.
4 We're a one-stop shop _ _ _ all your travel needs.
5 We provide cost-effective solutions _ _ _ the banking industry.
6 We are focused _ _ giving value to our clients.
7 We are actively involved _ _ every stage.
8 This will make a direct impact _ _ your bottom line.
9 We take a long-term approach _ _ value creation.
10 You have access _ _ your account online.

**5.4 Complete the sentences with verbs from the box.**

| advise  allow  assess  charge  customize |
|---|
| differentiate  handle  implement  ~~provide~~ |

1 We _____provide_____ a complete service.
2 We _____ a monthly fee of €500, all included.
3 Our IT solutions _____ you to maximize the use of data in your organization.
4 It is often difficult for a service company to _____ itself from the competition.
5 We _____ all the paperwork for you.
6 We can _____ the service to meet your needs.
7 Our consultants will _____ the security risks to your network, and then _____ you on the action you should take. If you wish, we will also _____ the solution you choose.

**5.5 Complete this email sent by a financial consultant to a potential client using the phrases in the box.**

| have immediate access    meet your needs |
|---|
| offer the full range    take a long-term approach |
| ~~handle your financial planning~~    charge an initial set-up fee |

To... Mr Richter
Send  Subject: Merlin Wealth Management

Dear Mr Richter

It was good to meet you on Tuesday – I thought we had a very useful discussion. I have been looking at my notes and studying the form that you completed and I have now made a detailed assessment of your financial situation.

As a married man with a family to support you want a reliable, well-established company to [1] _handle your financial planning_ . I believe that Merlin Wealth Management can provide you with a package that will [2] _____ .

We [3] _____ of wealth management services from investment funds to tax planning. We [4] _____ to building and protecting our clients' money, and we work closely alongside the client at every stage to make sure that you feel comfortable with every decision.

As I explained in the meeting, we [5] _____ of 2.5% of any money you invest with us, and then there is an annual management charge of 1.5%. You [6] _____ to your account online, and you can track the performance of the funds you choose to invest in.

I hope that you will choose Merlin as your Investment Manager, and I look forward to hearing from you soon.

Kind regards

Gillian Tett, Investment Consultant

**See page 146 for some discussion topics.**

# 6 Markets and competitors

## Markets

There are three basic areas of business.

- B2C (the business-to-consumer market: food retailing/consumer electronics, etc.)
- B2B (the business-to-business market: making parts for the auto industry/consultancy, etc.)
- B2G (the business to government market: defence and aerospace/big infrastructure projects, etc.)

There are many other ways that a company can define its market.

- The type of product (eg the mobile phone market, the property market, the stock market).
- A particular place (eg the German market).
- A particular group of people (eg teenage girls who like fashion, single professionals who like going out with their friends, families with young children).

Usually a company will have different products aimed at different sections/segments of the market. For example, to target different income levels a company might offer an economy model, a standard model and an executive model.

In the world of finance there are several specific markets: the stock market, the bond market, the foreign exchange market, the commodity market, and others. In finance a rising market is called a bull market, and a falling market is called a bear market.

Here is a list of adjectives that are often used with the word 'market'.

*booming/expanding/growing, competitive, declining, domestic, existing, foreign, free, global/international/ worldwide, healthy, huge, main, mass, niche/specialist, potential, profitable, protected, sluggish, total, wide*

*The market is **booming**. (= doing very well)*
*It's a **huge** market. (= very big)*
*It's a **niche** market. (= small and specialized)*
*The market is **sluggish** at the moment. (= slow)*
We say …
*a product is **on** the market*
*a company is **in** the market*
*there can be a market **for** a particular product*
*you hope to increase your **share of the market***
*the total market **is worth** €80 million a year*

## Competitors

Other companies who have similar products to yours are competitors. Competitors can be bigger or smaller in various ways:

- Revenue (= money from sales).
- Market share.
- Number of employees.
- Sales and distribution network.

The largest company is the market leader, but it is not always clear who this is. For example there may be a different leader for different product lines or in different markets.

Here are some adjectives often used with the words 'competitor', 'competition' and 'competitive'.

*closest/direct/main/major/nearest competitor*
*fair, fierce/strong/tough, healthy, open competition*
*extremely/highly/fiercely competitive*

*The iPhone is our **direct competitor**.*
*There is **fierce competition**, but it's **healthy** for the market because consumers benefit.*
*Retail banking is **highly competitive**.*

We say …
*compete **against** another company*
*win an order **against** the competition*
*be **in competition with** other companies*
*there is competition **among/between** companies*
*face competition **from** other companies*
*compete **for** a market*
*to succeed in business you need a **competitive edge/ competitive advantage** (= something that you do better than other companies in the same market)*

1  Read the text for general understanding.

2  Read it again and <u>underline</u> the words you don't know. Check their meaning.

3  Highlight words you know passively, but don't use actively. Choose some to write sentences of your own.

4  Check pronunciation at macmillandictionary.com

# Exercises

## 6.1 Underline the correct word in italics.

1 Our biggest market is the *France / French* market.

2 We're a *B2B / B2C* company. We sell specialist equipment to the telecommunications industry.

3 The price of oil was around $23 a barrel in 2001 and 2002. Today the figure is over $100. There's no doubt that oil is in a long-term *bear / bull* market.

4 We publish e-magazines for various *mass / niche* markets such as stamp collecting and extreme sports.

5 The Latin American pharmaceuticals market *is worth / values* $50 billion a year.

6 We have been *in / on* the market for over 20 years.

7 This product has been *in / on* the market since April.

8 It's a small company but we're growing fast. We hope to increase our *part / share* of the market to around 10% within the next three years.

9 Panasonic, Samsung and Sony are direct *competitors / concurrents* in the HDTV market.

10 The airline industry is *high / highly* competitive.

11 We were in competition *from / with* six other companies, but we gave the best presentation to their management team and won the contract.

12 In our market we *front / face* a lot of competition from low-cost producers in Asia.

## 6.2 Match a word describing a market on the left with a word with a <u>similar</u> meaning in the middle and their <u>opposite</u> on the right.

| | | |
|---|---|---|
| 1 domestic | open | declining |
| 2 existing | expanding | foreign |
| 3 free | current | mass |
| 4 growing | home | potential |
| 5 huge | specialist | protected |
| 6 niche | enormous | small |

## 6.3 Complete the sentences with a word from the left or right column in Exercise 6.2. Ignore the middle column.

1 In the next few decades nanotechnology is going to open up ___huge___ new markets in the areas of medicine, electronics and energy production.

2 We have to pay a lot of import duties to sell goods in their country, and their own domestic companies get a lot of government help. It's a very _____ market over there.

3 Why waste resources trying to enter new markets? Our _____ market is very big, and we need to establish our brand name at home first.

4 In the old days we used to talk about the '_____ market' – that means your products are aimed at everyone. These days it's different – we have different products for different sectors.

5 In my business there's very little interference or regulation from governments. It's a _____ market!

## 6.4 Complete each sentence with one of these words: *competitor, competition, competitive, competitiveness.*

1 We have a patent on this technology. It gives us a very important _____ advantage.

2 The long-term _____ of our economy depends on training and innovation.

3 Another brand of cola isn't a good idea – there would be very strong _____ from Coke and Pepsi.

4 Our closest _____ has improved their distribution network and is winning market share.

## 6.5 Complete the report extract written by the Marketing Director of a large supermarket chain. Use the words in the box.

| | | | |
|---|---|---|---|
| leader | line | price | position |
| research | trend | decline | entered |
| take over | | withdraw from | |

We've spent the last month doing extensive market [1] _____ – talking to customers in-store and asking them how we can improve our service. This research shows that customers want two things: first, more ready-made food, and second, better quality organic food.

In relation to the first point, we know that the market for ready-made food is growing rapidly. It already accounts for 8% of our total sales, up from 5% just three years ago. This [2] _____ is likely to continue, as the pressures of work mean that people have less and less time to cook meals for themselves. This doesn't mean that sales of fresh fruit and vegetables will disappear; it just means that they are likely to slowly [3] _____ .

This leads to the second point: organic food. We [4] _____ this market about ten years ago, and for a time sales were very strong. It even looked as if organic food would [5] _____ the fruit and vegetable market. However sales peaked and have now fallen to low levels.

The problem is that organic food is expensive – its [6] _____ will always be significantly higher than non-organic. This doesn't fit well with our market [7] _____ as a value-for-money supermarket with lower prices than our competitors. Given the low levels of sales, one option would be to [8] _____ the organic food market completely. However, I think this would be a mistake. We are the market [9] _____ and we can't simply stop selling this product [10] _____ . This matter needs further discussion.

**See page 146 for some discussion topics.**

# 7 Marketing – the four Ps

## What is marketing?

There is a well-known phrase that identifies the various areas of marketing. The phrase is 'the four Ps', and the Ps stand for product, price, place and promotion.

## Product

For a marketer, the most important things about a product are the following.

- Its *features* (= important and interesting things that will help to sell it).
- Its *benefits* (= how those features translate into a better experience for the user). Marketers often use the phrase 'value proposition' to mean the key benefits of the product.
- Its *USPs* (= unique selling points, in other words features that the competitors' products don't have).

## Price

A high price says to the market, 'this product is high-quality and exclusive'. If the quality really is good, and people enjoy the feeling of owning the brand, then some consumers will pay the high price. However, a high price often means fewer sales and less market share, and so identifying the exact price point for a product is an important issue. Usually a company has different products with different price points aimed at different segments of the market.

We say …

We need to **set our price points** carefully. (= charge as much as possible without damaging sales)

The cost price to us was €40, and we sell it in our stores for €80, so the **margin** (= percentage profit) is 100% and the **mark-up** (= amount added) is €40.

The **recommended retail price** (US: MSRP – manufacturer's suggested retail price) is €399, but you can often find it at a **discounted price**.

Our prices **range from** €1,250 for the standard/economy model **to** €1,950 for the deluxe/executive model.

We need to **cut/bring down/lower** our prices.

We need to **increase/put up/raise** our prices.

We **charge** €65 **per hour** for our services.

Our **fee** will be €8,450, all included.

## Place

This refers to the distribution channel, often referred to in marketing simply as 'the channel'. A customer can find a product in a retail outlet, such as a store or supermarket, but how did the product get there? What logistics operations were necessary (warehousing, handling, transportation)? How many intermediaries were there? Was there a distributor? an agent? a wholesaler?

All these people – logistics companies, intermediaries and retailers – are referred to as the 'channel partners'.

Direct marketing is a type of marketing with no intermediaries or outlets – it 'cuts out the middleman'. Direct marketing includes email marketing, catalogue shopping, direct mail, door-to-door leaflets, etc.

In the future m-commerce (using mobile devices as a shopping platform) will grow and take its place alongside e-commerce (using a computer).

## Promotion

There are many different forms of promotion.

- Online advertising (banner ads, flash animations, and search marketing that uses links on the results page of a search engine).
- Ads in the media (TV, magazines, newspapers).
- Outdoor advertising (billboards, buses).
- Promotional materials (brochures, catalogues, leaflets, flyers).
- Sponsorship (eg associating your logo with one particular football team).
- Sales promotions (special offers such as 'buy-one-get-one-free', coupons/vouchers, etc).
- Public relations.
- Word-of-mouth (especially important in the age of social networks on the Internet).
- Trade shows/trade fairs (especially in B2B).

We say …

**run** an advertising campaign

**place** an ad online/in a magazine

**make** a TV commercial

**sponsor** an event/a sports team

**attend** a trade fair

1 Read the text for general understanding.

2 Read it again and <u>underline</u> the words you don't know. Check their meaning.

3 Highlight words you know passively, but don't use actively. Choose some to write sentences of your own.

4 Check pronunciation at macmillandictionary.com

# Exercises

**7.1 Complete the text about a pizza service using the words in the box.**

| | | | |
|---|---|---|---|
| coupon | ~~delivery~~ | difference | guaranteed |
| leaflet | offer | online | range |

66 Near to my house there are two or three pizza stores, all offering home ¹ _delivery_ . I usually choose Pizza Place – I love their pizzas. They have a much better ² _____ of toppings than the others, and their pizzas are thin and crispy so you really taste the topping not the base. They put a ³ _____ through my door most weeks, and there's always some kind of special ⁴ _____ . For example, you can cut out a ⁵ _____ and use it in the store to get special deals on desserts and drinks. There's a code printed on the coupon so you can use it over the phone or to order ⁶ _____ . And every Monday they have a 'buy-one-get-one-free' offer. But the best thing about Pizza Place is their ⁷ _____ delivery time. They say that if they don't deliver in 30 minutes or less, it's free. None of the other pizza stores offer that, and when you're hungry it makes a ⁸ _____ . 99

**7.2 Use the text in Exercise 7.1 to underline the correct word in 1–2 below.**

1 Thin, crispy pizzas are a *feature / benefit*.
2 Being able to taste the topping not the base is a *feature / benefit*.

**7.3 Fill in the missing letters.**

1 If the quality is good and people enjoy the feeling of owning the b_ _ _d, then some consumers will pay a higher price.
2 Usually a company has different products aimed at different seg_ _ _ts of the market.
3 The cost price to us is €200 and we sell it in our store for €300. So the m_ _ _in is 50% and the m_ _k-up is €100.
4 Our prices ra_ _e from €600 to €900, depending on the model.
5 Professionals offering a personalized service, such as lawyers, don't really use the word 'price' with clients. Instead they say 'f_ _'.
6 We ch_ _ _e €90 per hour for our services.
7 Between the manufacturer and the end-user there are just two inter_ _ _iaries: a distributor and a retailer.
8 We use various retail out_ _ _s, including large supermarkets, small neighbourhood shops and kiosks.
9 Billboards are an example of _ _ _door advertising.
10 In the age of social networks such as Facebook, w_ _ _-of-m_ _th marketing is very important.

**7.4 Make word partnerships by matching an item from each column. One solution uses each word once.**

1 value
2 price
3 retail
4 distribution
5 channel
6 public
7 search
8 advertising

campaign
channel
engine
partner
point
outlet
proposition
relations

**7.5 Complete the sentences with a word partnership from Exercise 7.4.**

1 Looking at the competition, I think we should try a different _price point_ . Let's sell it for €49 instead of €54 and see what difference it makes.
2 In the summer we're going to run an _____ across various media: online, TV and magazines.
3 I think we need to expand our range of _____s to include small local shops.
4 As an online retailer, the logistics company we work with is a very important _____ . We use their warehousing services as well as their delivery services.
5 When people type 'Rome hotel', we want our name to appear on the first page of the _____ results.

**7.6 Complete the sentences with the verbs in the box.**

| | | | |
|---|---|---|---|
| aim at | attend | charge | handle |
| place | ~~set~~ | sponsor | translate |

1 We need to _set_ the right price point to maximize profits – not too high and not too low.
2 The consultants' fees are very high. They spent two days in the company and then _____d us €2,400 for a report which said nothing new.
3 Our advertising budget is limited and we have to be very careful about where we _____ this ad.
4 We have a reputation for high quality and high prices. But in the current economic climate I think we also need to _____ the value-oriented shopper.
5 It's possible to make this product with all sorts of additional features. The question is this: do those features _____ into benefits for the customer?
6 The cost of the stand is very high, but we have to _____ the Frankfurt trade fair every year. It's the best place to meet all our customers at one time.
7 In order to attract wealthy clients from the local area I think we should _____ the next season at the Opera House.
8 A lot of customers are calling to complain about damaged goods. We need to investigate how they're _____d at the warehouse and in transit.

**See page 146 for some discussion topics.**

# 8 Marketing strategy and brands

## Marketing strategy

The four Ps described in Unit 7 is a good way to look at the marketing of individual product lines over the short term. But a company also needs a longer-term strategy with realistic objectives in order to plan its overall marketing effort. The marketing strategy is likely to include the following.

- Collecting data to try to forecast (= say what is likely to happen in the future) market trends.
- Reviewing the positioning of the company. Which segments of the market does the company want to target (= aim at)? Who do the products appeal to (= who finds them interesting and wants to buy them)?
- Reviewing the company's existing product range to see how well it fits the needs of the market. Which products need a quick facelift? Which need a completely new model? Which need to be withdrawn from the market?
- Developing new products, working closely with production, R&D and sales staff.
- Doing market research to get feedback on existing products and ideas for new products. This may involve interviewing both existing customers and potential customers (= people who may become customers in the future).
- Analyzing and deciding how to respond to the behaviour of competitors.
- Allocating (= deciding how to use) resources. What should be the overall size of the marketing budget? How is this money going to be divided between the different promotional activities?
- Making decisions about sponsorship, for example deciding which sports/cultural activity to be associated with.
- Making decisions about endorsements, for example deciding which famous person is going to be 'the face' of the company or a certain product.
- Developing the corporate image in general.
- Developing and promoting individual brands (see next section).

### Note

*sponsor an event    sponsorship*
*endorse a brand    endorsement*

## Brand development

A brand is a product or group of products that has a well-known name. Some brands have the same name as the company, for example Google, BMW, Sony. Other brands have a different name to the company, for example Dove, Persil, Ben & Jerry's (all made by Unilever, which is not in itself a brand). A brand is usually associated with:

- A logo (= symbol of a company), for example Nike, Apple, McDonalds.
- A particular style of lettering, for example Disney, Carlsberg, Yahoo!
- A slogan (= short phrase that is easy to remember), for example *Life's Good* (LG), *Because we're worth it* (L'Oréal), *High Performance, Delivered* (Accenture).

A good brand has a personality, an identity, an image. It can be young and fun, conservative and safe, edgy (= radical) and innovative, warm and comforting, expensive and exclusive, soft and romantic. The idea is that consumers will get the feeling associated with the brand every time they use it.

Sponsorship and endorsements are very important to building a brand identity – you buy a product associated with a football team or movie star and you feel personally connected to the values and lifestyle they represent.

A 'white label product' is one produced by a company that no-one has heard of so that another company (usually a retailer) can put their own brand name on it. This is very common in supermarkets (with food) and also in consumer electronics and clothing. With the supermarket's name on it, the product is now called an own-label brand, or store brand.

Note these collocations with the word 'brand'.

*a **leading**/**top** brand*
*a **famous**/**favourite**/**popular**/**well-known** brand*
***promote** a **brand name***
***develop** a **brand identity**/**image***
*increase **brand awareness**/**recognition***
***brand loyalty** (= when people regularly buy the same brand and refuse to change)*

---

1 Read the text for general understanding.
2 Read it again and <u>underline</u> the words you don't know. Check their meaning.

3 Highlight words you know passively, but don't use actively. Choose some to write sentences of your own.
4 Check pronunciation at macmillandictionary.com

# Exercises

**8.1 Underline the correct word in italics.**

1 Our strategy must have a realistic *object* / *objective*.

2 We have to decide which segments of the market we want to *aim* / *target*.

3 We should do some market *investigation* / *research* to see what customers think about our brand.

4 The senior management team has decided to *allocate* / *delegate* fewer resources to promotional activities next year.

5 I hear that the company is looking for a new 'face' after the latest scandal. Even sports stars are human, and when you choose someone to *endorse* / *sponsor* your products, you always take a risk.

6 Our marketing budget is large, but not large enough to *endorse* / *sponsor* a team like Manchester United, Real Madrid or Bayern München.

7 We need a softer, more romantic image. Something that will *appeal to* / *attract to* women.

8 A brand is a product with a *known* / *well-known* name.

9 In today's world there are many *competing* / *competition* products with a similar price.

10 In a recession consumers buy cheaper products, or products on special offer. It's much harder to maintain brand *fidelity* / *loyalty*.

**8.2 Replace the underlined word or phrase with one word from the box. The meaning must stay the same.**

| | | | |
|---|---|---|---|
| awareness | behaviour | facelift | forecast |
| identity | ~~positioning~~ | slogan | withdraw |

1 I think our main competitor has changed their <u>decision about which segments to target</u> in the market. Now they have more exclusive items at a higher price. *positioning*

2 The range of white goods we introduced three years ago is doing well in the market. Maybe we just need to give them a <u>superficial redesign of the exterior</u> to make them look more contemporary.

3 The new advertising campaign isn't designed to produce immediate sales. Instead, we want to increase brand <u>recognition</u> at a more general level.

4 This line is looking old now and sales are very low. I think it's time to <u>remove</u> it from the market completely.

5 It's difficult to <u>predict</u> market trends exactly, but the computer screen might become less important as the mobile phone screen becomes more important.

6 We need to think of a good <u>short phrase that will stick in people's memory</u> to help launch the new brand.

7 We have spent a lot of money developing the brand. Now it has a clear <u>image that makes it different from the others</u>.

8 We are just a small company and we only started a few years ago. We can learn a lot by studying our competitors' <u>way of doing things</u> in the market.

**8.3 Complete the table below. This exercise includes some items from Unit 7.**

| | Verb | Noun | |
|---|---|---|---|
| 1 | promote | *promotion* | |
| 2 | compete | _____ | (activity) |
| | | _____ | (person) |
| 3 | distribute | _____ | (activity) |
| | | _____ | (person) |
| 4 | advertise | _____ | (long form) |
| | | _____ | (short form) |
| 5 | sponsor | _____ | (activity) |
| 6 | _____ | target | |
| 7 | recognize | _____ | |
| 8 | (be) loyal | _____ | |

**8.4 Complete the text about the Japanese store Muji using the words in the box.**

| | | | |
|---|---|---|---|
| appeals | brand | budget | packaging |
| range | solutions | ~~strategy~~ | word-of-mouth |

Is it possible to develop a brand by having 'no brand' as your [1] ___strategy___ ? The answer is yes, according to the Japanese retail company Muji, whose full name (Mujirushi Ryohin) means 'no brand quality goods' in English.

Muji sells a wide variety of household and consumer goods, yet you won't find their name on any of their products. Everything that they sell is just simple, modern and functional. All [2] _____ is minimal – designed not to make the product look more than it is. Clothes come in a limited [3] _____ of colours and have no patterns or designs; household goods and stationery are easy to use and practical. Inside the stores there is no marketing – just a Zen-like sense of calm. And their advertising [4] _____ is close to zero as Muji relies mainly on [5] _____ .

On their website Muji state that, 'As life gets more complex, the need for simple lifestyle [6] _____ becomes all the more necessary.' They explain that the idea behind 'no brand' is that 'the quality and credibility of each product speaks for itself – what you see is what you get'.

So Muji have developed a very clever brand strategy: functionality, a simple shopping experience, and an anti-brand image. In the age of brands this is a powerful differentiating factor.

Muji's brand identity [7] _____ strongly to people who don't like conventional marketing, and the [8] _____ (because that is what it is) is now expanding into Europe and North America.

**See page 146 for some discussion topics.**

# 9 Describing products

## Features

The features of a product are its selling points. Here is a list of 60 adjectives that can be used to talk about product features.

| | |
|---|---|
| adjustable | low-cost |
| affordable | low-risk |
| attractive | made-to-measure |
| best-selling | man-made |
| brand-new | mass-produced |
| built-in | modular |
| compact | off-the-shelf |
| convenient | one-touch |
| cost-effective | optional |
| customized | portable |
| easy-to-clean | practical |
| easy-to-maintain | real-time |
| economical to run | reliable |
| efficient | revolutionary |
| energy-efficient | secure |
| environmentally friendly | shock-absorbent |
| expandable | sophisticated |
| fully automatic | state-of-the-art |
| functional | stylish |
| hands-free | tailor-made |
| hard-wearing | time-saving |
| high-performance | trouble-free |
| high-quality | ultra-light |
| high-speed | unique |
| high-tech | up-to-date |
| innovative | user-friendly |
| integrated | waterproof |
| labour-saving | well-built |
| limited edition | well-designed |
| long-lasting | well-made |

Our financial products offer a **secure** home for your money, and are **tailor-made** to your own personal needs.

Our new range of clothing for the summer is **attractive, affordable** and **stylish**.

It's a **revolutionary, state-of-the-art** home cinema system. A useful feature is the **built-in** iPlayer access.

These running shoes are **waterproof** and **shock-absorbent**. They are available in a full range of sizes.

## Physical description of a product

In addition to describing the features of a product, you may also have to describe it physically, in particular its shape (= the form that it has), size (= dimensions), weight and materials.

To talk about shape we can use adjectives or nouns.

It's **square, circular**/round, **rectangular**, **L-shaped**, star-shaped.

It's in the shape of a **square, circle, rectangle, letter 'L'**.

To talk about dimensions we can use adjectives or nouns.

The product is 8mm **long**/**wide**/**high**/**deep**.
The **length**/**width**/**height**/**depth** of the product is 8mm.
It's 8mm **in** length/width/height/depth.
It's 40cm **in diameter**.
It **ranges** in height **from** 2m at one end **to** 3m at the other.

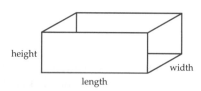

We might want to talk about area and volume.

It **measures** 60cm **by** 20cm. So that's 1,200 **square centimetres** (written as $cm^2$).
It **measures** 2m **by** 2m **by** 1.5m. So that's 6 **cubic metres** (written as $m^3$).

To talk about weight we say:

It **weighs** six kilos.
It's six kilos **in weight**. (NOT six of kilos)

To talk about materials we say:

It's **made of** aluminium, reinforced concrete, copper, fibreglass, glass, leather, moulded plastic, nanomaterials, rubber, steel, wood (US: lumber), etc.
It's a **composite material**. (= made of several things)
It's a new type of polymer.

Note these questions that a customer may ask:

What shape is it?    What size is it?
How long is it?    How wide is it?
Can you give me the dimensions?
How much does it weigh?
What's it made of?

---

1  Read the text for general understanding.

2  Read it again and <u>underline</u> the words you don't know. Check their meaning.

3  Highlight words you know passively, but don't use actively. Choose some to write sentences of your own.

4  Check pronunciation at macmillandictionary.com

# Exercises

**9.1 Match the adjectives 1–15 with the words a–o with a similar meaning.**

| | | | |
|---|---|---|---|
| 1 | functional | a | weighing very little |
| 2 | ultra-light | b | integral / fitted |
| 3 | expandable | c | high-tech / the newest |
| 4 | state-of-the-art | d | useful / practical |
| 5 | built-in | e | able to include other things in the future |

| | | | |
|---|---|---|---|
| 6 | innovative | f | available to buy without being ordered specially |
| 7 | off-the-shelf | g | strong / long-lasting |
| 8 | tailor-made | h | new / original |
| 9 | integrated | i | customized / personalized |
| 10 | hard-wearing | j | already combined in order to be more effective |

| | | | |
|---|---|---|---|
| 11 | labour-saving | k | water cannot pass through |
| 12 | water-proof | l | advanced in design |
| 13 | affordable | m | parts can be bought separately and then joined together later |
| 14 | sophisticated | n | reasonably priced |
| 15 | modular | o | makes it easier to do the job |

**9.2 Match the adjectives 1–5 with the products a–e they are most likely to describe.**

1 attractive, practical, stylish    `d`
2 labour-saving, reliable, economical to run
3 secure, low-risk, convenient
4 revolutionary, state-of-the-art, ultra-light
5 low-cost, functional, expandable

a financial product where you pay in money every month and get a guaranteed return after five years
b simple wine rack for storing nine wine bottles, with clips at the side to attach other units
c washing machine
d plate to hold sushi with a place to put chopsticks, designed by a top Japanese designer
e amazing new compact camera

**9.3 Find three adjectives from the Features list opposite for each product below. Do not choose adjectives already given in Exercise 9.2.**

1 a product aimed at 'green' consumers who want to save energy; protect the environment; and who hate the throw-away society.
2 a product aimed at parents with young children whose children make a mess with food and paint; who want to carry the product when they visit friends and relations; and who want a high quality of construction so that it doesn't break.
3 a product aimed at teenage boys who want something that works by itself without them doing anything; is very fast and powerful; and is produced in small numbers so that none of their friends have it.

**9.4 Underline the correct word in italics.**

1 The *features* / *characteristics* of a product are the important and interesting things that help to sell it.
2 Dimensions of a product *include* / *don't include* weight.
3 What *form* / *shape* is it?
4 What *dimension* / *size* is it?
5 How *length* / *long* is it?
6 What is its *length* / *long*?
7 How much does it *weigh* / *weight*?
8 What is the *weigh* / *weight*?

**9.5 Complete the sentences by writing one word in each space.**

1 How long is it?
   → It's 120 centimetres long.
   → It's 120 centimetres in _____*length*_____ .
2 How wide is it?
   → It's 15 centimetres wide.
   → It's 15 centimetres in _____ .
3 How _____ is it?
   → It's just 25 millimetres high.
   → It's just 25 millimetres in _____ .
4 How _____ is the hotel swimming pool?
   → It's around 2 metres in _____ .
   → It ranges _____ depth from 1 metre at one end to 2 metres at the other.
5 How much does it weigh?
   → It _____ a little over 2 kilos.
   → It's a little over 2 kilos in _____ .
6 What area of ground does it need?
   → Well, it measures 10 metres _____ 10 metres when it's constructed, so it will need 100 _____ metres of ground.
7 What is the _____ of the tank?
   → Let me see. It's 1.5 metres long by 1.5 metres wide by 4 metres deep. So that's 9 _____ metres.
8 What's it made _____ ?
   → Well, like most modern bicycles it's made of a _____ material – plastic reinforced with carbon fibre.

**9.6 Write the name of the material next to the object it is most likely to be made from.**

> reinforced concrete    copper    leather
> moulded plastic    nanomaterials    ~~steel~~

1 washing machine, bridge      *steel*
2 fizzy drink bottle, cheap toy    _____
3 pipe to carry water, wire, coin    _____
4 seat of a luxury car, shoe    _____
5 computer memory, high-tech clothing    _____
6 walls and floors of a tall building    _____

**See page 146 for some discussion topics.**

# 10 Customers

## Customer vs client vs consumer

In many cases the words 'customer' and 'client' can both be used. However:

- *Customer* is more common where there is a standard product or service, and also where cash is exchanged (eg in a shop or restaurant).
- *Client* is more common where the product or service is individually designed.

The word 'consumer' is more general and refers to anyone who buys things (rather than a customer of a particular company). Economists are interested in consumer demand, consumer confidence, etc. The consumer is also the end-user, whereas a customer/client may be another business or a distributor or agent.

## Pre-sales contact with the customer

This is the area of work of the sales department. Typical stages are:

Contact → Lead → Prospect → Customer

Contact can be made through many channels (eg a website enquiry, an existing customer). The sales consultant may:

**deal with**/**handle** *an enquiry*
**give**/**provide** *information*
**ask for**/**request** *information to find out the customer's* **needs**/**requirements**

A 'lead' is a piece of information or a person that helps you find new customers. The sales consultant may:

**follow up** *a lead* (= do more work on it)

A 'prospect' is a person who may become a customer. The sales consultant may:

*offer a* **customized**/**personalized**/**tailor-made** **solution**
*provide an* **individual package** *for a client*
**meet** (= satisfy)/**fail to meet** *the customer's needs or expectations*

And finally the customer may:

**make**/**place** *an order*
*make a* **repeat purchase** (= buy the same thing again)

## After-sales contact with the customer

Here the interaction with the customer will be very different, and might involve the following.

- Answering questions about payment and delivery. The activity of processing and shipping an order is called 'fulfilment'.
  *Unless we receive payment in full, we're unable to* **fulfil your order**.
- Explaining how to use the product.
- Discussing the terms of the warranty.
- Dealing with complaints. The person who handles the complaint will first apologize. Then, if the product is faulty and is still under warranty, the company will offer a repair or replacement. In other cases they may offer a refund or some other form of compensation.

Many companies do all this in a department with a name like Customer Services, Customer Care or Customer Support. Sometimes this department handles pre-sales enquiries as well.

## Loyalty schemes

The company wants loyal, satisfied customers who will come back again and again. This can be encouraged with a special loyalty scheme that offers various rewards. Existing customers may have a chance to win a prize if they order again, or a customer who hasn't placed an order for some time may be sent an email with a discount coupon.

## The Marketing Department and customers

The Marketing Department comes into contact with customers as part of market research. They want to get feedback on existing products and get ideas for new products. They might do the following.

- Carry out a survey, for example with an online questionnaire.
- Conduct a focus group (= a face-to-face discussion with a small group of consumers).

We say …

**carry out**/**conduct**/**do** *a survey*
**take part in**/**respond to** *a survey*
**fill in**/**fill out**/**complete** *a questionnaire*

1 Read the text for general understanding.

2 Read it again and <u>underline</u> the words you don't know. Check their meaning.

3 Highlight words you know passively, but don't use actively. Choose some to write sentences of your own.

4 Check pronunciation at macmillandictionary.com

# Exercises

**10.1 Complete each sentence with a word in the box. Several answers may be possible but choose the best one.**

| client    customer    consumer    end-user |

1 We offer financial advice to wealthy individuals. We have around 200 _____s on our books.
2 We manufacture children's toys and sell them to a distributor. The distributor supplies retail outlets all over Europe. So we never come into contact with the _____ .
3 I work in the retail business and people often bring back clothes simply because they don't like them. But we don't argue. We have a saying: 'the _____ is always right.'
4 When the economy comes out of recession, _____ demand for automobiles, holidays and luxury goods will pick up rapidly.

**10.2 Fill in the missing letters. A few words do not appear opposite.**

1 The customer buys from a su_ _lier (= seller). In American English the word 'ven_ _r' is also common.
2 Clients expect a pe_ _ _ _alized / cu_ _ _ ized / tai_ _ _-made service.
3 A sa_ _ _fied customer will often make a rep_ _t p_ _chase.
4 We can customize the product to meet your exact requ_ _ _ments.
5 We provide an individual pa_ _age to meet your sp_ _ _ic needs.

**10.3 In each group cross out the <u>one</u> word in italics that does not make a common verb + noun partnership.**

1 *deal with / handle / ~~meet~~ / respond to*     an enquiry
2 *carry out / find out / request / provide*     information
3 *do / fulfil / make / place*     an order
4 *attract / deal with / lose / offer*     a customer
5 *address / have / meet / satisfy*     somebody's needs
6 *offer / provide / reach / suspend*     a service
7 *deal with / do / handle / investigate*     a complaint
8 *carry out / conduct / enter / take part in*     a survey

**10.4 Underline the correct words in italics.**

1 If you 'handle' an enquiry or a complaint, you <u>*deal with it*</u> / *pass it to somebody else*.
2 If you 'provide' information, you *give / receive* it.
3 If you 'fulfil' an order, you *cancel it / ship it*.
4 If you 'meet' somebody's needs, you *discuss their needs with them / satisfy their needs*.
5 If you 'carry out' a survey, you *ask the questions / answer the questions*.

**10.5 Complete each mini-dialogue with the most appropriate phrase from the box.**

| deal with it    fill it in    follow it up    place it    provide it |

1 A: I spoke to someone on the reception desk. She was very chatty and gave me a good lead.
  B: When are you going to _____ ?
2 A: I have a Mr Rodriguez on the line. He sounds very angry. It's about the software he ordered.
  B: OK, give the phone to me. I'll _____ .
3 A: The information that I want is really very basic.
  B: I'm sorry but I'm just not able to _____ right now. Can I take your number and call you back?
4 A: I'm ready to make an order now. What should I do?
  B: The best way is to _____ online via our website.
5 A: Thank you very much, you've been very helpful.
  B: My pleasure. Just before you go, may I give you this customer satisfaction questionnaire? If you _____ and return it, you have a chance to win a prize.

**10.6 Match the words 'warranty' and 'guarantee' with their explanations below.**

1 _____ – refers to repair / replacement or a refund or general quality issues; it can be used as a verb.
2 _____ – refers to repair / replacement only; it cannot be used as a verb.

**10.7 Complete the text about customer loyalty schemes with the words in the box.**

| claimed    coupon    online    placed |
| points    ~~relationships~~    reward    scheme |

What is the best way to get customer loyalty? The first answer must be to give good overall service. But customer [1] *relationships* can also be strengthened with a special customer loyalty [2] _____ . These are programmes that use discounts, extra goods or prizes to [3] _____ customers for behaviour that benefits the business. For example, a local coffee bar might offer a free drink every tenth visit, or a mail-order company might offer a discount [4] _____ to customers who haven't [5] _____ an order for some time.

It's also common to give retail customers a loyalty card that is presented at the checkout (real or [6] _____) and is used to collect [7] _____ . Perhaps the best-known example of this is frequent-flyer programmes, although most points earned through these programmes are not [8] _____ .

**See page 146 for some discussion topics.**

## Orders

When an end-user makes an order they simply pay at the point of purchase. But in the business-to-business sector the following sequence is typical.

1 A customer makes an enquiry about a product and the price.
2 The supplier provides information and quotes/gives a price.
3 The customer makes/places an order. The order may be made by email, phone or fax, or may be made directly off/from a website.
4 The supplier confirms/acknowledges the order, processes it, and gives the customer a shipping date. Of course the goods may be out of stock, in which case there is a wait until they are in stock again.
5 The supplier ships the goods and issues (= produces + sends) an invoice.
6 A logistics company delivers the goods. Perhaps the customer has also tracked the shipment (= followed the progress of the goods) online.
7 On arrival, the customer checks the goods.
8 If the goods are in good condition, the customer pays the invoice. If they are damaged, there is a 'returns policy' for sending them back.

Note that 'ship' means send/dispatch by any means of transport, not just by ship.

Note that 'quote' and 'order' are used as both nouns and verbs:

*Can you give me **a quote**?*
*Can you **quote** me a price?*
*I'd like to place **an order** for 300 pieces.*
*I'd like to **order** 300 pieces.*

## Invoices

An invoice (or bill) is a document issued by a seller to a buyer. It requests payment for an order. A typical invoice contains:

- Date of the invoice and an invoice reference number.
- Name, contact details and tax details of the seller.
- Name and contact details of the buyer.
- Date that the products were shipped.
- Purchase order number (if the buyer has one which they want on the invoice).
- Description of the products.

- Unit price of the products.
- Total amount charged for the goods.
- Any extra amount for shipping (sometimes called 'postage and packing' for smaller items).
- Payment terms.

Note that 'charge' and 'invoice' are used as both nouns and verbs.

*Is there **a charge** for shipping?*
*How much do you **charge** for shipping?*
*Have you sent **the invoice**?*
*Have you **invoiced** them yet?*

## Payment

The invoice contains the payment terms, and these are the conditions of payment. If the customer pays early, there is often a discount, and if they pay late, there is a penalty. The invoice also shows the tax paid to the government (called VAT – value added tax – in BrE).

The method of payment can vary. A first-time business-to-business customer will often have to arrange a 'letter of credit' at their bank (business people just say 'l/c'). With an l/c the customer's bank makes a guaranteed payment as soon as the seller's bank presents certain documents (transport documents, invoice, etc). If there is a long-term business relationship with more trust, the customer will usually have an 'open account'. Here the customer pays later, after the goods are received, according to the terms of the contract.

The seller may:
**ask for/demand** payment **in advance/upfront**
ask for **cash on delivery** (COD)
ask for **prompt payment** (within 14 days of delivery)
ask for payment in 30/60/90 days **from date of invoice**
send a **reminder** (= an email or letter telling the buyer they must pay)

The customer may:
arrange a **bank transfer**
pay by **monthly instalments**
**delay** payment (pay later than is planned)
**defer** payment (arrange officially to pay later)
**settle** an account (= pay everything that is owing)

If the customer is late in paying, the seller might say:
*Your payment **is due**. (= it must be paid now)*
*Your payment **was due** two weeks ago.*
*Your payment is now **overdue**. (= it is late)*

1 Read the text for general understanding.
2 Read it again and underline the words you don't know. Check their meaning.
3 Highlight words you know passively, but don't use actively. Choose some to write sentences of your own.
4 Check pronunciation at macmillandictionary.com

# Exercises

## 11.1 Match verbs 1–8 with definitions a–h.

1 quote
2 ship
3 issue
4 track
5 acknowledge
6 deliver
7 charge
8 demand

a send / dispatch goods
b ask sb to pay money for a service
c follow the progress of sth
d say how much sth will cost
e take goods to a place
f say firmly that you want sth
g officially give / send sth
h tell sb you have received sth

## 11.2 Match nouns 1–8 with definitions a–h.

1 enquiry
2 order
3 goods
4 invoice
5 shipment
6 purchase
7 terms
8 penalty

a request for payment; bill
b amount of goods transported
c question to get information
d conditions
e (formal) process of buying
f request for goods to be sent
g punishment for breaking an agreement
h things produced for sale

## 11.3 Place the items in the list into the most likely sequence.

> confirms the order    issues an invoice    makes an enquiry
> quotes a price    sends a reminder    tracks the shipment

**Customer**

1 _____

places an order

5 _____ ;

checks the goods on
arrival; delays payment

settles the account

**Supplier**

2 _____

3 _____ ;

processes the order;
ships the goods;

4 _____

6 _____

## 11.4 One of the three phrases in italics does not exist or is not used. Cross it out.

1 I called them to make *a charge* / *a complaint* / *an enquiry*.
2 I asked them to give me *a quote* / *an enquiry* / *a price*.
3 Make sure that the *letter of credit* / *purchase order number* / *VAT* is clearly shown on the invoice.
4 The goods were *placed* / *shipped* / *dispatched* yesterday.
5 Our supplier has shipped the *bills* / *goods* / *products*.
6 They want us to pay 50% *in advance* / *upfront* / *up at the front*.
7 We paid the *bill* / *invoice* / *terms* on time.
8 Your payment is *due* / *overdue* / *overtime*.
9 Tell them we have cashflow problems and ask if we can *defer* / *delay* / *deliver* payment.
10 You have 30 days to *install* / *pay* / *settle* the invoice.

## 11.5 Complete this sequence of emails with the words in the boxes.

> contact    deliver    delivery    enquiry    order    quote

> I clicked on your ad on the Building Products website and got directed to your site. I am interested in your high-security doors for commercial properties. Do you make these doors with non-standard dimensions? If so, can you give me a 1_____? And can you also tell me how long it will take to 2_____ them?
>
> Thank you
> Patrick Murphy

> Dear Mr Murphy
>
> Thank you for your 3_____ sent from our website. Yes, we can make made-to-measure doors according to your specifications, but we require a minimum 4_____ of ten doors.
>
> The price will be the catalogue price plus 15%. 5_____ will be ten working days from a firm order.
>
> Please feel free to 6_____ me if you have any further questions.
>
> Marie Berger
> Sales Manager

> attached    disregard    invoice    overdue    records    terms

> Dear Ms Berger
>
> Following our phone call earlier today I can confirm that I want 20 security doors with the specifications given on the 7_____ document.
>
> I agree to the payment 8_____ and delivery dates we discussed.
>
> Patrick Murphy

a few weeks later …

> Dear Mr Murphy
>
> I note from our 9_____ that you have still not paid our invoice no. CMD6774 dated 12 March. The agreed terms were 30 days from date of 10_____ and so this payment is now 11_____ .
>
> Please arrange to transfer this money to our account as soon as possible.
>
> If you have already paid this invoice, please 12_____* this email.
>
> Yours
> Marie Berger

*ignore

**See page 146 for some discussion topics.**

# 12 Money

## Money, money, money

Below are just some of the things you can do with money. Notice the prepositions.

***borrow*** money (from a bank)
***cost*** (***us***) money (to cancel the event)
***earn*** money (from your job)
***have enough*** money (to live comfortably)
***invest*** money (in new technology)
***lend*** money (to a friend)
***lose*** money (by gambling/on a bad investment)
***make*** money (from home/by working hard)
***owe*** money (to the person who lent it to you)
***save*** money (on a flight by booking early)
***save up*** money (for a luxury cruise)
***spend*** money (on new office furniture)
***waste*** money (on lottery tickets – usually)
***win*** money (on the lottery – if you're lucky)

## Your money at the bank

Your employer pays your salary into your current account. Every month you receive a bank statement showing your transactions and the final balance. If you want to save money and earn interest on your savings, you will need a special account. You can withdraw money at a cash point/cash machine (AmE ATM). You can arrange an overdraft (= a temporary negative balance) for a small fee. If you have a negative balance, you are 'in the red'. Nobody likes being in debt/getting into debt and most people try to clear their overdraft as soon as possible.

In business the phrase 'line of credit' is more common than 'overdraft'. A line of credit can be given by a bank or a supplier.

You may need to take out/get a loan from the bank. Note that the bank lends you money, and you borrow money from the bank. The bank charges you interest on the loan and you pay interest on the loan. The interest rate is usually given as an APR (annual percentage rate) which shows the overall cost of credit including bank charges as well as interest. You repay the loan in monthly instalments.

To buy your own house you need to take out/arrange a special type of long-term loan called a mortgage.

## Spending money at the shops

Anna and Carla are out shopping on the last afternoon of a business trip.

Anna: *Look at these shoes. There's a **discount** (= reduction) **of** 50%. That's very good **value for money** – you'd **pay a lot more** in our country.*

Carla: *Really? **50% off**? That's a **real bargain**. Why don't you try them on? Hey, look at this blouse. No, it's too expensive – **I can't afford it.***

Anna: *Let me see the price. Wow! That's **a real rip-off** (= much too expensive). But you're coming back in January, right? It might be **in the sales**.*

Carla: *Look over here. This skirt is **on sale**. It's been **reduced by** €30.*

Anna: *Yes, but it's still expensive. **It's not worth it.** We saw something very similar **for sale** in the last shop.*

(At the checkout)

Anna: *Have you got any **local currency**? I've run out.*

Carla: *Just a few notes and a bit of **change**.*

Anna: *Never mind, I'll **pay by** credit card. (To the shop assistant) Can I have a **receipt** please?*

Note that 'for sale' means available to buy, while 'on sale' means available to buy at a cheaper price than normal.

Note the uses of 'pay'. We say …

| | |
|---|---|
| ***pay*** | *a lot of money for it, €80 for a dress, the bill at a restaurant, income tax* |
| ***pay for*** | *a meal, the drinks, my ticket, the taxi* |
| ***pay by*** | *card* |
| ***pay with*** | *my card* |
| ***pay in*** | *euros/dollars* |

## Money and budgets

A budget is an amount of money you have available to spend. Look at how to use the word 'budget'.

*The project **went over budget**.*
*The project **is on budget**.*
*The project **came in under budget**.*
*Is there any money **left in the budget**?*
*We have to **keep/stick to the budget**.*
*40% of the budget **goes on** labour costs.*
*The budget **for** next year has not been set.*
*We have budgeted €20,000 **for** advertising.*
('budget' is used as a verb in this last example)

---

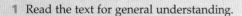

1 Read the text for general understanding.

2 Read it again and <u>underline</u> the words you don't know. Check their meaning.

3 Highlight words you know passively, but don't use actively. Choose some to write sentences of your own.

4 Check pronunciation at macmillandictionary.com

# Exercises

**12.1 Complete the sentences with a verb from list A and a preposition from list B.**

| A: | borrowed | ~~earned~~ | invested | lent |
|---|---|---|---|---|
| B: | ~~from~~ | from | in | to |

1 Last year I ___earned___ around €40,000 before tax ___from___ my job.
2 The bank _____ €25,000 _____ my colleague at work to pay for her MBA program.
3 My colleague at work _____ €25,000 _____ the bank to pay for her MBA program.
4 Last year we _____ a lot of money _____ a new IT system and it's really made a difference.

| A: | lost | owed | saved up | won |
|---|---|---|---|---|
| B: | by | for | on | to |

5 I heard that when they went bankrupt they _____ €2m _____ their creditors.
6 I know someone who _____ half a million _____ the lottery. Can you believe it? What luck!
7 My parents _____ €40,000 _____ a luxury cruise. They went all around the world.
8 He used to have a lot of money, but he _____ it all _____ speculating on the stock market.

| A: | cost | made | spent | wasted |
|---|---|---|---|---|
| B: | from | on | on | to |

9 While her children were small she _____ money for the family by working _____ home.
10 It _____ us a lot of money _____ get on the first page when people do a Google search.
11 I _____ money _____ that gym membership – I only ever went twice.
12 We _____ a lot of money _____ our holiday in the Seychelles but we really enjoyed it.

**12.2 Complete what Sandra says about her bank. Some letters have been given to help you.**

66 Every month my employer pays my [1]sa_ _ _y into my bank [2]a_ _ _ _ _t. I have a card and I can [3]wi_ _ _ _aw money at any cash machine. I'm not very good with money and I usually have an [4]ov_ _ _ _aft by the end of the month. I almost never have any [5]sa_ _ _gs. A few months ago I had to [6]b_ _ _ _w some money to buy a new car and the [7]in_ _ _ _st r_ _e was 8%. What a rip-off! Anyway, the arrangement is that I repay the [8]l_ _n in twelve monthly [9]in_ _ _ _ments. I hate being in [10]d_ _t but I had no choice. 99

**12.3 First rearrange the letters to make words connected with money. Then use the words to complete the sentences.**

| arffod | chgane | morggate | salse |
|---|---|---|---|
| baraign | ~~dicsnout~~ | recipet | wrtoh |

1 I asked the shop assistant for a ___discount___ and she gave me 10% off.
2 The _____ are on in January – things will be much cheaper.
3 I don't have enough money – I can't _____ it.
4 The price is so high! It's not _____ it.
5 It's really cheap. It's a _____ .
6 Here's the money. Can I have a _____ , please?
7 We took out a 25-year _____ to buy our house.
8 I'd like to give the hotel porter a tip. Do you have any _____ ?

**12.4 Complete the sentences with these prepositions: for, for, in, ~~on~~, on, over, to, under.**

1 Everything is going according to plan. The project is on time and ___on___ budget.
2 It would be nice to use better quality materials but we have to keep _____ the budget.
3 The budget _____ next year has not been set.
4 Around 50% of our total budget goes _____ labour costs.
5 Is there any money left _____ the budget?
6 Our Project Manager was really efficient. Believe it or not, the project actually came in _____ budget.
7 There were a lot of delays and other complications. The project went significantly _____ budget.
8 I have budgeted €600 _____ travel expenses.

**12.5 Each time A and B speak, they use one wrong word. Find the mistake and correct it.**

A: That last shop we went into was a real rip-~~out~~.
   *off*
B: You're right. I've seen exactly the same things for sell at the airport, but about half the price.
A: What about that shop over there? It says 'Italian fashion. 50% of!' Let's go in and have a look.
B: OK. That suit over there looks nice, and it's been reduction by €150.
A: Yes, it's a lovely suit. And very good value for price.
B: I'm going to try it on. I need a new suit and my salary has just gone into my account so I can ford it.
A: Make sure you keep the recipe. You should be able to claim back the tax at the airport.
B: It's only a small shop – I hope I can pay with card.
A: Don't worry. I have some local currents on me.

See page 146 for some discussion topics.

## Profit and loss

Companies have to produce accounts every year, and one of the most important is the income statement. It is also called the profit and loss account, or just the P&L. Here is a simplified version.

| money that comes into the company from sales | Revenue | |
| profit before other things are taken away | − Cost of goods sold | direct cost of making the goods, such as materials costs, labour costs |
| | *Gross profit* | |
| profit from the business activities of the company (of course the company can make a profit or a loss) | − Operating costs | general costs, such as rent, utilities, insurance, salaries of office staff, marketing |
| | *Operating profit* | |
| profit that remains after all costs and taxes are taken away | − Tax, depreciation, etc | tax: money paid to the government depreciation: loss in value of machinery, vehicles, etc |
| | *Net profit after tax* | |
| final amount that is left; it is used to reinvest in the company | − Dividends | money paid to the shareholders of the company |
| | *Retained profit* | |

Note the words 'gross' and 'net'. These words can be used for salary or weight as well as profit.

Note these alternative words.

revenue = turnover = sales income
operating costs = overhead = indirect costs
profit = earnings (formal)
a cost = an expense (formal)
spending = expenditure (formal)

Note that we say …

*make a* **reasonable/healthy/huge/record** *profit*
*make a* **slight/significant/substantial/heavy** *loss*
**first-quarter/half-year/annual** *profit*
*have an* **annual turnover of** *€15m*
*pay €2m* **in taxes**

## Assets and liabilities

A second annual account is the balance sheet. Here is a simplified version:

| Assets | Liabilities |
|---|---|
| Current assets | Current liabilities |
| Long-term assets | Long-term liabilities |
| | Shareholders' equity |

*Assets* are what the company owns. Current assets include cash and things that can be turned into cash quickly, such as accounts receivable (= money owed by customers). Long-term assets are things like machinery, vehicles and buildings.

*Liabilities* are what the company owes ('debts' in everyday language). Current liabilities are things that have to be paid quickly, such as accounts payable (= money owed to suppliers). Long-term liabilities are things like bank loans.

Now, imagine that the company stops doing business tomorrow. It uses all its assets to pay all its liabilities. Anything that remains belongs to the shareholders and would be returned to them. It is called shareholders' equity.

Note: Latin and German languages have words like 'active' and 'passive' for assets and liabilities. These are false friends.

We say …
*have* **total assets of** *€8m*
*have a* **healthy/strong** *balance sheet*
*have a* **high level of debt** *on your balance sheet*

## Cash

A third annual account is the cash flow statement. This shows the movement of real cash into and out of the company. A company can be profitable 'on paper' but have cash flow problems because of customers paying late, etc. A company needs real cash, not paper profits, to run its business day to day. This available cash, used to pay bills and salaries, is called working capital.

The three sets of accounts mentioned on this page are audited (= officially examined) each year.

1 Read the text for general understanding.

2 Read it again and underline the words you don't know. Check their meaning.

3 Highlight words you know passively, but don't use actively. Choose some to write sentences of your own.

4 Check pronunciation at macmillandictionary.com

# Exercises

**13.1 Underline the correct words.**

1 Another word for 'revenue' is *profit* / *turnover*.
2 Another word for 'profit' is *earnings* / *dividends*.
3 The word that means 'total before things are taken away' is *brute* / *gross*.
4 The word that means 'total after things are taken away' is *liquid* / *net*.
5 'Assets' are everything that the company *owes* / *owns*.
6 'Liabilities' are everything that the company *owes* / *owns*.
7 Money owed by the company to suppliers is called *accounts payable* / *accounts receivable*.
8 To keep the business running, pay its bills, etc a company needs *daily capital* / *working capital*.

**13.2 Rearrange the letters to make words and phrases from an income statement. Use the definitions in brackets to help you.**

1 cost of doogs losd      *cost of goods sold*
(direct cost of making the products eg materials costs)
2 opatering costs     ——————
(general costs eg utilities, marketing)
3 renevue     ——————
(turnover; money from sales)
4 ssrog prifot     ——————
(profit before other things are taken away)
5 oteparing prifot     ——————
(profit from the business activities of the company)
6 ten prifot after axt     ——————
(profit that remains after all costs and taxes are taken away)
7 divendids     ——————
(money paid to the shareholders)
8 decperiation     ——————
(loss in value of machinery, vehicles, etc)
9 axt     ——————
(money paid to the government)
10 renaited prifot     ——————
(profit that remains, after dividends have been paid, that can be reinvested in the company)

**13.3 Five of the items from Exercise 13.2 are given in the income statement below and five are missing. Fill in the missing items.**

1 ——————
– Cost of goods sold
2 ——————
– Operating costs
3 ——————
– Tax, 4 —————— , etc
Net profit after tax
– 5 ——————
Retained profit

**13.4 Put the phrases into order, from 1 (the best for your company) to 6 (the worst).**

| | | |
|---|---|---|
| *slight loss* | *record profit* | *reasonable profit* |
| *healthy profit* | *heavy loss* | *significant loss* |

Last year we made a …

1 ——————  ☺
2 ——————
3 ——————
4 ——————
5 ——————
6 ——————  ☹

**13.5 Read the text, then answer the questions below.**

What is shareholders' equity? On the very first day of the company's life it is the amount that the original founders of the business invested in the company. Let's imagine this is €100,000. This money, called the share capital, will be held at the bank in cash, waiting for the business activity to start.

So the balance sheet (BS) on Day 1 is very simple. On one side current assets are €100,000 and long-term assets are zero. On the other side, liabilities are zero (the business doesn't yet have any debt) and shareholders' equity is €100,000. The two sides of the balance sheet are equal. (That is why it is called a balance sheet.)

The company has a successful first year. The income statement shows a healthy net profit at the end of the year, and the shareholders decide to pay themselves a small dividend. After this, there is still a little money remaining to reinvest in the business (the retained profit). In the company's accounts this amount is transferred from the income statement to the balance sheet. In the BS it appears as an increase in shareholders' equity.

After several more years of successful trading the shareholders' equity is now quite large – each year it has grown by the addition of retained profits. But remember that shareholders' equity is only 'on paper'. It is not real money that we can see somewhere. Shareholders' equity is real only in the sense that there would be something left theoretically if the business stopped tomorrow and all the debts were paid using all the assets.

Why is shareholders' equity important? Because investors need to know approximately how much the business is worth. The simplest way to value a company is to say that it is the shareholders' equity right now plus (estimated) profits in the future.

**Now circle T (True) or F (False).**

1 Shareholders' equity = share capital + retained profits.      **T / F**
2 Shareholders' equity appears on the right of the BS because it is not an asset that belongs to the company. It is an amount that the company owes (theoretically) to the shareholders.      **T / F**
3 The value of the business is the same as the value of the shareholders' equity.      **T / F**

**See page 146 for some discussion topics.**

# 14 The language of trends

## Trends

A trend is the way a situation is developing or changing. We talk about trends in the financial performance of a company (sales, profits, costs, budgets).

*Sales **fell slightly last quarter**.*
*Profits **have risen 3% year-on-year**.*

We talk about trends in marketing.

*We saw some **growth in market share** last year.*

We talk about trends in the economy (inflation, interest rates, unemployment, house prices).

*There has been a **steady rise in inflation**.*

## Movement up and down

The most common verbs to describe movement up are: *go up, rise, increase, grow*. The irregular verb forms are:

*go up – went up – gone up*
*rise – rose – risen*
*grow – grew – grown*
The nouns are *rise, increase, growth*.

Look at these examples with verbs and nouns.

| | |
|---|---|
| *Sales **went up**.* | (no noun form) |
| *Sales **have risen**.* | *There has been **a rise** in sales.* |
| *Sales **increased**.* | *There was **an increase** in sales.* |
| *Sales **have grown**.* | *We've seen **some growth** in sales.* |

The most common verbs to describe movement down are: *go down, fall, drop*. The irregular verb forms are:

*go down – went down – gone down*
*fall – fell – fallen*

The nouns are *fall, drop*.

Look at these examples with verbs and nouns.

| | |
|---|---|
| *Sales **went down**.* | (no noun form) |
| *Sales **have fallen**.* | *We have seen **a fall** in sales.* |
| *Sales **dropped**.* | *There was **a drop** in sales.* |

## Verb forms

Remember that the past simple (*rose, fell*) is used for a time period that is finished. The present perfect (*have risen, have fallen*) is used for a time period that includes the present.

*Costs **rose** last year / in January.*
*Costs **have risen** this year / since January.*

## Using adjectives and adverbs

We often want to give more details about the size or speed of a trend. We can use basic words like *small, large, slowly, quickly* and also the words below.

**slight – slightly**: very small
**gradual – gradually**: slow and over a long period
**steady – steadily**: slow but continuing
**significant – significantly**: noticeable and important
**sharp – sharply**: large and sudden

Notice the two forms in the example sentences below: a) adjective + noun, then b) verb + adverb.

a  *There was a **slight rise** in profits.*
b  *Profits **rose slightly**.*

a  *There was a **small increase** in profits last year.*
b  *Profits **increased a little** last year.*

a  *We have seen **steady growth** in market share.*
b  *Market share **has grown steadily**.*

## Other types of movement

Sometimes there is no trend:

*Costs have **stayed the same / been stable**.*

Sometimes there is movement up and down:

*Prices have **fluctuated** all year.*
*Prices have **moved up and down within a range**.*

Sometimes there is a high point:

*Sales **peaked / reached a peak** in the second quarter and then fell for the rest of the year.*

We compare two points using 'be up / down'.

*Profits **were** 15% **down** on the previous year.*
('on' = compared to)

## Other points

Study these sentences and notice the prepositions and time phrases.

*Turnover went up **from** €38m **to** €42m – that's an increase **of** €4m.*
*Turnover went up (**by**) €4m.*
*Operating costs were stable **at** around €8.6m.*
*There has been a 2% increase **in** inflation.*
*Sales went up 1.5% **last quarter**.*
*Sales are up 6% **year on year**.*
*Here are the sales figures **for last month**.*

1  Read the text for general understanding.

2  Read it again and <u>underline</u> the words you don't know. Check their meaning.

3  Highlight words you know passively, but don't use actively. Choose some to write sentences of your own.

4  Check pronunciation at macmillandictionary.com

# Exercises

**14.1  Match graphs 1–6 with sentences a–f.**

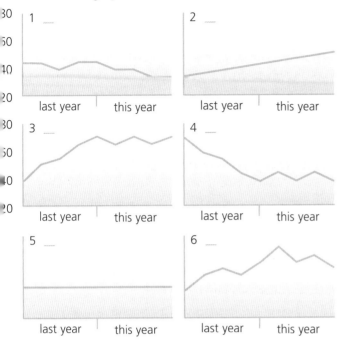

a  Sales peaked in the first quarter of this year.
b  Energy costs increased significantly last year.
c  Unemployment has risen steadily for the last two years.
d  Share prices have fallen slightly this year.
e  Interest rates have stayed the same for two years.
f  Profits dropped sharply last year.

**14.2  Complete the sentences with the correct form of the verb in brackets. It may be necessary to change the verb to a noun.**

1  Sales ___went up___ (go up) 12% last year.
2  Sales _____ (go up) 12% this year.
3  Profits _____ (rise) slightly last year.
4  Profits _____ (rise) slightly this year.
5  There has been a slight _____ (rise) in profits this year.
6  In the last two years our market share _____ (grow) steadily.
7  Last year our market share _____ (grow) steadily.
8  In the last two years there has been steady _____ (grow) in our market share.
9  Turnover _____ (fall) since January.
10  Turnover _____ (fall) in January.
11  In January we saw a significant _____ (fall) in turnover.
12  Costs usually _____ (increase) every year.

**14.3  Underline the correct words in italics.**

1  Costs have *stayed / rested* more or less the same.
2  Sales *had a peak / reached a peak* in March.
3  Market share has been *stability / stable*.
4  There has been a 2% *addition / increase* in inflation.
5  Turnover *fell / fell down* 5% last month.

**14.4  Complete the sentences with these prepositions: *at, for, from, in, of, on, to*.**

1  There was a 14% increase _____ profits.
2  Turnover went up _____ €25m _____ €28.7m. That's an increase _____ around 15%.
3  Market share remained the same _____ around 20%.
4  Sales are up 10% year-_____-year.
5  Here are the sales figures _____ last month.

**14.5  Complete sentence b so that it has the same meaning as sentence a.**

1a  Costs increased significantly last year.
 b  There was a _significant increase_ in costs last year.
2a  Profits dropped sharply last year.
 b  There was a _____ in profits last year.
3a  Inflation has risen gradually for the last two years.
 b  For the last two years there has been a _____ in inflation.
4a  Prices have fallen slightly this year.
 b  We have seen a _____ in prices this year.
5a  Market share has grown steadily over the last few years.
 b  We have seen _____ in our market share.

**14.6  Joelle is reviewing the financial performance of her company over the last two years. Complete the text with words from the box.**

> advertising budget    final figure    20% down
> increased significantly    percentage terms
> sharp drop    starting to rise    within a range

66  Last year was better than this year. If we begin by looking at annual turnover, it was around €40m last year, while this year it's €32m. That means in ^1_____ we're ^2_____ on last year. Luckily, the management team realized it would be a difficult year and every department was told to control its costs. Our ^3_____ for example, was cut from €5.8m to €2.1m. We also stopped replacing staff who left the company. That saved us a lot of money, but it meant that the workload of the remaining people ^4_____ . One thing that was very difficult to control this year was the cost of energy: oil prices moved up and down ^5_____ of $70 to $120 a barrel. Luckily our raw material costs stayed more or less the same.
Because of our success in controlling costs we did still manage to make a small profit this year. The ^6_____ will probably be around €2m – not too bad but it's a ^7_____ compared to last year. Looking ahead to next year, the business environment continues to be difficult. And we have a new challenge – inflation is now ^8_____ . 99

See page 146 for some discussion topics.

# 15 Numbers

## Numbers

Look at how to say numbers. The word 'and' (shown in brackets) is used in British English.

| | |
|---|---|
| 348 | three hundred (and) forty-eight |
| 21,000 | twenty-one thousand |
| 21,300 | twenty-one thousand, three hundred |
| 21,348 | twenty-one thousand, three hundred (and) forty-eight |
| 240,000 | two hundred (and) forty thousand |
| 8.5m | eight point five million |

Note these points.

- The words 'hundred', 'thousand', etc do NOT have an '-s' when used in numbers like those above. However they do have an '-s' in phrases like 'hundreds of people', 'millions of dollars'.
- 0 can be spoken as 'zero', 'nought' or 'oh' depending on dialect and context. The safest thing is just to say 'zero'.
- It is often easier to use approximate numbers:

| | |
|---|---|
| 390–410 | *around/about/roughly* 400 |
| 396 | *nearly/just under* 400 |
| 404 | *just over* 400 |

## + / - / x / ÷

Look at how to say mathematical operations.

| | |
|---|---|
| 8+2 | eight plus two |
| 8–2 | eight minus (take away) two |
| 8×2 | eight times (multiplied by) two |
| 8÷2 | eight divided by two |

To say the result use 'is' or 'makes' or 'equals'.

*Eight plus two **is/makes/equals** ten.*

## Money

Look at how to say amounts of money.

| | |
|---|---|
| €9 | nine euros |
| €9.50 | nine euros fifty |
| | OR nine euros and fifty cents |

Euros and dollars both have cents. Pounds have pence.

Different currencies have an exchange rate. You can ask:

*What's the **euro–dollar exchange rate**?*
*What's **the rate of** the euro **to** the dollar?*

In other contexts the word 'rate' means %.

*The inflation rate is 4%.*

## Fractions, decimals and percentages

Look at how to say fractions.

| | | | |
|---|---|---|---|
| ½ | a half | ⅓ | a third |
| ¼ | a quarter | ⅔ | two thirds |
| ¾ | three quarters | | |

***A quarter of our staff*** *are on short-term contracts.*
***Two thirds of the people*** *who responded to our survey wanted longer opening hours on Sundays.*

With more complicated fractions we say 'out of' instead of giving the fraction.

***Three out of ten people*** *who visited our website placed an order.* (NOT ~~three-tenths of the people~~)

With decimals use the word 'point' and say the numbers after the point individually.

| | |
|---|---|
| 2.56 | two point five six (NOT two point ~~fifty-six~~) |

With % use 'per cent'. The noun is 'percentage'.

*What **percentage profit** do you make on this product?*

With ratios use the word 'to'.

| | |
|---|---|
| 8 : 1 | eight to one |

*The **ratio** (proportion) **of** staff **to** managers in our company is around **eight to one**.*

## Measurements

Look at how to say measurements.

| | |
|---|---|
| 10mm | ten millimetres |
| 10cm | ten centimetres |
| 10m | ten metres |
| 10m² | ten square metres (area) |
| 5×2 | five by two (area/cross section) |
| 10m³ | ten cubic metres (volume) |

Don't use 'of' with units of measurement:

*two hundred euros/gigabytes*
(NOT ~~of~~ euros/~~of~~ gigabytes)

## Other points

Note the phrase 'on average'.

***On average*** *we assemble 80 cars a day.*

Note the prepositions in these examples.

*We had an increase **in** sales **of** 6%.*
*Sales increased **from** €14m **to** €16m.*

1 Read the text for general understanding.

2 Read it again and <u>underline</u> the words you don't know. Check their meaning.

3 Highlight words you know passively, but don't use actively. Choose some to write sentences of your own.

4 Check pronunciation at macmillandictionary.com

# Exercises

**15.1** Match the numbers with the way they are said.

1  790 ☐          4  70,900 ☐
2  7,900 ☐        5  79,000 ☐
3  7,990 ☐        6  7,900,000 ☐

a  seven thousand, nine hundred (and) ninety
b  seventy-nine thousand
c  seven hundred (and) ninety
d  seven million, nine hundred thousand
e  seventy thousand, nine hundred
f  seven thousand, nine hundred

**15.2** Write in words how you would say the numbers below. You can choose whether or not to include 'and'.

1  460 _____ *four hundred (and) sixty*
2  1,300 _____
3  6,950 _____
4  80,500 _____
5  73,000 _____
6  4,200,000 _____

**15.3** Write in words how you would say the mathematical operations below. There may be more than one correct answer.

1  37−5=32
   *thirty-seven minus five is (makes / equals) thirty-two*
2  12×3=36
   _____
3  143+68=211
   _____
4  480÷15=32
   _____

**15.4** Write in words how you would say the prices and measurements below.

1  €15.50 (two ways)      3  50cm$^2$
2  £4.60 (two ways)       4  15m$^3$

1  _____ or _____
2  _____ or _____
3  _____
4  _____

**15.5** Match the fractions, decimals, percentages and ratios with the way they are said.

1  2½ ☐     3  2.55 ☐     5  ¾ ☐     7  2:1 ☐
2  2.5 ☐    4  2.5% ☐     6  ⅔ ☐     8  ⁴⁄₂₅ ☐

a  two thirds
b  two point five per cent
c  two point five
d  two to one
e  three quarters
f  two and a half
g  four out of twenty-five
h  two point five five

**15.6** Write in words how you would say the fractions, decimals, percentages and ratios below. Use a separate piece of paper.

1  ⅓        3  6.75      5  12.5%     7  0.02
2  9.3      4  6:1       6  1¾        8  ¹³⁄₄₀

**15.7** Complete the sentences with these prepositions: *by, in, of, of, of, on, out, over, to, to.*

1  What's the exchange rate of the euro _____ the dollar?
2  Our turnover last quarter was just _____ €15m – €15.8m to be exact.
3  70% _____ the people we surveyed preferred strawberry to vanilla yoghurt.
4  Seven _____ _____ every ten people in our survey said they preferred strawberry to vanilla yoghurt.
5  _____ average US mobile subscribers send and receive 350 SMS messages a month.
6  We saw an increase _____ profits _____ 6.5% last year.
7  The gold to silver price ratio is usually around 50 or 60 _____ 1.
8  I need a piece of wood with a length of 2m and a cross section of 8cm _____ 4cm.

**15.8** The following report extract has eight mistakes. Find them and correct them.

## CUSTOMER SATISFACTION SURVEY

We carried out an email-based survey of customers who have ordered from our website in the last six months. 140 out a possible 873 customers replied. Of these 140 people, the ratio of existing customers to new customers was three by two.

Existing customers had made, for average, three purchases from the website over the six-month period.

Here are the main findings of the survey:

- Rough half of our customers are from the business-to-business sector.
- 85 percentage of customers were either 'satisfied' or 'very satisfied' with our service.
- The remaining 15% gave a variety of reasons for not being satisfied. However it seems that recently there has been an increase on the number of late deliveries and missing items.
- Three quarters the people who replied said they wanted more video on the site so that they could see our products in use.
- Many people suggested that we give more generous discounts. One regular customer suggested a 5% discount for orders with a value more than 1,000 of euros.

See page 146 for some discussion topics.

# 16 Time

## Time expressions

Here are some time expressions.

**Past**

| | |
|---|---|
| *in those days* | *a couple of days ago* |
| *many years ago* | *the other day* |
| *ages ago* | *just* (a short time ago) |
| *a little while ago* | *just now* (a moment ago) |

**Present**

| | |
|---|---|
| *at the moment* | *nowadays* (these days) |
| *right now* | *right away* (immediately) |
| *currently* | *for now* (for a short time) |

**Future**

| | |
|---|---|
| *in a minute* | *from now on* (starting now) |
| *as soon as possible* | *in a little while* (soon) |
| *in a few days* | *sooner or later* (someday) |

The word 'while' (used as a noun) means 'a period of time'.

*I saw her **a little while ago**.*
*I haven't seen her **for a while**.*

The word 'just' has two meanings with time.

*I've **just** had a good idea.* (just = a short time ago)
*Hang on, I'm **just** coming.* (just = now or very soon)

Here are some more useful phrases.

*It **lasted** for one hour.* (= it continued for one hour)
*It **took** me one hour.* (= I needed one hour)
*It's **over**.* (= it's finished)
*There are ten minutes **to go**.* (= ten minutes remaining)

The word 'by' is used to mean 'not later than'.

*I need your report **by** Friday.*

We often use 'by' with 'at the latest'.

*I'll call you when I know more information – **by** the end of next week **at the latest**.*

The phrase 'by the time' means 'when'.

***By the time** I arrived, the meeting had started.*

We use 'not … yet' to talk about something that has not happened, but probably will happen.

*I have**n't** decided **yet**.*
*Have you decided? – **Not yet**.*

Finally, note that we do not use the word 'actually' with a time reference. It means 'in fact/really'.

## Using the word 'time'

We can use the word 'time' with the verbs below.

***allow** time for sb to do sth*
***find** time to do sth*
***fix**/**set** a time for sth*
***(not) have enough** time to do sth*
***run out of** time* (= have no more time left)
***save** time by doing sth*
***spend** time on sth/doing sth*
***take** sb time to do sth*
***waste** time on sth/doing sth*

Notice that we *spend/waste/save/run out of* both time and money.

*We've **spent** a lot of **time** and **money** on this project.*

Here are more expressions with the word 'time'.

*for the time being* (= for a short period of time)
*in the meantime* (= until something happens)
*in two weeks'/five years' time* (= time from now)
*in time* (= early enough to do something)
*on time* (= at the correct time)

## Schedules and deadlines

A schedule is a plan of activities and when they will happen. Similar words are 'timetable' and 'programme'. A project can be:

***behind** schedule* (= late)
***on** schedule* (= going according to the plan)
***ahead of** schedule* (= early)

You can:

*have a **busy**/**tight** schedule*
***update** the schedule* (if it needs to be changed)
***build** something **into** the schedule*

We also use 'schedule' as a verb. It means 'arrange something at a particular time':

*Let's **schedule** another meeting for July.*

A deadline is a time or date by which you must complete some work. You can:

***set** a deadline*
*have a **strict** deadline* (= it must be obeyed)
*have a **tight** deadline* (= there is only just enough time)
***meet**/**make** the deadline* (= you finish on time)
***miss** the deadline* (= you don't finish on time)

1 Read the text for general understanding.

2 Read it again and <u>underline</u> the words you don't know. Check their meaning.

3 Highlight words you know passively, but don't use actively. Choose some to write sentences of your own.

4 Check pronunciation at macmillandictionary.com

# Exercises

## 16.1 Read the sentences and think about the meaning of the underlined word/s.

1 Are you looking for Claude? I saw him a little while ago – maybe he's gone for lunch.
2 OK, OK. I'm coming right away.
3 I was rushing and I made a mistake. From now on I'm going to be more careful.
4 I started working here ages ago. Let me see, it must be over 20 years now.
5 You can leave your bags in the hall for now.
6 Nowadays it's very difficult to find a secure job – things in the business world are changing so fast.
7 I was talking to Leyla the other day – she sends you her best wishes.
8 It's the best smart phone currently available.
9 I need to stay at the office to finish this report. I'll join you at the restaurant in a little while.

**Now match the underlined words with a word or phrase from the box with the same meaning.**

| a long time ago    a short time ago |
| at the present time    for a short time    immediately |
| recently    soon    starting now    these days |

sentence 1    *a short time ago*
sentence 2    _____
sentence 3    _____
sentence 4    _____
sentence 5    _____
sentence 6    _____
sentence 7    _____
sentence 8    _____
sentence 9    _____

## 16.2 Complete the sentences with *lasted* or *took*.

1 It _____ me a whole day to prepare the slides for the presentation.
2 The planning meeting _____ for two hours.
3 Last year the hot weather _____ until October.
4 It _____ them two days to send someone to fix the photocopier.
5 That printer cartridge only _____ for a week.
6 It _____ me over an hour to get to work this morning – the snow was terrible.

## 16.3 Underline the correct word/s in italics.

1 What a horrible experience! I'm glad it's *complete / over*.
2 If we want a stand at the trade fair, we need to let them know by Friday *at the last / at the latest*.
3 *In the time / By the time* I found their offices it was nearly five o'clock and everyone was going home.
4 Sorry, I *haven't spoken to my boss yet / yet haven't spoken to my boss* – I'll do it this afternoon.
5 Many people live until they're ninety *actually / nowadays*.

## 16.4 Match the beginnings of sentences 1–8 with their endings a–h.

1 Before we finish, let's fix a time   [e]
2 I won't have enough time to   [ ]
3 It looks like I've run out of time so   [ ]
4 At the weekend I like to spend time   [ ]
5 Don't waste your time   [ ]
6 If you could find some time   [ ]
7 You should allow time   [ ]
8 We could save a lot of time   [ ]

a for people to ask questions at the end of your talk.
b do it today, but I'll try to do it tomorrow.
c to help me with this new software, I'd be really grateful.
d I'll finish my presentation here.
e for the next meeting.
f trying to get everything absolutely perfect.
g meeting friends and relaxing.
h by taking a taxi direct to the conference centre and going to the hotel later.

## 16.5 Complete the sentences with these prepositions: *ahead, behind, for, into, of, on*.

1 Don't worry, we're _____ schedule – everything is going according to the plan.
2 I'm a little worried. According to the initial plan we're about a week _____ schedule.
3 Our Project Manager is doing a great job. Believe it or not, we're about a week _____ _____ schedule.
4 We calculate the time we need and then build an extra week _____ the schedule for safety – just in case anything goes wrong.
5 The meeting is scheduled _____ next Tuesday.

## 16.6 Complete the dialogue by writing one word in each space. Some letters are given to help you.

DANA: I'm going home now. Are you staying in the office and working late again?

KARL: Yes, I am. I have a [1]dead_____ that I don't want to [2]m_____ . I'm writing a report on the Barcelona project and it's very important that I finish it [3]o_____ t_____ .

DANA: I thought the Barcelona project was finished.

KARL: No, it isn't finished [4]y_____ .
There's still another few months to [5]g_____ .

DANA: Really?

KARL: Yes. It was originally planned to finish this month, but we're [6]b_____ sch_____ .

**See page 146 for some discussion topics.**

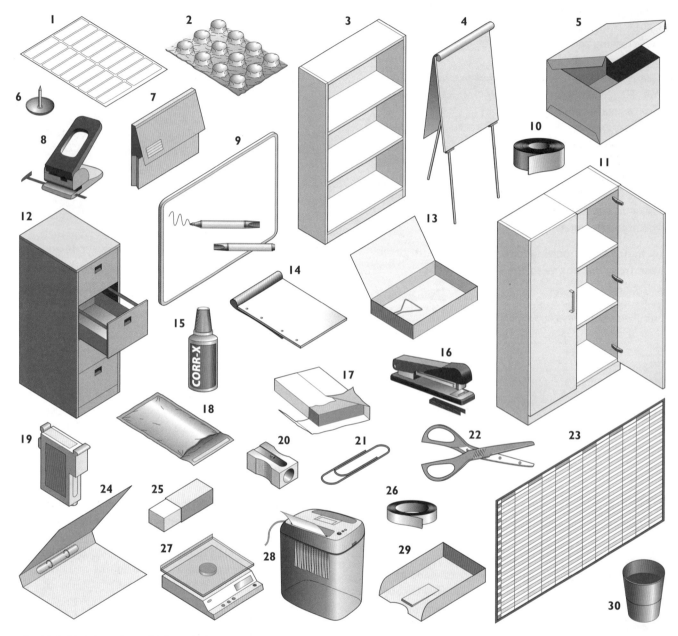

1 address labels (on a sheet of A4)
2 bubble wrap
3 bookcase with shelves
4 easel with flipchart
5 mailing box (with the lid open)
6 drawing pin
7 document wallet
8 hole punch

9 dry wipe board/whiteboard with markers
10 packing tape
11 stationery cupboard
12 filing cabinet (with one open drawer)
13 box file
14 pad of paper
15 correction fluid

16 stapler (with spare staples)
17 pack of copy paper
18 padded envelope
19 printer cartridge (containing ink or toner)
20 pencil sharpener
21 paper clip
22 scissors
23 wall planner

24 ring binder
25 rubber (BrE)/eraser (AmE)
26 sticky tape/sellotape
27 scales
28 shredder
29 tray
30 waste bin (BrE)/trash can (AmE)

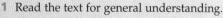

1 Read the text for general understanding.

2 Read it again and <u>underline</u> the words you don't know. Check their meaning.

3 Highlight words you know passively, but don't use actively. Choose some to write sentences of your own.

4 Check pronunciation at macmillandictionary.com

# Exercises

**17.1 Refer to the drawings on the page opposite. Complete each sentence with the name of the most appropriate object (or part of an object). Note that the gap may have two words (eg *paper clip*).**

1 They say these titanium _____*scissors*_____ will never need sharpening, but I don't believe it.

2 In the training room we have a _____ fixed to the wall (with a tray for markers) and also a _____ on an easel. We use PowerPoint as well, but the old technology is better for brainstorming and using ideas from the group.

3 I'm just preparing the handouts for the presentation. The paper is printed double-sided, and I'm going to fasten the pages together with two _____ at the side instead of one in the corner, so that the pages open like a book.

4 Hotels always put a pencil and a _____ of paper next to the room telephone in case you want to make any notes. But they never give you a _____ in case the pencil breaks!

5 You shouldn't use _____s to fix things to the wall – use Blu-Tack instead as it won't leave a hole.

6 Has the photocopier run out of paper again? The _____s of paper are over there in the _____ – don't worry, it's not locked.

7 Industrial espionage has been a big problem in our industry. Our policy now is to put all paper documents in the _____ after use – for reasons of confidentiality. If we throw something away in the _____, it could be found later.

8 As a freelancer I need a simple system to keep all my business receipts. I just throw them into a cardboard _____ where they stay until I do my tax return. It sits on one of the _____ of a bookcase at the side of my desk.

9 I've made a mistake with the postcode on this envelope. Can you pass me the _____?

10 Let's get a big _____ and put it right by the door so that everyone knows what's happening each day. We can even use colour-coded stickers for different kinds of events – it'll be fun!

11 I want to put these photocopies into a ring binder. Have you seen the _____?

12 If I want to send a book or DVD through the mail, I usually use a simple _____ to give it a bit of protection. But if it's something more delicate, then I use lots of _____ before putting it into a mailing box.

13 The word 'folder' is used in computer filing systems. A physical folder is anything that folds (= bends by pressing one part over another). One example might be a document wallet, another might be a _____ that holds punched documents firmly in place, and another might be the open folders that hang suspended from the drawers of a _____ .

14 I want to make sure this parcel doesn't come open in the mail. I don't think normal _____ will be strong enough to hold it – have you seen that roll of _____ anywhere?

15 The mailing cost of all these packages will depend on the weight. Let's take one and put it on the _____ to see how heavy it is.

16 These are the wrong address labels. We need the ones with sixteen labels per _____ .

17 At the conference registration they gave us a _____ to keep all our loose papers. It's quite useful, in spite of the horrible logo on the cover.

18 When you buy a printer nearly all the money goes to the retailer. The printer manufacturers make their money when you replace the _____s. It doesn't make any difference whether you use an ink jet printer, or a laser printer with _____ .

19 (*same word used three times*) Some people still organize their desks the old-fashioned way. They have an in _____ for documents recently received, a pending _____ for documents that are waiting for action, and an out _____ for documents that need to be filed (or for envelopes ready to be mailed).

20 The simple _____ is still in use to hold sheets of paper together. You can also use it for other things – like cleaning a pencil sharpener.

**17.2 Try to fill in the missing letters. The words are not given opposite but they are all related to computers and computer equipment.**

1 People are now used to touch-sc_ _ _n phones. Do they want to touch computer mon_ _ _rs in the same way? Possibly, but I think that the two traditional input dev_ _es (a mouse that you cl_ _k and a key_ _ _ _d where you t_ _e) will be with us for a long time.

2 I want a laptop with a long ba_ _ _ _y life, a hard d_ _ve with a large cap_ _ity, the latest op_ _ _ _ing system, a fast pr_ _ _ssor and a w_ _e screen. Oh yes, it should also be Bluetooth en_ _led. And as li_ _t as possible.

3 We use very little paper in the office, but we still need a h_ _d c_ _y of important documents.

4 The glare from the screen is hurting my eyes. Is it possible to t_ _n the bri_ _ _ness do_ _?

5 When I work from home I have to remember to sw_ _ch the w_ _cam o_ _ – I don't want colleagues to see me in my pyjamas!

**See page 146 for some discussion topics.**

# 18 Using the Internet and email

## Using the Internet

Here are some things that you might do while using the Internet:

*use your favourite* **browser** (IE, Chrome, etc)

*use* **default settings** ('default' = the way that something is done automatically if you do not change it; 'setting' = the position on a control panel)

*start at your* **home page**

**surf** (= look at pages on) *the Internet (or the Web)*

*go to/visit a* **website**

**browse** (= look around) *a* **website**, *looking at the individual* **web pages**

**scroll up** *and* **down** *the page using the* **scroll bar**

*use the Back and Forward* **buttons**

*open a* **new window** (or **tab**)

**type** *a* **search term** *into a* **search engine**

*type the* **URL** *directly into the address bar*

*use your* **Favorites** (or **Bookmarks**)

**block pop-ups** (or *temporarily* **allow** *them*)

*play a* **video clip**, *perhaps* **pausing** *it or* **restarting** *it*

*send a page (or a* **link**) *to a friend by email*

*select an item from a* **pop-up/drop-down menu** ('pop' = appear in a new window)

**click** (or **double-click** *or* **right/left-click**) *on a* **link** (or *on an* **icon**)

**register** *with a site, using an* **online form**

**sign in** (or **log in**) *to a site (or an email account); then* **sign out** (or **log out**) *of the site*

**enter a username** (or **user ID**) *and* **password**

**copy and paste** (= insert) *some text from the site into a document*

*copy and paste a graphics file onto your* **desktop**

**print** *a page, perhaps* **previewing** *it first*

**download** *a file, perhaps checking the* **progress of the download** *by looking at the* **status bar**

**upload** *some photographs to a* **social networking site** (such as Facebook or Twitter)

*make sure your* **internet security software** *is* **up to date**, *including the* **firewall** *and* **anti-virus/anti-spyware components**

**delete** *your* **browsing history**

These days people use the Internet on mobile devices, such as smart phones, as much as on computers. One feature of smart phones is the wide range of apps (= applications) available for download. Another trend is for software and data to be accessed 'in the cloud' (= stored on internet servers) rather than locally on a hard drive.

## Using email

There are two ways to use email. You can use a programme like Microsoft Outlook that downloads emails onto your hard drive and allows you to work offline. Or you can use webmail (like Yahoo! or Gmail) where you access your email online, including on a mobile platform. Many people do both.

You check your email to see if you have any new messages. They appear in your inbox. When you receive an email you can reply, forward it, save it, print it or delete it. If you save it, you can choose which folder (or sub-folder) to save it in. Also don't forget to check your spam folder occasionally – maybe there is something there that you want. If so, add that email address to your whitelist so that the spam filter ignores it.

*The first thing I do when I get to work is* **check my email**. *This is an interesting email – I'll* **forward it to you**.

When you write an email you can paste in text from another document, or insert a file such as a picture into the body of the email. You can also attach a file to an email – typical attachments being a Word document, Excel spreadsheet or photo. You can use a special symbol (like an exclamation mark) to give it high importance, or flag it (= mark it with a flag) to remind you that it needs to be followed up. You can save an unfinished email in your drafts folder if you want to work on it later.

***Please find attached*** *the sales report for March.*

Now the email is ready to send. You can send it to one person or several. If you 'cc' it to someone, then you send them a copy. If you 'bcc' it, then you also send a copy, but it is a blind copy so other recipients cannot see the name and email address. Email etiquette says that it's better to use bcc when sending a mass mailing for reasons of confidentiality. Don't forget the subject line – state the topic of the email very clearly so that the recipient can easily find it in their files later.

1  Read the text for general understanding.

2  Read it again and <u>underline</u> the words you don't know. Check their meaning.

3  Highlight words you know passively, but don't use actively. Choose some to write sentences of your own.

4  Check pronunciation at macmillandictionary.com

# Exercises

**18.1 Write S if the items are the same or very similar. Write D if they are different.**

1  the Internet / the web ............ [S]
2  a browser / a search engine ............ [ ]
3  your favorites / your bookmarks ............ [ ]
4  a link / an icon ............ [ ]
5  sign in to a site / log in to a site ............ [ ]
6  copy text / paste text ............ [ ]
7  download a program / install a program ............ [ ]
8  reply to an email / forward an email ............ [ ]
9  a file / a folder ............ [ ]
10 send somebody a copy / cc somebody ............ [ ]

**18.2 Underline the correct word in italics.**

1  *roll / scroll* up and down the page
2  use the Back and Forward *buttons / labels*
3  *block / prohibit* pop-ups
4  *click / press* on a link
5  *enrol / register* with a site
6  *enter / write* a password
7  *overview / preview* a page before printing
8  *send / transmit* an email
9  *delete / destroy* an email
10 *attach / enclose* a document

**18.3 Match an item on the left with an item on the right to make phrases from the text opposite.**

1  search            setting
2  default           networking
3  video             clip
4  drop-down         engine
5  social            menu

6  browsing          mailing
7  smart phone       history
8  drafts            line
9  mass              folder
10 subject           app

**18.4 Complete the sentences with a phrase from Exercise 18.3.**

1  Google is the most popular *search engine* .
2  Facebook and Twitter are ............... sites.
3  Move your mouse over the headings at the top of the page and you'll see a ............... .
4  You can use my laptop, but please don't change any of the ...............s.

5  Wait a moment while I look for the email I was writing earlier – OK, here it is in my ............... .
6  I have dozens of emails from you – what was the ............... of the one you're talking about?
7  I think we should do a ............... to all our customers about the special promotion next month.
8  I think Apple has always had the coolest ...............s and that's why the iPhone is doing so well.

**18.5 Complete the sentences with these prepositions:** *at, down, in, into, into, off, on, on, to, up.*

1  Why don't you go ............ our website and look ............ the video clips of our products?
2  You'll find the 'Contact us' link if you scroll right ............ to the bottom of the page.
3  The usefulness of the search depends on exactly which term you type ............ the search engine.
4  Just click ............ the link at the bottom of this email to go straight to our site.
5  I'm trying to access my webmail but it won't allow me to sign ............ .
6  I'm going to copy this paragraph from the site and paste it ............ an email to all my friends.
7  I'm just ............loading some photos of my holiday to Facebook.
8  I have all my emails stored ............ my hard drive, so I can access them even when I'm ............line.

**18.6 Complete the text using the words and phrases in the box.**

> bullets    capital letters    forwarded
> mobile device    recipients    remaining information
> Reply to All    ~~subject line~~

There are many unwritten rules of email etiquette in a business context. Here are some of the most important:

- Clearly state the topic in the [1] *subject line* . This helps people organize their email.
- Keep your messages short. They might be read on a [2] ............... where the screen size is small.
- Answer all the questions – don't leave the other person wondering if a second email is coming with the [3] ............... .
- Use paragraphing, [4] ..............., etc – it's much easier to read and respond to an email where the text is broken down into separate points.
- Don't copy every message you write to everyone in your team. Unnecessary messages are annoying. Similarly, when you answer an email do not overuse the [5] ............... button.
- Use Bcc when the [6] ............... don't know each other. It's not polite to give out someone's email address without their agreement.
- Avoid using [7] ............... for whole words. IT MAKES IT LOOK LIKE YOU'RE SHOUTING AND IT'S ALSO MORE DIFFICULT TO READ.
- Don't write anything you wouldn't say in public. Once the email has left your outbox it can be [8] ............... to anyone in the world. If in doubt, use the telephone.

**See page 147 for some discussion topics.**

# 19 Working conditions

This unit deals with some general areas related to working conditions. The topics of pay, benefits and motivation are covered in Unit 26.

## Working conditions

We know our ideal kind of workplace. It would have natural daylight; our own workstation in a spacious, well-equipped, open-plan office; comfortable furniture; air-conditioning (and central heating in cold countries); facilities such as a subsidized canteen, a crèche for small children, and a break-out area to sit and relax. This ideal workplace would be well-located so that our daily commute (= journey to and from work) is not too difficult, and in any case we would claim travel costs on expenses. Working hours would be reasonable: we would work a traditional eight-hour day, and be able to take 'time off in lieu' (AmE 'comp days' meaning 'compensation days') if we work more than the contracted hours.

But sadly reality is rarely like that. In the worst cases people work in small, noisy, cramped (= with not enough space) cubicles; the office is badly-equipped; staff work long hours with no overtime pay – even though they are entitled to it according to their contract; the working atmosphere is extremely stressful; and with the heavy workload many people suffer from burnout (= being tired or ill because of hard work).

## Work worries

You go for an interview and get what looks like your dream job. Congratulations! But after some time you realize that there are problems.

- *Having a bad boss.* Managing your boss is a skill you can learn – there are training courses called 'Managing Up'. The key is to understand your boss's priorities and communication style, and then target your behaviour towards him or her accordingly.
- *Difficult co-workers.* You don't choose the people you work with. Is there someone who gossips by the water cooler all day long? Is there an office joker who you find intensely irritating? And what about the glass-half-empty pessimist or the seen-it-all-before cynic who drain your energy away?

Protecting yourself from others involves a good awareness of office politics and how to get along with people.

- *Discrimination.* This is when a particular group of people is treated unfairly. In a recent survey, 22% of Americans said they had been unfairly denied a promotion or salary increase (AmE raise) because of their gender, race, age, religion or disability.
- *Bullying.* A bully is someone who deliberately frightens or upsets other people. A related area is sexual harassment ('harassment' = threatening or offensive behaviour).
- *Longer-term career management.* Nowadays nobody has a secure job, and you can't rely on your current employer for training and promotion. It's up to you to manage your own career.

## Health and safety

Workplace safety is an area covered by law, and all companies have to comply with (= obey) health and safety (H&S) regulations. H&S is a big issue in factories because of all the machinery, but there are dangers in every workplace. If anyone is injured at work, they can sue (= take legal action against) the company and demand compensation.

There is usually one person in a company with a specific responsibility for H&S. This person will work closely with the union (= the organization that is formed by workers to protect their rights). Responsibilities of the H&S Officer might include:

- Ensuring (= making sure) that there are signs and warning notices in appropriate places.
- Ensuring that protective equipment is issued and used – for example hard hats where objects could fall from above.
- Ensuring regular maintenance of equipment that could present a danger.
- Fitting and maintaining smoke alarms.
- Organizing regular fire drills, and maintaining fire alarms and fire extinguishers.
- Keeping floors free from hazards that could cause slips or falls.
- Identifying and training first-aiders who can help if someone is injured.

1 Read the text for general understanding.

2 Read it again and <u>underline</u> the words you don't know. Check their meaning.

3 Highlight words you know passively, but don't use actively. Choose some to write sentences of your own.

4 Check pronunciation at macmillandictionary.com

# Exercises

**19.1 Fill in the missing letters.**

1 a sp_ _ious, well-equ_ _ _ed, open-pl_ _ office
2 a sub_ _ _ized cant_ _n and a br_ _k-o_ _ area
3 cl_ _m travel costs on exp_ _ _es
4 take time o_ _ in li_ _
5 a small, noi_ _ _, cr_ _ped cub_ _le
6 be ent_ _led to over_ _ _ _ pay
7 understand your boss's pri_ _ _ties and co_ _ _ _ication sty_ e
8 have a good aw_ _ _ness of office pol_ _ _cs and how to get al_ _ _ with people
9 be unf_ _rly denied a pr_ _otion or salary inc_ _ _se.

**19.2 Find a word or phrase from Exercise 19.1 that means:**

1 paid in part to help reduce the cost _____
2 ask for something that you have a right to _____
3 money that you spend as part of your job and then get back from your employer _____
4 a small enclosed area in a room _____
5 (three words) have something as a right _____
6 knowledge or understanding of a situation _____
7 (two words) power relations between people at work on a day-to-day basis _____
8 when you are given a job at a higher level _____

**19.3 Match an item on the left with an item on the right to make phrases from the text opposite.**

| | |
|---|---|
| 1 comply with | the company because of an injury |
| 2 be injured | there are appropriate warning notices |
| 3 sue | compensation |
| 4 demand | regulations |
| 5 ensure that | at work |
| 6 issue | floors free from hazards |
| 7 organize | protective equipment |
| 8 fit | first-aiders |
| 9 keep | regular fire drills |
| 10 train | smoke alarms |

**19.4 Find a word or phrase from Exercise 19.3 that means:**

1 official rules _____
2 hurt in an accident _____
3 money someone is given because they have been injured or badly treated _____
4 written signs that give information _____
5 officially give something _____
6 repeated practice of what you should do in a dangerous situation _____
7 things that could be dangerous or cause accidents _____
8 people who give basic medical treatment as soon as someone is injured _____

**19.5 Fill in the missing letters.**

1 Your workpl_ _ _ is the building where you work.
2 Your workst_ _ _ _ _ is your desk with a computer.
3 Your worklo_ _ is the amount of work you have to do.
4 To go_ _ _p is to talk informally about other people's behaviour and private lives.
5 To refer to male or female, we can say ge_ _ _er.
6 Bu_ _ying is a big problem in schools as well as at work.

**19.6 Complete these health and safety rules using the words in the box.**

| | | | |
|---|---|---|---|
| assembly point | canteen | ~~clean and tidy~~ | hard hat |
| protective clothing | sign in | unauthorized | waste material |

1 The factory floor must be kept *clean and tidy* .
2 Factory workers must wear _____ at all times.
3 Before entering the construction site you must put on a _____ .
4 Put all _____ into the marked bins.
5 Food and drink can only be consumed in the _____ .
6 When you hear the fire alarm, go directly to the _____ . Do not stop to collect personal belongings.
7 Visitors must _____ at reception.
8 No _____ persons* are allowed to enter the storerooms or workshops.

* 'persons' is often used in official notices in place of 'people'

**19.7 Underline the correct or most appropriate word in italics. Be careful – sometimes the words are similar.**

In the field of people skills, managing your boss receives far less attention than managing people below you. Here are some useful tips for 'managing up':

● Don't bring a problem without bringing a solution. Better still, bring a [1]*group/range* of solutions.
● Give your boss some attention. Listen. Imagine what it is like to be him or her and what is important. Show [2]*empathy/sympathy*.
● When your boss asks a question, don't give too much detail. Instead, give a short answer and wait for any [3]*follow-up/furthermore* questions where needed.
● When your boss asks how things are [4]*going/running*, don't say everything's [5]*well/fine*. Start with the positives, certainly, but then move on to other areas. Your boss wants to know what can be fixed or improved to produce a better [6]*outcome/outlook*.
● When receiving criticism, don't [7]*argue/fight* or defend yourself. Try this strategy instead: first just shut up and listen; then ask clarifying questions (this turns the criticism into a [8]*chat/dialogue*); finally ask what changes you can make that will satisfy the criticism.

**See page 147 for some discussion topics.**

# 20 Your job

Your job is the particular work you do to earn money. You have a job title (such as Sales Consultant). The words 'post' and 'position' are more formal, and often used in job advertisements. The word 'occupation' is used on official forms.

Your job can be …

*badly-paid, boring, challenging, depressing, fun, glamorous, hard, interesting, rewarding, routine, secure, stressful, varied, well-paid, worthwhile*

## Describing your job

People might ask you:

*What do you do?*
*What kind of work do you do?*
*What do you do for a living?*

You answer *I'm a/an … +* the name of your profession and/or job title and/or business area.

*I'm an accountant.*
*I'm a Marketing Manager at a consumer electronics company.*

Note the prepositions:

*I work **in** a bank/an office.* (general place of work)
*I work **at** Head Office.* (specific place of work)
*I work **in** advertising/the fashion industry/the financial sector.*
*I work **for** Nestlé/an oil company.*
*I'm working **on** the design of …* (a project)
*I work **as** an engineer.* (profession)

To give a little more detail you can use the language in the box below.

---

**Describing your job**
*My job involves … (+ -ing form)*
*I spend a lot of/most of my time … (+ -ing form)*
*I deal with/handle …*
*My role is to …*
*I don't have much to do with …*

**Talking about what you personally control**
*I'm in charge of …*
*I'm responsible for …*
*I look after/take care of …*

**Talking about your boss**
*I report (directly) to …*
*My line manager is …*

---

*My job **involves** (= includes as a necessary part) visiting customers and discussing their needs.*
*I **deal with** customer enquiries.*
***My role is to** support the Sales Director.*
*I **don't have much to do with** the financial side.*
***I'm responsible for** strategy.* (NOT the responsible)
*I **report to** the Head of Customer Services.*

Note also the following words and phrases:

*I'm **working part-time** at the moment.*
*It's a **full-time** job – I work **nine to five**.*
*I'm on a **short-term/temporary contract**.*
*I'm on a **permanent contract**.*
*I'm **self-employed**. I work as a **freelance** consultant.*
*I'm **unemployed** right now, but I'm looking for a job as a …*
*I'm a student at the moment – I **graduate** next year.*

## Tasks and responsibilities

To give a detailed description of your day-to-day work, you might use phrases like those below.

***answer** hundreds of emails each day*
***develop** the business*
***do** market research*
***give** presentations*
***implement** the decisions of more senior managers*
***interview** job applicants*
***keep** computer files up to date*
***keep on top of** the paperwork*
***liaise** with my counterparts in other countries*
***make** decisions about budgets*
***make sure that** the IT network is working properly*
***maintain** all the equipment and machinery*
***manage** the production schedule*
***monitor** the production process*
***negotiate** with suppliers*
***organize** special promotions*
***prepare** the accounts*
***process** customer orders*
***recruit** new staff*
***set** sales targets and make sure they are met*
***solve** problems*
***supervise** the day-to-day work of my team*
***support** (or assist) the Marketing Director*
***write** quarterly reports*

---

1 Read the text for general understanding.

2 Read it again and <u>underline</u> the words you don't know. Check their meaning.

3 Highlight words you know passively, but don't use actively. Choose some to write sentences of your own.

4 Check pronunciation at macmillandictionary.com

# Exercises

**20.1 Match the adjectives describing jobs in the box with the most appropriate comment below.**

| boring | challenging | ~~hard~~ | glamorous |
|---|---|---|---|
| rewarding | secure | stressful | varied |

1 'The job I'm doing at the moment is not easy. I haven't done anything like this before.' _____hard_____

2 'I feel worried all the time – I just can't relax. Even when I come home I think about work.' _____

3 'Every day the same old thing. Nothing interesting ever happens in this office.' _____

4 'Yes, it's true that my job can be difficult at times – but I enjoy finding solutions to new problems. It makes things interesting.' _____

5 'In my job no two days are the same – different people to meet, new projects, different things to do. I never get bored.' _____

6 'I come home at the end of the day and I feel happy and satisfied. I know that I have really helped people in their lives.' _____

7 'I'm not worried about losing my job – even in a recession they will always need people like me.'

_____

8 'International travel, staying at five-star hotels, cocktail parties, meeting celebrities – I love my job!'

_____

**20.2 In the dialogues below there is <u>one</u> word missing in each question and each answer. Find the words and write them in the correct place.**

1 A: What you do?
  B: I'm lawyer specializing in mergers and acquisitions.
2 A: What kind work do you do?
  B: I work a scientist in the pharmaceutical industry.
3 A: What do you do a living?
  B: I work advertising.
4 A: What you doing at the moment?
  B: I'm working a project to improve the design and functionality of our website.
5 A: Is it a 9-to-5 full job?
  B: Yes, it is, but I'm a short-term contract – just for one year.
6 A: How do you deal a customer who has a serious complaint?
  B: If it's an important customer, I prefer to go to their office and talk to them to-face.
7 A: Who's charge of security in the building?
  B: We don't really have one person responsible that, but the reception staff check everyone who comes in.
8 A: Who do you report?
  B: My line is Mr Robert Louis-Dreyfus.

**20.3 Underline the correct word in italics.**

1 Your job is the work you do to *earn / gain* money.
2 What's your new job *name / title*?
3 What do you do *for your life / for a living*?
4 I'm working *on / with* an exciting new project.
5 I work *as / like* a financial analyst.
6 I'm looking for a new *job / work*.
7 I'm on a *short-term / short-time* contract.
8 I'm *autonomous / a freelancer*.
9 I *pass / spend* a lot of my time in meetings.
10 My role is *support / to support* the legal department.
11 I'm *responsible / the responsible* for maintaining the company website.
12 I take care *for / of* all the travel arrangements.

**20.4 Complete the sentences below using the words in the box. Note that a short line means a preposition.**

| care | charge | deals | handles | looks | responsible |
|---|---|---|---|---|---|
| takes | after | for | in | of | of | with |

Maria
is __ _____
is __ _____
___ ___
___ ___
___ ___
the sales side of the business

**20.5 Study the list of tasks and responsibilities at work a–o. Write each letter next to the name of the <u>most appropriate</u> department below. Find a solution that uses each item once.**

a attend trade fairs
b handle telephone enquiries
c keep on top of the paperwork
d make sure the whole supply chain is running smoothly
e maintain all the equipment and machinery
f manage cashflow
g meet and greet visitors to the company
h monitor quality
i organize special promotions
j organize training
k prepare the accounts
l recruit new staff
m run focus groups to test new products
n set budgets for different departments
o talk to the unions about pay and conditions

Sales and Marketing: ___ ___ ___
Production and Operations: ___ ___ ___
Finance: ___ ___ ___
Human Resources: ___ ___ ___
Administration: ___ ___ ___

See page 147 for some discussion topics.

# 21 Projects and teams

## The team

The success of projects depends on teamwork. The team leader should support team members, and every individual needs to be a good team player. You can:

*lead/head (up)/run* a team
*build/form* a team
*join* a team
*work together as* a team
*team up with* somebody (= work together with them)
*be a team leader/team member/team player*

Often your team includes external partners with whom you have common ground (= shared goals in certain areas). You work with them for your mutual benefit (= both sides gain something). When outside people are involved in the team and have the same goals, they are 'on board'.

*There is a lot of* **common ground** *between us – I think we can* **work together for our mutual benefit**.
*Welcome to the team. It's great to have you* **on board**.

## Time and money

Projects have a schedule (= time plan) and a deadline (= final date). You can:

*fall behind* schedule and then *catch up*
*be on* schedule
*finish ahead of* schedule
*agree/confirm/set/extend* a deadline
*meet/miss* a deadline

Projects also need a budget (= money available to spend). Before the project starts you can:

*estimate* (or *underestimate*) *costs*
*make a* **rough** (= approximate) *estimate of costs*

And once it is running you should try to:

*keep within* the budget
*stick to* the budget (also *stick to the schedule*)

## Getting started

At the beginning of a project you:

- Allocate resources (= decide how to use money, time, people and materials).
- Brief team members (= give them information and instructions).
- Delegate tasks.

If you are doing a project for an outside client, you:

- Meet with the client and discuss the specifications (= detailed instructions).
- Produce a breakdown (= detailed list) of the costs.
- Draw up (= prepare and write) a proposal and present it to the client.
- Get feedback from the client, and then modify the proposal based on the feedback.
- Discuss the details of the contract and then sign it once everything is agreed.
- Appoint subcontractors, usually after putting the work out to tender (= announcing publicly that work is needed and giving different companies the opportunity to bid for the work).

Finally you set a start date. If you have any issues (= problems), you might have to delay (= postpone/put back/push back) the start date.

## Progress

Everyone gets on with their work (= continues with it). The team leader gets regular updates from team members and makes sure that:
a) everything is on track (= developing in the right way and likely to be successful), and
b) everyone is kept in the loop (= kept informed).

- **Where are we with** *Phase 1 of the project?*
- *We've* **already** *done it./We have***n't** *done it* **yet**./*Don't worry, everything's* **on track**.

---

- *Is everything going OK?*
- *We* **had an issue** *with a subcontractor but we're* **back on track** *now.*

---

- *Can you send me* **regular updates***?*
- **Leave it with me.**

---

- **What's happening with** *Phase 2? I'm* **out of the loop**.
- *Good news. We're slightly* **ahead of schedule**. *And up to now we've managed to* **keep within the budget**.

---

- **How's everything going with** *Phase 3?*
- *We're* **short of time**./*Time's* **running out**.

1  Read the text for general understanding.
2  Read it again and <u>underline</u> the words you don't know. Check their meaning.
3  Highlight words you know passively, but don't use actively. Choose some to write sentences of your own.
4  Check pronunciation at macmillandictionary.com

# Exercises

**21.1 Match an item on the left with an item on the right to make phrases from the text opposite.**

| | | |
|---|---|---|
| 1 | be the team | estimate |
| 2 | be back on | resources |
| 3 | allocate | a start date |
| 4 | set | leader |
| 5 | make a rough | track |

| | | |
|---|---|---|
| 6 | be kept in | tasks |
| 7 | fall behind | within the budget |
| 8 | finish ahead | of schedule |
| 9 | delegate | schedule |
| 10 | keep | the loop |

| | | |
|---|---|---|
| 11 | find common | a proposal |
| 12 | brief (v) | ground |
| 13 | draw up | with our work |
| 14 | put work out | team members |
| 15 | get on | to tender |

**21.2 Complete the sentences with a whole phrase from Exercise 21.1.**

1 Juliana has little experience in this area. Is she ready to _be the team leader_ ?

2 It's difficult to give a detailed breakdown of the costs, but I think we can _____ .

3 We've had a few problems but we should _____ in a day or two.

4 We should know our budget next week. The senior management team are having a meeting on Monday to _____ for all the planned projects.

5 Phase 2 of the project is taking much longer than we thought. We're definitely going to _____ .

6 I won't be involved in the project on a day-to-day basis, but I would still like to _____ .

7 It's not vital that we stick exactly to the time plan – what really matters is the money side of things. We really have to _____ .

8 Everything's moving very quickly. Believe it or not I think we might even _____ .

9 I'm sure we can _____ with our competitors on the issue of internet piracy. We need to work together to do something about it.

10 Great! The contract is signed and the budget is in place. Now we can finally _____ .

11 We can't just offer this job to our usual subcontractor. EU legislation requires that we _____ .

12 On Monday morning there's a kick-off meeting to _____ on the new project.

**21.3 Rearrange the letters to make words. Use the definitions in brackets to help you.**

1 temarwok _____ _teamwork_
(the activity of working well together)

2 ddeanile _____
(a time or date by which you have to do something)

3 acallote _____
(decide to use money, time, etc for a particular purpose)

4 degatele _____
(give part of your work to someone else)

5 spificecations _____
(exact measurements or detailed plans)

6 brakewodn _____
(detailed information separated into different groups)

**21.4 Complete the sentences with these prepositions:** *back, between, on, on, to, to, up, up, up.*

1 Nicole is going to head _____ the Paris team.

2 Henrick, I'd like you to team _____ with Maxime.

3 There is a lot of common ground _____ us. I think we can reach an agreement.

4 Welcome _____ the team. It's great to have you _____ board.

5 We've fallen a little behind schedule – but no problem, I'm sure we can catch _____ .

6 We're _____ schedule to finish the project at the end of May, just as we promised.

7 We can't change the plans. We've agreed the schedule with the client and now we should stick _____ it.

8 There's been an unexpected problem. We're going to have to push _____ the start date by a week.

**21.5 Complete the dialogue by writing <u>one</u> word in each space. Some letters are given to help you.**

BULENT: What's happening with the Saudi construction project? I've been away for a couple of weeks and I'm out of the [1]l_____ .

AZIZ: Don't worry, everything is on [2]t_____ . We've had a meeting with the Qataris and they're fully on [3]b_____ now. They're going to invest 80 million dinars in the project.

BULENT: What about those guys in the Emirates?

AZIZ: They haven't contacted us [4]y_____ .

BULENT: Well, time is [5]r_____ out. We need to chase them. Can you deal with that?

AZIZ: [6]L_____ it with me.

BULENT: And [7]w_____ are we with the subcontractors?

AZIZ: We've put the work out to [8]t_____ . We've already had a number of bids.

BULENT: Good. I think we're in a position to [9]d_____ up a schedule for the whole project now.

AZIZ: I agree. At a [10]r_____ estimate I think we can begin the building work in May.

**See page 147 for some discussion topics.**

# 22 Plans and forecasts

## Planning in order to achieve a goal

In business the word 'plan' usually means a series of specific things to do in order to achieve (= succeed in) a particular goal or objective.

You can ... a goal.

*set, work towards, reach/achieve*

And your goals may be ...

*achievable, clear, specific, realistic, unrealistic*

Once you have clear goals, you can begin planning. You can ...

*develop/draw up/make/prepare a plan*
*present/propose/put forward a plan*
*discuss and then agree a plan*
*go ahead with a plan*
*implement (= put into action) a plan*
*review and then change/modify a plan*
*keep to/stick to a plan*
*abandon/cancel/drop a plan*
*shelve a plan (= decide not to use it, although you might use it later)*

A plan may:

*succeed/go smoothly, fail/go wrong*

And you can have a/an ... plan.

*ambitious, definite, detailed, five-point, long-term, short-term, strategic, three-year*

You may think that a plan is a good one, but have concerns (= worries).

During the planning process people may ask:

*How long will it take?*
*What's the timescale on this?*
*What's the next step?*
*What should we focus on first?*
*With limited resources, what should we prioritize?*

The outcome (= result) of the plan may mean success or failure for the business. There can be a/an ... outcome.

*favourable/positive/satisfactory/successful, negative/unfortunate, expected/likely, final*

Finally, all plans involve risks. You can ... risks.

*assess, accept, avoid, manage, take*

## Forecasts

A forecast is a statement about what is likely to happen in the future. The word 'forecast' can be a verb or a noun and is used when talking about business, the economy or the weather. The words 'predict/prediction' refer to a more personal view.

*We **forecast** sales of €5.6m next quarter.*
*We have a **sales forecast** of €5.6m next quarter.*
*I **predict** that the Board is going to fire the CEO.*

A forecast shows your expectations. Note that 'I expect' = 'I think it will happen' while 'I hope' = 'I want it to happen'.

***I expect** sales will improve next year – our product pipeline is very strong.*
***I hope** sales will improve next year, but it's unlikely because the patent on our bestseller runs out in December.*

It is also common to say:

***Hopefully**, sales will improve next year.*

## Time expressions for the future

You can talk about plans and expectations using phrases that show different degrees of probability.

> *We'll definitely .../We're certain to ...*
> *We're going to .../We intend to ...*
> *We'll probably .../We're likely to .../The chances are that we'll ...*
> *We might/may/could ...*
> *We're unlikely to .../We probably won't ...*
> *We definitely won't .../We have no intention of ...*

*The economy **is likely to** improve in the medium term.*
***The chances are that we'll** expand our production facility in Turkey in the coming months.*

Alternatively, you may simply say:

*It's difficult to forecast.*

Also note these time expressions.

*in the short/medium/long term*
*in the long run*
*in (or over or during) the next few weeks/coming months*

1 Read the text for general understanding.
2 Read it again and <u>underline</u> the words you don't know. Check their meaning.

3 Highlight words you know passively, but don't use actively. Choose some to write sentences of your own.
4 Check pronunciation at macmillandictionary.com

# Exercises

**22.1 Write S if the sentences are the same or similar. Write D if they are different.**

1 a What planning have you done?
  b What are your plans?     `S`

2 a We need to draw up a plan.
  b We need to prepare a plan.     ☐

3 a They've decided to go ahead with the plan.
  b They've decided to shelve the plan.     ☐

4 a The plan may be difficult to implement.
  b The plan may be difficult to change.     ☐

5 a The plan is going smoothly.
  b The plan is going wrong.     ☐

6 a What is the likely result?
  b What is the expected outcome?     ☐

7 a If we all work together, we can achieve our objectives.
  b If we all work together, we can reach our goals.     ☐

8 a We have to accept some risks.
  b We have to be cautious.     ☐

9 a I have one or two worries.
  b I have one or two concerns.     ☐

10 a What's the next step?
   b What should we focus on next?     ☐

**22.2 Complete comments 1–6 by filling in the missing letters.**

1 There's been a lot of changes to the plan and I really don't know if it will suc_ _ _d. I would say it's 50/50 whether or not we go ah_ _d.

2 We've rev_ _wed the plan carefully. I'm sorry, but our conclusion is that the g_ _ls are completely unr_ _ _ _ _tic – they're much too am_ _ _ _ous. And the whole thing involves ta_ _ng too many r_ _ _s.

3 We've s_ _ realistic goals and done most of the planning. The ch_ _ces are that we'_ _ start in a couple of months.

4 We have a de_ _ _led plan and it's def_ _ _ _ _ly going ahead. The imple_ _ _ _ation phase begins next month.

5 Unfortunately things aren't going acc_ _ _ing to plan. There is now a review process and the final out_ _ _e of that is not clear. We probably w_ _'_ begin until next summer, at the earliest.

**22.3 Now match each comment from the previous exercise with the time expressions below.**

☐ a They're certain to do it.
☐ b It's likely that they'll do it.
`1` c They might do it.
☐ d To be honest, they're unlikely to do it.
☐ e They have absolutely no intention of doing it.

**22.4 Complete the answers by writing either *expect* or *hope* in each space.**

Q: How long will it take to plan the sales campaign?
A: I [1]_____ it will take just a few weeks, but I [2]_____ it will be a month or more.

Q: And what do you think will happen as a result of the campaign?
A: Of course I [3]_____ that sales will rise significantly – maybe 15–20% – but I don't [4]_____ them to increase much more than that.

**22.5 Complete the story about an investment fund with the words and phrases in the box.**

| | | |
|---|---|---|
| abandoned | accept some risk | go wrong |
| implemented | in detail | long term |
| realistic objectives | taking risks | the outcome was |

Werner was one of our top investment analysts. For a long time he had this idea for launching a fund focused on emerging markets. He wrote a report describing his ideas [1]_____ , and he presented it to a meeting of senior managers. They talked about it and asked him a lot of questions. They wanted to make sure that he had [2]_____ for the fund. Eventually they said yes.

A few weeks later Werner's plans were [3]_____ . The fund was set up and we wrote to clients to give them the chance to invest. The problem was that very few clients were interested. It's because most of our clients are people over sixty who don't like [4]_____ , and emerging markets are by nature very risky. We didn't know what to do. One idea was to change the profile of the fund so that we only chose large, well-established companies. Werner disagreed – he said that we had to [5]_____ if we wanted the opportunity for greater profits in the [6]_____ .

Well, [7]_____ that we decided to follow the original ideas as planned, but to improve the marketing of the fund. Then disaster happened. Everything started to [8]_____ . There was a crash in the world's stock markets, and emerging markets fell the most. We closed the fund and Werner's ideas were [9]_____ . Now he's working for another company.

**22.6 Put the sentences below in order 1–6 to make a summary of the previous story.**

`1` He developed a plan.
☐ They thought about modifying the plan.
☐ They decided to stick to the plan, with some changes.
☐ He put forward the plan.
☐ They went ahead with the plan.
☐ They dropped the plan.

**See page 147 for some discussion topics.**

# 23 Problems, problems

## Using the word 'problem'

In the business world problems are often called issues to avoid sounding negative. In a more formal context you can refer to a problem as a 'matter' (= a situation you must deal with).

Here are some verbs often used with the word 'problem'.

*cause/create, be faced with, identify* a problem
*avoid/find a way around* a problem
*look into* (= investigate) a problem
*deal with/sort out* (= take action to solve) a problem

Here are some phrases with 'problem':

*We need to **take another approach to** this problem.*
*We need to **get to the root of** the problem.*
*I don't think you realize **the scale of** the problem.*

## Internal company problems

Day-to-day business problems include:

- Quality issues.
  *This machine **keeps on breaking down**.*
  *There are too many **defects** in this **batch** (= a group of products made or sent at the same time).*
- Problems with suppliers.
  *They've **let us down** – they're very **unreliable**.*
  *The parts **should have arrived** by now.*
- Problems with IT.
  *The network **is down**. (= not working)*
  *I can't **get** this software **to work**.*
- Equipment problems.
  *The photocopier **isn't working properly**.*
  *The printer has **run out of** ink.*
- A communication breakdown.
  *I think **there's a misunderstanding** here.*
  *I have absolutely no idea **what's going on** (= what's happening).*
- A shortage / lack of time.
  *I'm **getting nowhere** with this report.*
  *This is going to **take much longer** than I thought.*
- Colleagues who are difficult to work with.
  *I'm **fed up** with Alexander.*

If a colleague comes to you with a problem, you might ask questions to get to the root of the problem:

***What's the matter?*** *Is it serious?*
***What exactly*** *is wrong with it?*

Then you can suggest what to do next:

***Have you tried*** *looking at the FAQ (= Frequently Asked Questions) section on their website?*
***It sounds like*** *it's broken.* ***I think the best thing would be to*** *get a new one.*
***I'd*** *give them another call,* ***if I were you***.
***Perhaps you should*** *mention it to Alison.*
*Let's talk to Miguel. Maybe he can **come up with** something (= think of a solution).*
*In that case **you'd better** call their helpdesk.*
*Let me have a look. OK, **that should fix it/sort it out**.*

## Customer complaints

Customers can complain about …

- Delays in shipping a product.
  *The goods have**n't** arrived **yet**.*
- Damage to a product during shipping.
  *Some items are **broken/cracked/damaged/faulty/ scratched/substandard**. I want to return them.*
  *Please send a **replacement**.*
- Wrong or missing items on delivery.
  *You've sent the **wrong parts**. This is a real problem for us.*
- Mistakes on the invoice.
  *This is**n't the price we agreed**.*
- Faulty/defective parts in use.
  *The device **isn't working properly**.*
  *There's **something wrong with it**.*
  *Some parts **need replacing**.*
  *I want to **make a claim under the warranty**.*

The person who deals with the complaint might say:

*I really am very sorry about this. Can I **get some more details from you** so I can find out **what's going on**?*
*I'll **look into the matter** right now and **call you back**.*
*I'll **get back to you** (= contact you again) as soon as I can.*
*I'm sure we can **sort it out**.*
*Don't worry, we'll **replace it/refund your money**.*

Note the use of *I'll* or *we'll* in the phrases above to promise action.

In an email you should say sorry at the beginning and again at the end:

*Thank you for your email.* ***I am very sorry to hear that*** *you are having problems with …*
***I apologize again*** *for any inconvenience this may have caused.*

1 Read the text for general understanding.

2 Read it again and <u>underline</u> the words you don't know. Check their meaning.

3 Highlight words you know passively, but don't use actively. Choose some to write sentences of your own.

4 Check pronunciation at macmillandictionary.com

# Exercises

**23.1 Complete the sentences with these prepositions:** *around, back, into, on, on, out, up, up, with, with.*

1 We are faced _____ a serious problem.
2 I'm sure we can find a way _____ this problem.
3 Don't worry, I'll deal _____ it.
4 Don't worry, I'll sort it _____ .
5 If you give me all the details, I'll look _____ it.
6 This machine keeps _____ breaking down.
7 I need to find out what's going _____ .
8 I'm really fed _____ with Roberto.
9 Maybe Brad can come _____ with something.
10 I'll get _____ to you as soon as I can.

**23.2 Match the beginnings of sentences 1–6 with their endings a–f.**

1 We need to take another    [d]
2 We need to get to the    [ ]
3 I don't think you realize    [ ]
4 Our supplier    [ ]
5 This is going to take    [ ]
6 I think there's a    [ ]

a root of the problem.
b misunderstanding here.
c much longer than I thought.
d approach to this problem.
e has let us down – again.
f the scale of the problem.

**23.3 Look back at the previous exercise. Which sentence would you use if:**

1 the problem is continuing, and you want to suggest an alternative _1d_
2 you suddenly realize you will be staying late in the office tonight _____
3 you think that no-one has identified the real reason for the problem _____
4 you are very disappointed with the actions of a business partner _____
5 you think that no-one understands how serious the situation is _____
6 someone speaks to you in an angry way because someone else told them something you said _____

**23.4 Fill in the missing word in each sentence. Some letters are given to help you.**

1 What's the m_____r? Is it serious?
2 What exactly is w_____g with it?
3 Have you t_____d looking on their website?
4 The best thing w_____d be to get a new one.
5 I'd give them another call, if I w_____e you.
6 Perhaps you should me_____n it to Marta.
7 In that case you'd b_____r call their helpdesk.
8 Let me have a look. OK, that should f_____x it.

**23.5 Complete the mini-dialogues with the phrases in the box. C means Customer and S means Supplier.**

> damaged on arrival    it's faulty    it sounds like
> leave it    let me just check    missing items
> ~~placed the order~~    send a replacement

C: When will the goods arrive? We [1] *placed the order* over two weeks ago.
S: That's strange. [2]_____ with me and I'll get back to you as soon as I can.

C: There are some [3]_____ . You haven't sent everything that we ordered.
S: [4]_____ on the screen. Yes, that's right, we sent a part shipment with all the items we had in stock. The rest will follow in a week or so.

C: Some pieces were [5]_____ . They were broken and cracked.
S: [6]_____ a problem of bad handling in transit. I need to contact the courier about this.

C: There's something wrong with the part you sent. I'm sure [7]_____ .
S: OK, if you return it, we'll [8]_____ immediately or give you a credit note.

**Continue as before.**

> make a claim    refund your money    send me a sample
> the same fault    what's going on    working properly

C: The device isn't [9]_____ . I've tried looking in the manual but it doesn't help.
S: I'm sorry to hear that. Can I get some more details from you so I can find out [10]_____ ?

C: I want to [11]_____ under the warranty.
S: Of course, no problem. We can replace the item or [12]_____ – whichever you prefer.

C: All these products have [13]_____ – and they all come from the same batch that you sent.
S: That's strange – none of our other customers have reported any problems. Could you [14]_____ of one of the faulty products?

See page 147 for some discussion topics.

# 24 Strategy and leadership

## Strategy

Senior managers, with a strong involvement from the Board of Directors, have to develop a long-term strategy for the company.

The first step is to analyze the current situation. There are a variety of tools and techniques available to do this. Three of the best-known are given below.

1 *PEST analysis.* This looks at 'the big picture' in terms of the Political, Economic, Social and Technological factors that affect the whole business environment.

2 *Five Forces Analysis.* This looks at who has power in an industry by analyzing five factors:

- Supplier power. Can suppliers easily drive up (= force up) the prices you pay for your inputs?
- Buyer power. Can customers easily drive down (= force down) the prices of your products in the market?
- Competitor power. How many competitors are there and can they do what you do?
- Threat of substitution. Can your products easily be replaced with others that are cheaper, newer, or do the job better?
- Threat of new entry. Can new competitors easily enter the market and weaken your position?

3 *SWOT analysis.* This looks at the Strengths and Weaknesses of the company, and the Opportunities and Threats in the market.

Having looked at the current situation, you might consider:

- The growth of the company. Is the company going to grow organically, or are there possibilities for a merger, an acquisition or an alliance?
- New markets. Should the company enter any new markets, and if so, should it start from scratch (= start from nothing) or buy an existing local company?
- The product portfolio. Are there enough new products in the pipeline (= being planned) to take the place of those with declining sales? Does the company need to diversify its product offering? Or perhaps just focus on a few core (= very important), profitable areas?

- Cost control. Are there ways to cut costs internally? What about relocating some production?
- Image and reputation. What does the brand represent? How is the company seen by the outside world? How can we control these factors better?

You can have a/an … strategy.

*effective/successful, poor, clear, coherent, viable (= able to succeed), long-term, medium-term, broad/general/overall, market-oriented (= directed towards the market), high-risk/risky*

And you can … a strategy.

*design/develop, devise/come up with (= think of), propose, outline, adopt/decide on, implement, follow, change/revise, abandon*

Finally, a strategy can …

*be based on sth, be aimed at sth, be designed to do sth, consist of sth, involve sth, (not) work, fail*

The **overall strategy** is clear – but will it be **effective**? It seems very **risky**.

We've **developed** a **long-term strategy** which I'll **outline** in the meeting tomorrow.

Our strategy **is designed to** make us the number two company in the market in five years' time.

This strategy **consists of** four main elements.

## Leadership

Strategy is developed by leaders. Leaders are senior managers who use new ideas to create a vision and a sense of purpose (= a reason to succeed) for the organization. They 'think outside the box' (= think differently, from a new perspective).

But leaders don't only develop strategy. They also have strong people skills to inspire and motivate others to follow the strategy. They provide support and recognition, and encourage people to rise to new challenges.

You can be a/an … leader.

*born/natural, charismatic, dynamic/forceful, effective, strong, weak*

And you can show … leadership.

*clear, effective, outstanding, real, firm/strong, poor/weak*

1 Read the text for general understanding.

2 Read it again and <u>underline</u> the words you don't know. Check their meaning.

3 Highlight words you know passively, but don't use actively. Choose some to write sentences of your own.

4 Check pronunciation at macmillandictionary.com

# Exercises

**24.1 Match a word on the left with a word or phrase on the right with a similar meaning.**

1 strategy — replacement
2 opportunity — reason (to achieve something)
3 threat — takeover
4 factor — plan
5 substitution — thing that tests your skill
6 acquisition — thing that influences a situation
7 purpose — danger
8 challenge — chance

**24.2 Use a word on the left in Exercise 24.1 to complete these sentences.**

1 Working for Médecins Sans Frontières gave me a real sense of _____ in my life.
2 Cost and timing were the two most important _____s in our decision.
3 She's a lawyer specializing in mergers and _____s.
4 It may look difficult, but I'm sure you'll rise to the _____ and do very well.
5 In a SWOT analysis, a strength or a weakness is an internal issue (inside the company), whereas an _____ or a _____ is an external issue (in the market).

**24.3 Match an item on the left with an item on the right to make phrases from the text.**

1 develop a long-term — picture
2 look at the big — prices
3 analyze five — position
4 drive down — strategy
5 weaken your — factors

6 start from — pipeline
7 have products in the — world
8 focus on a few core — internally
9 cut costs — areas
10 be seen by the outside — scratch

**24.4 Complete the sentences with a whole phrase from Exercise 24.3.**

1 The new management team will soon *develop a long-term strategy* for the company.
2 The success of your company is clear for everyone to see. But it means you will attract new competitors, and that will surely _____ .
3 Before we get into a detailed analysis, I think we should first _____ .
4 We have absolutely no presence in the Chinese market and so we're going to have to _____ .
5 We should work with a communications company that knows about public relations. We need to _____ as socially responsible and environmentally friendly.
6 Our existing products sell well, but they are all coming to the end of their life cycle. The problem is we don't _____ to replace them.

**24.5 Match a word on the left with a word or phrase on the right with a similar meaning.**

1 effective — general, overall
2 coherent — full of energy and ideas
3 broad — exceptional
4 dynamic — working well and producing results
5 outstanding — clear, logical and consistent

6 develop — include (as a necessary part)
7 implement — suggest
8 outline — put into action
9 propose — create over a period of time
10 involve — give the main ideas

**24.6 Use a word on the left in Exercise 24.5 to complete these sentences.**

1 I don't have time to go into details, but I'll give you a _____ overview of the situation.
2 The Finance Director wants one thing and the Marketing Director wants something else. We need the CEO to listen to all sides and come up with a _____ strategy.
3 The Board have decided on a new strategy. Now it is up to us to _____ it.
4 He _____d the main ideas at the meeting and said he'd give more details soon.

**24.7 Read this text about emotional intelligence, then answer the questions below.**

It is often said that leaders have strong people skills. Recently the phrase 'emotional intelligence' (EI) has been used to talk about the same thing. When we say that leaders have a high degree of EI we mean that:

a They understand their emotions, trust their intuition, and are honest about themselves.
b They are good listeners and understand the wants, needs and viewpoints of other people.
c They are excellent communicators.
d They are easy to talk to, good at building teams, and good at resolving disputes between colleagues.
e They are self-motivated and like a challenge.
f They think before they act.
g They are comfortable with change where other people would be insecure because of the new situation.
h They don't feel they have to please other people all the time.

Which point a–h above is closest to the meanings below?
1 They have empathy. ☐
2 They have good social skills. ☐
3 They are self-aware. ☐
4 They have the ability to say 'no'. ☐
5 They are reflective, not impulsive. ☐

**See page 147 for some discussion topics.**

# 25 Hiring, firing and promotion

## Hiring and firing

The phrase 'hiring and firing' is used informally to refer to a company employing and dismissing people.

A company can … somebody.
*hire/take on/recruit/employ*

On the negative side, you can:
*be fired/be dismissed/be laid off/(BrE) be made redundant*

Or, your boss can say in a softer way: *We're going to have to let you go.*

We use 'be fired' and 'be dismissed' when you lose your job because you were incompetent or did something wrong. We use 'be laid off' when you lose your job because the company is not doing well and needs to downsize (= reduce its workforce). The company may ask some of its staff to take voluntary redundancy (AmE voluntary termination), in which case the staff will be offered a redundancy package (AmE termination package) of money and benefits.

Of course you may also leave/quit your job because you want to. In this case you resign/hand in your notice (= officially tell your employer you are going to leave).

I **resigned from** my last job because the company was badly managed and going nowhere.

## Unemployment

If you are unemployed/out of work you might be entitled to receive unemployment benefit (= money from the state). Being 'on the dole' is an informal way of saying you receive financial assistance from the government because you are unemployed.

I **lost my job** at the agency and now I'm **on the dole**. It's terrible – I've never been **out of work** before.

## Retirement

Retirement is the period of your life after you finish working. People often retire around 65 years old, or sometimes enter semi-retirement where they work less. The income you receive during retirement is your pension; you can get money from a state pension and/or a company pension and/or a private pension plan.

## Promotion

If the company moves you to a more senior position, you are promoted/get promotion. There are various ways that this can happen:

- It is the responsibility of the Human Resources department to develop and retain (= keep) its best workers. This is called talent management. One of the main ways to retain and motivate talented individuals is to offer them promotion.
- You can simply apply for promotion yourself.
- Some companies have an appraisal system/scheme (also known as a performance review system). This is a process of formally reviewing the work, progress and training needs of an employee. It often happens annually. At the appraisal meeting opportunities for promotion can be discussed.
- You can get a job in a new company at a higher grade (= level of job).
- Older-style companies have a career ladder where one of the reasons for promotion is simply length of service. However it is more common for a person to stay in the same job but move up by increments (= regular increases) on a salary scale.

He's just been **promoted to** Sales Director.
They **offered** him **a more senior position**.
He **applied for promotion** and he got it.
He was **passed over for promotion** (= not chosen, even though he wanted promotion).

## Executive search

At the very top management levels hiring does not usually take place through the usual recruitment process of public job advertisements and competitive interviews. Senior executives need a much more discreet (= careful and private) process. This is called executive search, or headhunting in everyday language.

An executive search agency – working for its anonymous client – makes informal contact with senior managers from other companies who might be interested in changing jobs. Possibilities are discussed, and eventually a shortlist of candidates is given to the client company. From this list one or two suitable people may be identified and introduced to the client company.

1 Read the text for general understanding.

2 Read it again and <u>underline</u> the words you don't know. Check their meaning.

3 Highlight words you know passively, but don't use actively. Choose some to write sentences of your own.

4 Check pronunciation at macmillandictionary.com

# Exercises

**25.1 Write S if the two phrases in italics have the same meaning. Write D if they are different.**

1 They have recently *taken on / hired* 50 new employees. ☐S☐
2 He was *laid off / made redundant* when they moved their Head Office to Geneva. ☐
3 They're going to *downsize / close* the company. ☐
4 She *left / quit* her last job because the pay was so bad. ☐
5 I might have to *go on the dole / receive a pension* for a short time until I find another job. ☐
6 He's been *out of work / retired* for nearly a year. ☐
7 There is a shortage of skilled people in my field, and companies have to make sure they *retain / promote* their staff. ☐
8 In my company your management grade and salary depend mainly on the results of the *appraisal meeting / performance review*. ☐

**25.2 Complete the sentences with the correct form of the word in brackets.**

1 At top management levels hiring does not usually take place through the usual _recruitment_ process. (recruit)
2 I was _____ when they downsized the company in the recession. (lay off)
3 They offered me voluntary _____ and I took it – it was time to find another job anyway. (redundant)
4 We have terrible problems with _____ in my town – it's very difficult to find a job. (employ)
5 I have all sorts of plans for my _____ – and not just playing golf and spending time with the grandchildren! (retire)
6 She was _____ last year. They raised her salary by more than 20%. (promotion)
7 There was a vacant position, he _____ for it and got it. I don't think there were any other candidates. (application)
8 Your salary depends partly on your _____ of service – obviously everyone expects a pay rise at the end of the year. (long)

**25.3 Complete the sentences with these prepositions: *from, in, off, on, on, out, over, to*.**

1 She was taken _____ to replace Barbara.
2 They're going to lay _____ some of the factory workers.
3 He handed _____ his notice and went off to India to study yoga.
4 She resigned _____ her job because of all the commuting – two hours there and two hours back.
5 I hope I won't be _____ the dole for long.
6 I hope I won't be _____ of work for long.
7 He was passed _____ for promotion – he's very bitter about it.
8 She was promoted _____ Head of Business Development.

**25.4 Match a word on the left with a word on the right to make phrases from the text opposite.**

1 redundancy      management
2 state           search
3 talent          pension
4 career          scale
5 salary          package
6 executive       ladder

**25.5 Complete the sentences with a phrase from Exercise 25.4.**

1 For the HR department, recruitment and selection is just the beginning. After that there is the whole area of _____ – performance reviews, training and promotion.
2 I was approached by an _____ agency the other day. I thought it was quite a compliment.
3 I've been doing the same job for five years and I'm nearly at the top of my particular _____ . If I want to earn more money, I'll have to move up the career ladder.
4 You can't just rely on the _____ when you retire. If you do, you'll suffer a big drop in your standard of living.

**25.6 Number the lines of the text in the correct order.**

a I'm a doctor – I work mainly with children and ☐1☐
b ago I got a job in a large teaching hospital. I ☐
c I find my job very rewarding. Around five years ☐
d better salary and the work is very challenging. ☐
e worked very hard because I wanted to be ☐
f promoted to consultant. Consultants have a much ☐

g However, every time a consultant's job became ☐7☐
h demanding and difficult to work with. It wasn't ☐
i just me. One colleague was fired for poor ☐
j available they gave it to someone else. I know ☐
k that my boss didn't like me. He was very ☐
l performance and another handed in her notice. ☐

m Then the hospital administration warned ☐13☐
n less but it's a much better working atmosphere. ☐
o us that they would have to lay off 10% of the ☐
p nearer to my home. The salary is slightly ☐
q resign. Now I'm working for a smaller hospital ☐
r staff because of restructuring. I decided to ☐

**25.7 The previous text includes the words *rewarding, challenging* and *demanding*. Write the correct word next to its definition below.**

1 difficult to do, but interesting and enjoyable

_____

2 needing a lot of time, ability and effort

_____

3 giving satisfaction, pleasure or profit

_____

**See page 147 for some discussion topics.**

# 26 Pay, benefits and motivation

## Pay

The words 'pay', 'salary', 'wage'/'wages' and 'income' all refer to the money an employee receives from an employer. You earn (NOT ~~win~~) money from your job. You win money on the lottery.

*Pay* is the most general word. A pay rise (AmE a raise) is when you get more money. Performance-related pay is when your pay depends partly on reaching (meeting/achieving) agreed targets.

*Salary* is used in the context of white-collar (= professional/office) jobs. Your basic salary is what you earn before extra payments such as overtime (= extra hours that are not part of your contract), sales commissions, car allowance, and any end-of-year bonus.

*Wage/s* is used in the context of blue-collar (= manual/factory) jobs and also casual jobs that are paid daily or weekly. The word 'wages' is also used for money earned by the whole workforce in a country: *Wages are lower in Vietnam than in China.*

*Income* refers to the total amount of money you receive in a year – it includes your salary but also money from investments, savings, etc.

Your payslip is the piece of paper that shows your gross pay (before anything is taken away), then all the deductions (such as income tax and social security), and finally your net pay (the amount you actually get in your pocket). The phrase 'take-home pay' is an informal way of saying 'net pay'.

*What's your **monthly/annual salary**?*
*How much **do you make** in a typical year?*
*What's the **weekly wage** in your bar job?*
*My **annual income** is 48,000 euros, **gross**.*
*I **earn** around 4,000 euros a month, **before tax**.*
*I **take home** around 3,000 euros a month.*
*When our factory workers **do overtime**, we pay them **time-and-a-half** (150% of the usual rate).*
*All our Sales Reps work **on commission**.*
*The company **made** a lot of **money** last year and we all got a big **end-of-year bonus**.*
*My **payslip** doesn't seem right this month – who should I ask about it?*

## Benefits

As an employee you can receive all sorts of benefits in addition to your salary. These include:

- A company pension scheme ('pension' = money you receive when you stop working because you are old).
- Health insurance. This is the most common benefit in the US where there is no national health service.
- Paid vacation and paid sick leave ('leave' = time away from work). In Europe these are a normal part of your contract. In the US they are considered as a benefit.

Then there are a whole range of other benefits, often called perks. These might include a company car, a laptop, a smart phone, going to conferences, training, gym membership, cheap meals in the company canteen, opportunities to work from home for a part of the week (teleworking/telecommuting), working flexible hours (flexi-time), etc. A perk can also be something much more general, as shown in the following sentence.

*One of the **perks of my job** is that I get to travel all over the world and meet interesting people.*

## Motivation

Pay and benefits are obviously very important motivators at work. But there are many other things that make people feel good at work, and managers should be aware of them. They include:

- Varied and interesting work, with control and responsibility in certain areas.
- A sense of achievement. This is the feeling of success when you do something good and impressive.
- Recognition (= public respect and thanks) by your managers and colleagues for work you have done.
- Feeling that the job you do is worthwhile (= is valuable and useful for society).
- Working with colleagues who you get along with (= have a good relationship with).
- Good working conditions.
- Opportunities for career development, personal growth, learning new skills, etc.

Sense of achievement, recognition, etc are often referred to as non-financial rewards.

1 Read the text for general understanding.

2 Read it again and <u>underline</u> the words you don't know. Check their meaning.

3 Highlight words you know passively, but don't use actively. Choose some to write sentences of your own.

4 Check pronunciation at macmillandictionary.com

# Exercises

**26.1 Underline the correct word in italics.**

1 I _earn_ / win a reasonable salary, and the benefits are very generous as well.

2 All our _employees_ / _employers_ will get a pay rise of 3% at the end of the year.

3 We have a system of performance-related _pay_ / _salary_ in my company.

4 This week I've done a lot of _late time_ / _overtime_ – I hope my boss wrote it down and they pay me for it.

5 I get 10% _bonus_ / _commission_ on every sale I make.

6 I'm working at a bar on the beach over the summer – the weekly _wage_ / _salary_ isn't great but it's good fun.

7 I earn around 50,000 euros a year. But that's _gross_ / _net_ – before they take away tax and everything else.

8 In my country we pay around 35% of our salary to the government as _commission_ / _tax_.

9 If I tell you my salary, it sounds like a lot – but you have to remember that my actual _take-away_ / _take-home_ pay is a lot less.

10 They give me some extra _advantages_ / _benefits_ such as pension contributions and a company car.

11 We have a company pension _scheme_ / _system_ where I pay in a certain amount and they match it.

12 I can take up to three days _illness_ / _sick_ leave without a doctor's note.

13 I get some nice _perks_ / _bonuses_ in my job – free meals and a 20% discount on all their products.

**26.2 Match a word on the left with a word on the right to make phrases from the text opposite.**

1 white-collar     bonus
2 pay     car
3 end-of-year     job
4 income     insurance
5 health     tax
6 company     rewards
7 career     rise
8 non-financial     development

**26.3 Complete the sentences with a phrase from Exercise 26.2.**

1 I wonder how long I'll be on this salary? I think I'll ask my boss about a ___pay rise___ when I get the chance.

2 The government came to power by promising to cut _____ and increase spending on health and education. How can they do both at the same time?

3 Pay and benefits are of course very important, but don't forget the _____ .

4 The starting salary isn't fantastic, but there are all sorts of opportunities for _____ – lots of training courses, the chance to work in different departments, and fast promotion if you show potential.

5 We offer private _____ to all senior managers as one of the company benefits.

**26.4 Rearrange the letters to make words. Use the definitions in brackets to help you.**

1 lavee     _leave_
(period of time when you are officially away from your job)

2 kerp     _____
(a small extra benefit you get in your job)

3 aveechiment     _____
(something good and impressive that you succeed in doing)

4 regoncition     _____
(public respect or thanks for your work)

**26.5 Complete each sentence with a word from Exercise 26.4.**

1 One of the _____ s of my job is the free gym membership – it's great for me as I love sport.

2 I have a lot of good ideas, but then my boss says they are his. It's really annoying. I don't think I get the _____ I deserve.

3 We don't get much annual _____ in my company – just 25 days, including public holidays.

4 We finished a major project last week and it was a great success. I have a real sense of _____ .

**26.6 Complete the text about a bonus scheme using the verbs in the box.**

| | | | |
|---|---|---|---|
| based | co-operate | fit | improve |
| ~~lost~~ | modify | motivate | reach |

" We used to have a bonus scheme that was based on an annual financial target for the whole company. The problem was that employees rarely got the bonus, so they [1] ___lost___ faith in the system. Also departments blamed each other for failure to [2] _____ the target. So we had to rethink everything.
  We wanted a new incentive scheme that would [3] _____ staff, encourage teamwork, and [4] _____ overall business performance. We discussed various options and in the end we decided to introduce quarterly, rather than annual, bonuses. This gave us the flexibility to [5] _____ targets every three months to [6] _____ the changing needs of the business. As you would expect, these targets were usually financial, but sometimes they were related to the success of projects or the launch of a new product. We also included a personal target for each employee, [7] _____ on their job specification.
  The new system has been running for a year now, and staff feedback has been very good. The quarterly goals maintain people's interest and so are far more effective, and departments now [8] _____ more because the goals are achievable. "

**See page 147 for some discussion topics.**

# 27 Cross-cultural communication

What are the main differences in the way that people from different cultures behave? Some are given below.

## Greetings and introductions

Level of formality is one area where cultures differ, and you often notice this on first contact with another person. Study the formal (F) and informal (I) versions below.

Greeting
F: *Good morning. My name is Linda Taylor. It's a pleasure to meet you.*
I: *Hi! I'm Linda. Nice to meet you.*

Introduction
F: *Feng, I'd like to introduce you to Olivia Dubois. Olivia is our Public Relations Officer.*
I: *Feng, this is Olivia. Olivia handles all our contacts with the media.*

Some cultures move quickly to first names, others continue to use titles and surnames (= family names) for many years as a sign of respect. If in doubt, start formally and use whatever the other person has on their business card. They (or you) might then say: *Please call me … .*

## Punctuality

For some cultures it's very important to be on time (= punctual). For others it's OK to be a bit late. If you are late, apologize fully and blame it on the traffic or parking.
*I'm so sorry, the traffic was really bad this afternoon.*

## Directness

If people say exactly what they think, they are direct. If they are more careful with their language, they are indirect. Both sides have good reasons. Direct people say it's easier to do business when everyone knows your real opinion. They think that indirect people hide their true feelings and so can't be trusted. Indirect people want to maintain harmony and avoid confrontation. They don't want the other person to 'lose face' (= be publicly embarrassed). When they disagree, it is done diplomatically. They think that direct people are rude.

The best solution in a new culture is to follow the example of the people you are with.

Here are some examples of direct (D) and indirect (I) language:

D: *Can you help me?*
I: *I wonder if you could help me?*

D: *That will be very difficult.*
I: *That's not going to be easy.*

D: *Can I open the window?*
I: *Would you mind if I opened the window?*

D: *No, that's not right.*
I: *Really? Are you sure?*

## Meals

Having a meal together is one of the best ways to break down barriers between cultures. And one of the best topics of conversation is … cross-cultural communication! Other safe topics are: food and drink, the city you are in, the history of the other country, and the current economic situation. A 'taboo' topic is one you must not talk about – obvious examples are party politics and jokes about the other person's religion or culture.

In some cultures a working lunch where you continue to talk business is normal, in others it isn't. An evening meal, however, is nearly always a purely social occasion.

## Humour

Humour (being funny) sometimes travels across cultures. It's OK to tell a funny story at dinner that doesn't offend anyone (= make them angry and upset). And laughing at yourself is a good way to put the other person at ease. However irony can be dangerous and is often misunderstood.

## Body language

Here are some physical actions that some cultures do more than others:

- Shake hands in the office every morning.
- Kiss someone on one (or both) cheeks.
- Make gestures (= head, arm and hand movements), wave your arms in the air, etc.
- Make/Not make strong eye contact.
- Slap someone on the back.
- Smile/Not smile.
- Stand close, and sometimes hold an arm.

1  Read the text for general understanding.

2  Read it again and <u>underline</u> the words you don't know. Check their meaning.

3  Highlight words you know passively, but don't use actively. Choose some to write sentences of your own.

4  Check pronunciation at macmillandictionary.com

# Exercises

**27.1 Underline the correct word/s in italics.**

1 Try to have good working *relations / relationships* with people from other cultures.
2 My name is Aga. It's *pleasant / a pleasure* to meet you.
3 Bjorn, I'd like to *introduce / present* you to Sergey.
4 My name is Josephine, but please *call me / say* Jo.
5 Avoid making people *lose face / lose their face*.
6 It's not very nice to be in a situation where you *are embarrassed / have shame* in public.
7 It's OK to *speak / talk* business at a working lunch.
8 Laughing at yourself can *put the other person at ease / make the other person easy*.
9 Irony is often *mistaken / misunderstood*.
10 Some people judge you by how firmly you *shake hands / shake the hands*.

**27.2 Match the cultural issues in the box with the comments below.**

| eye contact    humour    maintaining harmony |
| punctuality    titles    working lunch |

1 'A business contact in Japan took me out to dinner in Tokyo. I asked the waiter about the dish of the day. The waiter told me, and I said, "No, I don't like that." My Japanese host looked horrified.' _____
2 'We just grabbed a few sandwiches from a place round the corner and went back to the office.' _____
3 'When I worked in London I found that people used to make jokes in the middle of a business meeting – that just doesn't happen in my country.' _____
4 'We were supposed to start at 9am, and I got there ten minutes early. They were only just opening the building – the lights weren't even on.' _____
5 'He leant forward and stared at me in silence for several seconds, like he was looking into my soul or something. I felt very uncomfortable.' _____
6 'A German colleague once told me that over there a senior male university teacher with two PhDs could receive emails that begin 'Herr Professor Dr Dr Schmidt'. I wonder if it's true?' _____

**27.3 Complete sentence b) with <u>one</u> word so that the meaning is the same as sentence a).**

1 a) American business people are usually very relaxed and friendly – not at all official.
 b) American business people are usually very i*nformal* .
2 a) Indirect people disagree politely and sensitively.
 b) Indirect people disagree dip_____ .
3 a) Jokes about people's race are offensive and should not be told.
 b) Jokes about people's race are t_____ .
4 a) Italians are famous for their head, arm and hand movements that show their feelings.
 b) Italians are famous for their g_____ .

**27.4 Put the words into order to make examples of indirect language.**

a I wonder could you help me if for a moment?
 *I wonder if you could help me for a moment?*
b I'm very not happy about that.
 _____
c Unfortunately we've had problems little one or two.
 _____
d Could me tell you the restroom where is?
 _____
e With respect, be better wouldn't it to start next year?
 _____

**Now match sentences a–e with the direct versions below.**

1 I need your help. `a`
2 It's all a complete disaster. ☐
3 It's obvious that we should wait. ☐
4 I'm very angry about that. ☐
5 I need to go to the toilet. Where is it? ☐

**27.5 Read the text, then answer the questions below.**

What is culture? There are two helpful ways to see it: the X and the Y.

The X model of culture says that there are two parts to culture: the bigger part is below the surface – you can't see it. This includes values, attitudes, beliefs, history, etc. The smaller part is above the surface – you can see it. This includes food, dress, behaviour, music, art and architecture, etc.

The Y model of culture says that there are many different layers. Think of your culture at work. At the centre of the Y there is you as an individual (influenced by your family culture). Then, moving outwards, there is your team culture, company culture, functional culture (marketing, finance) and industry culture (banking, engineering). To this you might add your national (and/or regional) culture. All these elements make a contribution.

1 Can you guess the objects X and Y?
 X is an _____ and Y is an _____ .
 (There is a clue at the bottom if you need it).
2 The text includes the words 'values', 'attitudes', 'beliefs' and 'behaviour'. They are all useful words when discussing culture in a general way. Write the correct word next to its definition below.
 a the particular way that someone does something
 b a set of ideas that you think are true
 c your beliefs about what is important in life
 d opinions or feelings that you show by your behaviour

**See page 147 for some discussion topics.**

The first object is a titanic problem; the second will make you cry.

# 28 Business and the environment

## The environment

Here are some environmental problems.

- Climate change causing natural disasters, such as rising sea levels and floods.
- Household and industrial waste (= useless material that is left behind after a process) causing pollution of the air, the sea, rivers and lakes.
- Depletion (= reduction to a worrying level) of natural resources, such as fossil fuels and fresh water.
- Holes in the ozone layer caused by greenhouse gases.
- Loss of natural habitats causing the extinction (= destruction) of species.

But is business to blame for these problems? They are all consequences of industrialization and people's desire for rising living standards. Is it possible to stop this process? What happens when people from rich economies tell people from emerging economies that they can't have a better life because it will cause damage to the environment?

Most of these issues are controversial. For example there are some people who question whether climate change is really happening. And the decline in oil production may not be such a bad thing – renewable energy won't be developed while oil is cheap and easily available.

## The response of business

Business has responded to environmental issues in various ways. Often there is something simple to do that saves money anyway. An example would be hotels giving guests the choice to reuse towels that are wet but not dirty. This saves the hotel a lot of money on cleaning bills, but can be sold to the public as an environmentally friendly measure that saves water. Offices that have signs encouraging people to save energy by turning off lights or to re-use paper are also acting partly out of self-interest.

But there are many cases where business has made a genuine attempt to reduce its impact on the environment. The automobile industry is trying to use more and more recycled (= already used) and recyclable (= able to be re-used in the future) materials in its cars. Airlines are trying to cut carbon emissions (= substances that go into the air) from aircraft engines. Supermarkets are selling fish from sustainable (= able to continue for a long time) sources and give biodegradable plastic bags to customers. Engineering companies are trying to reduce pollution and waste. Oil companies are investing in alternative energy and biofuels.

Of course, companies don't do these things just to be nice. Nowadays consumers are very environmentally aware (= conscious) – they don't want to buy products that are harmful to the environment. Parents don't want to leave a damaged world to future generations. And companies do not want to become a target for environmental activists/pressure groups – their sales and profits can suffer just as much as their reputation.

A company can … environmental issues.
*avoid/ignore, face/address, tackle/deal with*

## Social responsibility

The environment is just one issue in the much wider area of 'corporate social responsibility' (CSR). CSR is interested in three things: people, planet, profit. It has been defined as 'the deliberate inclusion of public interest into corporate decision-making'.

As well as the environment, CSR includes areas such as:

- Having good working conditions for all employees, including factory workers in poor countries.
- Supporting local communities where the company operates.
- Being accountable (= in a position where you have to explain and justify your actions when questioned) and transparent (= clear and honest).

Most large international companies now spend a lot of time and money promoting their CSR – they realize that in the modern world it makes good business sense.

1 Read the text for general understanding.

2 Read it again and <u>underline</u> the words you don't know. Check their meaning.

3 Highlight words you know passively, but don't use actively. Choose some to write sentences of your own.

4 Check pronunciation at macmillandictionary.com

# Exercises

**28.1 Rearrange the letters to make words. Use the definitions in brackets to help you.**

1 wtase ___waste___
(unwanted material that is left after you use something)
2 deleption _____
(reduction to a level that is less than what you need)
3 hitabat _____
(place where an animal or plant normally lives)
4 reclyced _____
(used again, often for a different purpose)
5 stainusable _____
(able to continue for a long time at the same level)
6 biogradedable _____
(destroyed by natural processes, in a way that does not harm the environment)

**28.2 Complete each sentence with a word from Exercise 28.1.**

1 If you travel by ship, you will see lots of bottles made from non- ___biodegradable___ plastic on the surface of the sea.
2 The _____ of natural resources such as oil, forests and fish is becoming a major problem.
3 Economic growth is relatively easy – the difficult thing is to have _____ economic growth.

**28.3 Match a word on the left with a word on the right. Several answers may be possible but one solution uses each word once.**

| | |
|---|---|
| 1 industrial | resources |
| 2 climate | standards |
| 3 natural | change |
| 4 fossil | waste |
| 5 living | fuels |

| | |
|---|---|
| 6 emerging | emissions |
| 7 renewable | economies |
| 8 carbon | responsibility |
| 9 social | conditions |
| 10 working | energy |

**28.4 Complete each sentence with a phrase from Exercise 28.3.**

1 Have you noticed how the phrase 'global warming' has been replaced by '_____'? I wonder if scientists really know what is going on!
2 Coal, oil and gas are all _____ .
3 Environmentalists say we will have to reduce our _____ if the planet is going to survive, but I don't think anyone will be prepared to do that.
4 Wind, solar and wave power are all sources of _____ – but what about nuclear power? Is it in the same category?
5 These days corporate _____ is a very important issue for a company's image.
6 We need to improve _____ in the factory.

**28.5 Complete the phrases with one of these words: environment, environmental, environmentally.**

1 _____ issues / problems / activists
2 damage to / impact on the _____
3 _____ friendly measures / aware consumers

**28.6 Complete the sentences with verbs from the box.**

| act | blame | include | pay | reduce | ~~respond~~ |
|---|---|---|---|---|---|

1 Business needs to ___respond___ to environmental issues so that it is seen as part of the solution, not part of the problem.
2 Is it right to _____ business for environmental problems?
3 When business follows green policies, it _____s partly out of self-interest, but that's a good thing – it's an example of a win-win solution.
4 Many companies are trying to _____ their impact on the environment.
5 If you don't _____ attention to green issues, you can become a target for pressure groups.
6 CSR means that you _____ the public interest in your corporate decision-making.

**28.7 Read the text, then answer the questions below.**

CSR Europe is the leading business network for corporate social responsibility. It has around 80 multinational corporations and 30 national partner organizations as members. On its website it says that it is a platform for:

» Connecting companies to share best practice on CSR.
» Innovating new projects between business and stakeholders.
» Shaping the modern day business and political agenda on sustainability and competitiveness.

It has developed a European Roadmap for CSR that includes the following themes: innovation, equal opportunities and diversity, health and safety, environmental protection, mainstreaming CSR, involving stakeholders, leadership and governance.

**Find word/s in the text that match the definitions below. They appear in order.**

1 all the people that have an interest in the success of the business _____
2 (two words) the chance for everyone to succeed, without being treated differently because of their gender, race, age, etc _____
3 making an issue normal and acceptable _____
4 how a company is managed at the highest level
_____

**See page 147 for some discussion topics.**

# 29 CV (resume) and cover letter

## CVs and resumes

The word 'CV' is used in Europe, the word 'resume' in the US. A CV has to be personalized and there are many internet sites to help you do this: go to a search engine and type 'CV' or 'resume' followed by 'examples' or 'template' or 'tips'.

## Structure

Online recruitment sites and individual companies often have their own specific application forms. However if you do need to produce your own CV, here is some general information to help you.

● Many people put a summary at the top which is quick and easy to read and introduces the whole CV. Here is an example:

> *Currently working as a marketing assistant, I am now looking for wider experience and new challenges. With my creative problem-solving approach and excellent interpersonal skills I feel that I would make a good Marketing Manager. I have extensive knowledge of marketing strategies in the mobile communications industry.*

● Typical sections of the CV, in order, might be: Personal Data, Professional Experience, Skills, Other Interests, Education, References.
● Within the Professional Experience and Education sections use reverse date order (= most recent first).
● Here is an example that shows the first few lines of the Professional Experience section of the CV of an IT Project Manager:

### PROFESSIONAL EXPERIENCE

*[May 20xx – now]* Project Manager for IT projects at Ricobank, a Portuguese financial group (www.ricobank.pt). My job involves planning and controlling a wide variety of projects in the Information Technology area. As team leader I also coordinate the work of four team members.

Detailed list of projects at Ricobank:
* *[November 20xx – now]* Assessment of the data quality of the bank's customer database.
* *[June 20xx – now]* Implementation of a system to score customer loans according to defined risk criteria.

Notice how a general description of the current job is followed by more details as bullet points. Previous jobs would simply have the general description without further details.

In the body of your CV remember to focus on achievements (things you have done) rather than personal qualities which cannot be proved (*I am a team player, I work well under pressure,* etc). You can mention personal qualities in the summary, cover letter and interview.

For the Skills section you can list technical skills, management skills, people skills, language skills, etc. For the Other Interests section you can list a few things like sports or travel. For the References section many people simply write: *Available upon request.*

## Cover letter

When you apply for a job, your CV will often be accompanied by a cover letter. The structure should be something like this:

1 Say what job you are applying for and where you saw the advertisement.

*I am writing to apply for the position of ... advertised on the ... website/in ... magazine.*

2 Introduce yourself, referring to your experience.

*I have been working in the ... industry for five years and over this time have gained wide experience in ... . I believe this makes me an ideal candidate for the job.*

3 Describe how this particular job is right for you. Refer to your CV. Use a few key words from the advertisement.

*As you can see from my CV, I have a strong technical background in ...*
*I perform well in a results-driven environment, and am a good team player.*
*With my proven track record in financial control I feel that I could make a strong contribution to strategy and planning at Alpha International.*

4 Give your availability.

*I am available for interview at any time, but my preference is for late afternoon due to my current work commitments.*

---

1 Read the text for general understanding.
2 Read it again and <u>underline</u> the words you don't know. Check their meaning.
3 Highlight words you know passively, but don't use actively. Choose some to write sentences of your own.
4 Check pronunciation at macmillandictionary.com

# Exercises

## 29.1 Underline the correct word/s in italics.

1 Your *skills* / *experience* refers to your abilities – things you can do well as a result of practice. Examples include using a particular piece of software, speaking English, or being a good negotiator.

2 Your *skills* / *experience* refers to the knowledge you get by doing a particular job or activity. Examples include time spent in a particular industry, or working in a particular market.

3 A / An *applicant* / *candidate* is anybody who has sent a CV in response to a job advertisement.

4 A / An *applicant* / *candidate* is somebody who is being actively considered for the job.

## 29.2 Complete the sentences with the words in the box. Not all the words appear opposite.

> apply   ~~applicants~~   application   closing date   cover letter
> entry-level   experience   qualifications   position
> rates   rejected   updated   vacancy

1 At the bottom of this job description it says 'Previous __applicants__ need not apply'. I suppose that means your CV has already been looked at and _____ .

2 Employers always want people with lots of _____ – but how do you get it in the first place? I suppose you have to find an _____ job, but they are not very well paid.

3 I've filled in dozens of _____ forms, but no-one has called me for interview.

4 This candidate looks promising – their _____ include an MBA from INSEAD.

5 Look at this ad for an Office Administrator. It's only a temporary position but it says here 'good _____ of pay'.

6 I've just _____ my CV. Can you have a look at it and give me some feedback? It needs to be done soon – the _____ for applications is this Friday.

7 There's a great job on this job search website. It says at the bottom 'Please _____ by email with _____ and full CV'. I'm going to do that.

8 The word _____ is a formal way of saying 'job'. The word _____ means 'a job that is available'.

## 29.3 Cross out the one verb with a different meaning.

The company is *hiring* / *interviewing* / *recruiting* / *taking on* new staff.

## 29.4 Fill in the missing letters.

The Human Resources Department is responsible for recruit_ _ _ _ and select_ _ _.

## 29.5 Complete the sentences with the verbs in the box.

> apply for   call you for   fill in / out   matches
> register with   replied to   ~~search~~

1 Looking for a job is often called job _____search_____

2 If you _____ a job (or a place at university), you make a formal request for it.

3 Online recruitment agencies often have their own specific application forms which you _____ .

4 It's a good idea to _____ several online job sites. Some of them will even send you an email alert if a job appears that _____ your profile.

5 I _____ that job advertisement you showed me but I never heard anything.

6 After sending your CV you hope that the company will _____ interview.

## 29.6 Complete this cover letter (sent as an email) with the words in the box.

> attached   background   candidate
> challenges   high-pressure   interpersonal
> involved   notice   ~~reference~~   running

I am writing with [1] _____reference_____ to your advertisement on the job search website. My [2] _____ is in operations management in the hotel sector and I am currently Assistant Operations Manager at a prestigious hotel in Geneva. I support the OM in ensuring the smooth day-to-day [3] _____ of the hotel.

As you can see from the [4] _____ CV I have wide experience in hotel booking systems, collecting payments and handling money, managing housekeeping staff, and buildings maintenance. I am also actively [5] _____ in the organization of events, weddings and private dining on a weekly basis. I work well in the [6] _____ environment of a busy hotel and have excellent [7] _____ skills.

I feel I would be an ideal [8] _____ for this position as I am ready to move up to manager level and look forward to the new [9] _____ that the increased responsibility will bring.

I am available for interview at any time, but require some advance [10] _____ in order to arrange my work shifts.

I look forward to hearing from you.
Celine Perez

**See page 147 for some discussion topics.**

## Interview and selection

A panel of people (the interviewers) interview the candidates (the interviewees). The interview panel typically consists of someone from Human Resources, the line manager, and possibly other departmental managers. For many jobs there will be a first interview to narrow down (= reduce) the number of possible candidates to a shortlist of people who will be called for a second interview. After this the final decision will be made and the strongest candidate will be offered the job. There may then be a short period of negotiation over salary, working conditions, etc and the chosen candidate will either take up (= accept) or turn down (= refuse) the job offer.

## Assessment centres

Many people in their early twenties have similar CVs and a similar lack of experience, and a CV plus interview is unlikely to show who is the best person for a job. For older candidates the artificial context of a formal job interview may not show the person's real qualities. For these reasons many companies use an assessment centre as part of the selection process. This is typically a full day (or two) and includes social/informal events, information sessions, and tests and exercises designed to reveal your potential. The exercises might include a case study, a presentation and/or a group discussion.

## What the employer is looking for

In the interview (and at an assessment centre) the employer is usually looking for three things. First, they want to see evidence of the technical skills and background knowledge required to do that particular job. Second, they are looking for business skills such as the ability to achieve targets, meet deadlines and manage costs. Third, they want evidence of 'soft' personal skills, such as:

| | |
|---|---|
| teamworking | leadership |
| communication | influencing |
| motivation | listening |
| time-management | creativity |
| data analysis | initiative |
| decision-making | integrity |

Many interview questions – particularly the difficult ones – are designed to find out about your personal qualities in this third category.

## Typical questions

Here is a list of typical interview questions. If you are going for an interview in real life, first do the exercises opposite, then ask a friend/colleague to ask you all the questions below plus follow-up questions. Your friend will need your CV to refer to.

### First question + education

*Before we begin, tell me a little about yourself.*
*OK, so I see you studied … at university. Which part of the programme did you most enjoy? Why? Did you do a project in your final year?*

### Work history

*I can see from your CV that after university you worked as a … at … . What exactly did you do there? What did you learn from that job? Why did you leave?*

### Current job

*Can you tell me a little about the company where you work now? What exactly do you do there? What do you like about your job? Can you tell me about one or two of your most important achievements? Describe a challenge you faced – how did you deal with it? What personal and professional skills have you developed? Why do you want to leave?*

### The new job and the company

*Why did you apply to this company? Why do you want this job? What do you know about this business/this market? Why should we employ you in preference to the other candidates? You have very little experience of … – how will you deal with that? Are you prepared to travel/relocate?*

### Your personal qualities

*Let's finish by talking a little more about you as a person. What are your strong points? What are your weak points? Can you work under pressure? How would your friends describe you? What are your goals for the next five years?*

When you answer, give details and examples. So if the question is *Can you work under pressure?*, then the answer should be *Yes, I believe I can* followed by a description of a real situation where you were under pressure (eg time or budget pressure) and how you managed the situation.

---

**1** Read the text for general understanding.

**2** Read it again and <u>underline</u> the words you don't know. Check their meaning.

**3** Highlight words you know passively, but don't use actively. Choose some to write sentences of your own.

**4** Check pronunciation at macmillandictionary.com

**30.1 Rearrange the letters to make words. Use the definitions in brackets to help you.**

1 assssmeent   *assessment*
(making a judgement about a person or situation after thinking carefully)

2 aviechement   _____
(something impressive that you have done)

3 cellhange   _____
(something that tests your skill or ability, especially in a way that is interesting)

4 quatilies   _____
(positive features of a person's character)

**30.2 Read these eight interview questions and the suggested ways to answer.**

1 Q: *Tell me a little about yourself.*
A: This looks like an informal question to put you at your ease, but don't improvise. First impressions are very important. Give a three-part answer: who you are, your biggest strength, and why you are there. ☐

2 Q: *What do you like about your current job?*
A: In this case don't be too specific but use the question to show your friendly personality. ☐

3 Q: *Describe a challenge you faced.*
A: Describe how you handled one particular difficult situation. ☐

4 Q: *Why do you want to leave?*
A: You have to answer this in a way that is not too negative. Never criticize your current employer. ☐

5 Q: *Why do you want this job?*
A: Give an answer that refers both to the company and to your skills. ☐

6 Q: *What are your strong points?*
A: This question is a gift so make sure you use it well. Remember that you can mention both personal and business skills. ☐

7 Q: *What are your weak points?*
A: Turn a negative into a positive and show how you are willing to improve. ☐

8 Q: *Where do you see yourself five years from now?*
A: Show how you will continue to add value to the company. ☐

**Now match the actual words spoken a–h with the answers in 1–8 above. Write the letter in the box.**

a My job is a good entry-level position, but now I'm not really learning anything new. I would like new challenges and the opportunity for growth at a personal and professional level.

b I'm a Retail Manager with wide experience. I started as Assistant Manager but my employer saw that I was intelligent and hard-working and I was soon promoted. I worked in several stores and I learned a lot about leading a sales team. Now I'm looking for a more senior position in a large, international retail group.

c *Example 1* We were working on one particular project and it got behind schedule. I made some suggestions for how to get back on track, and we succeeded in solving all the problems very quickly.

  *Example 2* A long-term client was going to take their business to a competitor. I met with the client and was able to change how we handled the account on a day-to-day basis. We kept the business.

d I enjoy being with my colleagues – it's a great team. The atmosphere is fun and friendly but also hard-working at the same time. We really get a lot done.

e *Example 1* Once I gain additional experience, I would like to move on from a technical position to a management position. I think I have the potential to be a very good manager.

  *Example 2* I see myself as a top performing employee in a well-established organization, like this one.

f *Example 1* I'm a perfectionist, so sometimes I spend a little too much time checking my work. But I always leave time for this so that I don't miss deadlines.

  *Example 2* I know that I need to improve my typing skills, and I recently enrolled on a course.

g *Example 1* I'm enthusiastic and highly-motivated. I've exceeded my sales goals every quarter since I started with my current employer.

  *Example 2* My time management skills are very good. I'm a good planner and I'm organized and efficient when I work. I always meet my deadlines.

  *Example 3* I'm a quick decision-maker, but I'm also flexible enough to change plans if the situation changes. That's really important in a fast-moving environment.

h *Example 1* I'd really love to work here – this company is well-known in the industry for its successful strategies and its innovative solutions. With my skills I feel that I can make a real contribution here.

  *Example 2* This company is on the way up, and with my energy and dedication I'd like to be a part of your future success.

See page 147 for some discussion topics.

## Greeting people you know

When you greet people you know, you can say:

*Hi/Hey/Hello.*

*Good morning/afternoon.* (more formal)

This is often followed by:

A: *How are you?*
B: *I'm good/Fine thanks/Not too bad, and you?*
A: *Good/Fine.*

Of course Person B may not be feeling good:

A: *How are you?*
B: *Not too good, actually. I have a bit of a cold.*

When you know the other person very well the first few lines may be like the ones below.

A: *Hi, how's it going?*
B: *Not bad. And you?*

A: *Hey, what's up?* (= What's new)
B: *Same old thing. What about you?*

A: *How are things?*
B: *It's really busy at the moment. I guess you must have a lot of work yourself?*

A: *Long time, no see!*
B: *Yeah, it's been a while. What are you up to* (= doing) *these days?*

Or you may make reference to 'here and now' rather than make a greeting.

A: *Nice weather today.*
B: *Yes, lovely. I hope it stays like this for the weekend.*

A: *That's a nice scarf.*
B: *Thanks. I bought it at that new place on Market Street.*

Notice in the examples above how the replies help to develop the conversation.

## Greeting people you don't know

With people you don't know you can say:

A: *Excuse me, are you Mr Kovac?*
B: *Yes, that's right.*

A: *I don't think we've met. My name's Susan, Susan Atkins. I'm the Sales Rep for this area.*
B: *Nice to meet you Susan. My name's Felix.*

A: *Excuse me, is anyone sitting here?*
B: *No, it's free. Please sit down.*
A: *Thanks. Can I introduce myself? My name is Pedro Alvarez.*
B: *Nice to meet you, Pedro. I'm Ying Li.*

A: *I'm sorry, I didn't catch your name.*
B: *It's Anneka. And you are?*

After this the conversation depends on the context. For example at the airport:

*How was your flight?*
*Can I help you with your bags?*

Or more generally:

*Where are you from?*
*What do you do?*
*And who do you work for?*

Unit 34 'Small talk' covers this area in more detail.

## Introductions

If there are three people, then one person will take the lead in making the introduction. The social rules about using first name, or title + family name, vary. Follow the lead of the person making the introduction.

Sean: *Julie, have you met Simon before?*
Julie: *No, I don't think so.*
Sean: *I'll introduce you. Simon, come over here for a moment. I want you to meet someone.*
Simon: *Hi.*
Sean: *Simon, this is Julie, a colleague of mine from Belgium.*
Simon: *Nice to meet you, Julie.*
Julie: *Nice to meet you too, Simon.*
Simon: *I know Belgium well – I love the restaurants in Brussels. Whereabouts* (= where exactly) *are you based?*

Notice how Simon uses information supplied by Sean to develop the conversation.

Slightly more formal alternatives are:

*I'd like to introduce you to …*
*Pleased/It's a pleasure to meet you.*
*Pleased/It's a pleasure to meet you too.*

# Exercises

**31.1 Match the greetings 1–6 with the replies a–f.**

1 Good morning. My name's Martina Conti.  `d`
2 Hi, Nino, nice to see you again.  ☐
3 Excuse me, are you Mr Kovac?  ☐
4 Hello, Mr Zhu. How are you?  ☐
5 I don't think we've met. My name's Jo, Jo Atkins.  ☐
6 I'm sorry, I didn't catch your name.  ☐

a Fine thanks. And you?
b Nice to see you too.
c It's Jack Thompson. And you are?
d Pleased to meet you, Ms Conti.
e Nice to meet you Jo, I'm Miyu Tanaka.
f Yes, that's right.

**31.2 Complete the dialogues with the phrases in the box.**
**Dialogue 1**

| can I help you | ~~excuse me~~ | follow me | I'd appreciate it |
| how was your journey | | must be you | that's right |

MR D: [1] _Excuse me_ , are you Mr Moretti?
MR M: Yes, [2] _____ .
MR D: My colleague Pierre Leroy asked me to come to the station to pick you up. I thought it [3] _____ .
MR M: Oh, yes, Pierre said that someone would be here to meet me.
MR D: [4] _____ ?
MR M: Oh, the TGV is always very comfortable.
MR D: [5] _____ with your bags?
MR M Thank you. If you could take this one, [6] _____ .
MR D: Of course. We're going to take a taxi to our office. Just [7] _____ please.

**Dialogue 2**

| at home | enjoyed it | fine, thanks | good weekend |
| how are you | what about you | whereabouts | |

TATIANA: Hi, Chiara.
CHIARA: Hi, Tatiana. [8] _____ ?
TATIANA: [9] _____ . And you?
CHIARA: Fine. Did you have a [10] _____ ?
TATIANA: Yes, thanks. I just stayed [11] _____ but it was very relaxing. [12] _____ ?
CHIARA: I took the family to my parents' house in the country.
TATIANA: [13] _____ do your parents live?
CHIARA: Near Lake Como.
TATIANA: Wonderful. And how was it?
CHIARA: It all went very well. We [14] _____ .

**31.3 Put the words into order to make questions. Then use the questions to complete the dialogue below.**

Is free this seat?  _Is this seat free?_
And do do what you?  _____
Can I myself introduce?  _____
Who you do for work?  _____
Where from are you?  _____
What you about?  _____

MUKESH: Excuse me. [1] _Is this seat free?_
ELENI: Yes, it is. Please sit down.
MUKESH: Thanks. [2] _____ My name's Mukesh Patel.
ELENI: Nice to meet you, Mukesh. I'm Eleni Brakus.
MUKESH: [3] _____
ELENI: I'm from Greece. But I'm working here in London at the moment.
MUKESH: [4] _____ .
ELENI: I'm a bond trader. I work for an investment bank. [5] _____ .
MUKESH: I'm a financial analyst. I work in London.
ELENI: [6] _____ .
MUKESH: They're called Capital Investments. It's a small company. Perhaps you don't know it.
ELENI: Sometimes it's better to work for a small company.

**31.4 Underline the correct words in italics.**

PETRA: Adrian, have you [1]*one time met Johan Nilsson/met Johan Nilsson before*?
ADRIAN: No, I don't think [2]*it/so.*
PETRA: He could be a useful contact for you. I'll [3]*introduce/present* you. Johan, come over here for a moment. I [4]*like/want* you to meet someone.
JOHAN: Hi.
PETRA: Johan, [5]*here is/this is* Adrian Matthews. He works [6]*as/like* a journalist for the TechNet website.
JOHAN: Nice to meet you, Adrian.
ADRIAN: [7]*Nice to meet you too/The same to you,* Johan.
JOHAN: So, Adrian, you work for TechNet. It's a great website. What exactly do you [8]*do/make* there?

**31.5 🔊 01 You are going to hear eight phrases. Listen and repeat.**

## At the airport

The host (= person who makes the invitation) or a colleague of theirs meets the visitor at the airport.

*Welcome to Switzerland.*
*Let me help you with your bags.*
*Did you have a good flight?*
*Tim sends his regards, by the way. He's sorry he couldn't come to meet you in person.*
*Is this your first time in Zurich?*
*Will you have time to look around* (= see the city) *while you're here?*
*We'll catch a taxi to the hotel. You can freshen up, and then we'll have some lunch.*
*We'll go straight to our offices. I'll drop you off at your hotel later, after the meeting.*

## At reception

Sometimes a company receptionist welcomes the visitor, before the host appears.

The visitor might say:

*I'm here to see Mr Moser. My name's Luka Horvat.*
*I have an appointment with Mr Moser at ten o'clock.*

And the receptionist might say:

*Could you sign in* (= sign your name in a book on arrival) *here, please?*
*You need to fill in* (= write) *your details here.*
*Please put on this visitor's badge / ID card. Make sure you wear it at all times.*
*I'll let Mr Moser know you've arrived.*
*You can take a seat over there. Mr Moser will be down in a moment.*
*Can I get you a drink while you're waiting?*

## At the office

When the host welcomes the visitor at the office, phrases like these are typical.

*Come in.* (if the host is inside the room)
*Come through.* (if they enter together)
*It's good to see you again.*
*It's nice to finally meet you in person.*
*Let me take your coat.*
*Have a seat.*
*Would you like something to drink? Coffee? How do you like / take it?*
*How was your journey?*
*Did you find us* (= our office) *OK?*
*Where are you staying?*
*How long are you here for?*

The visitor might apologize for being late, or for the late arrival of another colleague.

*Sorry I'm late. My flight was delayed. Did you get my message?*
*My colleague is on her way – she just called to say her taxi is stuck in traffic.*

After the initial social conversation the host will move to the business part of the visit.

*Perhaps we can get started.*
*OK, let's get down to business.*

## Welcoming a large group

In some situations, such as a factory tour, a large group will visit at the same time. Someone from the company will usually make a short welcome speech using phrases like these.

*Good morning everyone. My name is Daniel Martin and I am the Public Relations Officer here at Magnum Engineering.*
*On behalf of Magnum it gives me great pleasure to welcome you here today.*
*I'll run through* (= quickly explain) *this morning's programme.*
*We're going to begin with a guided tour of the production facility. The tour should take around one hour.*
*We'll come back here for refreshments after we've been round the factory.*
*You'll have an opportunity to meet with Ms Hagen, our Production Manager.*
*After the tour we'll go to our other building where I will give you a short presentation.*
*I'll give you an overview of the company and our plans for the future.*
*You can leave your belongings* (= personal possessions) *here. I'll lock the room, but the company does not take responsibility if anything goes missing.*
*I'd now like to introduce you to Mr Meyer, one of our engineers, who is going to show you round the plant.*

The person leading the tour might then use phrases like these.

*Can I just go over a few safety rules?*
*For your own safety, please make sure you walk inside the yellow lines at all times.*
*Can I remind you that taking photographs is strictly prohibited.*
*OK, if you follow me, we'll begin the tour.*

# Exercises

## 32.1 Underline the correct words in italics.

1 Welcome *in* / *to* Switzerland.
2 Tim sends his *compliments* / *regards*, by the way.
3 Is this your first time *in* / *to* Zurich?
4 On *behalf* / *part* of Magnum, it gives me great pleasure *for* / *to* welcome you here today.
5 Can I *remember* / *remind* you that taking photographs is strictly prohibited.

## 32.2 Match an item on the left with an item on the right.

1 come          this badge at all times
2 drop          you in person
3 get           you off at your hotel
4 have          in
5 meet          you round the plant
6 show          an appointment
7 wear          down to business

## 32.3 Complete each sentence with a whole phrase from Exercise 32.2.

1 (*knock on door*) _____*Come in*_____ .
2 We've been emailing and talking on the phone for so long. It's nice to finally _____ .
3 OK, let's _____ . Did you get the document I sent with the list of points to discuss?
4 (*at the airport*) My car is over there. I'll _____ and then pick you up later.
5 After the meeting Mr Meyer, our Production Manager, is going to _____ . It's fully operational.

## 32.4 Match the beginning and end of each sentence.

1 Did you have a          regards, by the way.
2 Welcome                 time in Zurich?
3 Is this your first      good flight?
4 You can freshen         you with your bags.
5 Tim sends his           to Switzerland.
6 Let me help             to look around before you go?
7 Will you have time      up at the hotel, then we'll have some lunch.

**Now match lines 1–7 above with replies a–i below. Some lines have two replies.**

- [1] a Yes, it was fine.
- [ ] b Thanks, but I can manage.
- [1] c A bit of turbulence, but not too bad.
- [ ] d How is he?
- [ ] e Yes, it is.
- [ ] f Thanks – it's great to be here. And thank you very much for your invitation.
- [ ] g Maybe just a couple of hours on my last afternoon.
- [ ] h That sounds like a good plan. They only gave us a sandwich on the flight.
- [ ] i No, I've been here once before.

## 32.5 Continue as before.

1 Where are you          finally meet you in person.
2 It's nice to           something to drink?
3 Would you like         you get my message?
4 Did you find          are you here for?
5 Sorry I'm late. Did   staying?
6 How long              us OK?

**Match the lines and replies as before. Some lines have two replies.**

- [ ] a Yes, please. A coffee would be nice.
- [ ] b At the Marriott. It's very comfortable and I get Rewards points every time I stay there.
- [ ] c Just three days.
- [ ] d No problem. Your directions were excellent.
- [ ] e Yes, it's always good to put a face to a name.
- [ ] f I'm flying home tomorrow.
- [ ] g No, I'm fine thanks.
- [ ] h Yes, thanks for calling to let us know. There's no problem – I've just rearranged the programme a little.
- [ ] i Yes, the taxi brought me straight here.

## 32.6 Read this welcome speech. Fill in the missing words – some letters are given to help you.

> Good morning everyone. My name is Lotte Jacobs and I am the Public Relations Officer here at Wind Turbines International. On [1]b_____f of WTI it gives me great [2]pl_____ to welcome you here today. I'll just [3]r_____ through this morning's programme with you. We're going to begin with a guided [4]t_____ of the production facility. The tour should take around one hour, and afterwards we'll come back here for [5]ref_____s . Then at eleven o'clock our Production Manager Mr Schneider has kindly agreed to come and have a Q&A with you all. You'll also have an [6]opp_____y to meet with Mr Schneider in person as he will be joining us for lunch later.
>
> At around eleven thirty, after the Q&A, we'll all go to the main conference room in our other [7]b_____g where I will give you a short presentation. I'll give you an [8]o_____w of the company and our plans for the future. Again, there will be a chance for questions.
>
> OK, we'll begin the tour in a moment. You can leave your [9]bel_____s here. I'll lock the room, but I have to say that the company does not take [10]re_____y if anything goes [11]m_____g .
>
> For your own [12]s_____y , please make sure you walk inside the yellow lines at all times. And can I also remind you that taking photographs is [13]str_____y [14]pr_____d .
>
> OK, if you follow me, we'll begin the tour.

## 32.7 🔊 02 You are going to hear eight phrases. Listen and repeat.

In these mini-dialogues you will find examples of standard replies in Social English. See also Units 31, 34, 38 and 39.

## Offering/Being helpful

*Coffee?*
– *Yes please. Milk, one sugar.*
– *No thanks, I'm fine.*

*Can I give you a hand?*
– *Thanks. I'm having some problems here.*
– *It's OK. I can manage. It's under control.*

*Would you like me to call a taxi?*
– *Yes please, that would be very helpful.*
– *I've decided to walk. But thanks anyway.*

## Requesting

*Can I let you know tomorrow?*
– *Of course./Certainly./No problem.*

*Could you give me a hand?*
– *Yeah. Sure.*

*Do you mind if I open the window?*
– *No, not at all./Go ahead./Please do.*

## Thanking

*Thanks very much.*
– *You're welcome.*

*Thanks very much for everything. I really appreciate it.*
– *Don't mention it. It was my pleasure.*

*You did a great job.*
– *Thank you very much. That's very kind of you.*
– *I had a lot of help. It was a team effort.*

## Inviting

*Would you like to join us for dinner?*
– *I'd love to./That would be great.*
– *That's very kind of you, but I already have other plans. Another time maybe.*
– *Thanks for the invitation but I need an early night. My flight is at seven tomorrow morning.*

## Replying to 'sorry'

*I'm sorry, I can't come with you.*
– *Oh, that's a pity./Oh, what a shame.*
– *Oh well. Maybe next time.*

*I'm sorry. I broke it by mistake.*
– *Not to worry. These things happen.*

*Sorry, I can't make the appointment.*
– *No problem. Thanks for letting us know.*

*I forgot to bring my copy of the report.*
– *Don't worry./Never mind./It doesn't matter.*

## Congratulations

*I got the job!*
– *That's great news! Well done!*
– *Congratulations! That's fantastic!*

## Encouraging

*I'm feeling quite nervous before my presentation.*
– *Don't worry, you'll be fine.*

*This is quite difficult.*
– *Come on. Don't give up now. The worst is over.*

*I have a job interview tomorrow.*
– *Good luck. I'm sure you'll do really well.*

## Business situations

*Can we use another room?*
– *I'll just go and check.*

*Will you be there to give me your support?*
– *You can count on me.*

*Is this where we'll be working?*
– *That's right. Make yourself at home.*

*What do you think will happen?*
– *It's difficult to say at this stage.*

*Do you have his number by any chance?*
– *I might have. I'll have a look.*

*I heard they're going to give us all new laptops.*
– *I'll believe it when I see it.*

## Personal matters

*She's feeling very depressed about it.*
– *I understand. These things take time.*

*What should I do?*
– *Don't worry, it'll be all right. It's not the end of the world.*
– *If I were you, I'd just forget about it.*

## Other

*What's happening?*
– *I haven't a clue./Your guess is as good as mine.*

*They don't have the one you want.*
– *It's fine. It's no big deal.*

*Do you want to eat Italian or Chinese?*
– *It's up to you. They both sound good.*
– *I don't mind. You choose.*

*Which wine would you recommend?*
– *I'm probably not the best person to ask.*

*Let me pay.*
– *No, it's on me. I insist.*

*We have to go now.*
– *OK. Just hang on a minute.*

# Exercises

**33.1 Cover the opposite page with a piece of paper. Now tick ✓ the correct reply, a or b.**

1 More wine?
  a No thanks, I'm fine. ✓
  b No thanks, I'm well.

2 Can I give you a hand?
  a It's OK. I can do.
  b It's OK. I can manage.

3 Shall I get you a sandwich while I'm out?
  a I'm having lunch with a client. But thanks all ways.
  b I'm having lunch with a client. But thanks anyway.

4 Can I use the photocopier?
  a Of course.
  b Certain.

5 Do you mind if I sit here?
  a No, not at all. Go ahead.
  b Yes, of course. Go ahead.

6 Thanks very much.
  a You're welcome.
  b Your pleasure.

7 Would you like to join us for dinner?
  a I'd love it.
  b I'd love to.

8 Unfortunately I won't be at the conference next month.
  a Oh, what a shame.
  b Oh, what a loss.

9 I have a problem with my car. I'm going to be late.
  a I don't worry. These things happen.
  b Not to worry. These things happen.

10 Sorry, I have to cancel my appointment.
  a No problem. Thanks for letting us know.
  b No problem. Thanks for making us know.

11 I don't have an umbrella with me.
  a It doesn't matter. You can use this one.
  b It doesn't care. You can use this one.

12 We won the contract!
  a That's great news! Well made!
  b That's great news! Well done!

13 I have a job interview tomorrow.
  a Good fortune. I'm sure you'll do really well.
  b Good luck. I'm sure you'll do really well.

14 Is the meeting room free at the moment?
  a I'll just go and check.
  b I'll just control the situation.

15 Will you be there in the meeting?
  a You can count with me.
  b You can count on me.

16 What do you think will happen?
  a It's difficult to say at this stage.
  b It's difficult to say at this step.

17 I heard we're all going to get a pay rise.
  a I'll believe it when I see it.
  b I believe it when I'll see it.

18 There are so many things that could go wrong.
  a Don't worry, it'll be all fine.
  b Don't worry, it'll be all right.

19 My presentation was a disaster.
  a Don't worry, it's not the end of life.
  b Don't worry, it's not the end of the world.

20 He shouted at me. It was horrible.
  a If I were you, I'd just forget about it.
  b If I'm you, I'll just forget about it.

21 What's going on here?
  a Your guess is better than mine.
  b Your guess is as good as mine.

22 Do you want to walk across the park or take a taxi?
  a I don't mind. It's up to you.
  b I don't mind. You're up to it.

23 Let me pay.
  a No, it's on me. I insist.
  b No, it's with me. I insist.

24 We have to go now.
  a OK. Just wait on a minute.
  b OK. Just hang on a minute.

**33.2 Fill in the missing words. Some letters have been given to help you.**

1 Can I g___ _ive___ you a h_____?
  – It's OK. Everything's u_____er co_____l .

2 W_____ you like me to call a taxi?
  – Yes, please, that would be very he_____ful

3 Can I l_____t you k_____w tomorrow?
  O_____ c_____ . No problem.

4 Thanks very much for e_____ing . I really app_____te it.
  – Don't me_____n it. It was my pl_____e.

5 Would you l_____ to j_____ us for dinner?
  – That's very k_____ of you, but I already have other plans. An_____r ti_____ may_____ .

6 I'm sorry. I broke it b_____ mi_____e.
  – Not to worry. The_____ thi_____ ha_____n .

7 Is this where I'll be working?
  – That's right. M_____ y_____lf at h_____ .

8 Do you have his number b_____ a_____ cha_____?
  – I mi_____t have. I'll h_____e a l_____k .

9 She's feeling very depr_____ed about it.
  – I understand. These things t_____e t_____e.

10 Which wine would you recommend?
  – I'm probably n_____ the b_____t p_____n to a_____ .

**33.3 ● 03 You are going to hear eight phrases. Listen and repeat.**

# 34 Small talk

## Small talk

There are many situations in life and business when we need to make small talk (= informal conversation about unimportant things). We use small talk to find out the other person's personality, discover shared interests, and build trust. Active listening is very important in small talk (see Unit 56).

## Starting a conversation with strangers

To make small talk with strangers you can begin by referring to 'here and now', wait for the other person to reply, and then introduce yourself with *By the way*.

*This food looks good. Much better than you usually get at things like this. … By the way, I'm Patricia.*
*Are you here for the conference? … Look – the registration desk is over there. By the way, my name's Adam.*

You can also ask a question with 'do you mind':

*Excuse me, do you mind if I …*
*… join you?*
*… have a look at your conference programme?*
*… take one of your brochures?*

You then ask and answer questions to find out about each other.

### The event where you are now
*How are you enjoying the conference?*
*Did you go to the talk about …?*
*Do you know many people here?*

### Origins
*So where are you from originally?*
*Whereabouts (= Where exactly?) in Germany?*

### The city where you are now
*Is this your first time in Moscow?*
*How long are you here for?*
*Have you seen much of the city?*
*What do you think of the metro system?*

### Job
*What do you do, by the way?*
*Who do you work for?*
*And where are you based?*
*Have you always worked in the … industry?*
*What did you do before?*

Starting a conversation with people you know is much easier because you already have shared interests.

## Small talk topics

Some topics and phrases for small talk are given below. Other topics can be found in Units 35–36.

### Food and drink at a buffet meal
*Can I get you a drink/anything from the buffet?*
– *Thanks a lot. I'll have a white wine.*

*It all looks good. What do you recommend?*
– *The smoked salmon is very good.*
– *Try these. They're excellent.*
*I really like the way they do the salads/bread/fish here. In my country …*

### The weather
*What lovely/awful weather!*
– *Yes, beautiful/terrible.*
*Is it always as hot as this in October?*

### Talking shop (= talking about work)
*How's business?*
– *We're having a great year.*
– *Very busy, as usual. What about you?*

*Someone told me that Renova are going to …*
– *How interesting. Why do you think they …?*

*I hear you're thinking about … Is that right?*
– *Yes, that's right. The reason is …*

### Travel – past
*Have you been to Marrakesh? What was it like?*
*What did you think of the main square with all the street performers? I've heard that it's amazing.*

### Travel – future
*Are you going on holiday this year? New Zealand! Really!*
*That sounds wonderful. You must be looking forward to it.*

### Telling a story
*One time I met this guy/woman who …*
*A strange thing happened to me once.*
*Did I tell you about the time when …?*
– *Really? What happened next?*
– *That reminds me of the time when I …*

### Free time on the trip
*I might have a chance to do a bit of sightseeing/shopping before I leave.*
– *The old town is very interesting.*
– *There's a good museum/art gallery if you're interested in history/modern art.*
– *The local wine/cheese/handicraft is very good. It would make a good present.*

# Exercises

**34.1 Complete each phrase with a word from the box.**

| Are Can Do Have How Is What Where Who |
|---|

1  _Do_  you mind if I join you?
2  _____  are you enjoying the conference?
3  _____  this your first time in Cologne?
4  _____  long are you here for?
5  _____  do you do, by the way?
6  _____  are you based?
7  _____  you always worked in the auto industry?
8  _____  I get you a drink?
9  _____  do you recommend?
10  _____  lovely weather!
11  _____  's business?
12  _____  you been to Hong Kong?

13  _____  you here for the conference?
14  _____  you know many people here?
15  _____  are you from originally?
16  _____  you seen much of the city?
17  _____  do you work for?
18  _____  did you do before?
19  _____  about you? *(two possible answers)*
20  _____  interesting.
21  _____  was it like?
22  _____  happened next?

**34.2 Match 1–12 from Exercise 34.1 with the replies a–l below.**

- [1] a  No, not at all. Please sit down.
- [ ] b  Very busy, as usual. What about you?
- [ ] c  Just one more day. I fly back tomorrow evening.
- [ ] d  Try these. They're excellent.
- [ ] e  Yes, beautiful. It's much colder back home.
- [ ] f  I'm a design engineer in the auto industry.
- [ ] g  Very much. The quality of the presentations is very good and it's a great chance to network.
- [ ] h  No, never. I've always wanted to go.
- [ ] i  Thanks a lot. Is there any fruit juice?
- [ ] j  No, I've come here once before. It was just a quick visit, though.
- [ ] k  In Stuttgart.
- [ ] l  Yes, I have actually. Ever since leaving school.

**34.3 Find a word or phrase on the page opposite to complete these comments.**

1  To say 'Where exactly?' you can say _____ ?
2  A meal in which people get their food from a table and then walk away to eat it is called a _____ .
3  Talking about business in a social situation is called _____ _____ .
4  When someone is telling a story the person listening can say '_____ ?' It means 'I am interested and I want you to continue'.

**34.4 If a stranger makes a comment, we often use a similar (or stronger) adjective to agree. The example opposite is: *What lovely weather! – Yes, beautiful.***

**Use the words in the box to complete the replies below.**

| crowded  delicious  fascinating  freezing  massive |
|---|

1  Big, isn't it? – Yes, _____ .
2  Busy in here, isn't it? – Yes, really _____ .
3  Interesting talk. – Yes, _____ .
4  Cold today, isn't it? – Yes, _____ .
5  Food's nice. – Yes, _____ .

**34.5 Fill in the missing letters.**

1  The reg_ _ _ _ _ion desk is over there. B_ t_ _ w_ _, my name's Adam.
2  What a wonderful buffet. It all looks good. What do you rec_ _ _end?
3  So, what _ _ you _ _?
4  Is it always hot like this at this t_ _ _ of y_ _ _?
5  T_ _ these. They're excellent.
6  Excuse me, do you m_ _ _ if I ha_ _ a l_ _ _ at your conference programme? I'm Patricia by the way.
7  A strange thing ha_ _ _ _ed to me o_ _e.
8  Who do you w_ _ _ f_ _?
9  Have you been to Marrakesh? Yes? Wh_ _ was it l_ _e?
10  I really like the w_ _ they d_ the salads here.
11  You're going to New Zealand! That sounds w_ _ _ _ful. You must be l_ _ _ing for_ _ _d t_ it.
12  Some_ _e to _ _ me that Lexica are going to open a new production facility in Turkey.
13  And where are you ba_ _d?
14  That re_ _ _ds m_ of the t_ _ _ when I went for a job interview at a bank.
15  What did you think of the main square with all the street performers? I've h_ _ _d that it's am_ _ing.
16  What did you do be_ _re?

**34.6 Put the sentence numbers from Exercise 34.5 into the correct category below.**

| | |
|---|---|
| Introducing yourself | [1] [ ] |
| Job | [ ] [ ] [ ] [ ] |
| Food and drink | [ ] [ ] [ ] |
| The weather | [ ] |
| Talking shop | [ ] |
| Travel – past | [ ] [ ] |
| Travel – future | [ ] |
| Telling a story | [ ] [ ] |

**34.7 🌐 04 You are going to hear eight phrases. Listen and repeat.**

## Likes and dislikes

To ask a question about likes you can say:

*What sort / kind / type of music do you like?*

Notice how to reply when someone tells you their likes.

*I like jazz.*     *I don't like jazz.*
*– Me too.*     *– Me neither.*

There are ways to show different degrees of liking and disliking:

> ☺ *I adore it. / I love it. / I really enjoy it.*
>     *I quite like it. / I suppose it's OK.*
>     *I'm not very keen on it. / It doesn't really interest me. /*
>       *I'm not really into that sort of thing.*
>     *I don't like it very much. / It's nothing special. /*
>       *It's not really my kind of thing.*
> ☹ *I can't stand it. / I hate it.*

You can show degrees of liking and disliking with adverbs:

*I thought the film was **absolutely** brilliant.*
*I liked it **a lot**.*
*I didn't like it **at all**.*

Notice how the position of 'really' changes the emphasis:

*I didn't **really** like it.* (less strong)
*I **really** didn't like it.* (more strong)

## Free time

You can:

*go see a movie / a play / a band* (= a music group)
*go out for a meal / a drink*
*go clubbing / shopping / fishing*
*go to the park / beach / cinema / movies*
*go round / over to someone's house*
*go for a walk / a drive in the country*
*meet up with / get together with a few friends*
*have a few friends over for dinner*
*have a quiet night in and watch TV / a DVD*

To invite people to do these things you can say:

*Are you doing anything later?*
*Do you fancy going clubbing tonight?*
*Shall we go see a movie?*
*A few of us are …. Why don't you join us / come along too?*
*You can bring Sara – I'm sure she'd enjoy it.*

To reply you may want to express a preference:

*I think I'd prefer to …*
*To be honest, I'd (much) rather …*

## Interests and hobbies

You can …

*collect antiques, do gardening / the garden, do an evening course, go jogging, go swimming, go hiking* (= walking in the countryside), *join a health club, look round a gallery or museum, play football, play tennis, play cards, play in a band, read novels, take photographs, etc*

*collect stamps*       *cook*

*do yoga*       *paint*

*play computer games*       *play the guitar*

People also enjoy music (from hip-hop and rap to jazz and soul), films / movies (from action movies and thrillers to romantic comedies and period dramas) and the arts (= visual arts, literature and performing arts). The phrase 'performing arts' refers to arts performed live on a stage, and these include theatre, classical ballet, contemporary dance, opera and music of all kinds.

Many people like to do some kind of physical exercise to keep fit / in good shape and lose weight. But after the initial enthusiasm it's very easy to give up / quit (= stop doing it).

Notice the prepositions. We say …

*She's really **into** yoga.* (= is very interested in it)
*I'm really interested **in** photography.*
*My mother's very keen **on** gardening.*
*I'm a big fan **of** fifties American musicals.*

Also note: *It's interest**ing**. / I'm interest**ed** in it.*

# Exercises

**35.1 Underline the correct word in italics.**

1 Opera? Yes, I *love* / *love it*.
2 The restaurant? It was nothing *especial* / *special*.
3 The film? I didn't like it *at all* / *absolutely*.
4 I think *I prefer* / *I'd prefer* to eat after the film, not before.
5 I go to the gym to try to lose *weight* / *my weight*.
6 I'm not very keen *of* / *on* classical music.
7 To be honest, I'm not really *inside* / *into* football.
8 The art exhibition was a bit *bored* / *boring*.
9 I'm very *interested* / *interesting* in photography.
10 I love watching actors on *a platform* / *the stage*.

**35.2 Choose the right verb a–f to complete the phrases 1–6.**

| a do | b go | c have | d join | e keep | f play |
| --- | --- | --- | --- | --- | --- |

1 ☐ out for a meal; round an art gallery; shopping
2 ☐ a health club; your friends in the bar later
3 ☐ fit; in good shape
4 ☐ the garden; an evening course; yoga
5 ☐ football; computer games; the guitar
6 ☐ a few friends over; a quiet night in

**35.3 Complete the dialogue by using one word from list A and one from list B in each space.**

A: bring can't fancy join kind ~~me~~ me meet much shall

B: going her neither of rather stand ~~too~~ up us we

EMILY: That new movie with Scarlett Johansson is on at the cinema tonight.
IRENA: Oh yes, I like her.
EMILY: [1] *Me too* . Do you [2] _____ ?
IRENA: Maybe. What time are you thinking of?
EMILY: It begins at eight.
IRENA: I was going to [3] _____ with a few friends and then go clubbing afterwards. But Alex is going to be there and I [4] _____ him.
EMILY: [5] _____ . He's a real idiot.
IRENA: I don't know what to do now. To be honest, I'd [6] _____ see the film, but I promised Grace I'd go clubbing.
EMILY: You can [7] _____ as well – I'm sure she'd enjoy it. Why don't you ask her?
IRENA: I don't really like doing that type of thing. Everyone expects us to go clubbing.
EMILY: OK, no problem.
IRENA: Hey – why don't you [8] _____ tonight? It'd be great if you could come too.
EMILY: You know I'm not really into clubbing. It's just not my [9] _____ thing.
IRENA: OK. [10] _____ go and see the movie on Friday instead?

**35.4 Match the activities in the box with the comments below. You may have to check some vocabulary in a dictionary.**

| theatre | playing football | hiking | watching a movie |
| --- | --- | --- | --- |
| live music | gardening | yoga | looking round a gallery |

1 'We walked up the valley and reached the top of the hill where we were going to have lunch. Then the clouds came down and it started raining heavily. Luckily I had my waterproofs with me, but my backpack with the map in it got soaked.'
2 'I've seen the play a few times before, but this production was fantastic. The whole cast were superb, and some individual performances were outstanding. The stage design – the scenery and lighting – was also very well done.'
3 'He tried to tackle me but it was definitely a foul. The ref gave a free kick and I crossed the ball to Paulo on the other side of the pitch. He got past two defenders and took a shot – but it went wide.'
4 'I went to see this band last night – they were amazing. The singer kept jumping into the audience and crowd surfing, and the guitarist did some amazing solos. They played a lot of their last album, which I love, and previewed a track or two from their next album.'
5 'It's a difficult pose – you have to turn at the waist and keep your arms and legs in alignment. Often I just fall over! But the teacher gives me props – like a wooden block and a belt – to make it easier.'
6 'Basically it was a rom com. The usual plot – boy meets girl, but then they can't get together because of all sorts of obstacles. You can say it's a cliché, but it was very funny and they did it very well. I read the reviews and the critics didn't like it, but they are always so snobbish.'
7 'We have a lawn – I have to cut the grass every week in the summer – and around it there are borders with plants and shrubs. It's quite a lot of work to make it all look nice, but I love it – particularly in the spring when the trees are in blossom.'
8 'In one room there were some wonderful Impressionist landscapes, and in another some Italian Renaissance paintings – I liked one particular portrait from the late fifteenth century.'

**35.5 Find a word from Exercise 35.4 that matches each definition below. The words appear in order.**

1 All the performers in a play, film, etc _____
2 An attempt in sport to throw, kick or hit a ball (usually towards the place where you get a point) _____
3 A song or piece of music that is recorded _____
4 Events that form the main story of a book, film or play _____
5 Painting, drawing or photograph of a person _____

# 36 Home, city, country

## Home and family

You live in a house or an apartment (BrE a flat). A house is a building. The word 'home' is more emotional – it refers to all the people in the house and your pleasant feelings about them. It is also more general and can refer to the place where you grew up, the city/country where you live, etc.

*I don't like being away from home for too long – I start to miss my children.*
*I'm going to be at home this evening.*
*I work in Shanghai but I go home to the States a couple of times a year.*

To describe where you live you often refer to the number of bedrooms and the location.

*It's a two-bedroom apartment in the city centre.*
*It's a three-bedroom semi-detached house (= joined on one side only) in the suburbs.*
*It's a four-bedroom detached house (= not joined to another) in a small town outside the city.*

Your family consists of your immediate family (parents, husband/wife/civil partner, children, brothers and sisters) and your relatives/relations (aunts and uncles, cousins, nephews and nieces, etc). Note that the word 'cousin' does not have a different male/female form. Your in-laws are your husband's or wife's family, or your children's husbands and wives.

Different types of family include nuclear families (mother, father and children), single-parent families, extended families (where close relatives live nearby and have a big role in family life), and families with no children.

You can say:

*I was born and brought up (AmE raised) in Paris.*
*I grew up (= went from child to adult) in Paris.*
*I'm single/married/in a civil partnership/separated/ divorced/widowed.*
*I got married when I was 30.*
*Things didn't work out and we got divorced.*
*I live with my partner.*
*We're (not) a very close family.*
*I have two kids/children – a boy and a girl.*
*She looks just like her mother.*
*He's got his father's nose.*
*It runs in the family.*

## City

Here is some vocabulary to describe your city.

### City life
*be in a hurry/rush, cosmopolitan/multiracial atmosphere, stress, (no) sense of community, job opportunities*

### Places/Buildings
*commercial district, city centre (AmE downtown), housing estate, in the suburbs, interesting architecture, office block, on the outskirts (= areas furthest from the centre), residential area, surrounding area, tower block*

### Transport
*bus/cycle lanes, commute(r), get stuck in traffic, metro system, crowded/unreliable public transport, rush hour*

### Things to do
*entertainment, leisure facilities, nightlife*

### Problems
*begging, crime rate, homelessness, unsafe areas, pollution, vandalism*

### Talking points
*healthcare, immigration, (lack of) parking, population growth, property prices*

### Advice to tourists
*famous sights, go sightseeing, good time to visit, old town, souvenir/reminder/gift, spring/summer festival, tourist attraction*

## Country

Here is some vocabulary to describe your country.

### Economy
*main exports, main industries, north-south divide, road/ rail/air links, unemployment*

### Geography
*coast, countryside, interior, landscape, rural areas, scenery*

### History
*battle, be invaded by, defeated, established, fought with, gained/lost our independence, great moment, introduced, reunited, ruled, sixteenth/seventeenth century, terrible tragedy*

# Exercises

**36.1 Fill in the missing letters.**

1 Your mother and father are your p_ _ _ _ _s.
2 Your mother's and father's sisters and brothers are your a_ _ _s and u_ _ _ _s.
3 The children of the people who are the answer to #2 are your c_ _ _ _ _s.
4 Your husband's (or wife's) family are your i_-l_ _s.
5 Beyond your immediate family, the rest of your family are your re_ _ _ives/re_ _ _ions.

**36.2 Underline the correct word in italics.**

1 I *born / was born* in Stockholm.
2 I *brought up / was brought up* in Stockholm.
3 I *grew up / was grown up* in Stockholm.
4 I *got marriage / got married* when I was 28.
5 I live with my *companion / partner*.
6 He looks just *like / as* his father.
7 I'm going to be *at / in* home this evening.
8 I don't like being away *from / out of* home for too long.

**36.3 Match a word on the left with one on the right. Find a solution that uses each word once.**

| | |
|---|---|
| 1 city | system |
| 2 crime | estate |
| 3 cycle | rate |
| 4 housing | hour |
| 5 leisure | centre |
| 6 metro | attraction |
| 7 rush | area |
| 8 summer | lanes |
| 9 surrounding | facilities |
| 10 tourist | festival |

**36.4 Complete the sentences with a whole phrase from Exercise 36.3.**

1 If you want to find some nightlife, you have to go to the
   *city centre* .
2 I leave work quite late – around seven – but at least I miss the _____ .
3 Tourists who come to London often visit the _____ as well – places like Windsor Castle, Brighton and Oxford.
4 They put up CCTV cameras all over the city centre, and the _____ has definitely fallen.
5 The _____ in my town are quite good – we have a cinema, an ice rink, a swimming pool and a nice park where the children can play.
6 In cities like Amsterdam, Cologne and Copenhagen pedestrians have to be very careful. Not only are there roads to cross, there are _____ as well!
7 The locals don't go to the castle. It's really just a
   _____ .
8 Some years ago they built _____s all over the city. Unfortunately we have a lot of problems with gangs and drugs in those areas now.

**36.5 Jack is talking about his city. Complete what he says with the words in the box.**

| atmosphere ~~blocks~~ community commute crowded entertainment hurry locals lonely opportunities property stuck |
|---|

66 Let me describe my city. There's a downtown area – that's our central commercial district – with lots of office [1] *blocks* built in the sixties and seventies. There's also an old town that tourists like to visit during the day. In the evening it's the main area for nightlife, and the [2] _____ go to the restaurants and bars as well as the tourists.

The residential areas are all further out. As you move away from the centre, [3] _____ prices get cheaper. The problem is that if you live on the outskirts and work in the centre, you have to think about your daily [4] _____ . Public transport is very [5] _____ and there's a lot of stress, but what alternative is there? If you take your car into the centre, you get [6] _____ in traffic, and then when you arrive there's nowhere to park.

I don't have a family yet and most of the time I just work. But at the weekends I do get a chance to enjoy city life. There's a lot of [7] _____ on offer – cinemas, theatres, galleries, live music, comedy clubs, just about everything you can think of.

Of course city life has its downsides as well. Everyone's in a [8] _____ and no-one stops to talk. There's no real sense of [9] _____ . I have friends, but they live all over the city and I know very few people from my local area. If you don't know people, it can be a very [10] _____ life.

But in general I think I'm a city person. There are more job [11] _____ here than in a small town, and salaries are higher. And there's a real buzz on the streets – a kind of energy. There's a cosmopolitan, multiracial, tolerant [12] _____ – a kind of 'live and let live' philosophy. I like that. 99

**36.6 Cover the opposite page with a piece of paper. Now fill in the missing letters.**

1 In the int_ _ _or of the country we have some national parks with beautiful sc_ _ _ry. You should go there – there's a wonderful l_ _ _scape of mountains and lakes.
2 The statue you see over there is King Michael. In the fourteenth cen_ _ _y we were inv_ _ed by the Rubovians, and they ru_ _d a part of our country for fifty years. King Michael def_ _ _ed them in a great ba_ _le and the country was _ _united again. It was a gr_ _t mo_ _ _ _t in our _ _story.

## What's on the menu?

Here is a list of common types of food. Use a dictionary to check any unknown words.*

**Meat**

*beef, chicken, ham, lamb, pork, turkey, veal*

**Fish**

*cod, haddock, salmon, sardines, sea bass, sole, trout, tuna*

**Seafood**

*crab, prawns, shellfish (eg mussels), squid*

**Vegetables**

*aubergine (AmE eggplant), avocado, beans, broccoli, cauliflower, carrot, courgettes (AmE zucchini), cucumber, lettuce, mushrooms, onions, peas, peppers, potatoes, spinach, sweet potatoes, tomatoes*

**Fruit**

*apple, banana, cherry, clementine, grapes, kiwi fruit, lemon, mango, melon, orange, peach, pear, pineapple, plum, satsuma, strawberry, watermelon*

**Other**

*cheese, eggs, flour, garlic, herbs, noodles, nuts, olives, olive oil, pasta, spices, sugar, pancake/crepe, rice, vinegar*

## Describing food

Food can be prepared in many different ways. First you can …

*add something to it, cut it into slices, beat it, fill it, grate it, melt it, mince it, mix it, peel it, remove the skin, squeeze it, stir it.*

Then you cook the food in the following ways:

*bake, barbecue, boil, fry, grill, microwave, roast, smoke, steam, stew/casserole, stir-fry.*

After cooking the taste/texture can be …

*bitter, bland/tasteless, creamy, fatty, juicy, mild, oily, rich, salty, spicy/hot, sweet.*

When you order steak, common options are *rare, medium rare, medium* and *well-done*.

## Describing drinks

Water can be …

*bottled, sparkling, iced, mineral, still, tap.*

Wine can be …

*dry, fruity, full-bodied, light, red, refreshing, rosé, smooth, sparkling, sweet, white.*

If you are serious about wine, you will want to know the country/region of origin and the variety of grape. Alternatively, just order 'the house red' as a safe, inexpensive option. If it is corked (= has a bad taste because air has come into the bottle), send it back.

Beer comes in two types in English-speaking countries. European-style beer (light coloured, cold, with bubbles) is called lager. Traditional beer (darker, served at room temperature, without bubbles) is called bitter or ale. A Guinness-style beer is called a stout.

Beer can be bottled, or draught (= served with a pump from a large container). If you drink draught beer in a pub, you say whether you want 'a half' (approx 300 ml) or 'a pint' (600 ml).

## Talking about food

Food can be …

*fast, junk, fresh, frozen, healthy, homemade, organic, overcooked/undercooked, raw, seasonal.*

A meal can be …

*delicious, heavy, light, three-course.*

A diet can be …

*healthy, balanced, gluten-free, high-fibre, lactose-free, low-fat, vegetarian.*

And food/drink is no good if it is …

*burnt, not fresh, not ripe yet, off, stale.*

Here are some useful phrases:

*Is dinner nearly ready? I'm starving.*
*No more for me, thanks. I'm full.*
*I'll have a cup of tea, but no cake. It'll spoil my appetite.*
*I'm glad we went for a walk before dinner. It's really given me an appetite.*
*The salad dressing is made from oil, vinegar and mustard.*
*That was delicious – you must give me the recipe.*

*Many dictionaries (such as the *Macmillan Essential Dictionary*) have colour pictures of vegetables and fruit.

# Exercises

**37.1 Write the foods in the box under the correct headings.**

> aubergine   beef   cauliflower   cherry   chicken
> grapes   haddock   lamb   lettuce   mushrooms
> nuts   olive oil   pineapple   prawns   salmon   squid
> strawberry   trout   tuna   veal

**Meat**                  **Fish**

_____          _____

_____          _____

_____          _____

**Vegetables**            **Fruit**

_____          _____

_____          _____

_____          _____

**Seafood**               **Other**

_____          _____

**37.2 Find items of food on the page opposite that match the explanations below. The answers are not included in Exercise 37.1.**

1 In Italy people cut this meat into very thin slices and eat it raw – especially with melon. ___ham___
2 In Portugal people love to grill these small, silver fish.
   _____
3 This vegetable looks like a green cauliflower. People say it is one of the healthiest foods you can eat. _____
4 This long vegetable has a dark green skin. It is one of the main ingredients in ratatouille, along with aubergines, peppers and tomatoes. _____
5 If you can't find clementines, why not try _____s? They're very easy to peel and are usually seedless.
6 In Italy they call it pasta. In Asia they call it _____ . They look very similar to me!
7 Parsley, rosemary, thyme and basil are all _____

**37.3 Match the words in the box with the definitions below.**

> course   dish   meal   plate

1 an occasion when you eat, or the food that you eat _____
2 one of the parts of a meal _____
3 a flat dish that you use for eating or serving food _____
4 a) a round container used for holding food b) food cooked in a particular way _____

Now use each word once to complete the sentences below.
5 Breakfast, lunch and dinner are all _____s.
6 I had a starter, a main _____and a dessert.
7 Between your knife and fork on the table is your _____ .
8 Ratatouille is a French _____ .

**37.4 Choose the correct verb a–h to complete sentences 1–8.**

| a add | b cut | c fill | d melt |
|---|---|---|---|
| e mince | f peel | g squeeze | h stir |

1 ☐ a pancake with honey and lemon. Delicious!
2 ☐ vegetables and small pieces of meat in a pan over a high heat, and then add soy sauce and noodles. You will make a classic Chinese dish.
3 ☐ butter and sugar to flour to start making a cake.
4 ☐ a potato into long thin pieces to make french fries (BrE chips).
5 ☐ beef to start to prepare a bolognese sauce.
6 ☐ a banana or kiwi fruit because you can't eat the skin.
7 ☐ a lemon over your grilled fish so that all the juice comes out.
8 ☐ cheese over a low heat to make the classic Swiss dish called fondue.

**37.5 Underline the correct words in italics.**

1 Beer, coffee, lemons, tonic water and unsweetened cocoa all have a _bitter / salty_ taste.
2 If you prefer your fish cooked without any oil, ask for it to be _fried / grilled_.
3 If you want the vitamins to stay in the vegetables, it is better to _boil / steam_ them.
4 Food that has very little taste is called _bland / mild_. If you want a curry that is not too hot, then ask for it to be _bland / mild_.
5 When we cook bread or cakes in an oven, we use the word _bake / roast_. But when we cook meat or vegetables in an oven we use the word _bake / roast_.
6 What kind of water would you like? _With gas or without gas? / Still or sparkling?_

**37.6 One of the items in the list does not go with the noun at the end. Cross it out.**

1 _dry / full-bodied / light / pink / sparkling_        wine
2 _bottled / draught / local / fatty / refreshing_      beer
3 _fast / junk / overcooked / raw / tap_                food
4 _delicious / heavy / light / ripe / three-course_     meal

**37.7 Fill in the missing letters.**

1 Is dinner nearly ready? I'm sta_ _ing.
2 No more for me, thanks. I'm _ _ll.
3 No cake for me – it'll sp_ _l my app_ _ _te.
4 The salad dr_ _ _ing is made from oil, v_ _ _gar and m_ _tard.
5 That was delicious – you must give me the re_ _ _e.
6 If you order a drink in a pub, don't use the word 'beer' – it's too general. Instead, say 'I'll have a p_ _t of bi_ _er, please', or 'I'd like a h_ _f of l_ _er, please'. If you like Guinness, you will hope that the pub has dr_ _ght rather than bottled.

## 38 At the restaurant

### Basic vocabulary

The host invites the guest to go out for dinner. The host may call the restaurant first:

*I'd like to book/reserve a table for 8pm tonight, please.*
*I'd like a table for two, please.*
*Could I have a table by the window, please?*

On the table in the restaurant you will find: knife/fork/spoon, chopsticks, plate, side plate, soup bowl, napkin, water glass, wine glass, water jug, roll and butter, salt and pepper, menu and wine list.

The meal will have various courses: aperitif, starter, main course, dessert and coffee.

At the end of the meal you pay the bill (BrE)/check (AmE). Look to see whether a service charge is included – if not you can give a tip directly to the waiter (AmE server). And don't forget the most important phrase in Business English:

*Can I have a receipt, please?*

### Discussing the menu

As you discuss the menu you might want to say:

*It all looks very good.*
*You should try … They do it very well here.*
*It's a bit unusual. You may not like it.*
*I'm a vegetarian, although I sometimes eat fish.*
*I'm allergic to nuts/shellfish.*
*I like to choose a healthy option.*
*I'm not very hungry – I don't want a starter.*
*What are you having?*

The waiter might say:

*The specials are on the board over there.*
*It doesn't come with vegetables – you have to order them separately.*

Use the word 'the' to talk about specific food on the menu:

*I'll have the fish./I'm going for the fish.*

If an item looks unfamiliar, you may want to ask your host – or the waiter – some questions.

*What's it made of?*
*How's it cooked?*
*What does it taste like?*
*What does it come with?*

The vocabulary in Unit 37 is useful in answering these questions. Also note the phrase *It's a local speciality.*

When you've all decided, the host will say:

*Shall we order now?*

### Mini-dialogues with the waiter

Look at the questions and answers.

*Are you ready to order?*
– *Yes, I think so. I'll have the smoked salmon as my starter, and the chicken as my main.*
– *Not quite. Just give us a minute or two.*

*What would you like to drink?*
– *A bottle of the house white, please.*
– *Oh, and can we have a bottle of mineral water to put in the middle?*

*Would you like to see the dessert menu?*
– *Yes, I think so.*
– *Better not, I'm on a diet.*
– *No thanks, I'll just have a coffee.*
– *No thanks, can you bring the bill, please?*

### Phrases during the meal

At the start of the meal you might say:

*Enjoy your meal!/Bon appetit!*
*Please, help yourself.*
*Cheers everyone! – Cheers!*
*To Eva!/Here's to the project!*

Then during the meal you might say:

*Nice place. Do you come here often?*
– *I've been here a couple of times.*

*This is very good. How's yours?*
– *It's delicious/excellent.*

*Could you pass the water, please?*
– *Here you are.*

*Shall we have another bottle?*
– *I'm fine, but please go ahead.*

And for conversation topics look at Units 34, 35 and 36.

At the end of the meal you might say:

*Waiter, can we have the bill, please?*

*Let me pay.*
– *No, this one's on me. You paid last time.*

*I'll get this. You're my guest.*
– *Thanks very much. The next time in my country you will be my guest.*

*This is on me. I insist.*
– *Are you sure?*
*Yes, the company's paying.*
– *Well, that's very kind of you.*

*It was a fantastic meal.*
– *I'm glad you enjoyed it.*

# Exercises

**38.1 Fill in the missing letters.**

1 The person who makes the invitation is the h_ _t.
The person who accepts the invitation is the gu_ _t.
2 In Japan and China they eat with cho_ _ _icks, not a knife and fork.
3 Use a nap_ _n to keep clean.
4 The water in the middle of the table can be in a bottle or a _ug.
5 The Sahara is a desert. Ice cream is a d_ _ _ _t.
6 In British English people ask for the bill at the end of the meal; in American English they ask for the ch_ _ _.
7 The extra money you give the waiter is the t_ _.
8 The piece of paper that shows you have paid for something is a rec_ _ _t.
9 Someone who does not eat meat is a veg_ _ _ _an.
10 If you become ill when you eat something, then you are all_ _ _ic to it.
11 These days people want to eat h_ _ _thy food that is good for their body.
12 If you need to eat, you are hu_ _ry. If you need to drink, you are th_ _sty.
13 Dishes that do not appear on the menu every day are called the spec_ _ _s.
14 Food that is made in a particular restaurant or area and is always very good there is called a sp_ _ _ _ _ity.
15 When you ask for food or drink in a restaurant, you o_ _ _r it.

**38.2 Put the following into the most logical order.**

a  be shown to your table
b  make a reservation by phone
c  chat while you wait for the main course
d  have a coffee and a thin mint chocolate
e  have a starter
f  have a dessert
g  leave a tip on a side plate
h  look at the menu
i  order your food
j  ask for the bill

1 [b]  2 ☐  3 ☐  4 ☐  5 [e]  6 ☐  7 ☐  8 ☐  9 ☐  10 ☐

**38.3 Match an item on the left with an item on the right.**

1 a table for          course
2 house               list
3 local               plate
4 main                charge
5 service             two
6 side                red
7 soup                speciality
8 wine                bowl

**38.4 Complete each sentence by using a word from list A in the first space, and a word from list B in the second.**

| A: | *bring  enjoy  have  here's  hungry  order  place put  ready  specials  ~~try~~  unusual* |
|---|---|
| B: | *bill  board  ~~do~~  like  main  meal  middle  often order  portion  project  separately* |

1 You should ___try___ the beef – they ___do___ it very well here.
2 It's a bit _____ . You may not _____ it.
3 You have to _____ the vegetables _____ .
4 I'm not very _____ – I can only eat a small _____ .
5 The _____ are on the _____ .
6 Are you _____ to _____ ?
7 I'll _____ the chicken as my _____ .
8 Can we have a bottle of mineral water to _____ in the _____ ?
9 _____ to the _____ !
10 _____ your _____ .
11 Nice _____ . Do you come here _____ ?
12 Can you _____ the _____ , please?

**38.5 Complete the phrases by matching an item on the left with an item on the right.**

1 This is very good. How's      me pay.
2 Could you pass               dessert menu?
3 Shall we                     yours?
4 Would you like to see the    a fantastic meal.
5 Let                          a tip?
6 I'll get this. You're        the water, please?
7 It was                       my guest.
8 Should we leave              have another bottle?

**38.6 Complete the phrases by matching an item on the left with an item on the right.**

a  Better not, I'm            you enjoyed it.
b  Here you                   on a diet.
c  I'm glad                   go ahead.
d  There's no need. Service   delicious.
e  No, this one's on me. You  are.
f  I'm fine, but please       paid last time.
g  Thanks very much. I'll     is included.
h  It's                       invite you when you come to my country.

**38.7 Now match a question or comment from Exercise 38.5 (1–8) with a reply from Exercise 38.6 (a–h).**

1 [h]  2 ☐  3 ☐  4 ☐  5 ☐  6 ☐  7 ☐  8 ☐

# 39 Leaving and saying goodbye

## Ending a conversation at work

To end a conversation at work you can say:

*Well, I should get back to work now.*
*Anyway, I'd better get on. (= continue working)*
*I have to go now. I'll catch you later.*

## Mini-dialogues for leaving

With people you know well the lines of a leaving dialogue may be very short.

*See you tomorrow / later / soon / on Friday.*
*– OK. Bye.*

*Bye for now.*
*– Bye.*

*Bye Angela, I'm off. (= I'm going now)*
*– Bye. See you tomorrow.*

*Have a good weekend.*
*– You too. / Same to you.*

The words *Take care* and *Cheers* are also informal ways of saying goodbye.

With people you don't know well the lines are a little longer.

*It was nice meeting you.*
*– Nice to meet you, too.*

*It was really good to see you again.*
*– Same here. It was great working with you, as always.*

*Don't forget to keep in touch.*
*– I won't. And thanks again.*

*Thank you again for coming.*
*– Thanks for inviting me. I really enjoyed my trip.*

*Hopefully, see you next year.*
*– Yes. See you next time. I look forward to it.*

*If you're ever in Lisbon, give me a call.*
*– Thanks. Will do.*

*Goodbye. Have a safe journey.*
*– Goodbye. And thanks again for everything.*

Sometimes you need to get away quickly. One way is to say goodbye to everyone rather than individual people.

*OK, have a nice weekend everyone.*
*I've just come to say goodbye. I'm leaving now.*

If someone asks a last-minute question you can say:

*Can we leave it until Monday? I really have to go.*
*Call me tomorrow – we can discuss it then.*

## A full leaving dialogue

A full leaving dialogue, for example at the end of a business trip, might be something like this. First one person (usually the visitor) gives a warning that they need to leave.

*Is that the time? I think I should be going.*
*It's getting late. I have to be off now.*
*It's time to make a move (= leave).*

The host can reply:

*Oh, so soon?*
*Oh, already?*

The visitor gives a reason.

*I have a long day tomorrow. My flight leaves at 7.30 in the morning.*

The host shows interest and continues the conversation a little longer.

*Really? That means a 6.30am check-in. Will you get a chance to have breakfast in the hotel?*

After a short time the host makes a final 'thank you' and a reference to the success of the visit.

*Well, thank you very much for coming. I think we had a very useful meeting.*

And the visitor replies by thanking the host.

*Yes, the meeting was very good. And thanks very much for all your help these last few days. I really appreciate it.*

To which the host can reply:

*Not at all. It's been a pleasure.*
*Not at all. It was my pleasure.*

Now it's time for the visitor to make a second reference to leaving.

*Well, I really must be going now.*

The host replies by wishing the visitor a good trip.

*It's been very nice meeting you again. Have a good trip, and we'll be in touch.*

Finally someone says goodbye.

*See you in Hamburg in May. Bye.*
*Give my regards to everyone in Toulouse. Bye.*
*Goodbye. All the best.*

Notice at the start and end of this section how the phrases *I should be going* and *I really must be going* are more friendly than *I should go* and *I really must go*.

# Exercises

**39.1 Complete each phrase with the correct ending.**

1 Bye, Duncan. I'm            you later.
2 Don't forget to keep           get on.
3 Anyway, I'd better           meeting you.
4 Have a           in touch.
5 It was nice           give me a call.
6 I have to go now. I'll catch        off.
7 Thank you again          good weekend.
8 If you're ever in Lisbon,       for coming.

**39.2 Look back at Exercise 39.1. Match each comment 1–8 with the most appropriate reply a–h below.**

1️⃣ a  Bye. See you tomorrow.
☐ b  Thanks for inviting me – I really enjoyed my trip. We'll be in touch.
☐ c  Yeah, me too. I have that report to write.
☐ d  You too.
☐ e  I won't. And thanks again.
☐ f  Thanks. Will do.
☐ g  Nice to meet you, too.
☐ h  Yeah, at the meeting, if not before.

**39.3 Look back at Exercise 39.2. Find:**

1 Two dialogues where colleagues at work say goodbye at the end of the day. _1a_ _____
2 Two dialogues for ending a conversation at work in the middle of the day. _____
3 One dialogue where the people have just talked briefly for the first time and may not meet again. _____
4 Two dialogues at the end of a business trip where the people will probably meet again. _____ _____
5 One dialogue at the end of a business trip where the people may or may not meet again. _____

**39.4 Complete each phrase by matching an item on the left with one on the right.**

1 It was          be going.
2 I should get       great working with you.
3 Give           care!
4 I have          in touch!
5 Keep          back to work now.
6 Can we leave       forward to it.
7 I look          it until Monday?
8 It's time to make    my regards to Monique.
9 I really should     a move.
10 Take          a long day tomorrow.

**39.5 Fill in the missing letters.**

1 Goodbye! Have a s _ _ _ jou_ _ey!
2 Bye! S_ _ y_ _!
3 Goodbye. See you again s_ _e t_ _e.
4 Bye! T_ _e c_ _e. Give me a call when you get back.
5 Goodbye. I hope we m_ _t a_ _ _n s_ _n.
6 Bye! C_ _e b_ _k soon!
7 Goodbye and good l_ _k!
8 Bye f_ _ n_ _!

**Now match phrase numbers 1–8 with the most appropriate statements below.**

The other person is going on a journey. 1️⃣ ☐
The other person is moving to a new city/job/etc. ☐
You will meet again soon and the situation is informal. ☐ ☐
You are not sure if you will meet again. ☐ ☐ ☐

**39.6 Complete each space by using one word from list A and one from list B.**

| A: | *for get* ~~*getting*~~ *going long really should your* |
|---|---|
| B: | *appreciate be day everything help home* ~~*late*~~ *now* |

**Visitor**

a) Is that the time? It's ___*getting late*___ . I think I _____ going.
b) Goodbye. And thanks again _____ .
c) I'd love to carry on talking, but I've got a _____ tomorrow. I'm flying back to Jakarta.
d) Yes, the meeting was very positive. And thanks very much for all _____ these last few days. I _____ it.
e) Well, I really must be _____ .
f) It's a 14-hour journey, and then I have another hour to _____ from the airport.

**Continue as before.**

| A: | *at how in meeting so useful very* |
|---|---|
| B: | *all long meeting much soon touch you* |

**Host**

g) Well, thank you _____ for coming. I think we had a very _____ .
h) _____ is the flight?
i) It's been very nice _____ . Have a safe journey tomorrow, and we'll be _____ .
j) Not _____ . It's been a pleasure.
k) Oh, _____ ?

**39.7 Look back at Exercise 39.6. Put lines a–k into order to make a dialogue.**

| Visitor | Host |
|---|---|
| 1 a | 2 ☐ |
| 3 ☐ | 4 ☐ |
| 5 ☐ | 6 g |
| 7 ☐ | 8 ☐ |
| 9 ☐ | 10 ☐ |
| 11 b | |

## Greetings and introductions

### People you know

*How are you? – I'm good thanks, and you? – Good.*
*Did you have a good weekend?*
*Hi, how's it going?*
*How are things?*

### People you don't know

*I don't think we've met. My name's Susan Atkins. I'm the*
*Sales Rep for this area. – Nice to meet you Susan. I'm Ying Li.*

### Introductions

Anne: *Brian, come over here. I want you to meet someone.*
Brian: *Hi.*
Anne: *Brian, this is Claudia, a colleague of mine from*
*Austria.*
Brian: *Nice to meet you, Claudia.*
Claudia: *Nice to meet you too, Brian.*

## Welcoming visitors

### At the airport

*Welcome to Switzerland.*
*Let me help you with your bags.*
*Did you have a good flight?*
*Is this your first time in Zurich?*

### At the office

*It's nice to finally meet you in person.*
*Have a seat.*
*Would you like something to drink?*
*How was your journey?*
*OK, let's get down to business.*

## Small talk

### Talking to strangers

*This food looks good … By the way, I'm Patricia.*
*Excuse me, do you mind if I join you?*
*So where are you from originally?*
*How long are you here for?*
*What do you do, by the way?*
*Who do you work for?*
*And where are you based?*

### Topics

*Can I get you anything from the buffet?*
*What lovely/awful weather!*
*How's business?*
*Have you been to Marrakesh?*
*Are you going on holiday this year?*
*One time I met this guy/woman who …*
*A strange thing happened to me once.*

## Free time

*go see a movie/a play/a band*
*go out for a meal/a drink*
*go round/over to someone's house*
*meet up with/get together with a few friends*
*have a quiet night in and watch TV*

## Home, city, country

### Family

*I grew up in Paris.*
*I'm single/married/separated/divorced.*
*I have two kids/children – a boy and a girl.*

### City

*be in a rush, cosmopolitan atmosphere, stress, (no) sense of*
*community, job opportunities*
*bus/cycle lanes, commute(r), get stuck in traffic, crowded/*
*unreliable public transport*
*entertainment, leisure facilities, nightlife*

### Country

*main exports/industries, north-south divide*
*coast, countryside, landscape, scenery*

## At the restaurant

### Discussing the menu

*It all looks very good.*
*You should try … They do it very well here.*
*I'm a vegetarian, although I sometimes eat fish.*
*I think I'll have the fish.*

### Start of the meal

*Enjoy your meal!*
*Cheers everyone! – Cheers!*
*To Eva!*

### During the meal

*Nice place. Do you come here often?*
*This is very good. How's yours?*
*Shall we have another bottle?*

### End of the meal

*Waiter, can we have the bill, please?*
*This one's on me. You paid last time.*
*I'll get this. You're my guest.*

## Leaving

*Is that the time? I think I should be going.*
*See you later/tomorrow.*
*Bye for now.*
*Have a good weekend.*
*It was really good to see you again.*
*Don't forget to keep in touch.*
*Have a safe journey.*

# Exercises

**40.1 Look at the mini-dialogues below and think of one word for each space. Several answers may be possible.**

Hi Charles, [1]_____ are you?
– I'm good thanks, and you?
[2]_____ .

Hi, how's it [3]_____ ?
– Not [4]_____ . And you?

How are [5]_____ ?
– It's really [6]_____ at the moment.

I don't think we've [7]_____ . My name's Patricia Hwang. I'm the Sales Rep for this area.
– [8]_____ to meet you Patricia.

Anne: Brian, [9]_____ is Claudia, a colleague of mine from Austria.
Brian: Nice to meet you, Claudia.
Claudia: Nice to meet you [10]_____ , Brian.

Is that the time? I think I [11]_____ be going.
– Oh, so [12]_____ ?

Bye for [13]_____ .
– Bye. See you [14]_____ .

[15]_____ a good weekend.
– [16]_____ too.

It was [17]_____ good to see you again.
– Same here. It was great working with you, as [18]_____ .

Don't forget to keep in [19]_____ .
– I won't. And [20]_____ again for everything.

*These words give one possible solution: always, bad, busy, going, good, have, how, later, met, nice, now, really, should, soon, thanks, things, this, too, touch, you.*

**40.2 Fill in the missing letters.**

1 And wh__e are you bas__?
2 Did you have a good fl____t?
3 Excuse me, do you m____ if I j___n you?
4 Have a s__t.
5 How long are you here ___?
6 How was your j____ey?
7 Is this your first time __ Riga?
8 It's nice to finally meet you __ p____n.
9 OK, l__'s g__ d____t_business.
10 So where are you from orig_____y?
11 This food looks good. Much better than you usually get at things like this. B_t__w__, I'm Alan.
12 Welcome __ Latvia.
13 What __ you __, by the way?
14 Who do you work ___?

**40.3 Complete the comments with the words in the box.**

> a drink   commute   countryside   crowded
> go out for   grew up   in a rush   leisure
> main industries   meet up with   north-south
> night in   single   small town   stuck in traffic

1 At the weekends I like to _____ friends. Either we _____ a meal, or we go see a movie.
2 There's so much stress. Everyone's always _____ .
3 I _____ in a little town just outside Krakow.
4 I have a one-hour _____ every day – I always get _____ .
5 I'm _____ , but I have a long-term partner.
6 Our _____ are aerospace, automobile production and telecommunications.
7 Public transport is _____ and unreliable.
8 She invited me to go for _____ tonight, but to be honest I'd rather just have a quiet _____ and watch TV.
9 There are plenty of job opportunities – more than in a _____ .
10 There's a lot to do: entertainment, _____ facilities, nightlife.
11 We have a strong _____ divide.
12 In the interior we have some lovely _____ with beautiful scenery.

**40.4 Look back at Exercise 40.3. Match the comments above with the topics below.**

Free time        [1] [ ]
Family/Origins   [ ] [ ]
City             [ ] [ ] [ ] [ ] [ ]
Country          [ ] [ ] [ ] (economy/geography)

**40.5 Match the beginning and end of each phrase.**

| | |
|---|---|
| 1 Cheers | here often? |
| 2 This one's | everyone! |
| 3 Nice place. Do you come | looks very good. |
| 4 I'll get this. You're | your meal! |
| 5 I think I'll have the | on me. |
| 6 Enjoy | the bill, please? |
| 7 It all | try the lamb. |
| 8 This is very good. How's | fish. |
| 9 Can we have | my guest. |
| 10 You should | yours? |

**40.6 Look back at Exercise 40.5. Match the comments above with the topics below.**

Discussing the menu  [ ] [ ] [ ]
Start of the meal    [1] [ ]
During the meal      [ ] [ ]
End of the meal      [ ] [ ] [ ]

## Travel, trip, journey

*Travel* is the general activity of moving from one place to another. It is an uncountable noun and a verb.

*My new job involves a lot of **travel**.*
*I **travel** abroad on business around once a month.*

A *trip* is a short visit to a place.
*She's gone on a business **trip** to Zurich.*

The *journey* is the time spent travelling.
*Let's get an early night – we have a long **journey** ahead of us.*

## Tickets

You can book a flight either over the Internet or through a travel agency. Perhaps your secretary makes the booking for you. Your ticket can be single/one-way or return/round trip. It's a good idea to check-in online in advance, as it increases the chance that you get a good seat. Your seat may be window, middle or aisle.

## A typical flight

The taxi drops you off (= takes you by car and leaves you) outside the terminal building. You enter the terminal and find the self-service check-in machine. Enter your e-ticket reservation number or frequent flyer number, choose your seat from those still available/open (if you haven't already chosen), and the machine prints your boarding pass. If you have any checked baggage (= items to go in the hold), you go to the baggage drop-off point. Now follow the signs for 'Departures' and prepare for the security check. You may have to queue (AmE stand in line) for a little while, then you remove your belt and shoes, put your keys and laptop in a tray, and go through the scanner.

Now you're in the departure lounge. You can get some currency (= money used in a particular country), use your laptop, or just walk around and do some shopping. Keep checking the information screens to see the status of your flight. It might be delayed (= late). Soon you see the words you are waiting for: *Now boarding at Gate 14*. You walk to the gate and board (= get onto) the plane. Please don't wait until the final call (= last announcement). Find your seat and put your hand luggage in the overhead locker. Just before you take off (= leave the ground) the flight attendants/cabin crew will give a safety demonstration. Now you're in the air and can enjoy your flight! Let's hope there isn't too much turbulence.

You land (= come to the ground), get off the plane, and go through passport control. Follow the signs for baggage reclaim and collect your bags from the carousel/belt that has your flight number. Walk through customs and exit at the barrier in the arrivals hall. Is anyone there to meet you? Maybe it's a local contact who has come to pick you up (= collect you in a car), or maybe it's a taxi driver holding up a sign with your name on it.

If you travelled on a long haul flight, you may have jet lag (= feeling very tired after a long flight). You'll need a day or two to recover.

## On arrival: useful phrases

Here are some phrases to use when you arrive.

### Visitor
*You must be Vijay Chandra.*
*It's great to be here – thank you so much for organizing everything.*

### The local contact
*Let me help you with your bags.*
*How was your flight?*
*Is this your first time in India?*
(See also Unit 32.)

### Visitor to taxi driver
*Please drop me here – just before the lights.*
*How much is the fare (= money you pay to travel)?*
*Keep the change.*
*Make it forty.* (I will give you 40, which includes the tip)
*Can I have a receipt, please?*

## Word partnerships

Here are some verb + noun collocations.

***arrange/organize*** a trip
***cancel, cut short, extend*** a trip
***be away on/go on/make*** a trip
***come back from/return from*** a trip
***get a good deal on*** a ticket
***make*** a booking/reservation on a flight
***catch/miss*** a flight (NOT ~~lose a flight~~)
***wait for*** your flight (to be called)
***board*** the plane
***take*** a taxi, ***go by*** taxi

# Exercises

**41.1 Complete each sentence with one of these words: *travel, trip, journey.***

1  Did you enjoy your _____ to Disneyland?
2  My _____ to work takes around 45 minutes.
3  Have you made all the _____ arrangements for your trip to Paris?
4  It was a long, tiring _____ to Sydney – we had to wait four hours in Singapore for our connection.
5  I _____ to work every day on the metro.
6  I guess I make around ten business _____s a year in my job.

**41.2 Underline the correct word in italics.**

1  Did you have a good *travel / journey*?
2  I *booked / ordered* my flight on the Internet.
3  I prefer *an aisle / a corridor* seat as I get more leg room.
4  Excuse me, I think that's my seat. My boarding *pass / ticket* says seat 16A.
5  Oh no! The information screen says our flight is delayed *by / with* an hour.
6  Be quick – that was the final *call / calling* for our flight.
7  We were waiting on the runway for about 30 minutes before the plane finally *took off / took up*.
8  When you come out at the barrier, you'll see our driver holding a *sign / signal* with your name on it.
9  The taxi *bill / fare* was over 60 euros – I'm sure the driver didn't reset the meter before we left.
10  How much is the fare? 36 euros? OK – here's 40 euros. Keep the *change / small money*.
11  Make it 50, and can I have *a receipt / an invoice*, please?
12  I got a really good *deal / offering* on my ticket – it was about 25% less than the regular price.
13  There was a traffic jam on the way to the airport and I nearly *lost / missed* my flight.
14  I was just sitting there, *waiting / waiting for* my flight to be called.
15  I did some shopping in the *departing / departure* lounge.
16  You can book a hotel in the *arriving / arrivals* hall.

**41.3 Match an item on the left with an item on the right.**

| | |
|---|---|
| 1  make | you off at Terminal 1 |
| 2  be away | you up from Arrivals |
| 3  drop | security/passport control |
| 4  pick | a booking |
| 5  go through | on a trip |

| | |
|---|---|
| 6  walk | your bag in the overhead locker |
| 7  board | around and do some shopping |
| 8  put | short the trip |
| 9  follow | the plane |
| 10  cut | the signs for Baggage Reclaim |

**41.4 Complete each sentence with a whole phrase from Exercise 41.3.**

1  If I need to *make a booking* on a flight, my favourite Internet site is RidiculouslyCheapFlights.com.
2  It will be a great pleasure to welcome you to Lisbon. We'll take care of everything. A driver will _____ – he'll be at the barrier waiting for you.
3  The taxi will be here in five minutes. Don't worry – you should be at the airport in less than half an hour. I'll ask the driver to _____ .
4  I'm sorry sir, you have to _____ . It's part of the safety regulations.
5  There was an emergency at the factory – the workers were threatening to go on strike and my assistant was away on vacation. I had to _____ .
6  Before I _____ I always look around near the departure gate to see if there are any free newspapers.

**41.5 Match a word from list A with a word from list B.**

| A: | boarding  check-in  final  flight  frequent  jet  hand  overhead  passport  ~~terminal~~ |
|---|---|
| B: | attendant  ~~building~~  call  control  flyer  lag  luggage  locker  machine  pass |

**Now use a two-word phrase in each gap. Note that sentence e has two phrases.**

a  The taxi drops you off outside the *terminal building* .
b  Try to be friendly to the local colleagues who are there to meet you – even if you are suffering from _____ .
c  Enter the terminal and find the self-service _____ .
d  Before you go into the departure lounge, show your _____ to a security guard and then go through a scanner.
e  Board the plane and put your _____ in the _____ .
f  Enter your e-ticket reservation number or _____ number on the screen.
g  Pay attention while the _____s give a safety demonstration.
h  Check the information screen to see when your flight is going to board. Don't wait until the _____ .
i  When you land, go through _____ .

**41.6 Look back at Exercise 41.5 and put sentences a–i in order (according to what really happens).**

1 [a]  2 [ ]  3 [ ]  4 [ ]  5 [ ]  6 [ ]  7 [ ]  8 [ ]  9 [ ]

## Checking in

The guest (= person staying at the hotel) arrives at the hotel, walks into the lobby, and then goes up to reception/the front desk to check in. The receptionist/desk clerk needs to get (or confirm) various details. These may include: name and address, nationality, passport details, a signature on a registration form, room preferences (perhaps a particular view was requested), the rate quoted (= amount of money you were told you would pay), departure date and time, whether the person or the company pays, credit card details, and any loyalty programs that the guest belongs to. Once this is complete, the receptionist will give the guest the key card and explain a few things such as breakfast arrangements and the location of hotel facilities (health club, etc).

The guest may have some special questions to ask the receptionist:

*Can you get someone to help me with my luggage?*
*Can I have a wake-up call in the morning?*
*How far is the Expo Centre from here? Can I walk or should I take a taxi?*
*Could you tell me if there's a bank near here?*

The guest walks over to the elevator (BrE lift), goes up to their room, and unpacks their things. Perhaps it's time to have a nap (= short sleep), or to freshen up before meeting colleagues and going out.

## Hotel facilities

Here are some of the facilities that may be available in a hotel: business centre, swimming pool, gym/fitness room, laundry and dry cleaning, 24-hour reception, 24-hour room service, restaurant with regional food, complimentary (= provided free) newspaper, currency exchange, an airport transfer/shuttle, etc.

The room may be a double room (with a double bed), twin room (with two beds) or single room. Inside the room there may be coffee/tea making facilities, a separate sitting area, etc.

## Requests

If you need anything extra, you may need to contact reception or the room service clerk. You usually dial zero to speak to reception.

*Can I have an iron and ironing board sent up to my room, please? I need them as soon as possible.*
*Could you tell the housekeeping staff not to clean my room in the morning? I want to sleep late.*
*Is it possible to have breakfast sent up to my room?*
*Do you think you could call up to my room and let me know when my colleagues arrive?*
*Could I just ask you what time I need to be out of my room?*
*I'd be grateful if you could find out the weather forecast for tomorrow.*

## Complaints

Here are just some of the things that you may want to complain about:

- No reservation on arrival.
- Wrong room allocation – you wanted a room overlooking the sea.
- Poor housekeeping: room that hasn't been cleaned, dirty sheets, dirty towels, no spare blanket.
- Bathroom problems: shower not working, smell coming from the drains.
- Air conditioning or heater not working.
- Uncomfortable mattress or pillow.
- Noise from loud neighbours, or from an event happening in the hotel.
- Substandard restaurant.

Here are some tips on how to complain.

1 Take a photo with your mobile phone to help build your case. Then complain immediately – go down to the front desk and talk face-to-face.

2 Tell your story once, simply, and without exaggeration. Finish by identifying the solution you want (something fixed in your room or a new room?). Then be silent and wait for a response.

3 Remain calm and polite at all times. You will get better service more quickly.

4 If they cannot fix your problem immediately, be flexible about back-up solutions. How about using a shower in another room if you are in a hurry?

5 If it is a serious matter, keep notes of who you talked to, when, and what was said. Then when you get back home, write to the Hotel Manager and ask for a partial refund.

# Exercises

**42.1 Underline the correct word in italics.**

1  I'll be waiting in the *hall / lobby*, just in front of the reception desk.
2  Please fill in this registration form and *sign / signature* at the bottom where I have marked with a cross.
3  You are paying a special *charge / rate* for your room. It does not include breakfast.
4  Can you make sure I get my *fidelity / loyalty* points for this stay?
5  Can I have a *get-up / wake-up* call in the morning?
6  I have some clothes that need washing. Do you have a *laundry / laundering* service?
7  Please help yourself to a morning newspaper – it's *complimentary / a complement*.
8  Is there an airport *transfer / transportation*? When do they leave?
9  I would definitely recommend the hotel. It had very good *conditions / facilities*.
10  I'm sorry, my room is *incompatible / unsuitable* – it's right next to a noisy elevator.

**42.2 Fill in the missing letters.**

1  Is it possible to upgrade my room to one that has a v _ _ _ of the sea?
2  This price is not the price I was qu_ _ed when I called you last week.
3  The word 'elevator' is international, but in the UK you can also hear the word 'l _ _ _'.
4  I'll be down in half an hour – I just need to unp_ _k my things and fr_ _ _en up.
5  Can I change my euros into the local curr_ _ _ _?
6  Can I have an ir_ _ and ir_ _ing boa_ _ sent up to my room, please?
7  I'm sorry, but my room has not been cl_ _ _ed. The sh_ _ ts and tow_ _s are dirty.
8  It's cold and I might need a sp_ _e blanket tonight. I can't see one in the room.
9  There is an unpleasant sm_ _ _ in the bathroom – I think it's the drains. I would like to change rooms, please.
10  My room is cold. I tried to adjust the controls on the he_ _er but they don't work.
11  My pi_ _ow is too high. Do you have another one – if possible one with feathers?

**42.3 Can you remember the missing prepositions?**

1  (*you answer a call from the lobby*) I'll be _ _ _ _ in a few minutes – I just need to freshen _ _. Are we going _ _ _ for dinner or eating in the restaurant here?
2  (*you call room service*) Can I have a coffee and a croissant sent _ _ to my room, please?
3  (*you are complaining*) Can't I just use a shower in another room? I'm _ _ a hurry.

**42.4 Each sentence below contains one mistake (it might just be word order). Find it and correct it.**

1  Can I ~~to~~ have a wake-up call in the morning?
2  How distance is the Expo Centre from here?
3  Can I walk or would I take a taxi?
4  What time do you stop to serve breakfast?
5  I can have an iron sent up to my room, please*?*
6  I need it so soon as possible.
7  Could you tell to the housekeeping staff not to clean my room in the morning?
8  Is it possibility to have breakfast sent up to my room?

**42.5 Match the beginnings and endings of the phrases. Then use them to complete the dialogue between a receptionist (R) and a guest (G).**

| | |
|---|---|
| I'd like | someone to help me … |
| Can you | if you could … |
| Can you get | to check in |
| Could I just | of you |
| I'd be grateful | give me … |
| That's | ask you … |
| That's very kind | to follow the porter, … |
| If you'd like | right |

R:  Good morning, madam.
G:  Good morning. [1] *I'd like to check in* . I have a reservation in the name of Fiona Wilson, just one night.
R:  One moment. Right, I have it here. We've put you on the fourth floor, overlooking the hotel gardens.
G:  That sounds fine.
R:  And the rate you were quoted is €150 a night.
G:  [2] _____ .
R:  [3] _____ to fill in this registration form?
G:  Sure. Also, I have some heavy luggage in the lobby over there. [4] _____ with it?
R:  Yes of course. I'll get the porter to take it up for you. Was there anything else?
G:  Yes. [5] _____ a wake-up call tomorrow morning?
R:  Certainly. What time would you like?
G:  It needs to be 5.45am. My flight leaves at 8.00.
R:  No problem.
G:  [6] _____ book a taxi for me as well. I guess I need to leave around 6.30am to get to the airport for check-in at 7.00.
R:  Yes, 6.30 should be fine. At that time in the morning there's very little traffic. And I can ask room service to bring you a coffee and a croissant at 6 if you'd like.
G:  Oh, thank you very much. [7] _____ .
R:  I'll book the taxi right now. Here's your key card. [8] _____ he'll take you to your room.

# 43 Conferences and exhibitions

## Conferences

Are you a speaker/presenter who is giving a speech/ presentation/talk, or a participant/delegate who is attending (= going to) the sessions? If you are a speaker, then remember to look at Units 59-60.

There are many kinds of presentation, including:

- A workshop session. This is likely to be practical and aimed at improving skills.
- A seminar. This is a meeting for giving and discussing information.
- A round-table discussion. This is a discussion with several speakers, under the control of a moderator/ facilitator. One common format is where a panel of experts answer questions from the audience.
- An opening/closing address. This is a more formal speech given at the start/end of the conference. It may take place in a large auditorium.
- A keynote speech. This is an opening address that introduces the main issues to be considered at the conference.
- A plenary. This is a session attended by everyone at the conference.

The conference takes place at a venue (= place where a large event happens) such as a convention centre. After registration in the foyer/lobby, the day is organized into time slots with several sessions usually happening at the same time. Inside the venue there is an exhibition area where exhibitors have stands/booths to give information or sell their products. There will be somewhere for refreshments, and also several breakout areas with seating for people to sit and talk. This is very important – to most people the opportunity to network is just as important as attending the talks.

You walk away from the conference with all sorts of papers in your conference pack. There will be the promotional material you picked up on the stands, the handouts that the speakers gave out/passed round, and hopefully lots of business cards that you exchanged with useful contacts.

## Exhibitions and trade fairs

An exhibition often takes place in the same kind of venue as a conference, but here the emphasis is on the visitors walking around the stands and talking to the exhibitors. There may also be a few conference-style sessions to add interest. An exhibition may also be called an expo. A trade fair/trade show is very similar but is for one particular industry rather than the general public.

Exhibitors invest a lot of money in the event. Costs include rental of stand space, design and construction of displays for the stand, travel, accommodation, and promotional literature and items to give to visitors.

An increasing number of trade fairs are happening online, and these events are called virtual trade shows.

## Trade fair: useful phrases

Here are some phrases to use at a trade fair.

**Exhibitor**

*Can I help you? Please sit down. It's quieter over here – we can talk without being disturbed.*
*I see from your name badge that you work at …*
*I saw that you were looking at … . It's our latest model. You can see the quality.*
*What kind of thing are you looking for?*
*I think this model might suit your needs better.*
*We have it on display over there at the back of the stand.*
*Let me give you a catalogue/brochure – it explains everything we've talked about.*
*Here's my card – please feel free to email or call at any time. I'm here to help.*
*If you leave your details, I'll get our technical people to call you.*

**Visitor**

*I'm interested in … I work for a company that …*
*Can you tell me a little more about …?*
*We're thinking of changing our … and we want to see what is available on the market.*
*I'm already a customer of yours – I use your … .*
*I'd like to know what upgrades are available.*
*I'm not interested in buying at this stage, I just want to collect more information.*
*I was looking at a similar product on the stand over there – how is your product different?*
*Do you have any samples?*
*Is it available in other colours/sizes?*
*What are your usual delivery times?*
*What kind of after-sales service do you provide?*

*Let me give you a catalogue.*

# Exercises

**43.1 One of the three phrases in italics does not exist or is not used. Cross it out.**

1 I went to a very interesting ~~discourse~~ / speech / talk.

2 Which seminar / talkshop / workshop are you going to after lunch?

3 This year the conference is being held / is holding / is taking place in South Africa.

4 There's a talk I really want to go to at 11am. Do you mind if I'm not on the display / in the booth / on the stand for an hour or so?

5 The most useful thing about the conference was the opportunity to exchange contacts / make contacts / network.

6 Which session are you going to assist / attend / go to after lunch?

7 Before I pack my bags tonight I'm going to throw away most of the promotional literature / material / papers I was given.

8 We always have a stand at the Munich trade expo / trade fair / trade show.

9 This is our last / latest / most recent model. You can see the quality.

10 I think this model might be convenient for you / be what you're looking for / suit your needs.

**43.2 Fill in the missing letters.**

1 One common format for a round-table discussion is where a p _ _ l of ex _ _ _ _ s answer questions from the au _ _ _ _ ce.

2 A large hall for giving talks is sometimes called an au _ _ _ _ _ ium.

3 A ve _ _ e is a place where a large ev _ _ t happens.

4 Reg _ _ _ _ tion for the conference will take place in the foyer from 8am onwards. All delegates will be given a conference p _ _ k with the full programme.

5 A s _ _ _ d is a table or structure (often temporary) that is used for selling things or providing information. In American English the word 'b _ _ th' is also used.

6 Drinks and light snacks provided at an event are called ref _ _ _ _ ments.

7 The presenter often passes round a ha _ _ _ _ t at the start or end of their talk.

8 If you have a stand at a large trade fair and want to attract attention, try to make the dis _ _ ay on your stand look different to the others.

9 The cost of having a stand at the fair is very high when you add in travel and accommodation. We're looking at the possibility of vir _ _ _ l trade shows, online.

10 At a trade fair you are often given free sa _ _ _ es of a company's products.

11 This model is av _ _ _ able in a range of different colours.

12 Pl _ _ _ e f _ _ l f _ _ e to email or call me.

**43.3 Complete the sentences with these prepositions: at, for, in, in, on, on.**

1 I saw that you were looking _____ the photographs at the back of the stand.

2 What kind of thing are you looking _____ ?

3 We have a prototype _____ display over there.

4 Is it available _____ other sizes?

5 I'm interested _____ your hotel-catering equipment.

6 I saw a similar product _____ the stand over there.

**43.4 Complete the dialogue at a trade fair with the words in the box. E is an exhibitor and V is a visitor.**

| | | |
|---|---|---|
| a sample | at this stage | key features |
| leave your details | ~~name badge~~ | suit your needs |
| ideal solution | thinking of changing | |
| very advanced design | what is available | |

E: Can I help you? I see from your [1] name badge that you work at KLG. I must say your new product line is just fantastic.

V: Thanks very much. Actually we're [2] _____ the power units we use in our machines. I'm here at the fair to see [3] _____ on the market. I was just looking at the photographs behind the desk over there.

E: Yes, they show our new line of power packs. They feature state-of-the-art technology and a [4] _____ . We own the patent on the design.

V: Can you tell me a little more about the units?

E: Yes, of course. Please sit down. It's quieter over here – we can talk without being disturbed.

V: I must emphasize that I'm not interested in buying [5] _____ ; I just want more information.

E: No problem. I can run through the [6] _____ now, and then leave you with a brochure that you can look at later.

V: Fine.

E: Can I just ask what kind of power pack you are looking for?

V: Yes. We're going to need a 10 watt power supply, chassis mounted. It must have full universal AC input, from 85 to 264 volts. The space available is quite small – around 70 by 30 by 20 millimetres.

E: I see. I think I have the [7] _____ for you. Have a look at this item from our brochure – it would [8] _____ very well.

V: Yes, it does look like the kind of thing we need. Do you have [9] _____ I could take away and show to my colleagues back at the office?

E: Not here, but if you [10] _____ , I'll make sure we send one to you.

## Using the phone

In your house you might have a landline/fixed line phone. In your bag you might have a mobile phone/ smart phone (AmE cell phone). When you are speaking, you are 'on the phone'. You can also use your phone to send an SMS/a text message. The verb is 'to text someone'. When you take your mobile phone to another country it is called roaming – a foreign network will give you local coverage.

To make a phone call you select a name from your Contacts list or dial the number (= press the buttons) directly. If you succeed in making the call, you 'get through'. Sometimes you can't get through because the line is busy/engaged (= already in use), in which case you either hang up (= end the call) or go to voicemail and leave a message. You can also fail to get through because of a poor/weak signal, and of course you can dial the wrong number. Sometimes in the middle of a call you can be cut off (= disconnected unexpectedly).

We say …

*make a call*
*call/phone/ring* (BrE) *someone* (NOT call to somebody)
*give someone a call/ring* (BrE)

## Making a call: first words

Very often you speak immediately to the person you want.

*Is that Linda? Hi! It's Sebastian.*
*Hello Ramon! This is José from Sao Paolo here.*
*How are you? How's everything over there in Madrid?*

If you are not speaking to the person you want, you begin by saying your name and perhaps your company name as well.

*Good morning, my name is Finn Larsen.*
*Good morning. This is Finn Larsen from Bergen Energy Services.* (NOT I am Finn Larsen)

After that you ask for the person you want.

*Can I speak to Vera Pereira, please?*
*Can I have extension 738, please?*
*Could you put me through to* (= connect me to) *the Accounts Department, please?*

To get through to the right person you might have to say why you are calling.

*I'm calling to find out some information about your products.*
*The reason I'm calling is because of a problem we're having with some equipment made by your company.*
*I'd like to speak to someone about my account.*
*I'm calling in connection with an email you sent me.*
*I got a message on my voicemail and I'm returning the call.*

## Receiving a call: first words

If you answer a general company phone number, it creates a good image if you give your own name as well as that of the company.

*Good morning, Media International, Carla speaking, how can I help you?* (NOT Can I help you?)

If you answer a direct line inside a company, you can say where you are speaking from and give your own name.

*Sales Department, Simon speaking.*
*Lisa's phone, Simon speaking.*

If someone asks for you by name, you simply say *Speaking* (NOT Yes, I am/NOT Yes, it is).

You may have to transfer the call.

*I'll try her number for you. Stay on the line, please.*
*I'll just put you on hold for a moment.*
*Please hold* (= wait) *while I try to connect you.*
*Just a moment, please. I'll transfer you. The extension number is 7847 in case we get cut off.*

And sometimes the other person is not there.

*I'm sorry, there's no answer. I'll put you through to his voicemail.*
*The line is busy. Would you like to hold?*

The caller may ask for someone you know is unavailable.

*I'm sorry, she's …*
*… in a meeting.*
*… not at her desk right now.*
*… away from the office today.*

You can offer an alternative.

*Can I take a message?*
*Would you like to leave a message?*
*Would you like to call back after two?*
*Shall I ask her to call you back?*
*Is there someone else who can help you?*

# Exercises

**44.1 Underline the correct word in italics.**

1 I think I *dialled / made* the wrong number.
2 I tried calling her but I couldn't *get through / go through*.
3 The line was *engaged / occupied* – I'll try again later.
4 I need to *do / make* a call – will you excuse me?
5 Please *call me / call to me* on my mobile around five.
6 *Are you / Is that* Vassily? Hi! It's Miguel here.
7 Please *hang / hold* while I try to connect you.
8 I'll try her number. *Keep on / Stay on* the line, please.

**44.2 Match the beginnings of phrases 1–8 with their endings a–h.**

1 I'm calling to ☐ c
2 I'm calling in ☐
3 The reason I'm calling is ☐
4 Would you like to leave ☐
5 Would you like to call ☐
6 Could you put me ☐
7 Shall I ask ☐
8 Is there ☐

a a message?
b connection with the email you sent yesterday.
c find out some information about your services.
d through to the technical support team?
e her to call you back?
f because of a problem we're having with your software.
g someone else who can help you?
h back in an hour or so?

**44.3 Look back at Exercise 44.2.**

1 Which phrases are used by the person making the call?
  [1c] ☐ ☐ ☐

2 Which phrases are used by the person receiving the call?
  ☐ ☐ ☐ ☐

**44.4 Complete the sentences with these prepositions:**
*about, back, in, off, on, through, through, to, up, with.*

1 Melinda? Yes, I was _____ the phone to her yesterday.
2 After several tries I finally managed to get _____ .
3 I've been on hold listening to *The Four Seasons* for about 20 minutes. I'm going to hang _____ .
4 Sorry, I went through a tunnel and we were cut _____ .
5 I'm calling _____ connection _____ your advertisement.
6 I'd like to speak to someone _____ employment opportunities in your company.
7 I'll put you _____ _____ her voicemail.
8 Shall I ask her to call you _____ ?

**44.5 There is one mistake in each mini-dialogue. Find it and correct it.**

**Mini-dialogue 1**
A: Did you remember to phone ~~to~~ the printers?
B: Yes, I did it this morning.

**Mini-dialogue 2**
A: Do you have Mark's number? I need to make him a call.
B: Yes, I have it right here on my iPhone.

**Mini-dialogue 3**
A: Can I ask who's calling?
B: Yes, I am Sihem Benaouda from Algeria.

**Mini-dialogue 4**
A: Can I please to have extension 253?
B: Yes, I'll put you through.

**Mini-dialogue 5**
A: I'd like to speak to Angela Perez, please.
B: Just a moment while I transfer you. The extension number is 3281 in case we get cut.

**Mini-dialogue 6**
A: Can I speak to Ingrid, please?
B: Talking.

**Mini-dialogue 7**
A: I'm sorry, Mr Ohlson is not at his desk right now. Would you like to take a message?
B: No, it's OK, I'll call back later.

**Mini-dialogue 8**
A: Good morning, Delta Technology, Alex speaking, how can I help you?
B: Hello. Can you put me through the technical support team, please?

**Mini-dialogue 9**
A: How can I help you?
B: This is Goran Branković from Ljubljana. The reason I call today is because I have a small change I want to make to our last order.

**Mini-dialogue 10**
A: Could I speak to Sean Quinn, please?
B: The line is busy. Do you like to hold?

**44.6 🔊 05 You are going to hear eight phrases. Listen and repeat.**

Unit 44 gives some language for getting through to the right person. Once you have made contact, the language in this unit will be useful.

## The start of the call

This is the time to create a friendly yet business-like atmosphere. Starting in a professional way gives a good image and helps to build trust.

### Check it's a good time

This shows that you are thinking about the other person's needs.

*I know you're very busy. Is this a good time to talk?*
*Are you busy? I can call back later if you're in the middle of something.*

### Small talk

A few lines of social conversation helps to develop a good relationship.

*How's everything over there in Madrid?*
*I heard about … . That's great news!*

### Have an agenda

Establish the direction of the call right from the start.

*Did you get my email? I'm calling because I think it's easier at this stage to sort things out (= deal with things successfully) over the phone.*
*I think there are three things we need to discuss.*
*The first thing I want to talk about is … and the second is …*
*Do you have anything you would like to add?*

### Set a time limit

Again, this shows that you are thinking about the other person's needs.

*I'm calling to talk about … It should take around 15 minutes. Do you have the time now?*
*Do you have five minutes to go through (= look at carefully) the agenda for next week's meeting?*

## The middle of the call

This is the main part of the conversation and of course depends on each particular call. However there are three techniques that are always useful.

### Ask questions

Use questions to focus the conversation and explore alternatives.

*What are your reasons for thinking that?*
*So what exactly is the main issue here?*
*Instead of … why don't we …?*
*What if we … rather than …?*

### Summarize

Do this at regular intervals. Check details by referring to any notes you make during the call.

*I just need to make sure I understand everything you've said.*
*So what we've agreed so far (= up to now) is …*
*Perhaps I could summarize what we've said so far – to make sure I understand everything.*

### Email to confirm details

This is to double-check that you both understand the same thing.

*I'll send you an email to confirm the details.*

## The end of the call

At the end of the call the following language areas will be useful.

### Show that the call is finished

The word *Right* is a good way to signal the end of a topic or of the whole conversation.

*Right. I think that's all.*

### Confirm the key details

*So, I'll find out more about the likely costs, and you'll speak to Monique and let me know what she thinks. Is that right? Was there anything else?*
*So, we're meeting next Thursday at 2pm at your office. Before that I'm going to … and you're going to … OK? Have I left out (= not included) anything?*

### Thank the other person

Thank the other person for their time, help, call, enquiry or order. Note: *Thanks for calling* or *Thanks for your call* but NOT ~~Thanks for your calling~~.

*Well, thank you very much for taking the time to explain things.*

### Refer to future contact

Look forward to the next time you contact each other.

*I look forward to hearing from you in the first week of April. If I need to get in touch before then, what's the best time to call?*

### Leave a good feeling

Finish with a line of social English. Refer to any pieces of small talk from earlier in the conversation.

*Have a good weekend, and give my regards to John.*
*Enjoy your holiday! It sounds like it's going to be a lot of fun.*
*Have a good time at the theatre this evening.*
*Nice talking to you. Bye.*

# Exercises

**45.1 Match an item on the left with an item on the right to make phrases for the start of a call.**

1 good time
2 call back
3 in the middle
4 over there
5 sort things
6 have anything you would
7 Do you have the
8 go through

out over the phone
of something
time now
to talk
the agenda
later
like to add
in Stuttgart

**45.2 Complete the sentences below with whole phrases from Exercise 45.1.**

1 Do you have five minutes to *go through the agenda* for next week's meeting?
2 How's everything _____ ?
3 I'm calling to talk about arrangements for the conference. It should take around ten minutes. _____ ?
4 I know you're very busy. Is this a _____ ?
5 Did you get my email? I think it's easier at this stage to _____ .
6 That's all that I want to discuss. Do you _____ ?
7 Are you busy? I can _____ if you're _____ .

**45.3 Match an item on the left with an item on the right to make phrases for the end of a call.**

1 an email to
2 let me know as
3 Have I left
4 Thank you for
5 look forward to
6 the best time
7 give my
8 going to be a

taking the time
confirm the details
lot of fun
regards to Sue
soon as possible
out anything
hearing from you
to call

**45.4 Complete the sentences below with whole phrases from Exercise 45.3.**

1 Well, it was a very useful conversation. _____ to explain everything to me.
2 Enjoy your weekend! It sounds like it's _____ .
3 Good, I think the arrangements are all made now. Anyway, I'll send you _____ .
4 Good. So, I _____ in a couple of weeks. If I need to get in touch before then, when is _____ ?
5 So, before the next meeting I'm going to circulate the full report to everybody, and you're going to prepare a short PowerPoint presentation with a summary of the key issues. _____ ?
6 Have a good weekend and _____ .
7 So, you'll speak to the people at your end in Poland and _____ what they say.

**45.5 Fill in the missing letters.**

1 What are y_ _r rea_ _ _s for thinking that we should accept payment in other currencies?
2 We can't plan for every possible scenario. What ex_ _ _ly is the main i_ _ue here?
3 Ins_ _ _d o_ going to the Trade Fair this year, w_ _ d_ _' we do an internet marketing campaign?
4 Wh_ _ i_ we shipped the goods via Koper in Slovenia ra_ _er th_ _ Rotterdam? It would give us better access to Central European markets.

**45.6 Complete the sentences with these words: *around, as, as, back, for, in, out, over, through, to.***

1 I can call _____ later if you're in the middle of something.
2 I think it's easier if we sort things out _____ the phone.
3 Is this a good time to talk? I'd like to go _____ the plans for the product launch next month. It should take _____ 20 minutes I guess.
(*over* is possible for the first gap, but is not the answer)
4 Please let me know _____ soon _____ possible.
5 Is that right? Have I left _____ anything?
6 Thank you very much _____ all your help.
7 I look forward _____ meeting you in Zurich.
8 If I need to get _____ touch, when's the best time to call?

**45.7 Complete the missing words for the end of a call. The first letter is given to help you.**

ASTRID: [1]R_____, that's all I think. Let me just confirm the next steps. Before the next meeting I'm [2]g_____ t_____ look into the question of local agents in the Baltic region, and you're going to speak to Ginta and Teofilis.

MARKUS: Yes, that's right.

ASTRID: Was there [3]a_____ e_____ ?

MARKUS: No, I don't think so.

ASTRID: OK. Well, thank you very much for your [4]h_____ – I'm much clearer about everything now.

MARKUS: Thanks for [5]c_____ , and I [6]l_____ f_____ to seeing you at the meeting.

ASTRID: Yes, I'll see you there.

MARKUS: Have a good weekend and [7]g_____ my r_____ to Jean-Pierre.

ASTRID: I'll do that.

MARKUS: OK, nice [8]t_____ to you. Bye.

**45.8 ⊕ 06 You are going to hear eight phrases. Listen and repeat.**

# 46 Telephoning: common situations

## Messages

The simplest message is just about calling back later.

*She should be back in the office around two. Shall I ask her to call you back?*
*– Yes, please.*
*Does she have your number?*
*– Yes, she does.*
*When would be a good time for her to call you?*
*– Let's say two o'clock German time, which is three o'clock Romanian time.*

If you leave a longer message, speak slowly and carefully and leave time for the other person to write things down.

*Can I leave a message?*
*– Let me just get a pen. OK, go ahead.*
*Can you tell her that Emilia Raade called, from Finland. I'll spell it for you. Raade, R-double A-D-E.*
*– OK. And your number?*
*First you need the country code for Finland – that's 358. Then my number is 48 (pause) 792 (pause) double 5 (pause) 27. Have you got that?*
*– Yes, I've got that. And what's it in connection with?*
*I'm calling about …*

When you take a message, check information carefully and then repeat everything again at the end.

*Can I take a message? / Would you like to leave a message?*
*Can you spell that for me, please?*
*Is that E as in England or I as in Italy?*
*Can I read it back to you?*
*OK, let me just repeat everything to make sure it's correct.*

A good final line is:

*I'll make sure she gets the message.*

## Arranging a meeting

When you arrange a meeting you can ask open questions.

*Which day would be best for you?*
*Which day are you thinking of?*
*When would suit (= be convenient for) you?*

Alternatively you can make a concrete suggestion.

*How about Monday?*
*Does Wednesday look OK?*
*Are you free in the morning?*
*Shall we say ten o'clock?*

The other person may say no and suggest an alternative.

*Actually I'm quite busy around then. The next week would suit me better.*
*I'm tied up (= very busy) all day. Can you make Thursday instead?*

Finally you confirm by repeating the details.

*That sounds fine / good. I'll be there Thursday at nine.*
*Great. So, that's Thursday at nine, here at my office. I'll see you then.*

## Dealing with a complaint

Complaints are often handled by trained people in the Customer Services department. However if you find that you have to deal with a complaint, here is a sequence that you can follow.

### 1 Identify the problem
*What seems to be the problem?*
*Could you give me the details?*

### 2 Show empathy and apologize
*How annoying. I understand how you feel. I'm very sorry about this.*
*Yes, there definitely is a problem here. I really am very sorry. I must apologize on behalf of the company.*

### 3 Promise action
*I'll sort this out (= deal with it) right away.*
*I'll make sure this is put right immediately.*

### 4 Thank the caller
*Thank you very much for bringing this to our attention.*
*Thank you. This will help us to improve our service in the future.*

## Making a 'cold' call

Sometimes you want to call people you don't know – this is called a cold call. Sound confident so that the receiver feels they might lose something if they hang up. Mention your company name with pride in your voice and create a link between you and the receiver.

*Good morning, Mr Petrov. This is Mr Demir from Black Sea Resources in Turkey. I was given your name by … / We met briefly at … and you gave me your card.*

Try to mention a possible benefit to the other person right at the start.

*The reason I'm calling is to ask if anyone from your company will be attending the Petrochemicals Trade Fair in Moscow. I think there may be some very interesting opportunities for our two companies to work together.*

# Exercises

**46.1** **Match an item on the left with an item on the right to make phrases for telephone messages.**

1  call you
2  Let me just
3  the country
4  leave
5  I'll make
6  can you spell your
7  what's it in
8  read it

a message
connection with
back to you
back
code
repeat everything
sure
family name

**46.2** **Now use the whole phrases from Exercise 46.1 to complete the dialogue between Katalin and Jurgen.**

K: Hello, is Mr Louis Dreyfus there, please?

J: One moment. I'll put you on hold. I'm sorry, he's with a client at the moment. Shall I ask him to [1] *call you back* ?

K: I'm going to be busy for the next few hours. Can I [2]_____?

J: Of course. Let me just get a pen. OK, go ahead.

K: Can you tell him that Katalin Szili called, from Hungary.

J: Is that Katalin with C as in China or K as in Korea?

K: It's K as in Korea.

J: And [3]_____ for me?

K: It's Szili – that's S-Z-I-L-I.

J: OK, Katalin. And which company are you from?

K: From Magyar Software Solutions in Budapest.

J: Has Mr Dreyfus got your number?

K: Yes, but I'll leave it just in case. It's 36 – that's [4]_____ for Hungary – 17, 87, double 3, 49. Have you got that?

J: Can I [5]_____ to check? It's 17, 87, double 3, 49.

K: That's right.

J: And [6]_____ ?

K: It's about the network software that we're developing. Please tell Mr Dreyfus that I still haven't received the technical specifications we need. I did send an email yesterday but there was no reply. Can you ask him to send the specifications as soon as possible?

J: Of course, I'll do that. [7]_____ to make sure it's correct. The message is that Katalin Szili called from Magyar Software Solutions. You need the technical specifications for the network software as soon as possible.

K: That's right.

J: No problem, Katalin, [8]_____ that Mr Dreyfus gets the message.

K: Thank you very much for your help.

J: Thank you for calling. Goodbye.

**46.3** **Match each beginning of a phrase with two endings on the right.**

1  Which day would be
2  Actually I'm
3  Does Wednesday
4  That sounds

look OK?
quite busy around then.
best for you?
fine.
suit you?
tied up all day.
the most convenient?
good.

**Which phrases above are:**

a  open questions [1]     c  saying 'no' [ ]
b  suggestions [ ]        d  saying 'yes' [ ]

**46.4** **Match the beginning with the end of the phrase.**

1  Are you
2  I'll be
3  Shall we
4  So, that's
5  Can you
6  How about

say ten o'clock?
make the week after?
meeting for lunch?
free anytime next week?
four o'clock at your office.
there Friday at nine.

**Which phrases above are:**

a  open possibilities [1] [ ]
b  definite suggestions [ ] [ ]
c  confirmations [ ] [ ]

**46.5** **Put the lines into order to make a conversation.**

[1] a  Jack: Which day would be best for you?
[5] b  Jack: Yes, Thursday may be possible. Can you make an early morning meeting?
[ ] c  Jack: Sorry, Monday's no good. I'm tied up all day.
[ ] d  Jack: Great. So that's Thursday at 8.30am here at my office.
[ ] e  Jack: Shall we say 8.30am?

[8] f  Sara: Yes, that sounds fine.
[ ] g  Sara: Let me check my schedule. How about Monday?
[ ] h  Sara: I think so. What sort of time are you thinking of?
[ ] i  Sara: OK. Let's see. What about Thursday instead? Are you free on Thursday?
[ ] j  Sara: That's right. I'll see you then. Bye.

**46.6** **Read aloud the phrases in 'Dealing with a complaint' opposite. Then cover the page opposite and fill in the missing letters.**

1  What s___s t_ b_ the pr____m?
2  Could you gi__ m_ the de____s?
3  I must ap_____ze.
4  I'll s___ this o__ right away.
5  I'll m___ su__ this is p__ri__t immediately.
6  Thank you very much for br___ing th__ to our a____ion.

**46.7** 🌐 **07 You are going to hear eight phrases. Listen and repeat.**

# 47 Telephoning: conference calls

## What is a conference call?

A conference call/teleconference/audioconference is a telephone call between more than two people. A web conference/video conference is more complex, and can include live video, instant messaging, making presentations, sharing your desktop and files, etc.

## Chairing a conference call

Discussion is controlled by a chairperson/moderator, and much of the language needed is the same as for chairing a face-to-face meeting. Of course it is more difficult because you cannot see the other people. The phrases below will help you.

### Starting the conference call

*Welcome to the conference call. My name is Dirk Willems and I'm the chairperson for this call. It's a pleasure to be here. Can you all hear me?*

*I will begin by saying all your names. When you hear your name please introduce yourself briefly to the others. I need to check that everyone can hear everyone else.*

*Thank you. Now some information about the call. Michael will be taking the minutes* (= making a written summary of the meeting). *As for timing, I'd like to finish by four o'clock.*

*Before we begin I want to establish some ground rules* (= basic rules that govern behaviour) *for the call. First, please introduce yourself before you speak – and that means every time. Second, please try not to interrupt other people. I want to run this call as a Q&A* (= Question and Answer). *Louisa will begin by giving a short project update and then there will be a chance for questions.*

*OK. Let's get started. Petra, I think you are going to introduce the first item.*

### Managing the discussion

A key role for the chair is to make sure that everyone has a chance to speak.

*Hans-Peter, what do you think?*
*I'd like to hear Sara's views now. Sara?*
*I want to bring Felix in at this point.*
*Sorry, Erik. Could you let Sophia finish?*
*What do people think about this? Any comments?*

The chair has to keep the discussion moving.

*I think we're digressing* (= moving away from the main point). *Can we come back to the agenda* (= list of items to discuss) *please?*
*Let's make a decision. I propose that we … . I will now ask everyone if they agree. Elias? Inge?*
*OK. The next item on the agenda is: business development.*

There may be communication problems.

*Adriana, I'm sorry, could you slow down a little?*
*Please speak up, Davide. We can't hear you very well.*
*Please wait a moment. It's very difficult if everyone speaks at the same time.*
*There's a lot of background noise. If necessary, use your mute button* (= control that turns off the microphone) *when you're not speaking, or move with your mobile phone to a quiet area.*

### Closing the conference call

At the end of the call the chair should summarize and review action points. Finish by making a reference to the success or usefulness of the call and thanking everyone for their input.

*OK. I think we've covered everything. Before we finish, let me summarize the main points.*
*There are some tasks to do/action points before the next call. Bob, you agreed to … and Julia, you will …*
*Good. I think we made a lot of progress today. Thanks to everyone for your input. We will finish now.*

## Participating in a conference call

Here are some tips.

- Prepare what you are going to say before the call. Your time is limited and you may only get one chance to make your point.
- Say your name before you speak. Then speak more slowly and more clearly than usual.
- Don't be embarrassed to ask a question if you don't understand.

*Eva speaking. I'm sorry, could you repeat that?*
*This is Lars. What exactly did you mean when you said 'one or two problems'?*
*Nina here. Could you say a little more about that? I want to make sure I understand you.*
*This is Daan. Sorry, could I just remind everyone to say their name before speaking?*

- Be prepared to block an interruption.

*This is João speaking. Sorry for interrupting, but can I come in* (= interrupt) *here?*
*– Eva again. I want to finish what I was saying, then I'll hand over* (= give control) *to you, João.*

# Exercises

**47.1 Fill in the missing words. Some letters are given to help you.**

Discussion during the conference call is controlled by the [1] _chairperson_ . It is a good idea for this person to establish some [2]gro_____ ru_____ right at the start – for example by asking everyone to [3]intr_____ themselves every time they speak, and also by telling participants not to [4]interr_____ other people.

At the start of the call the chairperson will say who is going to take the [5]min_____ , and will remind people of the [6]tim_____g. In fact, making sure the call doesn't go on too long is one of the most important jobs for the chairperson – there may be many items on the [7]ag_____ and when people talk in a meeting they often [8]dig_____ and lose sight of the main point.

At the end of the call the chairperson will [9]summ_____ the main points again. It is particularly important to remind people of any [10]tas_____ they agreed to do.

**47.2 Put the words into order to make sentences for starting a conference call.**

1 I will saying begin by all your names.
_____I will begin by saying all your names._____

2 I need to hear that everyone can check everyone else.
_____

3 Michael be taking will the minutes.
_____

4 I'd like by finish to four o'clock.
_____

5 Before I want we begin to establish some rules ground.
_____

6 Please speak before you introduce yourself.
_____

7 Please not to interrupt try other people.
_____

8 Petra, I think introduce you are going to the first item.
_____

**47.3 Use a verb from list A and an adverb from list B to complete the sentences below.**

| A: | ~~come~~ come hand slow speak |
|---|---|
| B: | ~~back~~ down in over up |

1 I think we're digressing. Can we _come_ _back_ to the agenda, please?
2 I'm sorry, Adriana, you're speaking very fast. Could you _____ _____ a little?
3 Davide, we can't hear you very well. Can you _____ _____ please?
4 Lars speaking. Sorry for interrupting, but can I just _____ _____ here for a moment?
5 Eva again. I want to finish and then I'll _____ _____ to you, Lars.

**47.4 Complete this extract from a conference call using the words and phrases in the box.**

| any comments   behind schedule   control costs |
|---|
| did you mean   I was saying   related issue |
| project update   repeat that |

LUCA: OK. Let's get started. I want to run this call as a Q&A. Emma will give a short [1]_____ and then answer questions. Emma, over to you.

EMMA: Thanks, Luca. Overall, the project is going well. The client is very happy with the quality of our work. However we have had one or two problems and we're running about one week [2]_____ . It's nothing to worry about – I think we can get back on track quite easily. On the financial side of things, we're managing to [3]_____ well and we're working within our budget up to now.

IVAN: This is Ivan speaking. Hi Emma. I'm pleased that things are going well, but what exactly [4]_____ when you said 'one or two problems'? You only mentioned the time schedule. Is there anything else?

EMMA: Emma again. Well, it's a [5]_____ . We're having some problems with the subcontractor who's doing our electrical work. They keep disappearing – presumably to do work on other sites.

JOÃO: João speaking. Sorry for interrupting, but can I come in here? I thought we had a contract with those guys. If they walk off the job, they must be breaking the contract.

EMMA: I want to finish what [6]_____ . We had discussions with them earlier this week and we raised this matter. They assure us that they'll fulfil the terms of the contract as agreed.

DIEGO: Diego speaking. I'm sorry, my English is not too good. You speak very fast! Could you [7]_____ ?

EMMA: Of course. The subcontractors say there is no problem.

DIEGO: OK, I understand now. Thanks, Emma.

LUCA: What do other people think about this issue with the electrical subcontractor? Has anyone worked with them before? [8]_____ ?

## Making a call

### First words

*Good morning. This is Finn Larsen from Bergen Energy Services.*

*Can I speak to Vera Pereira, please?*

*Could you put me through to Vera Pereira, please?*

### First words (someone you know)

*Is that Linda? Hi! It's Sebastian.*

*Hello Ramon! This is José from Sao Paolo here.*

### Reason for calling

*I'm calling in connection with …*

*The reason I'm calling is …*

*I'd like to speak to someone about …*

### Start of call

*Is this a good time to talk? I can call back later if you're in the middle of something.*

*How's everything over there in Madrid?*

*Did you get my email? I'm calling because …*

*I'm calling to talk about … It should take around 15 minutes. Do you have the time now?*

### End of the call

*So, I'll … And you'll … Is that right? Was there anything else?*

*I'm going to … and you're going to … OK? Have I left out anything?*

*Well, thank you very much for taking the time to answer all my questions.*

*Have a good weekend, and give my regards to …*

*Right. That's all I think. Nice talking to you. Bye.*

## Receiving a call

### First words

*Good morning, KP International, Maria speaking, how can I help you?*

*Sales Department, Maria speaking.*

### Transferring a call

*I'll try her number for you. Stay on the line, please.*

*Please hold while I try to connect you.*

*The extension number is 7847 in case we get cut off.*

*I'm sorry, there's no answer. I'll put you through to his voicemail.*

### Taking a message

*I'm sorry, she's in a meeting / not at her desk right now.*

*Shall I ask her to call you back?*

*Would you like to leave a message?*

*Let me just get a pen. OK, go ahead.*

*Can you spell that for me, please?*

*Can I read it back to you?*

*And what's it in connection with?*

*OK, let me just repeat everything to make sure it's correct.*

*I'll make sure she gets the message.*

## Arranging a meeting

### Questions and suggestions

*Which day would be best for you?*

*How about Monday?*

*Are you free in the morning?*

*Shall we say ten o'clock?*

### Giving an alternative

*Actually I'm quite busy around then. The next week would suit me better.*

*Can you make Thursday instead?*

### Confirm

*That sounds fine. I'll be there Thursday at nine.*

*So, that's Thursday at nine, here at my office. I'll see you then.*

## Conference call

### Chairing

*Welcome to the conference call. My name is Dirk Willems and I'm the chairperson for this call.*

*Before we begin I want to establish some ground rules for the call. First, please introduce yourself before you speak. Second, …*

*OK. Let's get started. Petra, I think you are going to introduce the first item.*

*I'd like to hear Anton's views now.*

*Sara, what do you think?*

*I want to bring Felix in at this point.*

*What do people think about this? Any comments?*

*I think we're digressing. Can we come back to the main point?*

*OK. The next item on the agenda is …*

*Please wait a moment. It's very difficult if everyone speaks at the same time.*

*OK. I think we've covered everything. Before we finish, let me summarize the main points.*

*There are also some tasks to do / action points before the next call. Bob, you agreed to … and Julia, you will …*

*Thanks to everyone for your input. We will finish now.*

### Participating

*Eva speaking. I'm sorry, could you repeat that?*

*This is Lars. What exactly did you mean when you said …?*

*Nina here. Could you say a little more about that?*

# Exercises

## 48.1 Complete the sentences with the words in the box.

| call back later | how can I help | in connection with |
|---|---|---|
| over there | put me through | speaking |

a I'm calling _____ the email you sent me.
b Could you _____ to the accounts department, please?
c Good morning, ACT International, Lena speaking, _____ you?
d How's everything _____ in Dubai?
e Sales department, Stanislaw _____ .
f I can _____ if you're in the middle of something.

## Continue as before.

| get cut off | give my regards | left out |
|---|---|---|
| on the line | Right | taking the time |

g Have a good weekend, and _____ to Tony.
h (after summarizing) Have I _____ anything?
i I'll try her number for you. Stay _____ , please.
j Well, thank you very much for _____ to answer all my questions.
k _____ . That's all I think. Nice talking to you, and enjoy your holiday – you deserve it. Bye.
l The extension number is 3428 in case we _____ .

## Continue as before.

| Actually | How about | Shall we |
|---|---|---|
| instead | sounds fine | would suit me |

m _____ Monday afternoon?
n _____ say nine o'clock?
o _____ I'm quite busy around then.
p The next week _____ better.
q Can you make Thursday _____ ?
r That _____ . I'll be there Thursday at nine.

## 48.2 Look back at Exercise 48.1.

1 Which one sentence from a–f could be said by either the caller or the receiver? ☐
2 Which two sentences from a–f are said by the receiver? ☐ ☐
3 Which two sentences from g–l would be said if the people already know each other well? ☐ ☐
4 Which two sentences from g–l would be said by a receptionist who answers all calls? ☐ ☐
5 Which one sentence from m–r is a polite way of saying 'no'? ☐
6 Which two sentences from m–r are used to give alternatives? ☐ ☐

## 48.3 Match the beginning and the end of each sentence.

1 She's not                    leave a message?
2 Let me just get             in connection with?
3 Would you like to           at her desk right now.
4 Shall I ask her             back to you?
5 I'll make sure              that for me, please?
6 Can I read it               she gets the message.
7 And what's it               a pen.
8 Can you spell               to call you back?

## 48.4 Complete the dialogue with the sentences from Exercise 48.3. Write them in full to help you remember.

ELIZA: Can I speak to Yvonne Roche, please?
PIM: I'm sorry, [1] *She's not at her desk right now* . I think she's in a meeting. [2] _____ when the meeting finishes?
ELIZA: Actually I'm busy all afternoon – it won't be easy to contact me.
PIM: [3] _____ ?
ELIZA: Yes please.
PIM: [4] _____ . OK, go ahead.
ELIZA: So, this is Eliza Ksiazek from BSL speaking.
PIM: [5] _____ ?
ELIZA: Yes, my first name is Eliza, like it sounds, and my family name is Ksiazek, K-S-I-A-Z-E-K. Have you got that?
PIM: [6] _____ to check? E-L-I-Z-A, K-S-I-A-Z-E-K.
ELIZA: That's right.
PIM: [7] _____ ?
ELIZA: It's about the market research that Yvonne wants my company to do. There are some things that need clarifying. Perhaps she could give me a call tomorrow.
PIM: OK. Let me just repeat everything to make sure it's correct. Eliza Ksiazek from BSL called about the market research. You want Yvonne to call you tomorrow.
ELIZA: Yes, that's right.
PIM: OK Eliza, [8] _____ . Thank you for calling. Bye.

## 48.5 Fill in the missing letters.

1 Please int_ _ _ce yo_ _ _ _lf before you speak.
2 I think we're digressing. Can we c_ _e b_ _k to the m_ _n p_ _t?
3 The next i_ _m on the ag_ _da is the financial report for the last quarter.
4 OK. I think we've co_ _ _ed everything. Before we finish, let me su_ _ _ize the main points.

## 49 Emails: basics

### Subject line

The subject line should be a short, clear summary of the contents of the email. This is important when people look for old emails in their folders.

### Opening

You can begin with *Hi/Hello* + first name, or just the person's first name, or no name at all – just start the message immediately. For more formal openings see Unit 52.

There might then be one or two short sentences of social English such as:

*It was good to speak to you yesterday.*
*Hope you're well.*
*Great to meet you last week.*

### Introducing the subject of the email

Next comes the reason for writing. If you are replying to another person's email, or following up a phone call, you can say:

*Thanks for this. Sorry I haven't got back to you (= replied) sooner.*
*Thank you for your email requesting information about ...*
*Re (= regarding)/About our phone call the other day ...*
*Further to/Following our call, ...*

If there is no previous context, then begin with:

*I'm writing about ...*
*Just a short note to let you know that ...*

It can help to establish a context if you mention the name of a third party who you both know:

*I understand from Hiroto that ...*
*I was given your email address by Claudette Blanchard at Global Networks.*

### Clarifying

You may not understand what the other person wants. If so, your first response is to clarify (= make things clear).

*Thanks for the email, but I'm not sure what action you want me to take. Can you please clarify?*
*Are you saying that ...?*
*I understand that you want me to ... Is this right?*

### Body of email

Here are some typical phrases.

#### Ask for information

*Could you/Please send me ...*
*I'd like to know ... In particular, ...*
*I need ... asap (= as soon as possible).*

#### Give information

*Re the info you wanted, here is ...*
*Have a look at this. Then please forward it to the other team members.*
*I've spoken to ... and she says that ...*

#### Give news

*Good news! You'll be pleased to hear that ...*
*I have some bad news. Unfortunately, ...*

#### Ask for action/help

*Could you ...?/Could you do me a favour?*
*Thanks – I'd really appreciate your help on this.*

#### Offer action/help

*Do you want me to ...?*
*Shall I ...?*

#### Attach a document

*Please find attached ... Could you have a look and let me know what you think? I'd be grateful for any suggestions.*

#### Apologize

*Sorry about ... It was my fault entirely.*
*I'll make sure it doesn't happen again.*

#### Promise action

*I'll ...*
*I'll look into it. (= try to discover the facts)*
*I'll chase it up. (= find out what is being done)*

#### Suggest action

*How about ... (+ -ing)?*
*Perhaps you could ...*
*We might also need to ... What do you think?*
*Let me know what you think.*

If you think of a point that is not directly related to the body of the email, you can use *BTW* (= by the way).

*BTW – give my regards to Henrik when you see him.*

### Closing

If appropriate, show that you are available to give more help:

*Please get back to me (= contact me again) if you need more information.*
*If you need any help, just let me know.*

Make a reference to the next contact:

*I'll be in touch soon.*
*Let's talk soon.*
*I'll give you a call sometime next week.*
*Are we still OK for Friday?*
*See you at the conference!*

The final line can be *Best wishes/Best regards/Kind regards* + your name, or just your name.

# Exercises

## 49.1 Underline the correct word in italics.

1 How *are / go* things over there in Riyadh?
2 It was *fine / good* to speak to you yesterday.
3 Just a note to *let / make* you know that the publicity material is back from the printers.
4 I *understand / have knowledge* from Dieter in Hamburg that you have some data on the recent sales promotion.
5 Thanks for this. Sorry I haven't *got you back / got back to you* sooner.
6 Please get back to me if you need more *information / informations*.
7 Let's *talk / talking* soon.
8 *I give / I'll give* you a call sometime next week.

## 49.2 Match the beginning and end of each phrase. Find a solution that uses every item.

a Please        do me a favour?
b I need        send me the sales figures?
c How about        send you the sales figures?
d Could you        send me the sales figures.
e Could you        send you the figures when I get them.
f Re        the sales figures asap.
g I'll        the sales figures, I've attached …
h Shall I        asking Pam to send us the figures?

## 49.3 Look back at Exercise 49.2. Find:

1 Three phrases that ask for information ☐ ☐ ☐
2 One phrase that gives information ☐
3 One phrase that asks for help ☐
4 One phrase that offers help ☐
5 One phrase that promises action ☐
6 One phrase that suggests action [c]

## 49.4 Complete the sentences with the words in the box.

> appreciate    attached    chase    clarify
> forward    further    ~~pleased~~    unfortunately

1 Good news! You'll be ___pleased___ to hear that we won the Datura contract. I'll send more details soon.
2 I have some bad news. _____ , we didn't get the Zeta contract.
3 _____ to our call, here is an estimate for the work you require.
4 I'm not sure what this means. Can you please _____ ?
5 Could you do me a favour? I need all the background info you have on Data Services Inc. Thanks – I'd really _____ your help on this.
6 Have a look at this. Then please _____ it to the other team members.
7 Please find _____ my report on quality issues at the Haiphong plant.
8 Leave this with me. I'll _____ it up and get back to you when I know what's happening.

## 49.5 Complete the sentences with these prepositions: *about, back, for, in, into, on, to, up.*

1 I'm writing _____ the issues you raised in the meeting.
2 Thanks for this. Sorry I haven't got _____ to you sooner.
3 Please forward this _____ the other team members.
4 I'd really appreciate your help _____ this.
5 I'd be grateful _____ any suggestions.
6 I'll look _____ it and find out what's going on.
7 I'll chase it _____ and see what progress has been made.
8 I'll be _____ touch soon.

## 49.6 Put paragraphs a–d in each email into the most likely order. Write the order at the bottom.

---

| ✉ | To... | Emma Dubois |
|---|---|---|
| Send | Subject: | Re: meeting with Mr Gupta |

Hi Emma

**a** They asked a lot of questions about price, and about customization of our products for the Indian market.

**b** Just a short note to let you know that the meeting with Mr Gupta and his business associates was a great success.

**c** Thanks in advance.

**d** I'd like to know whether we can offer them a more basic product at a lower price. Could you look into this?

Daniel

---

| ✉ | To... | Daniel Williams |
|---|---|---|
| Send | Subject: | Re: meeting with Mr Gupta |

**a** I'll see you on Thursday anyway – let's discuss it further then.

**b** I've spoken to the production guys and they've put together a few ideas. Have a look at the attached document and let me know what you think.

**c** Dan – thanks for this. Sorry I haven't got back to you sooner.

**d** What's the next step? Shall I set up a conference call between you, me and the Production Manager?

Best wishes
Emma

---

| ✉ | To... | Emma Dubois |
|---|---|---|
| Send | Subject: | preparation for conference call |

**a** Following our discussion on Thursday, I've now made some comments on the doc you sent. I'm attaching it again here – you'll see my comments in red.

**b** Btw give my regards to Axel when you see him.

**c** If you need anything else before the call, just let me know.

**d** Please forward this doc to everyone who will be attending the conference call.

Daniel

---

1st email: 1 [b]   2 ☐   3 ☐   4 ☐
2nd email: 1 ☐   2 ☐   3 ☐   4 ☐
3rd email: 1 ☐   2 ☐   3 ☐   4 ☐

**See page 148 for some writing tasks.**

## Arranging a meeting

To arrange a meeting you can begin by asking an open question.

*Perhaps we can arrange a meeting to discuss things in more detail?*

*When would suit (= be convenient for) you?*

*When can you make it?*

Alternatively you can suggest a time yourself.

*How about Thursday at 9am at my office?*

*I'm available at the following times – let me know if any of them are good for you.*

To reply to a suggestion you can say:

*Friday's fine by me. Shall we say 12.30? I'll take you to lunch.*

*I'm out of the office in the morning, but any time in the afternoon would be fine.*

*Sorry, but I can't make it on Thursday.*

A meeting is often confirmed by email, after being arranged by phone (Unit 46).

*Further to our call, I'm writing to confirm the details of our meeting next Weds.*

*I'll see you in Reception at 12.30.*

*I've booked a table at … It's quiet, so we can talk.*

There may already be a meeting, and you are inviting someone else to attend it.

*If you can come, I'll send you the agenda and the minutes from the last meeting.*

*Let me know if you can make it and I'll be in touch with the details.*

You may need to rearrange the meeting.

*I'm really sorry, but I've had to change my plans.*

*Unfortunately, … (+ reason). It means we need to rearrange the meeting. I wonder if we could move it to Monday instead?*

## Follow-up after a meeting

With a more formal meeting it is common to circulate the minutes to all the participants.

*Thank you for attending the meeting on Friday. I think it was very useful. I know that we do not all agree on the different proposals. However, I hope that we can find a solution that suits us all.*

*Please find attached the draft (= not yet finished) minutes of the meeting.*

*Can I have any comments by the 14th, so I can finalize the minutes and prepare an agenda for the next meeting?*

## Invitations

You may want to invite someone to a special event.

*We would like to invite you to …*

*… the launch of our new range of children's toys.*

*… an open evening at our new production facility.*

*… attend a seminar on risk management.*

*The event takes place on 5 March and will start at 2pm. The venue is … A map and full programme are attached.*

*Light refreshments will be provided.*

*We would be delighted if you could come. Please let me know if you are able to attend by 14 February.*

To reply you can say:

*Thank you for inviting me to … I would be delighted to come and I am looking forward to it very much.*

Or alternatively:

*Thank you for your kind invitation. Unfortunately I have something else in my schedule for that day. In any case, I am sure that the launch / open evening / seminar will be a great success.*

*Please keep me on your mailing list as I would be interested in attending similar events in the future.*

## Arrangements before a business trip

Before a trip the visitor confirms the travel details.

*Please find attached my travel plans. As you can see, I am arriving on flight LH6758 at 12.25, Terminal 2.*

*I will take a taxi and go straight to the hotel. I look forward to meeting you in the lobby of the hotel at 12 noon.*

The host also has things to confirm.

*We've booked a taxi to meet you at the airport – the driver will be waiting at the exit barrier in Terminal 1.*

*We'll leave a folder at Reception for you. It will have the agenda for the meeting and some background documents.*

*I look forward to seeing you next week.*

*Have a good journey.*

## Follow-up after a business trip

It is common to write and thank the host.

*Thank you very much for your hospitality in Stockholm. I really enjoyed the trip and you made me feel very welcome.*

*It was great to finally meet everybody.*

*It was a very useful meeting, and I am much clearer now about …*

*Your ideas about … are all excellent.*

*I'm sure it's going to be a fantastic project and I look forward to working with you very much.*

# Exercises

**50.1** Andrei (A) and Barbora (B) arrange to meet by phone. Put the lines of the call into order. Write the lines in full on a separate sheet of paper. Start like this:

1 A: *Perhaps we can arrange a meeting to discuss things in more detail?*

2 B: *Yes, that sounds like a good idea.*

A: ~~Perhaps we can arrange a meeting to discuss things in more detail?~~

A: Sorry, but I can't make it on Thursday. Is Friday any good?

A: OK. When would suit you?

A: Good. Shall we say 12.30 at my office? I'll take you to lunch.

B: ~~Yes, that sounds like a good idea.~~

B: Perfect. I'll see you then. Bye.

B: How about Thursday 17th?

B: Yes, Friday's fine by me.

**50.2** Andrei writes a follow-up email to Barbora. There are eight mistakes in the email (missing word, extra word, wrong form, wrong spelling). Find the mistakes and correct them.

To... Barbora Novakova
Subject: meeting Friday 18 May

Further our call, I'm writing to confirmation the details of our meeting on Friday 18 May.

I see you in Reception at 12.30, and take you to lunch. I've booked a table at a nice little Italian place round the corner. It's quite, so we can to talk.

I've detached a map that shows you how to find our office. It's very easy to get here – the taxi driver will know it.

I look forward seeing you.

Best wishing
Andrei

**50.3** Andrei writes another email to Barbora. There are six mistakes. Find them and correct them.

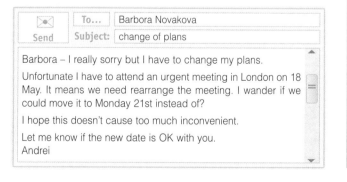

To... Barbora Novakova
Subject: change of plans

Barbora – I really sorry but I have to change my plans.

Unfortunate I have to attend an urgent meeting in London on 18 May. It means we need rearrange the meeting. I wander if we could move it to Monday 21st instead of?

I hope this doesn't cause too much inconvenient.

Let me know if the new date is OK with you.
Andrei

**50.4** Fill in the missing letters.

1 Perhaps we can arrange a meeting to discuss things i_ mo__ det__l?

2 When would s__t y__?

3 Sorry, but I c__'_ m__e i_ on Thursday.

4 Sh_ _ _ w_ s_ 12.30 at my office?

5 I'm re___y so__y but I have to ch___e my p__ns.

6 I wo__er if we co__d move it to Monday ins___d?

**50.5** A real estate company is sending an invitation to a special event. Complete the email with the words in the box.

| attend | click | delighted | event |
| --- | --- | --- | --- |
| ~~launch~~ | link | refreshments | venue |

We would like to invite you to the ¹ *launch* of our new city-centre apartment block. There are 50 units for sale, including two-bedroom and three-bedroom apartments. Please ² _____ on the ³ _____ below to visit our website and see a video tour of the apartments.

The ⁴ _____ takes place on 5 March and will start at 2pm. The ⁵ _____ is the ballroom of the Park Hotel. A map and full programme are attached.

Light ⁶ _____ will be provided.

We would be ⁷ _____ if you could come. Please let me know if you are able to ⁸ _____ by 14 February. You can either reply to this email or call me on the number below.

**50.6** Lana is confirming travel arrangements with Felix. Put paragraphs a–e into the most likely order.

Hello Felix

**a** The taxi will take you straight to your hotel. We'll leave a folder at Reception for you. It will have the agenda for the meeting and some background documents.

**b** Have a good journey.

**c** It's great that you have finally sorted out your travel plans for next Monday. I look forward to welcoming you here in Slovenia.

**d** I'll meet you in the lobby of the hotel at 12.30 and we'll go together to our office. My mobile number is below in case you need to contact me. I think that's all – let me know if I've forgotten anything.

**e** I understand from your email that you're arriving on flight OS7031 at 10.45am. We've booked a taxi to meet you at the airport – the driver will be waiting at the exit barrier.

Best regards
Lana

1 c    2 ☐    3 ☐    4 ☐    5 ☐

See page 148 for some writing tasks.

## Making contact

Start by saying how you got the contact.

*I'm emailing you from your website.*
*We met at the Trade Fair and you gave me your card.*
*You name was given to me by … She mentioned that you might be a good person to contact re online publishing.*

Then introduce your own company, and say how the other person can benefit.

*Please let me introduce myself and my company. My name is … and I am the regional Business Development Manager for … We are a leading provider of … I think there are a number of ways in which our two companies may be able to collaborate.*
*We are a major manufacturer of … We are currently reviewing our list of suppliers for parts and components.*

Say what you want.

*I wonder if I could call you to discuss possible areas of interest?*
*I would like some information about customizing your products. In particular, I would like to know …*
*It would be great to have an opportunity to show you some of our products.*

## Sending information

The supplier sends information.

*Thank you for your email requesting information about our accountancy services.*
*Following our conversation earlier today, I am writing to give you more details of our investment products.*
*Please find attached a catalogue and a price list.*
*As you will see, we have a special offer running at the moment.*
*If you would like to place an order, please call our customer order line on …, or if you have any further questions, please do not hesitate to contact me either by email or telephone.*

## Specific questions

Sometimes the customer will have more detailed questions and will write another email.

*Thank you for sending … We are interested in … however there are one or two things I need to clarify before going ahead with a firm order.*
*What exactly does the price include?*
*Are they available in other sizes / colours?*
*How soon can you ship the goods?*
*Is there a discount for large quantities?*
*Do you have a minimum order?*
*What are your terms of payment?*
*Can you send me a copy of your warranty in French?*

The supplier should reply point by point.

*The price includes everything, including shipping.*
*I am sorry but that line is discontinued.*
*We offer next-day shipping on receipt of a firm order.*
*We require a letter of credit or 50% of the total amount in advance.*
*We offer a 5% discount for orders over €10,000.*
*Our terms of payment are 50% in advance, 50% after 30 days.*

## Orders

The customer places an order, and the supplier confirms that the goods are shipped.

*We can confirm that your goods have been shipped. You can track the shipping details by clicking the link below.*

## Problems

Customers might complain about delays in shipping, wrong or missing items on delivery, etc.

*My order reference number JN9773 has still not arrived. You promised delivery within ten working days.*
*We ordered … but you sent …*

The supplier deals with the issue.

*I am very sorry that you have not yet received your order.*
*I will look into the matter immediately and get back to you within 24 hours.*
*Please accept my apologies for … The problem was due to …*
*The items you ordered were temporarily out of stock at our warehouse.*
*I can assure (= promise) you that the goods were shipped today.*
*As a goodwill gesture we would like to offer you 5% off your next order.*
*I apologize again for any inconvenience this has caused.*

Alternatively, it might be the supplier who complains.

*Our invoice number 897003 is still unpaid.*
*Our records show an outstanding (= not yet paid) amount of €3,000. When can we expect payment?*

The customer deals with the issue.

*According to our records, it was paid …*
*I'll check with the bank.*
*Apparently, there was a query on the invoice – that is why we haven't paid it yet.*
*I'll arrange for a bank transfer immediately.*
*Please send me your IBAN and BIC.*

# Exercises

**51.1 Put the words into order. Write the sentences in full to help you remember.**

1  It would great be to have an opportunity to show you some products of our.
   It _____

   _____

2  Following our earlier today conversation, I am writing you to give our services more details of.
   Following _____

   _____

3  If you any questions further have, please do hesitate to not contact me.
   If _____

   _____

4  There are two or one things I need to going ahead before clarify with a firm order.
   There _____

   _____

5  We require a credit of letter or in advance 50% of the total amount.
   We _____

   _____

6  We offer a discount 5% for orders €10,000 over.
   We _____

7  You can details the shipping track by link the clicking below.
   You _____

   _____

8  I will get back to the matter immediately and look into you within 24 hours.
   I _____

   _____

9  I for any inconvenience again apologize this has caused.
   I _____

10  Apparently, a query there was on the invoice – that is why we yet haven't it paid.
   Apparently, _____

**51.2 Look back at Exercise 51.1 again. Find a word that matches each definition below. The words appear in order.**

1  additional; more (slightly formal)  _further_
2  make clear  _____
3  need (slightly formal)  _____
4  follow the progress of  _____
5  investigate (phrasal verb: two words)  _____
6  contact again (phrasal verb: three words)  _____
7  tell someone you are sorry  _____
8  question (in order to check something)  _____

**51.3 Match the words in the box with the definitions.**

> ~~discount~~   invoice   terms of payment
> IBAN and BIC   warranty   letter of credit

1  reduction in the usual price  _discount_
2  numbers that identify a bank account (needed for making international bank transfers)  _____
3  conditions you agree when making a commercial contract  _____
4  written agreement to repair or replace a product if there is a fault  _____
5  a promise by a customer's bank to pay a supplier's bank after the goods are shipped  _____
6  document giving details of goods that have been bought and how much you must pay  _____

**51.4 Match the beginning and end of each phrase. Then use them to complete the various email extracts.**

introduce          assure you
leading            my apologies
I can              myself
price              with a firm order
going ahead        be interested
place              list
Please accept      provider
you might          a small order

> Please let me ¹ _introduce myself_ and my company. My name is Lars Peeters and I am the regional Sales Representative for Financial Data Corporation. We are a ² _____ of market data and analytics to financial institutions.
>
> You name was given to me by Marie Martin at the Financial Trade Show in Paris. Marie mentioned that ³ _____ in our products.

> Thank you for sending your catalogue and ⁴ _____. We are interested in stocking your range of children's toys. However, there are one or two things I need to clarify before ⁵ _____ .
>
> a) What exactly does the price include? In particular, does it include shipping?
> b) Do you have a minimum order? We want to ⁶ _____ initially to see how the products are received by the market.

> ⁷ _____ for the late delivery of your office furniture. The items you ordered were temporarily out of stock at our warehouse.
>
> However, they are now back in stock and ⁸ _____ that the goods were shipped today.
>
> If I can be of further assistance, please do not hesitate to contact me.

**See page 148 for some writing tasks.**

# 52 Emails: formal language

## Neutral vs formal

In business people usually write emails in a neutral style which is simple, direct, brief and friendly. Units 49–51 all show this neutral style. There is also a more formal style that is careful and polite, and uses longer, standard expressions. This style may be appropriate in some situations, for example if you want to make a good impression on someone outside the company, or you want to ask a favour from a colleague.

## First line

Neutral emails begin with just the name, or *Hi/Hello* + name, or no name at all. Formal emails open with *Dear* + *Mr/Mrs/Ms* + family name. *Ms* is used for a married or unmarried woman, *Mrs* for a married woman only. You can also write *Dear* + first name to be a little less formal.

## Formal phrases: examples

Study these examples. A neutral (N) version is given first, then a more formal (F) version.

### Opening
N: *Hope you're well.*
F: *I hope you are well.*
N: *Great to see you again.*
F: *It was a pleasure meeting you last week.*
N: *Thanks for the email.*
F: *Thank you for your email of 12 January.*
N: *Sorry for not getting back to you.*
F: *My apologies for not replying sooner.*
N: *Just a note to say …*
F: *I am writing to let you know that …*
N: *About the meeting:*
F: *I am writing with regard to the meeting.*
N: *Re our conversation last Fri, …*
F: *Further to our conversation last Friday, …*

### Body of email
N: *Good news!*
F: *I am pleased to say that …*
N: *Please send me …*
F: *I would be grateful if you could send me … OR I would appreciate it if you could send me …*
N: *Can you … ?*
F: *I wonder if you could …?*
N: *Are you saying that …?*
F: *If I understand correctly, you're saying that … Is that right?*

N: *Shall I find out …?*
F: *Would you like me to find out …?*
N: *Sorry, but I can't …*
F: *Unfortunately, I am unable to …*
N: *Sorry about …*
F: *I would like to apologize for …*
N: *I'll look into it and get back to you.*
F: *I will investigate the matter and contact you again shortly.*
N: *Can we meet …?*
F: *Perhaps we could meet …?*

### Closing
N: *If you need anything else, just let me know.*
F: *If you require any further information, please do not hesitate to contact me.*
N: *Speak to you soon.*
F: *I look forward to hearing from you.*
N: *See you at the conference.*
F: *I look forward to meeting you at the conference.*

## Last line

Neutral emails end with *Best wishes/Kind regards* or a friendly comment like *Thanks again* or *See you soon.* Then the writer puts their first name.

Formal emails end with *Yours sincerely* (BrE) or *Sincerely* (AmE). Then the writer puts their full name.

## Other points

Formal emails avoid contractions. Write *I am/you have/there is* instead of *I'm/you've/there's.*

Formal emails use longer words with a Latin origin. Compare:

| | |
|---|---|
| *chance – possibility* | *need – require* |
| *get – receive* | *now – currently* |
| *give – provide* | *main – principal* |
| *help – assistance* | *money – financial resources* |

Formal emails use indirect questions. Compare:
N: *Can we change the time of the meeting?*
F: *Would it be possible for us to change …?*
N: *What is their market share?*
F: *Can you tell me what their market share is?*
N: *Do you want to join us for dinner?*
F: *Would you like to join us for dinner?*
N: *Is the presentation to the client going ahead as planned?*
F: *Do you know if the presentation to the client is …?*

# Exercises

**52.1  Underline the correct word in italics.**

1  *Dear* / *Hi* Mr Kovacs.
2  *Kind regard* / *regards*.
3  *Your* / *Yours* sincerely.
4  I hope you are *well* / *fine*.
5  I *could* / *would* be grateful if you *could* / *would* send me an application form for the job.
6  I would *appreciate it* / *appreciate* if you could resend the file. The one I have now doesn't open.
7  *Do* / *Would* you like me to book a taxi to pick you up from the airport?
8  I *ask* / *wonder* if you could do me a favour?
9  Unfortunately I am *unable* / *impossible* to meet you as planned next week.
10  If I understand correctly, *you're saying* / *you say* that you are not prepared to invest any more money in this project. Is that right?
11  If you *inquire* / *require* any further information, please do not hesitate to contact me again.
12  I look forward to *hear* / *hearing* from you.

**52.2  The words in bold below have been mixed up and put in the wrong sentences. Move them back to the correct sentence.**

1  I hope you are **hearing**.        *well*
2  It was a **wonder** meeting you last week.  _____
3  My apologies for not **well** sooner.  _____
4  **Unfortunately** to our conversation last Friday, I have now spoken to Michael.  _____
5  I would **pleasure** it if you could send me the CVs of the candidates we're going to interview.  _____
6  I **appreciate** if you could have a word with Mr Gonzalez when you see him?  _____
7  **Further** I am unable to attend the meeting next week.
   _____
8  I look forward to **replying** from you soon.  _____

**52.3  In each sentence one word (or abbreviated word) is missing. Add the missing word in the correct place.**

1  How's ⋀ going?   *it*
2  Thank you your email of 12 January.
3  Sorry for not getting back you.
4  I am writing regard to the meeting.
5  I be grateful if you could send me your latest price list.
6  If I understand correctly, you're saying that the final price will be higher – is right?
7  I would like to apologize the poor service you received.
8  I look into it and get back to you.
9  If you need anything else, just let know.
10  If you require any further information, please do hesitate to contact me again.
11  See you the conference.
12  I look forward meeting you at the conference.

**52.4  Look at the patterns for indirect questions.**

| Can we …? | → Would it be possible for us to …? |
| What …? | → Can you tell me what …? |
| Do you want to …? | → Would you like to …? |
| Do they …? | → Do you know if they …? |

**Now use the patterns to change the sentences below.**

1  What is your best offer?
   →  *Can you tell me what*  your best offer is?
2  Do you want to be on the stand at the trade show?
   →  _____ be on the stand …?
3  Do they have a presence in the Turkish market?
   →  _____ have a presence …?
4  Can we renegotiate that part of the contract?
   →  _____ renegotiate …?
5  What did Mr Chen say at the meeting?
   →  _____ Mr Chen said …?

**52.5  First read this email which is written in a neutral/ friendly style.**

Thanks for your email of Sep 30th and sorry for not getting back to you.

I am writing about the meeting next week where you're going to come to our offices to present your web design services to me and some colleagues. Two points:

First, as you wanted, here's a document with the names and job titles of everyone who will be at the meeting. Good news – our Managing Director Ms Lena Holmberg can now come.

Second, please show us in the meeting a working example of website analytics. I think we're not analyzing our website traffic very well, and we would like some help in this area.

If you need any more information, just let me know.

See you next week.

All the best
Marta Lopez

**Now rewrite the email in a more formal style by replacing the underlined phrases with phrases from the box. Write in full on a separate piece of paper.**

> *I feel that at the moment we are not*   *Thank you*
> *I look forward to seeing you*   *with regard to*
> *please do not hesitate to contact me again*   *myself*
> *as effectively as we might*   *professional guidance*
> *I would be grateful if you could*   *my apologies*
> *I am pleased to say that*   *require any further*
> *will now be able to attend*   *replying sooner*
> *Kind regards*   *be present*   *September*
> *requested*   *I attach*   *you are*

**See page 149 for some writing tasks.**

## Opening

*Hi Bob / Hello Bob / Bob / no name at all*
*It was good to speak to you yesterday.*
*Hope you're well.*

## Introducing the subject

### with previous context
*Thanks for this. Sorry I haven't got back to you sooner.*
*Further to / Re (= regarding) our call the other day ...*

### no previous context
*I'm writing about ...*
*Just a short note to let you know that ...*

## Body of email

### Ask for information
*Could you / Please send me ...*
*I'd like to know ... In particular, ...*

### Give information
*Re the information you wanted, here is ...*
*I've spoken to ... and she says that ...*

### Ask for action/help
*Could you ...?*
*Thanks – I'd really appreciate your help on this.*

### Offer action/help
*Do you want me to ...?*
*Shall I ...?*

### Attach a document
*Please find attached ...*

### Apologize
*Sorry about ... It was my fault entirely.*
*I'll make sure it doesn't happen again.*

### Promise action
*I'll ... / I'll look into it. / I'll chase it up.*

### Suggest further action
*How about ...*
*Perhaps you could ...*
*We might also need to ...*
*Let me know what you think.*

## Closing

*Please get back to me if you need more information.*
*I'll be in touch soon.*
*I'll give you a call sometime next week.*
*Btw (= by the way) – give my regards to Henrik.*
*Best wishes / Best regards / Kind regards* + your name, or
   just your name.

## Arranging a meeting

*When would suit you?*
*When can you make it?*
*How about Thursday at 9am at my office?*
*Friday's fine by me. Shall we say 12.30?*
*I'm really sorry, but I have to change my plans.*
*I wonder if we could move it to Monday instead?*

## Invitations

*We would like to invite you to ...*
*The event takes place on 5 March and will start at 2pm. The
   venue is ... A map and full programme are attached.*
*Light refreshments will be provided.*
*Please let me know if you are able to attend by 4 March.*
*Thank you for inviting me to ... I would be delighted to
   come and I am looking forward to it very much.*
*Thank you for your kind invitation. Unfortunately I have
   something else in my schedule for that day.*

## Commercial

### Supplier sends information
*Thank you for your email requesting information about ...*
*Following our conversation earlier today, I am writing to
   give you more details of our ...*
*Please find attached a catalogue and a price list.*

### Customer asks specific questions
*What exactly does the price include?*
*Are they available in other sizes / colours?*
*How soon can you ship the goods?*
*Is there a discount for large quantities?*
*Do you have a minimum order?*
*What are your terms of payment?*

### Supplier replies to questions
*The price includes everything, including shipping.*
*We offer next-day shipping on receipt of a firm order.*
*We require a letter of credit or 50% of the total in advance.*
*We offer a 5% discount for orders over €10,000.*
*Our terms of payment are 50% in advance, 50% after 30 days.*

### Problems: customer complains
*My order reference number ... has still not arrived.*
*We ordered ... but you sent ...*

### Problems: supplier replies
*Please accept my apologies for ... The problem was due to ...*
*I will look into the matter immediately and get back to you
   within 24 hours.*
*I apologize again for any inconvenience this has caused.*

# Exercises

**53.1 Complete the sentences with the pairs of words in the box.**

| back / sooner | be / touch | do / favour | give / call |
| --- | --- | --- | --- |
| ~~let / know~~ | Please / attached | Re / here | Sorry / fault |

1 Just a short note to __*let*__ you __*know*__ that everything's OK for Tuesday.
2 Thanks for this. Sorry I haven't got _____ to you _____ .
3 _____ the info you wanted, _____ are the sales figures broken down by region.
4 Could you _____ me a _____ ?
5 _____ find _____ the artwork for next year's brochure.
6 _____ about the mix-up with the hotel reservation – it was my _____ entirely.
7 I'll _____ in _____ soon.
8 I'll _____ you a _____ sometime next week.

**53.2 Continue as before.**

| able / attend | change / plans | delighted / forward |
| --- | --- | --- |
| event / place | refreshments / provided | Shall / say |
| | When / make | wonder / instead |

1 _____ can you _____ it?
2 _____ we _____ 12.30 at my office?
3 I'm really sorry, but I have to _____ my _____ .
4 I _____ if we could move it to Monday _____ ?
5 The _____ takes _____ on 5 March and will start at 2pm.
6 Light _____ will be _____ .
7 Please let me know if you are _____ to _____ by 4 March.
8 I would be _____ to attend and I am looking _____ to it very much.

**53.3 Continue as before.**

| apologize / inconvenience | available / sizes |
| --- | --- |
| discount / quantities | exactly / include | letter / credit |
| look / matter | order / arrived | terms / payment |

1 What _____ does the price _____ ?
2 Are they _____ in other _____ ?
3 Is there a _____ for large _____ ?
4 What are your _____ of _____ ?
5 We require a _____ of _____ .
6 My _____ reference number KO8763 has still not _____ .
7 I will _____ into the _____ and get back to you within 24 hours.
8 I _____ again for any _____ this has caused.

**53.4 Read the email sequence below. Each email contains <u>five</u> mistakes (missing word or short form of a word, extra word, wrong word, wrong form). Find the mistakes and correct them.**

**Email 1**

> Hi Aditya
>
> It was good to speak you yesterday. Hope you well.
>
> Could you sending me the name of that market research company you mentioned? I like to know more about them. In particularly, how long did it take them to write the report, and how much did they charge you?
>
> Thanks
> Melanie

**Email 2**

> Hi Mel
>
> Re the information you wanted, here is it the website of the market research company. It took them about two weeks to write the report, and they charged €1,800. Please get back me if you need more information about them.
>
> On another matter – could you do me some favour? Can you talk to the Finance Director and try to get an idea about the size of the budget for the new projects we discussed? There's no point spending time on the planning if the resources aren't be there.
>
> Thanks – I'd appreciate it your help on this.
>
> Aditya

**Email 3**

> Aditya
>
> Thanks this. Sorry but I haven't got back to you sooner.
>
> The website details were very useful and I'm in touch with the market research company. They seem very good.
>
> Re the budget for the new projects, I've spoken the FD and he says that no decisions have been taken yet. I think we should be proactive here. How about if you and I prepare an estimate of the budget we going to need? That way we get to shape the discussion at an early stage.
>
> Let me knowing what you think.
>
> Mel
>
> Btw – who got that job at Head Office?

**Email 4**

> Mel
>
> Yes, good idea re the budget. Let put some figures together. I give you a call over the next few days to arrange a meeting.
>
> Do you want it me to invite Reza to the meeting as well? His input would be very useful.
>
> About the Head Office job – I'm not sure who got it. I'd be very interested to know myself. I chase it up and let know.
>
> A.

**See page 149 for some writing tasks.**

## Using the word 'meeting'

A meeting is about/on a particular issue/matter/topic/subject. A 'matter' is a serious issue you have to deal with.

You …
*meet* (with) someone
*have a meeting with* someone
*arrange/set up/schedule/call* a meeting
*go to/participate in/attend* a meeting
*have/hold* a meeting at a particular time and place
*miss* a meeting (= fail to go to it)
*postpone/reschedule* a meeting
*cancel/call off* a meeting
*meet up with* a friend to do something together

You can have a/an … meeting.

*angry/heated/stormy, brief/short, lengthy/long, fruitful/productive/successful, crucial/key/vital, formal/informal, face-to-face, frequent/regular, weekly/monthly, initial/preliminary/preparatory, crisis/emergency/urgent, kick-off, follow-up*

Note these phrases:
*the purpose/aim of the meeting*
*the outcome/result of the meeting*

An 'appointment' is an official arrangement to see someone at a particular time. It may be a meeting (with a bank manager) or not (with a doctor).

## Before the meeting

Somebody arranges a meeting – they invite people to attend (= be present). It is probably this person who will then be the chair/moderator/facilitator when the meeting takes place. The chair draws up/prepares a list of points/items to be discussed. This list is called the agenda of the meeting. The agenda is usually circulated to participants before the meeting. Items may be added or removed before or during the meeting.

## The start of the meeting

The chair opens the meeting. The meeting might begin by appointing someone to take the minutes (= make a written summary of the meeting). This written summary can also be called a Memorandum of Meeting (MoM in everyday speech). In a formal meeting, where the participants don't know each other, the chair might then go round the table and ask everyone to introduce themselves. At this point the chair announces who sends apologies (= has said they cannot attend and is sorry not to be there). The next steps are to agree/approve the minutes of the previous meeting and then to review the agenda for the current meeting.

The chair sets a time limit for the meeting and goes over any 'housekeeping points' (practical things such as a reminder to put mobile phones into silent mode, whether there will be a break for refreshments, where the restroom/bathroom is, etc).

## During the meeting

In the meeting you … issues.

*consider/deal with/discuss/examine/look at/tackle*

You can discuss an issue …

*in depth/in detail, briefly, at length*

A 'point' in a meeting is a fact or opinion. You can … a point.

*make/raise, clarify, emphasize/stress*

And a point can be …

*good/interesting/valid, central/crucial/key, important, controversial*

In the decision-making part of the meeting you can …

make   *a suggestion, a proposal, a recommendation*
reach   *an agreement, a compromise, a conclusion, a decision*

Note the differences:

*a suggestion* (just an idea – nothing definite)
*a proposal* (an official, detailed plan or suggestion)
*a recommendation* (a piece of advice)

A compromise is when people accept less than they really want in order to reach an agreement.

## The end of the meeting

The chair has to make sure that the meeting doesn't run over time (= finish late). At the end of the meeting there is often a review of action points – who will do what before the next meeting. Different tasks are assigned (= officially given) to different people. The time for the next meeting is then set (= decided) and the chair closes the meeting/brings the meeting to a close. Alternatively it might be adjourned (= temporarily stopped) for a short time or until a later date.

# Exercises

**54.1 Each word in italics below is wrong. There could be one extra letter, or one changed letter, or one missing letter. Write the correct word/s in full at the end.**

1 A meeting can deal with a variety of different *tissues / topigs / sujects*. _issues/topics/subjects_

2 A formal way to say 'be at' a meeting is *'atten'* a meeting. _____

3 If you fail to go to a meeting, you *mish* it. _____

4 The *pupose* of the meeting is the *rason* why you are there. _____ / _____

5 The *outdome* of the meeting is its result. _____

6 The chair of the meeting can also be called the *modelator* or the *facsilitator*. _____ / _____

7 The list of *idems* to be discussed at the meeting is called the *adenda*. _____ / _____

8 If the chair asks everyone in turn to speak, we say that they *do roun then zable*. _____

9 In a meeting you might *agreet / approde* the minutes of the previous meeting before you begin. _____ / _____

10 At the start of the meeting the chair briefly mentions any *mousekeeping oints*. _____

11 Another way to say *'ephasize* a point' is *'struss* a point'. _____ / _____

12 A *keg* point is one that is *scentral* to the discussion. _____ / _____

**54.2 Replace each word in bold with a word in the box that has a similar meaning.**

| | | | | | |
|---|---|---|---|---|---|
| attend | call off | chair | close | deal with | draw up |
| ~~hold~~ | miss | postpone | raise | set | set up |

1 Where will we **have** the meeting? _hold_

2 He'll **come to** the meeting as well. _____

3 Sorry, I will **not come to** the meeting. _____

4 We'll **arrange** a meeting with Frank. _____

5 Who is going to **lead** the meeting? _____

6 I'll **prepare** the agenda for the meeting. _____

7 We'll have to **delay** the meeting. _____

8 We'll have to **cancel** the meeting. _____

9 We need to **discuss** three main issues. _____

10 It's a very interesting point that you **make**. _____

11 We should **decide** a time limit. _____

12 I think we can **finish** the meeting now. _____

**54.3 Complete each sentence with the most likely word – either *suggestion* or *proposal*.**

1 We've had two meetings with the client and we're now in a position to make a detailed _____ .

2 It's just a _____ , but why don't we go back to the client with a modified design that is cheaper?

**54.4 Make phrases by matching each verb 1–9 with a group of words a–i below.**

| | | | | | |
|---|---|---|---|---|---|
| 1 arrange | [c] | 4 cancel | [ ] | 7 reach | [ ] |
| 2 book | [ ] | 5 go | [ ] | 8 send | [ ] |
| 3 bring | [ ] | 6 make | [ ] | 9 take | [ ] |

a round the table to see if everyone agrees; over something again to make sure you understand

b your apologies to the organizer of the meeting; the minutes to everyone after the meeting

c to have a meeting at a particular time; the tables and chairs inside the meeting room

d a room for a meeting; a table at a restaurant

e an interesting point at the meeting; progress at the meeting; a decision; a suggestion

f place (= happen); notes at the meeting; the minutes of the meeting

g a meeting because the boss is sick; an appointment because you are sick

h an agreement; a compromise; a conclusion; a decision

i the meeting to a close; a copy of the agenda to the meeting

**54.5 Replace each word in bold with a word in the box that has a similar meaning.**

| | | | | | |
|---|---|---|---|---|---|
| brief | face-to-face | follow-up | heated | informal | lengthy |
| monthly | preliminary | productive | regular | urgent | vital |

1 It was a very **angry** meeting. _____

2 I had a **short** meeting with Emma. _____

3 It was a **long** meeting – over two hours. _____

4 I think the meeting was very **successful**. _____

5 It's a **crucial** meeting. You must be there. _____

6 It was a very **relaxed** meeting. _____

7 I want to meet them **in person**. _____

8 We need to set up **frequent** meetings. _____

9 We have a sales meeting **every month**. _____

10 The **initial** meeting went very well. _____

11 We need to call an **emergency** meeting. _____

12 We need a **second** meeting to check on how things are going. _____

**54.6 Complete the phrases with these prepositions: *at, for, in, into, over, with*.**

1 put your phone _____ silent mode

2 have a break _____ refreshments

3 deal _____ some important issues

4 discuss something _____ detail

5 discuss something _____ length

6 run _____ time and finish later than planned

# 55 Meetings: basic phrases

## Starting

To begin a discussion just say:

*Right / So / OK / Right then / Well / Let's get started.*

If there has been some social conversation first, then you can say:

*OK, let's get down to business.*

To introduce the subject of the meeting say:

*We're here to decide …*
*The purpose / aim of this meeting is …*
*The reason we're here today is …*

## Giving an opinion

You can just give an opinion with no special phrase OR you can introduce it with:

*I think / I feel / I'd say (that) …*

Use a longer phrase to emphasize that it is a personal opinion. The underlined words are stressed in speech.

*From my point of view, …*
*The way I see it, …*
*As far as I'm concerned, …*

You can introduce a comment with a short word or phrase like those below. This signals to the listener what kind of thing you are going to say.

**Something is obvious**
*Obviously / Of course / Clearly …*

**Something is surprising but true**
*Actually / In fact / As a matter of fact …*

**You are uncertain**
*Apparently / It seems that / They say that …*

**You are being honest**
*To be honest / Frankly / To tell the truth …*

**Emphasizing an important point**
*Basically / The point is / The main thing is …*

**Other phrases**
*Unfortunately / Luckily / I'm pleased to say that / Hopefully / Presumably / Between you and me …*

## Agreeing and disagreeing

While someone else is talking we say small words to let them know that we are listening and agree.

*Right. / That's right. / True. / That's true.*
*Absolutely. / Exactly. / Definitely.*
*Yes, good point. / Yes, good idea. / Yes, I agree.*

To disagree just say:

*But / However / Then again …*

Alternatively, use *Yes, but* or a variation of it:

*That's true, but …*
*Yes, you have a point, but …*
*I can see what you're saying, but …*

You can correct factual information with *Actually*:
*Actually, I'm Scottish, not English.*

To disagree more directly you can:

**Use open questions**
*Really? Do you think so? Are you sure?*

**Ask challenging questions**
*But what would happen if …?*
*Have you thought about the risk involved?*

**Use a fixed expression**
*I'm not sure about that.*
*That's not really how I see it.*

## Managing the conversation

You may want to:

**End a topic**
*OK. So I'll … (+ action point) then.*
*Anyway, … (+ conclusion).*

**Change the topic**
*Right / So / Anyway. Now what about …?*
*OK, shall we move on to discuss …?*

**Invite someone else to speak**
*What about you?*
*What do you think?*

**Interrupt**
*Can I just come in here?*
*Sorry, can I just say something / ask a question?*

**Block an interruption**
*Can I just finish my point?*
*Perhaps we can come back to this later?*

**Go back to a previous topic**
*Anyway, as I was saying …*
*Anyway, getting back to what I was saying before …*

## Finishing

To signal that you want to end the discussion say:

*Right / So / Anyway … (followed by a pause)*

A longer alternative is:

*I think that's as far as we can go today.*

Finally talk about the next steps and review action points:

*I think the best way forward is …*
*So, before the next meeting I'm going to … and you're going to …*

# Exercises

**55.1 Underline the correct word in italics.**

1 OK, let's *get started / make it start*.
2 OK, let's *be down with / get down to* business.
3 The *object / purpose* of this meeting is to discuss the market research findings that I circulated to you.
4 The *motive / reason* we're here today is to discuss improvements to the company website.
5 *From / In* my point of view, it would be better to finance this project out of the existing budget.
6 *As far as I'm concerned / As it concerns me*, the timescale for this project is too short.
7 Yes, *you have reason / you're right*.
8 Yes, *I agree / I am agree* with you.
9 OK, shall we *move to / move on to* discuss what kind of promotional materials we're going to use?
10 Can we *come back / come back to* this point later?
11 I think that's *as far as / so far as* we can go today.
12 I think the best *manner / way* forward from here is to approach existing customers and see how much they would pay for this extra service.

**55.2 Match each item on the left with the one on the right with the closest meaning. Be careful because several phrases may have a similar meaning.**

| | |
|---|---|
| 1 Actually | The point is |
| 2 Apparently | As a matter of fact |
| 3 Basically | Of course |
| 4 Frankly | It seems that |
| 5 Hopefully | Sorry to say, but |
| 6 Obviously | I imagine |
| 7 Presumably | With any luck |
| 8 Unfortunately | To be honest |

**55.3 In each mini-dialogue cross out the word in italics that is less likely or not possible.**

1 A: The new model is a big improvement.
   B: *Of course / Hopefully* it's a little more expensive.
2 A: Did you go to the Frankfurt Trade Fair?
   B: *Unfortunately / The main thing is* I didn't go this year. It's a shame because I always find it very interesting.
3 A: Do you think she'll get the job?
   B: *Apparently / To be honest*, I don't think so.
4 A: I haven't heard of them before.
   B: *Actually / With any luck*, they're the fourth biggest company in the market.
5 A: Who's going to be the new Team Leader now that David has left?
   B: *Basically / Presumably* they'll give the job to Freya – she's the most obvious person.
6 A: What's going to happen?
   B: *It seems that / Frankly* I don't care. I'm already applying for other jobs.

**55.4 Match the beginning and end of each phrase.**

| | |
|---|---|
| 1 OK, let's get | what you're saying |
| 2 I can see | of this meeting is |
| 3 So, what | sure about that |
| 4 As far | down to business |
| 5 The purpose | about |
| 6 I'm not | as I'm concerned |

| | |
|---|---|
| 7 Anyway, as I | happen if |
| 8 Can I just | as we can go |
| 9 I'm | was saying |
| 10 I think that's as far | say something |
| 11 I think the best | going to recommend |
| 12 What would | way forward |

**55.5 Complete this meeting extract using the phrases in Exercise 55.4 (phrases 1–6 are used first).**

CHAIR: Is everybody here now? [1]*OK, let's get down to business*. Do you all have a copy of the agenda? Good. [2]_____ to talk about what we're going to do with the net profit we made from last year's trading. Miki, would you like to begin?

MIKI: Thank you. There are really just two options, either to return it to the shareholders as dividends or to reinvest it in the business. [3]_____ , we should return it to the shareholders. We paid a very small dividend last year.

LOUIS: [4]_____ , Miki, but we're at a crucial stage with the business and we need money for our expansion plans.

MIKI: [5]_____ . I think it's too soon and too risky to expand right now – we need a period of consolidation.

LOUIS: [6]_____ all those new projects we discussed last week?

*Later in the same meeting ...*

LOUIS: [7]_____ *Anyway, as I was saying* earlier, I think a reasonable compromise would be to return half the profits to the shareholders.

TINA: [8]_____ ? The shareholders are expecting more than that.
[9]_____ they start questioning how we run the company?

CHAIR: [10]_____ with this discussion today. [11]_____ is for me, as CEO, to meet with the chairman of the Board and sort out the final details. But in principle [12]_____ a much bigger dividend.

**55.6 🔘 08 You are going to hear eight phrases. Listen and repeat.**

## Ask for repetition

To ask someone to repeat something say:

*Sorry? / Excuse me (AmE)?*
*Sorry, I missed that. What did you say?*
*Sorry, I didn't catch that.*
*Could you say that again?*

Note that the single word *What?* sounds rude.

If you want repetition of a longer, more complicated idea you can say:

*I'm sorry, could you go over that again?*

## Use your own words to check

A common way to check understanding is to rephrase what the other person said using your own words.

*Are you saying …?*
*Do you mean …?*
*So, in other words, … . Is that right?*

## Say you don't understand

If you don't understand the other person's ideas, you can say:

*Sorry, I don't follow you.*
*Sorry, I'm not with you.*
*Sorry, I don't quite see what you mean.*

Another case is where you thought that you did understand, but now you have doubts. Negative questions are common here.

*Maybe I've got it wrong. I thought you said …*
*Isn't it …?*
*Don't you mean …?*
*Shouldn't that be …?*

## Make your own meaning clear

If you realize that other people don't understand you, then stop and begin again in a different way.

*I mean / What I mean is …*
*In other words …*
*What I'm trying to say is …*

If there is a serious breakdown in communication, take responsibility for it yourself. You can say:

*Perhaps I didn't make myself clear. Let me put it another way.*
*My mistake. I should have said …*
*I think there's a misunderstanding here. What I meant was …*

## Ask for more detailed information

What the other person says is often too general, and you need more specific information.

*Can you say a bit more about that?*
*Can you be a little more specific?*
*Can you put a figure on that?*
*What kind of timescale are we talking about?*

If you want more details about particular key ideas, you can say:

*What do you mean by 'quite expensive'?*
*You say 'very profitable'. What exactly do you mean by that?*

## Active listening

Active listening means giving your full attention to what the other person is saying, and using short words, sounds and comments to show you are interested.

*Right. / Yes. / Yeah. / Yuh. / Mhm. / Uhuh.*
*Exactly. / Absolutely. / Of course. / Yes, you're right.*

Use two-word questions (auxiliary + subject) to encourage the other person to keep talking.

*Did you? / Are they? / Was it?*

Echo key words and then make a short comment.

*Eight thousand euros? That's a lot of money.*
*All over the world! They're obviously very successful.*
*Next Friday? That doesn't give you much time.*

Make a personal response:

**Show interest**
*Really? / That's interesting. / How interesting.*

**Show surprise**
*Really! / Wow! / That's amazing! / You're kidding, right?*

**React to good news**
*That's fantastic! / That's wonderful! / That's great news! / Well done!*

**React to general bad news**
*Oh dear. / That's a pity. / That's a shame. / That's bad news.*

**Show sympathy (more personal)**
*I'm sorry to hear that. / That's awful.*
*Never mind. / These things happen.*

Very often a personal response is just a single word:

*Amazing! / Correct. / Excellent! / Fantastic! / Fine. / Good. / Great! / Interesting. / Really? / Right. / True.*

# Exercises

**56.1 Match each beginning with all its possible endings. Then write the phrases under the most appropriate heading below.**

Sorry, I
Can you

'm not with you.
be more specific?
say that again?
don't follow you.
don't see what you mean.
go over that again?
didn't catch that.
say more about that?
missed that.
put a figure on that?

**Asking for repetition**
1 _____
2 _____
3 _____
4 _____

**Saying you don't understand**
5 _____
6 _____
7 _____

**Asking for more detailed information**
8 _____
9 _____
10 _____

**56.2 Add the word/s in brackets to each sentence in the right place. They make the sentences less direct.**

1 (just) Can you ʌ say that again?
    *just*
2 (a little) Can you be more specific?
3 (quite) Sorry, I'm not with you.
4 (just) Can you go over that again?
5 (quite) Sorry, I didn't catch that.
6 (just, a bit) Can you say more about that?

**56.3 Complete the mini-dialogues with phrases from the box. Write them in full to help you remember.**

> Are you saying    Can you be a little more specific?
> Can you put a figure on that?
> My mistake. I should have said    Sorry, I missed that.
> ~~What exactly do you mean by that?~~
> What I'm trying to say is
> What kind of timescale are we talking about?

1 A: We're known throughout the software industry for the high quality of our products.
  B: You say 'high quality'. *What exactly do you mean by that* ?
  A: We have ISO 25,000. It's the international standard.
2 A: Forty thousand euros? Don't you mean thirty thousand euros?
  B: _____ thirty.

3 A: The new product is selling very well in some European markets, but not in others.
  B: _____ ?
  A: Yes – it's selling well in Benelux and Germany, but not so well in Spain and Italy.
4 A: Before we can install the new lighting system, we'll have to remove the old one. Then there's all the redecoration once the work is finished.
  B: _____ ?
  A: Around four months to do the job properly.
5 A: Their Head Office is in Saskatchewan.
  B: _____ . What did you say?
  A: I said their Head Office is in Saskatchewan. It's a province of Canada. They're a Canadian company.
6 A: There have been some new developments. The situation is different now.
  B: _____ the future of the project is in doubt?
  A: No, I'm just saying things are more complicated.
7 A: The underlying principles behind the general concept are reasonably sound, but there will be numerous obstacles to overcome on the way to successful implementation.
  B: Sorry, I don't follow you.
  A: _____ it's a good idea in theory, but I'm not sure it will work in practice.
8 A: Our sales forecasts show that demand for this product is falling.
  B: _____ ?
  A: Yes, we estimate a drop of 25% in total sales this year.

**56.4 Complete each mini-dialogue with one item from list A and one from list B.**

| A | B |
|---|---|
| ~~Jennifer!~~ | That's fantastic! Well done! |
| Really? Was it? | Oh dear. That's bad news. |
| Did you? | ~~I haven't seen her for ages.~~ |
| 20%? | Never mind. Another day. |
| I'm sorry to hear that. | I'm not surprised – it was very good. |

1 A: I spoke to Jennifer last week.
  B: *Jennifer! I haven't seen her for ages.*
2 A: Oh, I never told you. I got promoted last month.
  B: _____
3 A: Their share price has fallen 20% over the last month.
  B: _____
4 A: It was their most effective advertising campaign ever.
  B: _____
5 A: I can't make it tomorrow – my little boy has the flu.
  B: _____

**56.5 🌐 09 You are going to hear eight phrases. Listen and repeat.**

# 57 Meetings: developing the discussion

## Building an argument

To persuade people to support your opinion you might need to build your case point by point.

### List points one by one
*First / Firstly / First of all …*
*Second / Secondly …*
*Lastly / Finally / Last but not least …*
*There are three reasons: one …, two …, and three …*

### Add another point
*Also / In addition …*
*As well as that …*
*Moreover …*

### Show both sides of an argument
*In general …, although …*
*On the whole …, but …*
*In most cases …, however …*
*On the one hand …, on the other hand …*

### Show a consequence
*So / Therefore …*
*Because of this …*
*And as a result …*

### Say the main point in a simple way
*Basically …*
*The thing is …*
*To put it simply …*
*In short / To cut a long story short …*

### Emphasize with *What* + *be*
*What we need is …*
*What we can't do is …*
*What this means is …*

Also note these structures:
*What we'll do is this: …*
*What's going to happen is this: …*
*Here's what we'll do: …*
*Here's what's going to happen: …*

### Introduce a different point
*In relation to / In terms of / On the subject of …*
*As far as … is concerned …*

### Review and conclude
*On balance …*
*At the end of the day …*
*Taking everything into consideration …*

## Making a suggestion

Use *should* to make a strong suggestion. The negative *shouldn't* can sound very direct – instead say *I don't think you should*.

*You should ask for a pay rise – you've been here a year and your performance has been excellent.*
*I don't think you should mention this to anyone else – it's very sensitive business information.*

By adding *Perhaps* or *Maybe* or *I think* you make the suggestion less strong.

*Perhaps we should leave this discussion until the next meeting?*

Use *could* to make a suggestion. With a question or a negative question the suggestion becomes more open.

*We could introduce the product in one region first and see how it sells.*
*Could we / Couldn't we try to renegotiate the contract?*

Here are some other ways to make suggestions.

*What about / How about* (+ verb ending in *-ing*)
*Shall we …? / Let's …*
*Why don't we … ? It might be worth trying.*
*It's just an idea, but what if we…?*

## Accepting and rejecting suggestions

If you think it's a good suggestion, you can say:

*I really like that suggestion.*
*Yes, I think that would work very well.*

If you don't like the suggestion, you can say:

*I'm not sure about that.*
*I can see one or two problems with that.*
*It sounds interesting, but I don't think it would work in practice.*
*There are too many unknowns. What would happen if …?*

## Reaching a decision

The meeting will discuss the 'pros and cons' (= advantages and disadvantages) of each suggestion. The chair will then make a decision.

*On balance, I think we should go with Martin's idea. Is everyone happy with that?*
*Taking everything into consideration, it seems to me that Mei's suggestion is the best. Does everyone agree?*

Finally the meeting will discuss action points.

*So, what are the next steps?*
*So, the next thing to do is …*
*Mehmet, can we leave you to prepare an action plan to discuss at the next meeting?*

# Exercises

**57.1 Match an item on the left with an item on the right with a similar meaning.**

| | | |
|---|---|---|
| 1 | On balance | What we should do is |
| 2 | In general | In relation to |
| 3 | We should | As a result |
| 4 | On the subject of | Moreover |
| 5 | Basically | At the end of the day |
| 6 | In addition | In short |
| 7 | However | On the whole |
| 8 | Therefore | On the other hand |

**57.2 Underline the correct word in italics.**

1 It's true that option B is a little more expensive. *However / Therefore*, cost isn't the only factor we have to consider.

2 So, that's decided. Now, *in general / on the subject of* online advertising, how are we going to reach mobile users who have smart phones?

3 They're a very well-known company and they have a good reputation in the market. *In addition / However* we have worked with them before and there were no problems. So I think we should use them again.

4 It's going to need hundreds of hours of management time, it's very risky, and it doesn't fit with our long-term strategy. *Basically / On the other hand* it's just not a good idea.

5 *In general / Moreover* publishers are moving more and more to the e-book format, although I think many people will still prefer a real, physical book.

6 We've spent a lot of money on the product launch – it's going to be at the Sheraton, our most important clients will be there, and there will be journalists as well. *On the whole / Therefore* we need to do everything possible to make sure it's a success.

**57.3 Fill in the missing letters. The words you make are very simple, basic words.**

1 *In addition* and *Moreover* are another way of saying _ _ _ .

2 *However* and *On the other hand* are another way of saying _ _ _ .

3 *Therefore* and *As a result* are another way of saying _ _ .

**57.4 Fill in the missing letters.**

1 To begin a list of points we can say *First* or *First_ _* or *First o_ a_ _* .

2 To say that the final item in a list is still important we can say *L_ _ _ but not l_ _ _ _ _* .

3 To compare two different ideas we can say *O_ the o_ _ _ _ _ _, but _ _ the other _ _ _ _* .

4 To say the main point in a simple way we can say *To cu_ a lo_ _ sto_ _ sho_ _* .

5 To introduce the topic of finance, we can say *As f_ _ as finance is con_ _ _ned* .

6 To review and conclude we can say *Taking ev_ _ _ _ing into cons_ _ _ _ation* .

**57.5 Look at the pattern in the box.**

> We should recall the products immediately and do full safety checks.
> a → What we should do is recall the products …
> b → Here's what we should do: recall the products …

**Now use the same patterns to change the sentences below. Note that the verb 'should' in the examples above is replaced by other verbs below.**

1 We need to call all our clients in person and reassure them that the news reports are false.
   a → _____ call all our clients …
   b → _____ : call all our clients …

2 We'll replace the faulty item immediately and give you 10% off your next order.
   a → _____ replace the faulty item …
   b → _____ : replace the faulty item …

3 We can't just sit here and wait.
   a → _____ just sit here and wait.
   b → _____ : just sit here and wait.

**57.6 Fill in the missing letters.**

1 I think we _ _ould / _ould take another approach. What a_ _ _t do_ _ _ some market research first, before we invest all our resources in this project?

2 Could_'_ we ask our colleagues in the Singapore office to help us? L_ _'_ contact them and see what they say.

3 _ _ _ll we have a coffee break now?

4 Why _ _ _'t _ _ open a part of our online resources to the general public? It m_ _ _t be w_ _th try_ _ _.

**57.7 A meeting has been discussing investment opportunities in the Gulf. The chair is reviewing and concluding. Complete his comments with the words in the box.**

> ~~first of all~~   it seems to me   pros and cons
> sounds interesting   the next steps   too many unknowns
> what would happen   work in practice

❝ 1 *First of all,* we looked at the Dubai option, and I think we discussed all the 2 _____ in some detail. Personally I think the Dubai option would work very well. Then we discussed the Qatar option. This 3 _____ , but I don't think it would 4 _____ . Finally we considered Oman. I'm not sure about Oman. There are 5 _____ . And we don't have very good connections there – 6 _____ if we lost the support of our local partners? So, taking everything into consideration, 7 _____ that Dubai is the best option. Does everyone agree? Good. Now then, what are 8 _____ ? ❞

## Starting

*Right./Let's get started.*
*OK, let's get down to business.*
*The purpose of this meeting is …*
*The reason we're here today is …*

## Opinions

*I think/I feel …*
*From my point of view …*
*Obviously/Of course …*
*Actually/In fact …*
*Apparently/It seems that …*
*To be honest/Frankly …*
*Basically/The point is …*

## Building an argument

*First/Second/Lastly …*
*Also/As well as that …*
*In general …, although …*
*On the whole …, but …*
*So/Therefore …*
*Because of this …*
*In relation to/In terms of …*
*On balance …*

## Showing interest

*Right./Exactly./Of course.*
*Did you? Are they? Was it?*
*Really?/That's interesting.*
*That's fantastic!/That's wonderful!*
*Oh dear./That's a pity.*

## Agreeing and disagreeing

*Right./That's right./Absolutely./Exactly.*
*Yes, good point./Yes, good idea.*
*That's true, but …*
*I can see what you're saying, but …*
*Really? Do you think so?*
*But what would happen if …?*
*I'm not sure about that.*

## Managing the conversation

*Right. Now what about …?*
*OK, shall we move on to discuss …?*
*What about you?*
*What do you think?*
*Can I just come in here?*
*Sorry, can I just say something?*
*Can I just finish my point?*

*Perhaps we can come back to this later?*
*Anyway, as I was saying …*
*Anyway, getting back to what I was saying before …*

## Checking and clarifying

### Ask for repetition
*Sorry, I missed that. What did you say?*
*Sorry, I didn't catch that.*
*I'm sorry, could you go over that again?*

### Use your own words to check
*Are you saying …?*
*So, in other words, … . Is that right?*

### Say you don't understand
*Sorry, I don't follow you.*
*Sorry, I'm not with you.*
*Maybe I've got it wrong. I thought you said …*

### Make your own meaning clear
*What I mean is …*
*What I'm trying to say is …*
*My mistake. I should have said …*

### Ask for more detailed information
*Can you say a bit more about that?*
*Can you be a little more specific?*
*You say 'difficult'. What exactly do you mean by that?*

## Suggestions

*We/You should/could …*
*What about (+ -ing)*
*Shall we …?/Let's …*
*Why don't we … ?*
*I think that would work very well.*
*I can see one or two problems with that.*
*There are too many unknowns/risks.*

## Finishing

*Right/So/Anyway …*
*I think that's as far as we can go today.*
*On balance, I think we should … Is everyone happy with that?*
*Taking everything into consideration, it seems to me that …*
*Does everyone agree?*

## Action points

*So, what are the next steps?*
*I think the best way forward is …*
*Julie, can we leave you to prepare an action plan to discuss at the next meeting?*
*So, before the next meeting I'm going to … and you're going to …*

# Exercises

**58.1 Match the beginning and end of each phrase. Then write the whole phrase next to item 1–9 below with the closest meaning.**

| | |
|---|---|
| Because | well as that |
| Of | the whole |
| In | course |
| In | fact |
| Shall | of this |
| As | seems that |
| On | be honest |
| It | terms of |
| To | we |

1 Actually _____
2 Also _____
3 Apparently _____
4 Frankly _____
5 In general _____
6 In relation to _____
7 Let's _____
8 Obviously _____
9 Therefore _____ *Because of this*

**58.2 Complete the sentences with phrases from Exercise 58.1 Write both possibilities to help you remember.**

1 There have been some important new developments with the Danube project. *(show a consequence)*
   _Therefore / Because of this_ I'm calling an urgent meeting for next Monday.

2 Our investments have lost 15% of their value over the last quarter. *(be honest)* _____ it could have been worse.

3 *(speak generally)* _____ I agree with what you're saying, but there is one point I'm not sure about.

4 Vendo would be a better supplier for us. They have a good record for quality and their prices are reasonable. *(add another point)* _____ they have very fast delivery times.

5 Our legal department said the contract was OK, but there have been quite a few alterations since then. *(make a suggestion)* _____ ask them to have another look at it?

6 Our competitor's product now has more market share than ours. *(show something is surprising but true)* _____ it's been selling very well for some time but we never really noticed.

7 Product development costs and manufacturing costs should be around €400,000. *(introduce a different point)* _____ marketing, we'll probably need another €200,000.

8 Their Sales Director is leaving. *(you are uncertain)* _____ he's been offered a job in Hong Kong.

**58.3 Match the beginning and end of each phrase. Then write the whole phrase next to phrase a–h below with the closest meaning.**

| | |
|---|---|
| What | the next steps? |
| Can I just | come in here? |
| Can you be a | to what I was saying |
| So, in other | didn't catch that. |
| So what are | words, … . Is that right? |
| Sorry, I don't | follow you. |
| Sorry, I | little more specific? |
| Getting back | about you? |

a Anyway, as I was saying … _____
b Are you saying …? _____
c Can I just say something? _____
d Can you give a few more details? _____
e So what is the best way forward? _____
f Sorry, I missed that. _____
g Sorry, I'm not with you. _____
h What do you think? _____ *What about you?*

**58.4 Look back at the previous exercise. Which pair of phrases would you use if:**

1 You don't understand. __g__
2 You want to ask for repetition. _____
3 You want to use your own words to check. _____
4 You want to ask for more detailed information. _____
5 You want to invite someone else to speak. _____
6 You want to interrupt. _____
7 You want to go back to a previous topic. _____
8 You want to discuss action points. _____

**58.5 Fill in the missing letters.**

a Can we leave you to pr_ _are an a_ _ion p_ _n?
b I'm sorry, could you g_ o_ _ _ that again?
c I think that's a_ f_ _ a_ we can go today.
d OK, let's get d_ _ _ to bu_ _ _ _ _ _.
e OK, shall we m_ _e o_ to di_ _ _ss …
f Perhaps we can co_ _ b_ _ _ t_ this later?
g Taking e_ _ _ _thing into co_ _ _ _ _ _ation, it s_ _ _s to me that …
h The pur_ _ _e of this m_ _ _ _ _g is to …

**58.6 Look back at the previous exercise. Which phrase would you use if:**

1 There has been some social conversation and now you want to start the meeting. _____
2 You want to introduce the subject of the meeting. _____
3 You want to change the topic. _____
4 You want to ask for repetition. _____
5 You want to block an interruption. _____
6 You want to say the meeting is nearly finished. _____
7 You want to review and conclude. _____
8 You want someone to do something before the next meeting. _____

# 59 Presentations: an introduction

There are many books and training courses on how to give presentations. But even without training you can give a good presentation if you a) have a real passion for your subject matter, b) have information that is genuinely interesting to your audience, and c) speak clearly and use your voice to emphasize key points.

## Planning the content

When planning the content of your talk, begin by writing down the 'take home message'. This is the summary of your talk that you want the audience to remember. Write it as three short bullet points, and consider making this your final slide. Once you have it, work backwards and build your talk so that everything relates to this key message.

Plan the start and finish carefully. Typical ideas for the opening are:

- Thank the organizers for inviting you.
- A reference to 'here and now' (the occasion/the place/the audience).
- Ask a question that is in the minds of the audience and that you will answer in your talk.

To close you might finish with the slide showing your 'take home message' plus a new, more personal, final comment that relates to it. Then remember to thank the audience for coming.

## Preparing your slides

You can download a free template (= basic layout and design for every slide) from the internet, or create your own. When preparing the individual slides, remember to keep the amount of text on each slide to a minimum. Use keywords, and then give more explanation in your talk. You can include more detail in your handouts.

Make use of visuals: use images, short video clips, graphs and charts, colours. But don't over-use them – you don't want to distract the audience. Images should reinforce your message – they shouldn't be decoration.

## Equipment

To give your presentation/talk you'll need your laptop with the presentation saved on it, a projector with a spare bulb, a screen, and the right cables to connect them all together. An extension lead is also useful if the power socket on the wall is some distance away. You may be speaking using a microphone (perhaps a small wireless clip microphone that attaches to your clothing), and your voice will be heard through speakers. Some or all of these things may be provided by the venue, and often all you have to bring is your presentation saved on a memory stick.

It can be useful to have a flipchart or whiteboard in the room as well – for example for writing up ideas that come from a Q&A (= question and answer) session at the end of the talk. You'll also need any handouts you plan to distribute.

Remember to get to the room early to test all the technology, adjust the projector, stand on the stage and see how it feels, arrange the seating, check that there is a glass of water, etc.

## Performance

You want your talk to sound convincing, and also to maintain your audience's attention. To do this you need to:

- Be yourself. Let your natural enthusiasm for the subject express itself. Don't hide your personality behind your content or your slides.
- Speak freely. Never read your slides word by word.
- Speak with confidence: clearly, calmly, slowly and strongly.
- Maintain eye contact with the audience, smile and look around the room frequently. There may be other examples of body language that you personally should or shouldn't do, but the problem is that most of them are outside your control once you start speaking. Perhaps ask a colleague to attend one of your presentations and then give you advice on how to improve.
- Pause often, for example after making a key point or when showing a new slide. Allow the audience time to think, digest information, understand a visual, make notes, make a connection with their personal experience, etc.
- Use your voice to create impact. First decide which key ideas you want to stress. Then, as you speak these words, say them with emphasis for maximum impact. Pause just afterwards – allow the audience time to absorb the idea. See Exercises 59.2 and 59.3.
- Use a few public speaking techniques. In particular use rhetorical questions (where you ask a question and then answer it yourself), and repetition of words and phrases. The extracts in Exercises 59.2 and 59.3 show examples of both.

# Exercises

**59.1 Match the words in the box with the comments.**

> extension lead    flipcharts    handouts    keywords
> ~~projector~~    slide    stage    template

1 Are you sure It's powerful enough to give a clear image on the screen from the back of the room? _projector_
2 I haven't decided whether to give them out at the beginning or at the end of my talk. _____
3 You'll be speaking up there. _____
4 Let's get two or three and put them at the sides of the room and by the door. During the break people can write comments and questions on them. _____
5 This one is going to be difficult to read from the back of the room – the font size is quite small. _____
6 The projector and laptop are going to be here. But the socket is over there. Can you find a technician and tell him what we need? _____
7 All my slides are based on a standard design that the company gives us. It has our logo at the top. _____
8 My final slide will just have three bullet points saying: Innovation, Design, Technology. _____

**59.2 Look at the presentation extract in the box. Note that it is unpunctuated. Places where the speaker could pause for impact are marked with // and key words to be stressed are underlined.**

> Take a look at this slide // you have a bucket // a few rocks // some small stones // some sand // and some water // now // put the rocks in the bucket // is it full // no // put the small stones in around the rocks // is it full // no // put the sand in // give it a shake // is it full // no // put the water in // now it's full // you got everything inside the bucket // well done // my talk this morning // ladies and gentlemen // is about time management // the point is this // do the main tasks first // or the sand and water issues will fill up your day // if you leave those big rocks until last // you might not even have space for them.

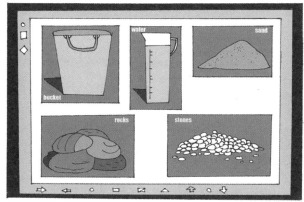

**Practise reading the text aloud several times. Create maximum impact.**

**59.3 Study the presentation extract below. Note that it is unpunctuated. Write // where you will pause and <u>underline</u> key words you will stress.**

> I want to ask you a question what is the difference between data and information I'll tell you the difference data are infinite in number they cost almost nothing and are worth almost nothing information on the other hand is meaningful data it is a key ingredient in decision making and is enormously useful and valuable to managers but how exactly do you turn data into information the answer is with business intelligence software and ladies and gentlemen we are one of the world's leading providers of that software.

**Check in the Answer Key. Your version may be slightly different but equally good. Then practise reading the text aloud several times.**

**59.4 Read the article, then underline the correct word in italics in the comment below.**

## How (NOT) To Give a Presentation

**Want to know how to give a great presentation? Here are some Top Tips to help you.**

* Begin by establishing how impressive you are. Make sure the audience knows all about your wonderful achievements. Promote your company at every opportunity. After all, this presentation is about you.
* Explain in detail what you are going to talk about, before you get to the main contents. You know how people love reading the table of contents in a book? It builds suspense. It's exciting.
* Get the audience on your side by using that joke you heard last week. It's got a clever double meaning and everyone will understand it and find it hilarious.
* Every slide should be packed with information. Use as many bullet points and words as possible. If you can't fit everything onto one slide, try a smaller font. Feel free to use several slides to explain things properly.
* Read aloud every word on your slides. Audiences have difficulty reading, particularly if the font size is small, and it's your responsibility to help them.
* Summarize everything at the end. Audiences forget things so easily. Spend the last few minutes patiently going over everything they just heard and saw.
* If you run out of time at the end, keep going. The audience paid good money to see your presentation, so make sure they see it all. Your time is important.
* Don't take any questions. The content and quality of your presentation speaks for itself.

Comment: the author of this article is being _serious / ironic_.

## First few words

Welcome everyone warmly. Thank the organizers. Make a reference to 'here and now' to relax the audience and show your human side.

*Good morning everyone and thanks for coming.*
*I'm very happy to be here. It's always a pleasure to visit …*
    *(+ say something nice about the place where you are)*
*I hope that after the coffee no-one will fall asleep during my presentation!*
*Before I begin, I'd like to thank the organizers for inviting me here today. In particular, a big thank you to Marissa for making this event possible / all her hard work behind the scenes.*
*Can everybody see the screen?*
*Can you hear me at the back of the room?*
*Let me start by saying a few words about myself.*

The audience needs to know whether they should ask questions during or after your presentation.

*My presentation this morning will take around 30 minutes, and that will leave plenty of time for questions at the end.*
*Please feel free to ask questions during my presentation – just put up your hand.*

And it may be helpful to mention the different areas you will cover.

*I've divided my talk into three parts. First I'll give you an overview of … Then I'll look at … And finally I'll talk in a little more detail about …*

## Starting the main presentation

Start with something to get attention: a question that is in the minds of the audience, a visual, a surprising statistic, a story, a quote (for ideas type 'business quotes' into an internet search engine).

*The title of my presentation is … Why did I choose this title? Because …*
*This morning I'm going to talk about … This is an issue that affects us all.*
*Take a look at this picture. What does it tell you about …?*
*Somebody once said that … (+ quote)*

## Developing a point

The language for 'Building an argument' in Unit 57 will be relevant here. Also:

*To give you some background, let me explain …*
*I'd like to stress one very important point.*
*To give you an example of what I mean, …*

## Rhetorical questions

A rhetorical question is one that you answer yourself. It is a way to get the interest of the audience.

*So what's the problem? The problem is …*
*So what's the solution? The solution is …*
*What exactly is Critical Path Analysis? CPA is …*
*What does this mean in terms of costs / business opportunities / planning for the future? It means …*
*So what should we do? My answer is simple. We should …*

## Digressing and returning

In the middle of speaking you often want to talk about something different for a moment. This is called digressing. Afterwards you return to the main point.

*To digress for a moment, …*
*Going back to what I was saying before, …*

## Changing the subject

Signal clearly to the audience where one subject ends and the next one begins. You might want to ask for questions before moving on.

*OK, that's all I want to say about … Does anyone have a question? Yes, the gentleman at the back. Yes, the lady over there.*
*I'd like to move on to my next point.*
*That brings me to my next point, which is …*
*Turning now to a different matter, …*

## Referring to visuals

Make sure any graph, chart, diagram or table is clearly labelled (eg the units on the two axes). Give the audience a few moments to study it before you start talking about the details.

*Have a look at this next slide. The horizontal axis shows … and the vertical axis shows …*
*As you can see, …*
*You'll notice on the diagram that …*
*The figures clearly show that …*

## Finishing

It is common to end with a review / summary.

*OK, just before I finish, let me go over the main points again.*
*So, to sum up / summarize, …*
*That brings me to the end of my presentation.*
*Thank you very much for listening and I hope you found it useful / interesting.*
*Are there any questions?*

# Exercises

**60.1 Complete each sentence with a word from the box. Find a solution that uses each word once.**

| affect | bring | digress | divide | have |
|--------|-------|---------|--------|------|
| notice | show | ~~start~~ | stress | take |

1 Let me _start_ by saying a few words about myself.
2 My presentation will _____ around 30 minutes.
3 I've _____d my talk into three parts.
4 This is an issue that _____s us all.
5 I'd like to _____ one very important point.
6 And in a moment I will take you on a tour of the factory. To _____ for a moment, can I just check that you've all signed in at reception?
7 That _____s me to my next point.
8 _____ a look at this next slide.
9 You'll _____ on the diagram that there is very little space available for the cooling fan.
10 The figures clearly _____ that demand for oil is still rising.

**60.2 Put the words into order to make sentences from a presentation.**

1 Good morning for coming and everyone thanks.
   _Good morning everyone and thanks for coming._
2 I'd like to inviting the organizers for thank me here today.
3 Can you back me at the hear of the room?
4 Please ask free to feel questions during my presentation.
5 So does what this mean in costs of terms?
6 That's all I want to market about changes in the say.
7 Let me go again the main points over.
8 Thank you for very much listening and I hope it found you useful.

**60.3 Complete the phrases with these prepositions: *about, at, at, back, for, for, of, of, on, to, up.***

1 Good morning and thanks _____ coming.
2 Can you hear me _____ the back _____ the room?
3 I'll leave time at the end _____ questions.
4 First I'll give you an overview _____ the company, then I'll look _____ our new range of products, and finally I'll talk _____ opportunities for customization based on your own specific needs.
5 Going _____ to what I was saying before.
6 I'd like to move _____ to my next point.
7 Turning now _____ a different matter.
8 So, to sum _____, our values are these: Innovative Solutions, Strategic Partnerships and Global Vision.

**60.4 Match the beginning and end of each phrase.**

| It's always | in a little more detail |
| I'll give | free to ask questions |
| I'll talk | a pleasure |
| Please feel | you an overview |

| I'd like to move | me to the end |
| That brings | to stress |
| The figures | on now |
| And I'd like | you an example |
| To give | clearly show that |

**Now use the phrases to complete the presentation extract below. The first four phrases are used first.**

❝ Good morning everyone and thanks for coming. I'm very happy to be here. [1] _It's always a pleasure_ to visit the Czech Republic – I have many good friends here.

Before I begin I'd like to thank the organizers for inviting me here today. In particular, a big thank you to Tomas for all his hard work behind the scenes.

OK. My presentation this morning will take around 40 minutes. [2]_____ during my presentation, and there will also be time for questions at the end.

I've divided my talk into three parts. First [3]_____ of Smart Think Consultancy. Then I'll look at the area that is, I think, of most interest to you – Business Process Outsourcing. And finally [4]_____ about some ideas for BPO for your own company, based on the initial research we have done.

*Later in the presentation*
[5]_____ one very important point. We do deliver value to our clients. This next slide lists some of the companies we have worked with. Next to each name is an estimate of money saved as a result of our recommendations. [6]_____ using the services of Smart Think makes a direct impact on profitability and business success.

*Later in the presentation*
OK, that's all I want to say about Smart Think. [7]_____ to the subject of Business Process Outsourcing. What exactly is Business Process Outsourcing? It is using outside companies to handle your routine business activities – the ones that are not central to your mission. It leaves you free to do what you do best: product development, operations, sales and marketing. [8]_____ of what I mean, let's look at Human Resources outsourcing.

*Later in the presentation*
Right. [9]_____ of my presentation. Thank you very much for listening and I hope you found it useful. Are there any questions? ❞

**60.5 ⏻ 10 You are going to hear eight phrases. Listen and repeat.**

# 61 Word families: verbs and nouns

If you know a word in different grammatical forms (eg verb, noun, adjective) you can express yourself in a more varied way.

We **compete** against several larger companies.
**Competition** in my industry is very strong.
This market is very **competitive**.

## Changing a verb to a noun

You can use a suffix (= letters added at the end of a word) to change a verb into noun. Some common suffixes are given below. There may be other small differences at the end of the word as well.

**-ion, -sion, -tion, -ation, -ication, -ition**

apply – application        innovate – innovation
compete – competition      motivate – motivation
decide – decision          produce – production
discuss – discussion       qualify – qualification
explain – explanation      repeat – repetition

**-ment**

achieve – achievement      improve – improvement
advertise – advertisement  invest – investment
employ – employment        manage – management

**-ance**

appear – appearance        maintain – maintenance
insure – insurance         perform – performance

**-al**

arrive – arrival           refuse – refusal

**-y**

apologize – apology        discover – discovery
deliver – delivery         recover – recovery

Examples
When are they going to **decide**?
When are they going to make a **decision**?
Our shareholders will **invest** another half a million euros.
We need to make a substantial **investment** in new technology.
The whole sales team **performed** well last year.
My salary depends on my **performance**.
I hope the economy **recovers** soon.
We need to see a **recovery** in the economy before employing more staff.

Some verbs can make more than one noun. For example the verb 'produce' has the nouns 'production' = 'the process of making things in large quantities' and 'productivity' = 'the efficiency of production'.

## More verbs changing to nouns

The suffixes below are less common, but the words are all important in business vocabulary.

advise – advice            fly – flight
analyze – analysis         grow – growth
behave – behaviour         lose – loss
choose – choice            sell – sale(s)
complain – complaint       sign – signature
criticize – criticism      succeed – success
fail – failure             store – storage

Examples
I think we should **choose** option B.
I think option B is the better **choice**.
We **sell** a lot of this particular model.
**Sales** of this model are very strong.

## Words for people, jobs, etc

Nouns for people are often based on a root word with -er, -or, -ist, -eer, -ant and -ian.

advertis**er**, advis**er**, lawy**er**, mana**ger**
competit**or**, direct**or**, innovat**or**, invest**or**
econom**ist**, pharmac**ist**, special**ist**, scient**ist**
engin**eer**, mountain**eer**, pion**eer**
account**ant**, applic**ant**, consult**ant**
electric**ian**, politic**ian**, statistic**ian**, technic**ian**

And note these irregular forms: analyst and critic.

The ending -ee means 'someone who receives something'. So:

an employ**ee** receives employment from an employ**er**
an interview**ee** is asked questions by an interview**er**
a train**ee** receives training from a train**er**

## Adjectives part of the same word families

Many verbs from the previous sections make an adjective with -ing or -ed: growing, failed, improved, etc.

It is a **growing** problem for us.
This is an **improved** version of our earlier model.

There are other suffixes used to make adjectives: achiev**able**, analyti**cal**, apologet**ic**, competit**ive**, criti**cal**, innovat**ive**, manage**able**, product**ive**, success**ful**, etc.

He was very **apologetic** when I saw him.
With enough resources this problem is **manageable**.

# Exercises

**61.1 Look at nouns 1–10 below and write the verb form. All the verbs appear on the page opposite.**

1  apology  _apologize_
2  application  _____
3  arrival  _____
4  competition  _____
5  decision  _____
6  delivery  _____
7  explanation  _____
8  investment  _____
9  performance  _____
10  production  _____

**61.2 Complete the sentences with a word from Exercise 61.1. The word may be a noun or a verb.**

1  What time does your flight ___arrive___ ?
2  We've been discussing this issue for weeks. In the meeting tomorrow we finally have to take a _____ .
3  I heard that the Sales Director is leaving the company. Why don't you _____ for his job?
4  We don't have any of these items in stock right now, but we're expecting a _____ sometime next week.
5  It's our supplier on the phone. They can't ship our order until next week and they are calling to _____ . Do you want to speak to them? *(two possible answers)*

**61.3 Look at nouns 1–10 below and write the verb form. This time the verbs do not appear opposite.**

1  assistance  _assist_
2  communication  _____
3  guidance  _____
4  identification  _____
5  measurement  _____
6  reduction  _____
7  repayment  _____
8  requirement  _____
9  variation  _____
10  withdrawal  _____

**61.4 Complete the sentences with a word from Exercise 61.3. The word may be a noun or a verb.**

1  The bank has agreed to lend us the full amount, and we have to _____ the loan in two years.
2  What's going on? Why is there so much _____ in the figures from week to week?
3  The equipment isn't working properly but I can't _____ exactly where the fault is.
4  I don't know if the new machine will fit at the side of the assembly line. We'll have to _____ the space very carefully.
5  Yes, your products are certainly well-designed. But I must tell you that we have a very specific _____ in relation to quality assurance.
6  Consumer groups say the product isn't safe. I think we'll have to _____ it from the market.

**61.5 Complete the sentences with the correct form of the word in brackets.**

1  I just need your ___signature___ (sign) here at the bottom of the page.
2  Install a good security solution for your IT network or let hackers enter the system – the _____ (choose) is yours.
3  If you want to _____ (success) in this business, you need to focus on the customer.
4  Over the last year we have seen significant _____ (grow) in revenues.
5  The best _____ (advise) I can give you is this: bring your boss solutions, not problems.
6  Some of these pieces have defects – I'm going to call them this afternoon to _____ (complaint).

**61.6 Continue as before. This time the words you need are all adjectives.**

1  It's been a very _____ (success) year for us. Profits and market share are both up.
2  Our latest aero-engines feature an _____ (innovate) new technology.
3  Things are going well and I think the annual sales targets are definitely _____ (achieve).
4  We have a skilled and highly motivated workforce. It's our most important _____ (compete) advantage.
5  Thank you for coming. I thought it was a very _____ (produce) meeting.
6  She has a Masters in Financial Economics and her _____ (analyze) skills are excellent.

**61.7 Complete the words for people and types of jobs by filling in the missing letters. Items 11–15 do not appear opposite.**

1  econom _ _ _
2  account _ _ _
3  competit _ _
4  engin _ _ _
5  law _ _ _
6  electric _ _ _
7  consult _ _ _
8  advertis _ _
9  direct _ _
10  analy _ _
11  visit _ _
12  suppli _ _
13  assist _ _ _
14  administrat _ _ _
15  particip _ _ _

**Continue as before. Some words do not appear opposite.**

16  We had over fifty applic _ _ _s for the job, but after looking at all their CVs we've reduced that to a shortlist of six interview_ _s.
17  Let me explain our distribution channel. We are the manufactur_ _, and we supply the distribut_ _s. They sell to retail_ _s who sell to the end-us_ _s.
18  Our company has over 200 employ_ _s working at Head Office.
19  I'm going to open my own McDonalds restaurant. I've decided the best way to have my own business is to become a franchis_ _.
20  Our technology has a patent, but if you want to use it, you can pay an annual fee and become a licens_ _.

## Changing an adjective to a noun

You can use a suffix (= letters added at the end of a word) to change an adjective into noun. Some common suffixes are given below. There may be other small differences at the end of the word as well.

### -ity

| | |
|---|---|
| able – ability | necessary – necessity |
| available – availability | possible – possibility |
| equal – equality | popular – popularity |
| flexible – flexibility | reliable – reliability |
| major – majority | secure – security |

### -ness

| | |
|---|---|
| aware – awareness | fit – fitness |
| busy – business | friendly – friendliness |
| careless – carelessness | polite – politeness |
| dark – darkness | thick – thickness |
| effective – effectiveness | weak – weakness |

Examples
*Our adventure holidays are **available** with a wide range of extras.*
*Customers often can't find our products in the shops – we need to improve their **availability**.*
*The marketing campaign is going to be very expensive. How do we know that it will be **effective**?*
*I have to question the **effectiveness** of all the money we spend on marketing.*

## Changing a noun to an adjective

In the examples below a noun changes into an adjective with a suffix.

### -al

| | |
|---|---|
| accident – accidental | origin – original |
| critic – critical | option – optional |
| economy – economical | politics – political |
| finance – financial | profession – professional |
| influence – influential | season – seasonal |
| nation – national | try – trial |

### -ent, -ant

| | |
|---|---|
| confidence – confident | importance – important |
| difference – different | intelligence – intelligent |
| efficiency – efficient | patience – patient |

### -ic

| | |
|---|---|
| apology – apologetic | pessimism – pessimistic |
| economy – economic | problem – problematic |
| enthusiasm – enthusiastic | realism – realistic |
| optimism – optimistic | science – scientific |

Examples
*What are young people wearing this **season**?*
*Demand for ice cream is very **seasonal**.*
*We've improved the **efficiency** of the process.*
*The process is now much more **efficient**.*
*The business relationship is full of **problems**.*
*The business relationship is very **problematic**.*
Some nouns can make more than one adjective. For example the noun 'economy' has the adjectives 'economic' = 'relating to the economy' and 'economical' = 'not costing much money'. And note that the study of the economy is called 'economics'.

Also note these adjectives formed from numbers: *twentieth, thirtieth, hundredth*, etc.

## Verbs part of the same word families

Many words from the previous sections make a verb with 'be' + adjective: *be aware, be possible, be realistic, be efficient,* etc.

## Dimensions: adjective, noun, verb

With dimensions the adjective form is often the simplest and most common. Note carefully how to build the other forms.

| adjective | noun | verb |
|---|---|---|
| deep | depth | deepen |
| high | height | heighten |
| long | length | lengthen |
| short | shortness | shorten |
| thick | thickness | thicken |
| wide | width | widen |

Examples
*The steel bar is five metres **long**.*
*The **length** of the steel bar is five metres.*
*My talk at the conference was quite **short** – only 40 minutes including questions at the end.*

*The previous speaker finished late and I had to **shorten** my talk.*

# Exercises

**62.1** Look at the table below and write the missing form. The nouns end in *-ness* or *-ity* and the adjectives end in *-al* or *-ic*.

| noun | adjective |
|---|---|
| 1 accident | *accidental* |
| 2 apology | |
| 3 _____ | aware |
| 4 _____ | effective |
| 5 enthusiasm | |
| 6 _____ | major |
| 7 _____ | necessary |
| 8 optimism | |
| 9 _____ | polite |
| 10 _____ | reliable |
| 11 season | |
| 12 try | |

**62.2** Complete the sentences with a word from Exercise 62.1. The word may be a noun or an adjective.

1 I see that the sixties hippy look is very much in fashion this _____ season _____ .

2 You can have the product on a _____ basis to see if you like it.

3 The process is quick, cheap and produces the results you want. It's both efficient and _____ .

4 It's a private company, and the _____ of the shares are held by the founder of the company and his close family members.

5 German cars are generally considered to be very _____ .

6 The project has run into some problems, but I am _____ that there is a solution.

7 I'm sorry – I owe you an _____ . I was in a bad mood yesterday and I'm sorry for what I said.

8 We will have to make cutbacks. We have no choice. It's _____ for our survival.

**62.3** Look at the adjectives below, then fill in the nouns. Some of the words do not appear opposite.

| | |
|---|---|
| 1 confident | confide_ _ _ |
| 2 efficient | efficie_ _ _ |
| 3 important | importa_ _ _ |
| 4 creative | creativ_ _ _ |
| 5 frequent | frequen_ _ |
| 6 similar | simil_ _ _ _ _ |

**62.4** Complete the sentences with a word from Exercise 62.3. The word may be an adjective or a noun.

1 Model 800 is very _____ to model 600, but it has more capacity and is designed for commercial use.

2 It's her first job after university and she's a bit lacking in self-_____ .

3 Thanks to the _____ and imagination of our marketing team we won a prize for Innovative Product of the Year.

**62.5** Complete the sentences with the correct form of the word in brackets.

1 The success of this product is _____ critical _____ (critic) to our survival.

2 Like every organization we have our strengths and our _____ es (weak).

3 I don't expect the _____ (economy) situation to improve until next year at the earliest.

4 I studied _____ (economy) at university.

5 Nowadays when you buy a car you have to think about whether it's _____ (economy) to run.

6 Next year we will celebrate the _____ (hundred) anniversary of our company.

**62.6** Complete the dialogue in a car manufacturing company with the words in the box.

| | | | |
|---|---|---|---|
| deep | depth | high | heighten |
| long | length | short | shorten |

PETRA: Here are the latest design ideas for our next generation of electric powered cars.

ERIK: The styling looks great. But the car is meant to be easy to park. I'm a little worried about its [1]_____ .

PETRA: Why? It's 4200 mm [2]_____ . That's about the same as a VW Golf.

ERIK: But electric cars need to be smaller. Can't we [3]_____ the vehicle?

PETRA: That would be very difficult. We'd have to completely change the interior of the car. I think it's [4]_____ enough as it is.

ERIK: Changing the interior may be a good idea anyway. For tall people there isn't much space – I think it would be better to [5]_____ the roof by about 30 mm.

PETRA: The roof needs to be [6]_____er above the passengers' heads?

ERIK: Yes. And the car could be a little wider as well.

PETRA: Let me get this right. First you want a smaller overall size from front to back to make it easier to park, but then you want a larger interior.

ERIK: Yes, we can do it if we completely remove the back seat. There would only be space for the driver and front passenger, but it would give us a really [7]_____ boot*.

PETRA: Well, it's true that the [8]_____ of the boot would be a great selling point. I'll ask the design guys to see what they can come up with. It's certainly an interesting solution.

*AmE trunk

Unit 62 gave adjectives with the suffixes *-al*, *-ent*, *-ant* and *-ic*. This unit gives adjectives with other suffixes. Note that in this unit the root word may be a noun or a verb, whereas in Unit 62 it was always a noun.

**-able**

| | |
|---|---|
| *accept – acceptable* | *manage – manageable* |
| *achieve – achievable* | *predict – predictable* |
| *advise – advisable* | *profit – profitable* |
| *believe – believable* | *reason – reasonable* |
| *change – changeable* | *rely – reliable* |
| *consider – considerable* | *value – valuable* |
| *enjoy – enjoyable* | *vary – variable* |

**-ary**

| | |
|---|---|
| *budget – budgetary* | *inflation – inflationary* |
| *imagine – imaginary* | *second – secondary* |

**-ible**

| | |
|---|---|
| *response – responsible* | *sense – sensible* |

**-ive**

| | |
|---|---|
| *compete – competitive* | *imagine – imaginative* |
| *create – creative* | *produce – productive* |
| *effect – effective* | *sense – sensitive* |
| *execute – executive* | *support – supportive* |
| *expense – expensive* | *talk – talkative* |

**-ous**

| | |
|---|---|
| *ambition – ambitious* | *luxury – luxurious* |
| *danger – dangerous* | *number – numerous* |
| *disaster – disastrous* | *suspicion – suspicious* |

**-ward**

| | |
|---|---|
| *back – backward* | *up – upward* |

**-y**

| | |
|---|---|
| *fun – funny* | *noise – noisy* |
| *health – healthy* | *rain – rainy* |
| *luck – lucky* | *wealth – wealthy* |

Examples

*Thanks for your help, I can **manage** on my own now.*
*The problem is serious, but **manageable**.*
*We **produce** 200 vehicles a day at this site.*
*With the new technology our workforce is a lot more **productive**.*
*The product recall was a public relations **disaster** for Toyota.*
*The product recall was **disastrous** for Toyota.*
*There's a high level of **noise** in the factory.*
*The factory is very **noisy**.*

The adjectives above ending in *-able* show that something can be done. For example, something *believable* can be believed.

Note also that two adjectives are formed from 'sense': *sensitive* (= reacting quickly or strongly; easily hurt; showing that you care) and *sensible* (= reasonable and practical). These words are easily confused.

## Adjectives with *-ful* and *-less*

Some adjectives are formed by adding the suffixes *-ful* or *-less* to a root word. The meaning is 'with' or 'without' something.

| | |
|---|---|
| care | *careful / careless* |
| harm | *harmful / harmless* |
| help | *helpful / helpless* |
| hope | *hopeful / hopeless* |
| power | *powerful / powerless* |
| use | *useful / useless* |

Examples

*Our products are not **harmful** to the environment.*
*He thinks his joking is **harmless** fun, but some people are quite offended.*
*I'm **hopeful** we can sign the contract next week.*
*There's nothing we can do. The situation is **hopeless**.*

Sometimes only one of the suffixes is used:

| | |
|---|---|
| end | *endful / endless* |
| forget | *forgetful / forgetless* |
| gratitude | *grateful / grateless* |
| point | *pointful / pointless* |
| skill | *skillful / skillless* |
| stress | *stressful / stressless* |
| success | *successful / successness* |

## Adjectives with *-ish* and *-like*

The suffixes *-ish* and *-like* both mean 'similar to' or 'approximately'. Here are some examples.

*childish* (behaviour)
*bluish* (colour)
*fortyish* (age of someone)
*businesslike* (attitude to something)
*dreamlike* (state of mind)
*lifelike* (painting)

*A life-like painting*

# Exercises

**63.1 Look at the root words 1–8 below and write the adjective form. The suffixes may be *-able*, *-ive* or *-ous*.**

| | | |
|---|---|---|
| 1 | accept | accept *able* |
| 2 | compete | competit_____ |
| 3 | expense | expens_____ |
| 4 | number | numer_____ |
| 5 | product | product_____ |
| 6 | profit | profit_____ |
| 7 | suspicion | suspici_____ |
| 8 | value | valu_____ |

**63.2 Complete the sentences with a word from Exercise 63.1. The word may be the root word on the left or the adjective on the right.**

1 Her experience of the Chinese market makes her very ___*valuable*___ to the company.
2 General Electric are a huge industrial, engineering and services conglomerate. Their product lines are far too _____ to list.
3 The unions voted to _____ a pay increase of 4%. That's in line with the rate of inflation.
4 As a service company, labour costs are our biggest _____ .
5 I do all the difficult tasks as soon as I arrive at work – like most people I'm more _____ in the morning.

**63.3 Continue as in Exercise 63.1. Write adjective forms on the right. This time the words do not appear opposite, but the choice of endings is the same: *-able*, *-ive* or *-ous*.**

| | | |
|---|---|---|
| 1 | change | change_____ |
| 2 | disrupt | disrupt_____ |
| 3 | fame | fam_____ |
| 4 | invent | invent_____ |
| 5 | impress | impress_____ |
| 6 | memory | memor_____ |
| 7 | mystery | mysteri_____ |
| 8 | suit | suit_____ |

**63.4 Complete the sentences with a word from Exercise 63.3. The word may be the root word on the left or the adjective on the right.**

1 Every few years a ___*disruptive*___ technology comes along which completely transforms business. Automobiles, plastics and personal computers are all examples.
2 How on earth did I save the wrong presentation on my USB drive? I just don't know – it'll always be a _____ .
3 The project will begin in November. When would be a _____ time to have a kick-off meeting?
4 I'm going to wear an Armani suit at my job interview. You know what they say: 'Dress to _____ !'
5 If you're going to the UK in April, take a raincoat as well as a light jacket. You never know – the weather is very _____ at that time of the year.

**63.5 Complete the second sentence with one word so that it has the same meaning as the first sentence. Use the adjective form of the underlined word.**

1 Many companies <u>compete</u> in our market.
Our market is very ___*competitive*___ .
2 Many people with a lot of <u>wealth</u> have a second home in the south of France.
Many _____ people have a second home in the south of France.
3 There would be a <u>danger</u> if we entered the market without doing more research first.
It would be _____ to enter the market without doing more research first.
4 We will have to cut back some projects for reasons connected to the <u>budget</u>.
We will have to cut back some projects for _____ reasons.
5 Our last marketing campaign had a great <u>effect</u>.
Our last marketing campaign was very _____ .
6 I'm not surprised she became Director of Marketing. She has a lot of <u>ambition</u>.
I'm not surprised she became Director of Marketing. She is very _____ .
7 What you're saying makes a lot of <u>sense</u>.
What you're saying is very _____ .
8 This device quickly <u>senses</u> pollutants in the water.
This device is _____ to pollutants in the water.

**63.6 One word in each sentence is wrong. Cross it out and write the correct word.**

1 It's a delicate situation. We'll have to be very ~~careless~~.
___*careful*___
2 We need a new photocopier – this old one is useful. The paper keeps getting stuck. _____
3 Thanks for all your help. I really am very grated.
_____
4 She's the President of the Chamber of Commerce and a powerless figure in the city. _____
5 That's what I don't like about my job – the endingless meetings. _____
6 Why continue talking to them? It's completely pointful. Let's refer the matter to our lawyers. _____

**63.7 Fill in the missing letters.**

1 We're going to introduce a new snack bar made from biscuits, chocolate and caramel. It will be soft and sweet and have a yellow_ _ _ brown colour inside.
2 Try not to get angry when you make a complaint. It's better to keep a business_ _ _ _ attitude at all times.

A 'prefix' is a group of letters added to the beginning of a word to change its meaning. Some common prefixes are given below.

### co-/com-/con-
*co-/com-/con-* mean 'with' or 'together': *cooperate, co-worker, combine, compatible, conference, confirm, connect, context*

### de-
*de-* means 'opposite' or 'reduce': *decaffeinated, decentralized, demotivated, deregulate, devalue*

### dis-
*dis-* means 'opposite' or 'negative': *disagree, disappear, disapprove, disconnect, discontinued, discourage, dislike*

### inter-
*inter-* means 'between': *interactive, intermediary, international, interview*

### mis-
*mis-* means 'wrongly' or 'badly': *miscalculate, misinform, misjudge, misinterpret, mismanage, mistake, misunderstand*

### mono- and multi-
*mono-* means 'one': *monolingual, monopoly, monorail, monotonous*
*multi-* means 'many': *multicultural, multinational, multi-purpose, multitasking*

### over- and under-
*over-* means 'too much': *overcharge, overcook, overestimate, overqualified, overwork*
*under-* means 'too little' or 'not enough': *undercharge, undercook, underestimate, underuse*

### pre- and post-
*pre-* means 'before': *prearranged, predict, preliminary, prepackaged, prepare, prepaid*
*post-* means 'after': *postgraduate, postscript*

### pro- and anti-
*pro-* means 'in favour of': *pro-European*
*anti-* means 'against': *anti-European, anti-theft device, antiwar protestors*
*anti-* can also mean 'opposite': *anticlockwise, anticlimax, antisocial*

### re-
*re-* means 'again': *redesign, renegotiate, replace, return, review, rewrite*

### sub-
*sub-* means 'below' or 'under' or 'less': *subcommittee, subcontract, substandard, sub-zero*

### un-
*un-* means 'opposite': *unload, unlock, unpack, unscrew*

## Prefixes to make negative adjectives

The opposite or negative form of an adjective can be made with *dis-, il-, im-, in-, ir-, non-* or *un-*.

*disabled, dishonest, disloyal, disorganized*
*illegal, illogical*
*impatient, impolite, impossible, impractical*
*incompetent, inconvenient, independent, inexperienced, indirect, inefficient, informal*
*irregular, irrelevant, irresponsible*
*non-essential, non-existent, non-negotiable, non-refundable, nonsense, non-standard*
*unable, unacceptable, unbelievable, uncertain, uncompetitive, unemployed, unfair, unfortunate, unhealthy, unpopular, unpredictable, unprofitable, unreliable, unsuccessful, unusual*

Examples
*Our local agent wants some money in cash to help with the customs clearance. It's completely **unacceptable**. It's not just **dishonest**, it's **illegal**.*

Prefixes to make negative verbs have already been given above: *de-, dis-, mis-* or *un-*.

## Other points

Note that many words have a prefix but the root word does not exist without it: *combine, connect, predict, prepare, underneath*, etc. The prefix does still keep its meaning in these cases.

Note also that a few prefixes have a hyphen (*pro-European, sub-zero*) while others can be written with or without (*co-worker/coworker*). Check in a dictionary if you are not sure.

*Pro*

*Anti*

# Exercises

**64.1 Fill in the missing letters to write the correct prefix. The following are used once each:** *anti-, com-, con-, de-, dis-, inter-, mis-, mono-, multi-, under-, pre-, re-, sub-, un-.*

1  _com_ bine
2  _____centralized
3  _____clockwise
4  _____continued
5  _____contract
6  _____estimate
7  _____firm
8  _____interpret
9  _____liminary
10 _____load
11 _____mediary
12 _____negotiate
13 _____poly
14 _____tasking

**64.2 Complete the sentences with a word from Exercise 64.1.**

1  Thank you for calling and I look forward to seeing you in Paris next week. I'll _confirm_ my flight time by email in a day or two.
2  Have you heard the news? They want to _____ the whole contract because of what they call 'changed circumstances'.
3  The full test results are not yet in, but the _____ data I have here show that the drug reduces cholesterol by around 40%.
4  We believe that local managers are the best people to understand their own markets. So decision making is _____ and only a small number of people work at Head Office.
5  They say that women are better at _____ than men, and that Brazilians are the world experts!
6  Traffic restrictions make life very difficult for shops in the city centre. Delivery vans can only _____ in the evening and at night.
7  I'm sorry, that model of pushchair has been _____ . But we do have the new range over there in the corner – have you seen them?
8  The cost of raw materials is rising, and the factory workers are demanding higher wages. I think your budget for production costs is an _____ .

**64.3 One of the four words in each group does not exist or is not used. Cross it out.**

1  delegate ~~demit~~ demotivate destroy
2  comparate compromise commuter component
3  mismanage misjudge misunderstand missucceed
4  discourage disapprove distake dislike
5  undersleep undercook undercharge underuse
6  overweight oversided overcrowded overworked
7  prepackage predict prearrange prefirm
8  unturn unscrew unlock unpack

**64.4 Complete each sentence with a word from Exercise 64.3. The words appear in order.**

1  To make progress with this negotiation we're going to have to make a _____ .
2  I think I _____d him. Now I know him better I can see that he's very good at his job.
3  I don't want to _____ you, but many people have tried that before and failed.
4  The meeting room on the first floor is very _____d. I think it would be better with a fridge and a microwave – for staff to use at breaktimes.
5  Who knows where the dollar will be against the euro a year from now? It's very hard to _____ .
6  Be careful. If you _____ the back of the machine, you might break the terms of the manufacturer's warranty.

**64.5 Fill in the missing letters.**

1  If something is not *successful*, it is _ _successful.
2  If something doesn't *exist*, it is _ _ -existent.
3  If something is not *efficient*, it is _ _efficient.
4  If something is not *predictable*, it is _ _predictable.
5  If something is not *popular*, it is _ _popular.
6  If something is not *essential*, it is _ _ -essential.

**64.6 Choose the correct word to fill each gap from A, B, C or D below.**

1  We're pretty _B_ in this office. You don't have to wear a suit unless you're meeting a client.
   A formal                  B informal
   C unformal                D deformal
2  The Board of Directors has set up a ____ to look into the possibility of a merger with GKN.
   A undercommittee          B multi-committee
   C subcommittee            D intercommittee
3  Our high labour costs and long holidays make us ____ in the global economy. It's a problem.
   A subcompetitive          B decompetitive
   C recompetitive           D uncompetitive
4  The pieces you need are ____ and we'll have to set up our machines for a special production run.
   A substandard             B non-standard
   C unstandard              D antistandard
5  Outsourcing our whole recruitment and selection process to an outside agency is probably a bit ____ .
   A impractical             B inpractical
   C unpractical             D mispractical
6  This product line has been ____ for years. It's time to replace it with something more modern.
   A interprofitable         B multiprofitable
   C misprofitable           D unprofitable
7  I think the sales assistant ____ me. The till receipt says €189.50 but I'm sure everything cost less than that.
   A overcharged             B undercharged
   C supercharged            D multi-charged

# 65 Word families: revision/extension I

Units 61–64 explored word families. Units 65–66 revise and extend this language area with an alphabetical list of business words. Note that adverbs (*commerce – commercially, direct – directly – indirectly*, etc) are not included.

**ABLE**
*be able* (v)
*ability* (n)
*inability* (n)
*able* (adj)
*unable* (adj)

**ACCEPT**
*accept* (v)
*acceptance* (n)
*acceptable* (adj)
*unacceptable* (adj)

**ACHIEVE**
*achieve* (v)
*achievement* (n)
*unachievable* (adj)
*achievable* (adj)

**ACT**
*act* (v)
*activate* (v)
*action* (n)
*activity* (n)
*active* (adj)
*inactive* (adj)

**ADD**
*add* (v)
*addition* (n)
*additional* (adj)

**ADVISE**
*advise* (v)
*advice* (n)
*adviser* (n)
*advisable* (adj)
*unadvisable* (adj)

**AGREE**
*agree* (v)
*disagree* (v)
*agreement* (n)
*disagreement* (n)
*agreeable* (adj)
*disagreeable* (adj)

**ANALYZE**
*analyze* (v)
*analysis* (n)
*analyst* (n)
*analytical* (adj)

**APPLY**
*apply* (v)
*application* (n)
*applicant* (n)
*applicable* (adj)

**ASSIST**
*assist* (v)
*assistance* (n)
*assistant* (n)

**ATTRACT**
*attract* (v)
*attraction* (n)
*attractive* (adj)

**AVAILABLE**
*be available* (v)
*availability* (n)
*available* (adj)
*unavailable* (adj)

**BENEFIT**
*benefit* (v)
*benefit* (n)
*beneficial* (adj)

**BUDGET**
*budget* (v)
*budget* (n)

**COMMERCE**
*commercialize* (v)
*commerce* (n)
*commercial* (adj)
*uncommercial* (adj)

**COMPETE**
*compete* (v)
*competition* (n)
*competitor* (n)
*competitive* (adj)
*uncompetitive* (adj)

**DECIDE**
*decide* (v)
*decision* (n)
*indecision* (n)
*decisive* (adj)
*indecisive* (adj)

**DELIVER**
*deliver* (v)
*delivery* (n)

**DIFFER**
*differ* (v)
*difference* (n)
*different* (adj)

**DIRECT**
*direct* (v)
*direction* (n)
*director* (n)
*direct* (adj)
*indirect* (adj)

**DISTRIBUTE**
*distribute* (v)
*distribution* (n)
*distributor* (n)

**ECONOMY**
*economize* (v)
*economy* (n)
*economist* (n)
*economics* (n)
*economic* (adj)
*economical* (adj)

**EFFICIENT**
*be efficient* (v)
*efficiency* (n)
*inefficiency* (n)
*efficient* (adj)
*inefficient* (adj)

**EMPLOY**
*employ* (v)
*employment* (n)
*unemployment* (n)
*employer* (n)
*employee* (n)
*employed* (adj)
*unemployed* (adj)

**EXPENSE**
*expense* (n)
*expenses* (n)
*expenditure* (n)
*expensive* (adj)
*inexpensive* (adj)

**EXPLAIN**
*explain* (v)
*explanation* (n)
*explanatory* (adj)

**EXPORT**
*export* (v)
*export* (n)
*exporter* (n)

**EXTEND**
*extend* (v)
*extent* (n)
*extension* (n)
*extensive* (adj)

**FINANCE**
*finance* (v)
*finance* (n)
*financier* (n)
*financial* (adj)

**GROW**
*grow* (v)
*growth* (n)

# Exercises

**65.1 Complete each sentence with the correct form of the word in capital letters at the end.**

1 It's an interesting offer, but our _ability_ to respond is limited by our lack of resources. (ABLE)

2 Yes, we'll begin production on _____ of a firm order from you. But we also need a payment guarantee in the form of a letter of credit from your bank. (ACCEPT)

3 We have an excellent team and I'm sure we can _____ the results we want. (ACHIEVE)

4 Taking the company from a small family firm to a listing on the Frankfurt Stock Exchange was a great _____ . (ACHIEVE)

5 Our main business _____ is customs clearing, shipping and forwarding. (ACT)

6 If you want to extend the warranty to two years, there is a small _____ cost. (ADD)

7 Can I give you some _____ ? Don't burn your bridges. You may meet the same people in a different context in a few years' time. (ADVISE)

8 It's always _____ to check with your boss first before you take a decision that could have serious consequences for the business. (ADVISE)

9 Is everyone in _____ with this decision? Good, then let's move on to the next item on the agenda. (AGREE)

10 It was an interesting presentation. The speaker gave an _____ of the impact of internet piracy on the publishing industry. (ANALYZE)

11 He works for UBS as a financial _____ . His speciality is the government bond market. (ANALYZE)

12 The job looked interesting so I filled out the online _____ form. Now I'm waiting to hear from them. (APPLY)

13 In order to _____ candidates with the right skills and experience we will have to offer a good salary with good working conditions. (ATTRACT)

14 I'm sorry – my computer is showing that the model number you want is _____ . I think it's been replaced with model number KX4000. (AVAILABLE)

15 Low-paid workers will _____ from the new law that raises the minimum wage. (BENEFIT)

16 What is the total size of our marketing _____ ? (BUDGET)

17 We didn't _____ for the increased raw material costs. (BUDGET)

18 Yes, we have a working prototype. The challenge now is to _____ it on a larger scale. (COMMERCE)

19 We can give you a high-quality, customized product at a _____ price. But we need a minimum order of 10,000 pieces before we can go ahead. (COMPETE)

20 _____ in this industry is very strong. It's a real battle to gain every single point of market share. (COMPETE)

**65.2 Continue as before.**

1 I need some time to think about this. Can I give you my _____ on Monday? (DECIDE)

2 We're out of stock right now, but I'm expecting another _____ on Monday. (DELIVER)

3 Sorry, you'll never convince me. We'll have to agree to _____ . (DIFFER)

4 She's a _____ of the company. She owns around 12% of the shares and sits on the Board. (DIRECT)

5 We have our own _____ network. We supply local agents who sell directly to the end-user. (DISTRIBUTE)

6 I studied _____ at university. (ECONOMY)

7 As a student, I just need a small car – something reliable and _____ . (ECONOMY)

8 The truth is that our production process is very _____ . There are too many defects and there's too much waste. (EFFICIENT)

9 Our investment in new technology is aimed at improving _____ across the whole organization. (EFFICIENT)

10 I lost my job in January and I've been _____ for around three months. (EMPLOY)

11 I'm an _____ of the company, but most of the people I work with are independent freelancers who just work on individual projects. (EMPLOY)

12 I keep all my taxi receipts and meal receipts when I travel abroad. I can claim them back as _____ . (EXPENSE)

13 We have to import all our raw materials at great _____ . (EXPENSE)

14 I'll send you an _____ document that gives the background to the project. (EXPLAIN)

15 I agree with you to some _____ , but there are one or two issues I'm still not sure about. (EXTEND)

16 The bank has agreed to _____ our credit line. (EXTEND)

17 How are we going to _____ this project? (FINANCE)

18 Immigration is by far the biggest factor in population _____ . (GROW)

**65.3 On the opposite page you will see that 'export' has the same form as a verb and a noun. However, the stressed syllable is different:**

(verb) *Their flowers are ex<u>port</u>ed all over the world.*
(noun) *Oil is their largest <u>ex</u>port.*

**There are a few other words like this. <u>Underline</u> the stressed syllable in the word in italics:**

1 We *record* all contacts with clients in our Customer Relationship Management database.

2 We have no *record* of this transaction on our system.

3 The goods are *transferred* from our central warehouse to the various retail outlets.

4 Real Madrid's striker went to Manchester United for a *transfer* fee of 91 million euros.

This unit continues the list of word families for business words. Note that adverbs are not included (*legal – legally – illegally, success – successfully – unsuccessfully*, etc).

**IMPRESS**
*impress* (v)
*impression* (n)
*impressive* (adj)
*unimpressive* (adj)
*impressed* (adj)
*unimpressed* (adj)

**INDUSTRY**
*industrialize* (v)
*industry* (n)
*industrialization* (n)
*industrialist* (n)
*industrial* (adj)
*industrialized* (adj)

**INFLATE**
*inflate* (v)
*inflation* (n)
*inflated* (adj)
*inflationary* (adj)

**INFORM**
*inform* (v)
*misinform* (v)
*information* (n)
*misinformation* (n)
*informative* (adj)
*misinformed* (adj)

**INNOVATE**
*innovate* (v)
*innovation* (n)
*innovator* (n)
*innovative* (adj)

**INSURE**
*insure* (v)
*insurance* (n)
*insurer* (n)
*insurable* (adj)
*uninsurable* (adj)

**INTRODUCE**
*introduce* (v)
*introduction* (n)
*introductory* (adj)

**INVEST**
*invest* (v)
*investment* (n)
*investor* (n)

**KNOW**
*know* (v)
*knowledge* (n)
*known* (adj)
*unknown* (adj)
*knowledgeable* (adj)

**LEGAL**
*legalize* (v)
*legality* (n)
*legislation* (n)
*legal* (adj)
*illegal* (adj)

**MANAGE**
*manage* (v)
*management* (n)
*manager* (n)
*manageable* (adj)
*unmanageable* (adj)

**NEGOTIATE**
*negotiate* (v)
*renegotiate* (v)
*negotiation* (n)
*negotiator* (n)
*negotiable* (adj)
*non-negotiable* (adj)

**OFFER**
*offer* (v)
*offer** (n)
*offering** (n)

**OPERATE**
*operate* (v)
*operation* (n)
*operator* (n)
*operating* (adj)
*operational* (adj)

**OPT**
*opt* (v)
*option* (n)
*optional* (adj)

**PREFER**
*prefer* (v)
*preference* (n)
*preferable* (adj)

**PRODUCE**
*produce* (v)
*product* (n)
*production* (n)
*productivity* (n)
*producer* (n)
*productive* (adj)
*unproductive* (adj)

**PROFIT**
*profit* (v)
*profit* (n)
*profitability* (n)
*profitable* (adj)
*unprofitable* (adj)

**RELY**
*rely* (v)
*reliability* (n)
*reliable* (adj)
*unreliable* (adj)

**SATISFY**
*satisfy* (v)
*satisfaction* (n)
*satisfied* (adj)
*satisfactory* (adj)
*unsatisfied* (adj)
*unsatisfactory* (adj)

**SHARE**
*share* (v)
*share* (n)

**SPONSOR**
*sponsor* (v)
*sponsor* (n)
*sponsorship* (n)

**STRONG**
*strengthen* (v)
*strength* (n)
*strong* (adj)

**SUCCESS**
*succeed* (v)
*success* (n)
*successful* (adj)
*unsuccessful* (adj)

**SUIT**
*suit* (v)
*suitability* (n)
*suitable* (adj)
*unsuitable* (adj)

**SUPPORT**
*support* (v)
*support* (n)
*supporter* (n)
*supportive* (adj)

**SUPPLY**
*supply* (v)
*supply* (n)
*supplier* (n)

**WEAK**
*weaken* (v)
*weakness* (n)
*weak* (adj)

*Note: either 'offer' or 'offering' can be used for all the products that a company has available on the market.

# Exercises

## 66.1 Complete each sentence with the correct form of the word in capital letters at the end.

1 Yes, your sales growth is certainly *impressive* . How have you done it? (IMPRESS)
2 I was in Sao Paolo about ten years ago, and I visited again earlier this year. The changes that I saw made a big _____ on me. (IMPRESS)
3 Vietnam, Cambodia and Laos have now started on the road to _____ . (INDUSTRY)
4 Mumbai is the economic capital of India. It is the centre of _____ and commerce. (INDUSTRY)
5 Consumer prices rose by 2.2% in August compared with a year ago, showing that _____ pressure in the economy is building. (INFLATE)
6 This data shows the earth is cooling, not warming. It's a very emotional issue and people will accuse us of spreading _____ about climate change. (INFORM)
7 Thank you, your presentation was very _____ . I'm much clearer now about your overall aims and objectives. (INFORM)
8 _____ that leads to increased productivity is the main way to increase wealth in an economy. (INNOVATE)
9 It's a very _____ idea – I like it. Now we need to ask managers in other departments how it would impact their own work. (INNOVATE)
10 The CEO wants to buy a Picasso to hang in the boardroom. Have you any idea how much it would cost to _____ that kind of thing? (INSURE)
11 We offer financial products in the areas of investments, pensions and _____ . (INSURE)
12 I will make just a few _____ comments before handing over to the President of Business Link who has kindly agreed to give the opening speech at our conference. (INTRODUCE)
13 I hope she doesn't leave. Her _____ of the Russian market is a great advantage for us. (KNOW)
14 This is all very new for us. We're going into _____ territory. (KNOW)
15 There has to be a question mark against the _____ of what they're doing. (LEGAL)
16 There's a lot of government _____ in the area of health and safety at work. (LEGAL)
17 It's a difficult situation, but it's _____ as long as it doesn't get worse. (MANAGE)
18 I'm sorry, our price is _____ . It's company policy to quote a fixed price and then stick to it. However we do have some flexibility with our terms of payment. (NEGOTIATE)
19 He's a very skilled _____ . He listens carefully and uses his natural charm if there's a problem. It seems to work. (NEGOTIATE)
20 I'll give you a quick overview of the history of our company, then tell you about our market _____ . (OFFER) *(two answers)*

## 66.2 Continue as before.

1 I deal mainly with _____ issues. Company strategy is decided by the people on the top floor. (OPERATE)
2 Our accounts show that last year revenue was €56 million, gross profit was €19 million, and _____ profit was €8 million. (OPERATE)
3 Air conditioning is standard on this car, but an electric sunroof and heated leather seats are _____ . (OPT)
4 The product will be ready to launch in October, but my _____ is to wait until November to catch the Christmas market. (PREFER)
5 We have 24-hour continuous _____ at this site. (PRODUCE)
6 It was a very _____ meeting. We covered a lot of important areas. (PRODUCE)
7 From what I hear, one of our main competitors is in serious trouble. We have to be quick and try to _____ from this situation. (PROFIT)
8 Finally, after three years, it looks like the company will make a small _____ this year. (PROFIT)
9 It's a very _____ business. We work on margins of around 30 per cent. (PROFIT)
10 The most important thing with a business partner is trust. They have to be honest and _____ . (RELY)
11 The key issue for us is _____ , not price. We need to know that components, equipment and systems will function without failure for the time period that we specify. (RELY)
12 Good! Another _____ customer. Let's hope they tell all their friends. (SATISFY)
13 I'm sorry, your work over the last six months has been _____ . I've spoken to you about this several times and given you plenty of opportunity to improve. We're going to let you go. (SATISFY)
14 I have to _____ my office with this guy from marketing who uses really strong aftershave cologne. (SHARE)
15 We want to work with you on equal terms. We will split the costs 50/50, and of course you'll get an equal _____ of the profits. (SHARE)
16 We've just signed a _____ deal with the local opera house. Our logo will be on all their publicity for the next season. (SPONSOR)
17 As a manager she's a real perfectionist. Sometimes it's a _____ but often it's a weakness. (STRONG)
18 You need skill and determination to _____ in this business. And more than a little luck. (SUCCESS)
19 I regret to inform you that your application for the above position has been _____ . (SUCCESS)
20 When my father was ill my boss was very _____ . She let me take some unpaid leave to be with him in hospital. (SUPPORT)

## 67 Compound nouns

### What is a compound noun?

A compound noun is formed from two nouns, or an adjective and a noun. Here are some examples:

Group A

| | |
|---|---|
| bank account | credit card |
| distribution channel | insurance company |

Group B

| | |
|---|---|
| fast food | private sector |
| human resources | mobile phone |

Group C

| | |
|---|---|
| baby-sitter | dry-cleaning |
| brother-in-law | editor-in-chief |

Group D

| | |
|---|---|
| database | sunglasses |
| email | timetable |

You can see that there are four ways to form a compound noun. The compound nouns in group A have two nouns written as separate words. Those in group B are formed by an adjective and a noun. Those in group C are two words joined by a hyphen. Those in group D are single words made of two parts. There are no definite rules about how to write a compound noun, and if in doubt, you should check in a good, modern dictionary. Note that the form can change over time – for example when email first started it was written as 'e-mail'.

The most common form is two separate nouns, and the following examples all have this form.

### Compound nouns for key business words

**advertising**

| | |
|---|---|
| advertising agency | advertising campaign |
| advertising budget | advertising slogan |

**business**

| | |
|---|---|
| business card | business objectives |
| business contact | business opportunities |
| business deal | business partner |
| business interests | business relationship |
| business lunch | business trip |

**costs**

| | |
|---|---|
| labour costs | production costs |

**customer**

| | |
|---|---|
| customer care | customer profile |
| customer complaints | customer requirements |
| customer enquiries | customer satisfaction |
| customer loyalty | customer service(s) |
| customer needs | customer support |

**market**

| | |
|---|---|
| market forces | market sector |
| market leader | market share |
| market price | market survey |
| market position | market trends |
| market research | market value |

**price**

| | |
|---|---|
| price cut | price rise |
| price list | cost price |
| price range | retail price |
| price reduction | wholesale price |

**product**

| | |
|---|---|
| product design | product line |
| product development | product range |
| product features | product specifications |
| product launch | product quality |

**production**

| | |
|---|---|
| production capacity | production plant |
| production costs | production problems |
| production level | production process |
| production line | production target |
| production plan | production volume |

**sales**

| | |
|---|---|
| sales consultant | sales rep (representative) |
| sales figures | sales report |
| sales forecast | sales target |
| sales manager | sales team |
| sales performance | sales technique |
| sales presentation | sales volume |

Examples

This **market research** indicates some interesting new **business opportunities**.

Our competitor is making **price cuts** across their whole **product range**.

This **production plan** is based on last year's **sales figures**.

The **advertising campaign** is targeted at people with a very specific **customer profile**.

# Exercises

**67.1 Match each word on the left with two words on the right to make compound nouns. Several matches may be possible, but find a solution that uses each word on the right once only.**

agency
capacity
deal
1 advertising
enquiries
2 business
launch
3 customer
leader
4 market
objectives
5 product
plant
6 production
range
service(s)
share
slogan

**67.2 Complete the sentences with a compound noun from Exercise 67.1.**

1 L'Oréal have a very well-known _____advertising slogan_____ : 'Because we're worth it'.
2 Google is the _____ in online search.
3 The assembly plant is designed to produce 200 vehicles a day, but we're running at just 60% of the _____ right now.
4 We have just negotiated a very good _____ with a new customer in Turkey.
5 The staff who deal with _____ by phone or email are the first point of contact between a customer and the company.
6 Sony have a _____ that includes TVs and home cinema, computers, games consoles, camcorders and cameras.

**67.3 Cross out the one word in italics that does not make a common compound noun with the word on the right. Not all the compounds are given opposite.**

1 advertising / ~~business~~ / sales        campaign
2 advertising / price / production        costs
3 business / cost / market        price
4 market / price / product        range
5 business / customer / production        relationship
6 product / production / sales        target

**67.4 Complete the sentences with a compound noun from Exercise 67.3.**

1 We're promoting the new line with magazine advertising, street posters and special discounts. It's the biggest _____sales campaign_____ we've ever done.
2 We could set up the new factory in Vietnam _____ are cheaper than in China.
3 It was impossible to get a discount. We had to pay the full _____ .
4 This year Nokia's shares have traded between €7 and €12. That's a very wide _____ .
5 They have been our main supplier of raw materials for over ten years. We have a long _____ .
6 I'll get an end-of-year bonus of 20% if I meet my _____ .

**67.5 Answer the questions below.**

1 Is an 'advertising budget' …?
   a) an amount of money
   b) a plan for how to spend the money
   c) either, depending on the context
2 Is an 'objective' …?
   a) something you say to show that you disagree
   b) an aim that you want to achieve
3 Find 'customer needs' on the page opposite. Which other compound noun in the same section has the same meaning but is more formal?
4 Find 'market research' on the page opposite. Which other compound noun in the same section is one way of doing this research (by asking questions)?
5 Fill in the missing letters in this definition: market share is the per _ _ _ _age of total sales in a market that a company or product has.
6 Is the 'wholesale price' …?
   a) the basic cost of producing the product
   b) the price that the customer pays after a discount
   c) the price paid by a retailer (who will then sell again to the end-user)
7 Put these three stages into the order in which they happen: product development, product launch, product design.
8 Match each of these compound nouns with its correct definition below: product features, product specifications.
   a) important and interesting things that will be the main selling points of the product
   b) exact measurements or a detailed plan about how a product should be made
9 Is a production plant …?
   a) a living thing with leaves and roots
   b) a large factory
10 Is a sales forecast …?
   a) a report describing past sales
   b) a prediction of future sales

# 68 Compound adjectives

## What is a compound adjective?

A compound adjective is an adjective formed from two (or more) words. They are usually written with a hyphen. Here are some examples:

| | | |
|---|---|---|
| air-conditioned | ice-cold | part-time |
| day-to-day | last-minute | second-hand |
| duty-free | long-distance | short-term |
| fed-up | never-ending | so-called |
| first-class | north-east | upside-down |
| full-length | off-peak | worldwide |

If the adjective is written alone, not before a noun, there is usually no hyphen.

*It was a **first-class** seat.*
*I traveled **first class**.*
*Here's our most **up-to-date** sales report.*
*Unfortunately this report isn't **up to date**.*

Many compound adjectives have 'well' or 'badly' as the first word.

*a well-known (company)*
*a well-made / badly-made (product)*
*a well-paid / badly-paid (job)*
*a well-written / badly-written (report)*

It is common to have a number as the first word.

| | |
|---|---|
| two-door (car) | four-wheel (drive) |
| three-bedroom (house) | five-star (hotel) |
| 18th century (palace) | six-month (project) |
| 24-hour (supermarket) | eight-year-old (boy) |
| half-finished (report) | 20-minute (walk) |
| one-way (street) | 30-page (contract) |
| two-year (MBA) | 50-euro (note) |
| three-hour (delay) | multi-million-dollar (deal) |

## Describing people

Many compound adjectives describe a person's appearance or personality.

| | |
|---|---|
| dark-haired | middle-aged |
| down-to-earth (= practical) | open-minded |
| easy-going (= relaxed) | strange-looking |
| good-looking | self-confident |
| kind-hearted | self-motivated |
| left-handed | well-dressed |

## Describing products

In business English there are many compound adjectives to describe products and services.

| | |
|---|---|
| brand-new | old-fashioned |
| cutting-edge | out-of-date |
| hard-wearing | state-of-the-art |
| high-speed | time-saving |
| high-tech | trouble-free |
| labour-saving | up-to-date |
| long-lasting | user-friendly |
| man-made | well-built |
| mass-produced | well-made |

Examples
*It's the very latest **cutting-edge, state-of-the-art** technology.* (= extremely new, modern and advanced)

The following adjectives are used to describe the quality and price of a product.

| British English | American English |
|---|---|
| up-market | upscale |
| down-market | downscale |
| top-of-the-range | high-end |
| bottom-of-the-range | low-end |

We can also say that a product is 'good value-for-money' or 'good value' (= a good relationship between quality and price).

## Other common compound adjectives

| | |
|---|---|
| cost-effective | long-term / short-term |
| energy-saving | round-table (discussion) |
| fast-growing | time-consuming |
| government-funded | well-established |
| hand-held | well-maintained |
| high-level | well-run |
| high-profile | worst-case |
| interest-free (loan) | year-round (use) |

Examples
*It's been a very **time-consuming** problem, but finally I think we have a solution that is simple and **cost effective**.*
*They're a **well-established**, **well-run** company.*

*What are the risks? What's the **worst-case** scenario?*

140

# Exercises

**68.1 Match a word on the left with a word on the right to make compound adjectives.**

| | | |
|---|---|---|
| 1 | badly- | called |
| 2 | duty- | down |
| 3 | full- | free |
| 4 | last- | known |
| 5 | off- | length |
| 6 | short- | made |
| 7 | so- | minute |
| 8 | upside- | peak |
| 9 | well- | term |

**68.2 Complete the sentences with a compound adjective from Exercise 68.1.**

1 They're a _____ , highly-respected company with some of Europe's leading companies as their clients.
2 We need to save money, but cutting our advertising budget is just a _____ solution.
3 I was going to stay at home this weekend, but I made a _____ decision to come to the conference.
4 When I called them I was put on hold for over 20 minutes. Their _____ 'customer care' department doesn't care about anyone.
5 In my country you can get _____ electricity at much lower cost. You use the electricity during the night, but if you've got a storage heater it's OK.

**68.3 Look at the compound adjectives with a number as the first word on the opposite page, plus the example nouns (eg two-door car). Complete the sentences using phrases from that section.**

1 What are you doing! Don't turn down there! It's a _one-way street_ ! Why don't you let me drive?
2 That's not the right change. The scarf cost €18 and I gave you a _____ .
3 We used to live in a small apartment in the city centre. Then we found out that my wife was pregnant and we moved to a _____ in the suburbs.
4 There was a _____ with the flight. Luckily I had my laptop with me and I could do some work.
5 You can catch a taxi, or go on foot if it's a nice day. It's a _____ from the station – you just go up the main street and turn left when you get to the park. Our offices are 200 metres down that road.
6 The company has a big _____ in the Middle East starting next month. They're probably going to send me as I don't have any family commitments.
7 All these interruptions are really annoying – I have a _____ that I need to complete by the end of today.
8 I think I'm going to take a break in my career and do a full-time _____ .

**68.4 Match a word on the right with a word on the left to make compound adjectives.**

| | | |
|---|---|---|
| 1 | brand- | date |
| 2 | high- | fashioned |
| 3 | mass- | free |
| 4 | old- | friendly |
| 5 | second- | hand |
| 6 | trouble- | new |
| 7 | up-to- | produced |
| 8 | user- | speed |

**68.5 Complete the sentences with a compound adjective from Exercise 68.4.**

1 To celebrate my promotion I bought a _brand-new_ Ferrari.
2 No, that's the _____ way of doing things. These days we use the Internet for everything.
3 It's a very _____ website – you can find the information you want and place orders very easily.
4 Construction has started on a _____ rail link between London and Edinburgh.
5 Luckily I've had a _____ computer for several years. But I always check that I have _____ anti-virus software.

**68.6 Fill in the missing letters in these sentences.**

1 This is our t__-of-the-r__ge executive model.
2 I never watch TV. I think it's awful. All the programmes are so d__n-ma___t.
3 It's a very upsc__e store – I could never afford to shop there.
4 Supermarkets that sell l__-end products – like WalMart, Aldi and Lidl – have done very well in the recession.
5 Have you seen this offer of two nights in Paris at a four-star hotel for €100? It's great va__e for money.

**68.7 Complete the sentences below using adjectives from the section opposite called 'Other common compound adjectives'.**

1 A German engineering company is selling all its old machines. I think we should buy them – I'm sure they've been _well maintained_ .
2 Scientists are working on a _____ device that allows crime scene investigators and others to quickly conduct DNA tests from almost anywhere.
3 They're building the golf course in an ideal location. It'll have _____ use. I think we should invest.
4 It's a _____ agency that offers _____ loans to small businesses to help them improve their energy efficiency.
5 The project could be very profitable, but it's also very risky. I think we should have a _____ discussion with all the team members to look at what we would do in a _____ scenario.

## What is a collocation?

A collocation is a pair or group of words that are often used together. There are many types of collocation. Here are some examples:

verb + noun
*make an arrangement, set up a business, reach a decision*
adjective + noun
*fixed cost, part-time job, competitive advantage*
noun + noun
*insurance company, business plan, information technology*
sentence heads
*What exactly do you mean by …?, Give my best wishes to …*
fixed expressions
*Last but not least, Time is money, See you later.*

The English language is full of collocations, and every unit of this book includes many examples. Why are they important? Because learning words individually is only half the story. You also have to learn how words combine with each other. And if you can learn the whole collocation as one item – instead of thinking of the individual words one-by-one – your speech will become more fluent.

This unit and the next unit focus on verb + noun collocations.

## Collocations for key business words

### company

Somebody or something can … a company.

| | |
|---|---|
| *buy/take over* | *leave/resign from* |
| *close down* | *manage/run* |
| *establish/set up/start* | *reorganize/restructure* |
| *join* | *work for* |

And a company can …

| | |
|---|---|
| *be in trouble* | *go out of business* |
| *expand/grow* | *make/manufacture* sth |
| *go bankrupt/bust/under* | *offer/provide* sth |
| *go into liquidation* | *run into difficulties* |

### contract

Somebody can … a contract.

| | |
|---|---|
| *alter/amend* | *get out of* |
| *break* | *go over/review* |
| *(re)negotiate* | *keep to* |
| *draw up* | *renew* |
| *enter into* | *sign* |
| *finalize* | *terminate* |

And a contract can …

| | |
|---|---|
| *be worth …* | *come to an end/expire* |
| *come into effect/start* | *run until …* |

### costs

Somebody or something can … the cost/costs

| | |
|---|---|
| *absorb* | *figure out/work out* |
| *bring down/cut/reduce* | *pay/meet* |
| *cover* | *spread* |

And costs can …

| | |
|---|---|
| *be associated with …* | *go down/up* |
| *fall/rise* | *stay (more or less) the same* |

### customer/client

Somebody or something can … customers/clients.

| | |
|---|---|
| *attract* | *look after/take care of* |
| *deal with* | *lose* |
| *entertain* | *serve the needs of* |

The sentences below show some of these collocations in use, and others not mentioned above.

*His father **set up the company** twenty years ago.*
*I **work for a company** in the **hospitality sector**.*
*I knew that **the company was in trouble**, but I didn't know they had **gone out of business**.*
***The company went bust** last year. Sad, really.*
*Our **legal department** is **drawing up the contract**.*
*I'd like to **go over the details** one more time.*
*This **contract** could **be worth** millions!*
*The **contract comes into effect** on the first of March and **runs until** the end of October.*
*We can **absorb** some of the extra **costs**, but not all of them.*
*We should **cover** our **costs** if we can sell 3,000 units, then after that we begin to **make a profit**.*
*It would be easier if we could **spread the costs** between ourselves and our **business partners**.*
***The costs associated with** buying a house are quite high.*
*We should be able to **attract** a lot of **new customers** with our '**buy-one-get-one-free**' promotion.*
*I **deal with** our large **corporate clients**.*

# Exercises

**69.1 Complete Claudia's description of her family company with the words in the box.**

| closed down | expand | grew | join | leave |
|---|---|---|---|---|
| ~~makes~~ | restructure | run | set up | take over |

66 It's a medium-sized business in the north of Italy that ¹ _makes_ leather goods. My father ² _____ the company over 30 years ago – I wasn't even born then! Nowadays he doesn't really ³ _____ it on a day-to-day basis – he leaves that to my brother – but of course he gives advice when it's needed.

At first the company ⁴ _____ organically, increasing sales year after year. But about ten years ago my father took an important strategic decision. It was to ⁵ _____ one of our competitors that had run into difficulties. Of course putting the two companies together wasn't easy, and my father had to ⁶ _____ everything, including the management team. That was when they asked me to ⁷ _____ them. They said they needed someone with my language skills and background in sales to ⁸ _____ the business.

Well, it wasn't an easy decision – I was working for another company at the time. But in the end my father persuaded me to ⁹ _____ that company, and I'm glad I did. Do you know why? I drove past their offices the other day and it looks like the company has ¹⁰ _____ ! The building is empty and the sign above the gate has gone. It's a shame really. 99

**69.2 Look at the words the speaker says. Then complete the comment below using a word from the box.**

| amend | get out of | keep to |
|---|---|---|
| draw up | go over | ~~renegotiate~~ |

1 'The situation is completely different now. The old agreement is not valid any more.'
She wants to _renegotiate_ the contract.
2 'There are one or two things here that I'm still not clear on. Can you explain it again?'
He wants to _____ the contract again.
3 'Before we finalize things, there are one or two points that we would like to change.'
She wants to _____ the contract.
4 'OK, the details are all agreed in principle, now we need to get everything in writing.'
Now the legal department need to _____ the contract.
5 'Is there any way we can avoid doing this?'
He wants to _____ the contract.
6 'I hope they do what they said they would do.'
She hopes they will _____ the contract.

**69.3 Underline the correct word in italics.**

1 If you agree to a minimum order of 10,000 pieces, we will *meet* / *spread* the cost of customizing the product in the way you explained.
2 The company we use for all our transport and logistics has told me their prices will be going up. We'll have to try to *absorb* / *cut* some of the extra cost ourselves. I don't think we can pass it all on to our customers.
3 It's a very complex project involving a lot of people and a lot of resources. I'm using a spreadsheet to help me *figure out* / *pay* all the costs.
4 They are offering us very attractive terms of payment – 20% on delivery, 40% after 30 days, and the remainder after 60 days. That will help to *cut* / *spread* the cost.
5 Sales have been disappointing and we're not going to make a profit. The good news is that we should at least *cover* / *figure out* our costs, so it's not a complete disaster.

**69.4 One word in each sentence is wrong. Cross it out and write the correct word at the end.**

1 Our customer services team deal ~~for~~ people who call us with an enquiry or a complaint. _with_
2 He was forced to resign of the company when his boss saw his Facebook page. _____
3 There are a lot of costs associated to doing all your Research and Development internally. These days we outsource most of it. _____
4 A lot of small shops in the town centre have gone out from business since the hypermarket opened. _____
5 I'd like to go across the contract again if you don't mind. There are still some points that need clarification. _____
6 I take care from all our customers in the north of the country. _____
7 We try to serve the needs with the whole community. _____
8 The contract runs by the end of the year, then after that we can renew it if we want to. _____

**69.5 Write one of these words in each space to make adjective + noun collocations: *company, contract, costs, customer*.**

| considerable | | limited | |
|---|---|---|---|
| fixed | 1 _____ | parent | 3 _____ |
| hidden | | start-up | |
| unnecessary | | well-run | |

| exclusive | | key | |
|---|---|---|---|
| major | 2 _____ | potential | 4 _____ |
| two-year | | regular | |
| valid | | satisfied | |

**Check the meaning of any unknown adjectives in a good dictionary.**

This unit continues the list of verb + noun collocations from Unit 69.

## Collocations for key business words

**market**

Somebody or something can … the market.

| | |
|---|---|
| *analyze/research* | *corner* |
| *be driven out of* | *flood* |
| *break into/enter* | *take over* |
| *come onto* | *withdraw from* |

And the market can …

| | |
|---|---|
| *be booming* | *disappear/dry up* |
| *be vulnerable to …* | *grow* |
| *decline* | *shrink* |

**order**

Somebody or something can … an order.

| | |
|---|---|
| *authorize* | *get/receive* |
| *call about* | *make/place/put in* |
| *cancel* | *process* |
| *confirm* | *ship* |

And an order can …

| | |
|---|---|
| *be delayed* | *come in* |
| *be late* | *go out* |

**price**

Somebody or something can … a price/prices.

| | |
|---|---|
| *agree on/agree to* | *guarantee* |
| *bring down/cut/lower* | *hold down* |
| *charge* | *increase/put up/raise* |
| *establish/fix/set* | *push down* |
| *give/quote* | *push up* |

And prices can …

| | |
|---|---|
| *be tied to …* | *fluctuate/vary* |
| *go up/rise* | *range from … to …* |
| *go down/fall/drop* | *start at …* |

**product**

Somebody or something can … a product.

| | |
|---|---|
| *advertise/promote* | *launch/roll out* |
| *customize* | *make/manufacture* |
| *design/develop* | *market* |
| *discontinue* | *modify* |
| *distribute* | *sell* |
| *export/import* | *sell out of* |
| *improve/upgrade* | *test* |

And a product can …

| | |
|---|---|
| *be in/out of stock* | *sell out* |
| *sell badly* | *sell well* |

**production**

Somebody or something can … production.

| | |
|---|---|
| *be in* | *go into/start* |
| *cut/cut back* | *increase/step up* |
| *delay/hold up* | *speed up* |
| *disrupt/interrupt* | *transfer* |

**sales**

Somebody or something can … sales.

| | |
|---|---|
| *affect* | *increase/boost* |
| *generate* | *push up* |
| *hit* | *win/lose* |

And sales can …

| | |
|---|---|
| *account for …* | *go up/increase/rise* |
| *be down/up* | *grow* |
| *exceed …* | *improve/recover* |
| *go down/drop/fall* | *reach …* |

**staff**

Somebody or something can … staff.

| | |
|---|---|
| *appoint* | *have/employ* |
| *be in charge of* | *hire/recruit/take on* |
| *be responsible for* | *lose* |
| *develop/train* | *motivate* |
| *fire/lay off/dismiss* | *supervise* |

The sentences below show some of these collocations in use, and others not mentioned above.

*They own the patent and it's a very specialized product area – basically they've **cornered the market**.*

*It's very difficult to **do business** over there – I think we'll have to **withdraw from the market**.*

*The **stock market is vulnerable to** an increase in **interest rates**.*

*A large **order** has just **come in** from Poland.*

*We're trying to **hold down prices** as long as we can.*

*Our **prices range from** €100 **to** €250 per piece.*

*We'll be **launching the product** in France and **rolling it out** across the rest of Europe later.*

*The cold weather has **hit sales** of **summer clothes**.*

*The new promotion has really **boosted sales**.*

*North American **sales account for** 40% of the total.*

***Sales figures** have **exceeded our expectations**.*

*We need to **appoint** a new **Training Manager**.*

*I'm **in charge of a team** of eight people.*

*We had to **lay off** a lot of **employees** in the last recession.*

# Exercises

**70.1 Match two words on the left with each word on the right to make verb + noun collocations. Find a solution that uses each word on the left once only.**

1  come onto
2  customize
3  disrupt
4  employ
5  lay off
6  put in
7  sell out of
8  ship
9  start
10 take over

a product
production
the market
staff
an order

**70.2 Complete the sentences with a verb + noun collocation from Exercise 70.1.**

1  If the recession continues, we will have no alternative. We'll have to *lay off staff* .
2  This is just the prototype. I expect the final version will actually _____ in the spring of next year.
3  We can't _____ until we've set up all the machines. The factory manager says it will take a day to do that.
4  The plasma TVs are selling very well in all our stores – I _____ for another 50 last week.
5  In this catalogue you can see our full range of small gift items. We can easily _____ – for example we can put your company logo on any item.

**70.3 In each group cross out the one word in italics that does not make a common verb + noun collocation.**

1  *analyze / break into / export / flood*  the market
2  *cancel / confirm / develop / process*  an order
3  *agree on / charge / set / win*  a price
4  *design / employ / roll out / upgrade*  a product
5  *distribute / generate / hit / push up*  sales

**70.4 Complete the sentences with a verb in italics from Exercise 70.3**

1  Cheap imported goods are ___ _____ing the market.
2  My screen shows your order is being _____ed right now. It should leave our warehouse within the next few days.
3  No, I can't give you a special discount. We have to _____ our customers the market price or we'd go out of business.
4  We'll _____ the new software over the summer – first in the States and then in Europe and Asia.
5  Our main competitor has much better distribution in our key market. I'm sure it's going to _____ our sales.

**70.5 Look at the words spoken by speaker A. Then underline the correct words in italics spoken by speaker B.**

1  A: The market for this product is becoming smaller and smaller.
   B: Yes, it certainly is *booming / shrinking*
2  A: Two years ago this product was flying off the shelves; now we sell maybe one a month.
   B: Yes, the market really has *dried up / grown*.
3  A: Have you shipped the order yet?
   B: Yes, it *came in / went out* yesterday.
4  A: You export most of your production. Is there an exchange rate risk in your business?
   B: Absolutely. Our prices in foreign markets *are tied to / range from* the value of the euro against the local currency.
5  A: We're beginning to see signs of inflation in the economy.
   B: Yes, prices are beginning to *raise / rise*.
6  A: My friend told me about the new range of Prada shoes. I can't see them in the store.
   B: I'm sorry, they've completely *sold out / sold well*. We're expecting some more next week.
7  A: How are sales doing?
   B: Very well. We've already *grown / reached* our year-end target of €80,000.
8  A: Do you do well in Latin America?
   B: Oh yes, sales in Brazil *account for / improve* something like 10% of our total revenue.

**70.6 Fill in the missing letters.**

1  In the US it's easier to find a job, but easier to lose it. It's a 'h_ _ _ and f_ _ _' culture.
2  There's been a delay with some key components and it will h_ _ _ up production. When they arrive we'll have to sp_ _ _ up everything to recover the lost time.

**70.7 Write one of these words in each space to make adjective + noun collocations: *market, order, price, product, production, staff.***

| attractive | | | best-selling | | |
|---|---|---|---|---|---|
| average | 1 | | finished | 4 | |
| cost | | | high-quality | | |
| retail | | | household | | |
| | | | | | |
| administrative | | | competitive | | |
| full-time | 2 | | domestic | 5 | |
| temporary | | | specialist | | |
| well-qualified | | | worldwide | | |
| | | | | | |
| initial | | | annual | | |
| repeat | 3 | | full | 6 | |
| outstanding | | | mass | | |
| urgent | | | small-scale | | |

# Speaking practice

## Discussion topics

### Unit 1 Page 7
Draw an organigram (organization chart) of your company. Use it to explain your organization structure, the relation between the different departments, etc. Mention key individuals within the structure and what they do.

### Unit 2 Page 9
Have you ever worked for a small company or tried to start your own business? Perhaps you have friends or family members in that situation. Tell the story of the company's start-up and growth. If it had problems or failed, explain why.

### Unit 3 Page 11
Use the headings in the unit to prepare and then give a presentation about your own organization. Ask for questions at the end.

### Unit 4 Page 13
Say what you know or have read about these topics: modern manufacturing methods; the globalization of supply chains; quality.

### Unit 5 Page 15
Choose one industry in the service sector. (There is a list at the start of the unit, or think of one not on the list.) Use this industry as an example to discuss the topics in the section 'Issues for the service sector'.

### Unit 6 Page 17
What market/s does your company operate in? Use various ways to define 'market', as suggested in the unit. Who are your main competitors? How do you compete against them?

### Unit 7 Page 19
Choose one particular product or product line that your company sells. What are the four Ps?
Alternatively, choose a product that is not connected with your work but that you know a lot about.

### Unit 8 Page 21
Choose a strong, well-known brand name. What is the image of the brand? How does the company build this image? What other elements of the company's marketing strategy do you know about? How are competitors reacting?

### Unit 9 Page 23
Hold up a product from your bag or in the room. Describe its features, and describe it physically.
Now describe a product at home that you recently bought.
Now describe one of your company's products.

### Unit 10 Page 25
What is the pre-sales and after-sales process in your own company? What areas are typically discussed between customer and company at each stage?

### Unit 11 Page 27
What is the process of orders, invoices and payment between your company and your suppliers? And between your company and your customers? What problems can occur at each stage? How do you deal with them?

### Unit 12 Page 29
Look at the list of verbs used with 'money' at the start of the unit. Use four of them to write true sentences about yourself (write about your habits or recent experiences). Read them aloud and discuss them.

### Unit 13 Page 31
If you work in finance, explain the main points in your organization's P&L and BS last year.
If you don't, turn to the unit and cover all the explanations of the words on the P&L and BS. Just leave the accounts showing. Now explain the meaning of the different words.

### Unit 14 Page 33
Choose a topic from the first section of the unit and a time period (eg sales of one of your products over two years, or house prices over five years). Draw a graph, remembering to label the X and Y axes. Exact figures on the Y axis do not matter. Explain the graph.

### Unit 15 Page 35
Write down on a piece of paper one of each of the following: a very large number, a mathematical operation, a very specific amount of money (with cents or pence), a fraction, a decimal, a percentage, a ratio, a measurement. Choose things that mean something to you personally. Now explain why you've written down those particular numbers. Why are they important?

### Unit 16 Page 37
Choose a few expressions from the unit that you can use to talk about your work (or life). Include examples from all three sections of the unit. Use the expressions in full sentences and then discuss them.

### Unit 17 Page 39
Describe all the equipment in your office. For each item say what you use it for.

## Unit 18 Page 41
Describe a typical internet session at work. Which sites do you visit most often? Which pages on that site? What do you do on the site?
Now describe a typical internet session at home.

## Unit 19 Page 43
Describe the working conditions in your office. What one single thing would make them better? Why?
Have you ever had work worries like those mentioned in the unit? Tell the story.
Is H&S an important issue at your organization? Why?

## Unit 20 Page 45
Describe your job. Before you start, make a few notes with phrases you want to use.

## Unit 21 Page 47
Describe a recent project you were involved in. Include details of schedules and budgets, getting started, progress, team members, and deadlines.

## Unit 22 Page 49
Give an example of a plan that you made at work (or in your life) that had a successful outcome. Describe the planning process, including development, discussion, implementation, review, changes made, etc. Also mention any risks involved and how you managed the risks.
Write down three forecasts related to your job, or your life, or world events – with the maximum time period being the last week of your English course. At the end of the course read them out and see which ones came true.

## Unit 23 Page 51
Describe an internal company problem you recently had.
Describe an internal company problem you are currently having.
What do your customers typically complain about? How do you deal with the complaints?
What do you typically complain about with your suppliers? How do they deal with it?

## Unit 24 Page 53
Do a PEST analysis and/or a Five Forces Analysis and/or a SWOT analysis of your organization.
Who develops the strategy for your organization? How much do you know about the strategy? What leadership qualities do your senior managers have?

## Unit 25 Page 55
What is the process of hiring and firing in your organization? How were you hired?
How do people get promotion?
If you could make one change to the hiring process and one to the promotion process, what would they be?

## Unit 26 Page 57
What benefits and perks do you receive?
Excluding pay and benefits, what else motivates you at work?

## Unit 27 Page 59
Talk about your experience of working in cross-cultural teams. What was easy? What was more difficult?
'When in Rome, do as the Romans do'. But is it possible to change your behaviour and personality?

## Unit 28 Page 61
Do you think that 'green' issues are important? Does your organization think they are important?
What do you do in your personal life to help the environment? What does your organization do?
Does your organization actively promote its activities in the field of CSR? Does it encourage managers to consider people and planet as well as profit?

## Unit 29 Page 63
Bring in your CV and show it to your colleagues/teacher. Work together to look at alternative layouts, different styles of language, etc. In particular aim to include achievements, and make them quantified (with numbers) where possible.

## Unit 30 Page 65
Tell the story of an interview you once went to. Did you get the job?
Cover the words spoken a–h in Exercise 30.2 with a piece of paper, but leave 1–8 showing. Brainstorm how you would answer the same questions. Then write these answers in more detail.

# Writing practice

## Email 1

- Write an email to Filip, a business partner, following a phone call with him yesterday. In the call you talked about business opportunities in Indonesia.
- Say that it was an interesting conversation and ask him to send you the link to the article he mentioned.
- During the call he talked about going to Jakarta on a fact-finding mission – clarify whether he wants you to go as well, and when this might be.
- You said during the call that you would find out about market research companies that specialize in Indonesia – promise you will do this.
- Suggest that you arrange a meeting with the commercial attaché at the Indonesian embassy – ask him what he thinks about this idea.

*When you finish, 'send' your email to a colleague in class for them to reply. You reply to any email you receive. Invent all the details.*

## Email 2

- You are the Project Manager of the Turbina project, which is developing technology to produce energy from the power of waves.
- Write an email to Maria, a colleague in the Sales Department, about the progress of the project. Things are going well.
- Ask Maria if she has any comments, and suggest that you call her in a day or two to discuss her input to the project in the future.
- You need some help preparing a PowerPoint presentation about the project for clients. Does Maria know anyone in her office who is good at using PP and has the time to help you?

*When you finish, 'send' your email to a colleague in class for them to reply. You reply to any email you receive. Invent all the details.*

## Unit 50 Page 105

### Email 1

- You work as a designer in the fashion industry. Write an email to Denise, a business partner, who works as a buyer in a large retail chain.
- Refer to your new range of formal evening clothes and say that you are sure they will sell very well.
- Say that you have to rearrange the time of the meeting with her to discuss the marketing campaign.
- Apologize and explain why.
- Suggest a new time, and give other times if this is not convenient.

*When you finish, 'send' your email to a colleague in class for them to reply. You reply to any email you receive. Invent all the details.*

### Email 2

- Next week you are going to visit the Istanbul office of your company. Write an email to Mehmet, a colleague in your Istanbul office, about your travel plans.
- Confirm your flight details.
- Thank Mehmet for arranging a taxi to meet you at the airport – ask him where the driver will be and how you will recognize the driver.
- Give your mobile phone number, and ask for Mehmet's in case you need it.
- Ask Mehmet to send you the program for your visit.

*When you finish, 'send' your email to a colleague in class for them to reply. You reply to any email you receive. Invent all the details.*

### Unit 51 Page 107

### Email 1

- You work for Computer Solutions, a company that helps businesses use their IT systems more effectively.
- Write to Bottom Line Accountancy Services, a small firm working in your city. You would like to arrange a meeting with them to present your services.
- You are sure that you can add value to their business.
- You have worked with many other local companies and you attach a document with details of your previous work and testimonials from satisfied clients.

*When you finish, 'send' your email to a colleague in class for them to reply. You reply to any email you receive. Invent all the details.*

## Email 2

- You recently received a copy of an office equipment catalogue with the business card of the local Sales Representative (Martina Thomas) attached.
- Write an email to Martina, asking for more information. In particular you are interested in their new range of 'BackRest' office chairs that offer support to your back.
- You want to know a) if the chairs really do offer back support and what evidence there is for this, b) if there are any discounts for large orders (you may want 40 chairs) and c) if the fabric on the chairs can include your company logo as a design feature.
- Suggest a time for Martina to call you to discuss things in more detail.

*When you finish, 'send' your email to a colleague in class for them to reply. You reply to any email you receive. Invent all the details.*

## Unit 52 Page 109

You work for a web design company. Write an email to a potential new client who came to see you last week. Use a formal (careful, polite) style to make a good impression.

- Open in a friendly way and refer to the meeting last week.
- Apologize for not writing sooner.
- Say why you are writing (you need more information from them before you can give a quote to redesign their website).
- Ask them to send you a diagram showing the structure of the new site, and also a sketch of the various pages.
- Check that you understand their needs (they said they don't want to sell anything directly from the site, but they want a way for users of the site to find a local retailer. Is that right?).
- Offer to find out the cost of a sponsored link on Google when people search for their product.
- Say that you are unable to provide advice on how to run an email marketing campaign as you are only a web design company. However you will investigate this.
- Close by saying they can contact you if they need more information.
- Say you look forward to hearing from them.

## Unit 53 Page 111

This is a review unit and now is the chance to practise a few emails similar to the ones you write in your real-life job.

- You may want to practise some emails you really have to send this week. Write a first (draft) version. Then work with your teacher and colleagues to try to improve them.
- Alternatively, you may want to work on some emails you have already written. Look in the Sent folder of your computer at work, print out a few emails, and bring them in to class. Work with your teacher and colleagues to try to improve them.
- When you finish, everyone in the class can put their emails on the walls around the room. Go round and read all the emails.

# Listening exercises

## 1 An interview with an accountant

### Exercises

**1 Fill in the missing letters or underline the correct word in italics.**

1 The three financial reports produced by a company are the inc_ _ _ st_ _ _ment, the bal_ _ _ sh_ _ _ and the cash flow statement. The first of these can also be called the pr_ _ _ and lo_ _.

2 Marketing is *a direct cost / an indirect cost*.

3 When people refer to 'the bottom line', they mean *gross profit / operating profit / net profit*.

4 Out of the net profit the company pays divi_ _ _ds to sh_ _ _holders and reinvests the rest in the company for future growth.

**2 ⊕ 11 Now listen to the interview and compare your answers.**

**3 Listen again with your eyes closed. Then listen a third time while you follow the script (page 154).**

**4 Discuss any interesting issues.**

## 2 An interview with a B2B commercial director

### Exercises

**1 Answer the questions.**

1 Who do you think are the customers of a B2B pharmaceutical company? Choose two.
   a) people who are ill          c) hospital managers
   b) doctors                      d) pharmacies

2 The Commercial Director believes in giving staff more responsibility. How do you think he does this? Choose one.
   a) letting area managers organize the recruitment and selection of their own sales representatives
   b) letting area managers be like entrepreneurs inside the company, producing a business plan for their region

3 The Commercial Director thinks that sales representatives in the pharmaceutical sector should be more like consultants. Do you think this approach is easier with doctors or pharmacists?

**2 ⊕ 12 Now listen to the interview and compare your answers.**

**3 Listen again with your eyes closed. Then listen a third time while you follow the script (page 154).**

**4 Discuss any interesting issues.**

## 3 An interview with a bank manager

### Exercises

**1 Answer the questions.**

1 Imagine you are the branch manager at a busy bank but you don't have enough employees. Your staff are demotivated and there is no sense of teamwork. Think of an unusual way to bring your staff together every week for team building and sharing information.

2 You have a meeting with each employee every quarter to discuss their performance and career development. Write down two or three issues that you might discuss in the meeting.

**2 ⊕ 13 Now listen to the interview and compare your answers.**

**3 Listen again with your eyes closed. Then listen a third time while you follow the script (page 155).**

**4 Discuss any interesting issues.**

## 4 An interview with an events organizer

### Exercises

**1 The events organizer organizes exhibitions to promote her country's products abroad. Decide whether these statements are true (T) or false (F).**

1 She has one team in her home country, and another team in the export market.                                    T / F
2 An exhibitor can also be a sponsor.                          T / F
3 She organizes all the flights and shipping of large items herself.                                             T / F
4 There are seminars and round-table discussions at the exhibition, not just stands with products.               T / F
5 The usual venue is a large exhibition centre near an airport.                                                   T / F
6 The exhibitions are open to the general public.             T / F
7 Sometimes she overspends, but this is OK as long as the event is a success.                                     T / F
8 Government ministers are sometimes on the stands to persuade people to buy.                                     T / F

**2 ⊕ 14 Now listen to the interview and compare your answers.**

**3 Listen again with your eyes closed. Then listen a third time while you follow the script (page 156).**

**4 Discuss any interesting issues.**

## 5 An interview with a specialized manufacturer

### Exercises

**1 The manufacturer does a simple SWOT analysis of his company. Write next to each item below one of these letters: S (Strength), W (Weakness), O (Opportunity), T (Threat).**

1 A lot of experience in the market ____
2 Demotivated employees ____
3 Economic recession ____
4 Look for new markets ____
5 Unknown name and so no brand power ____
6 A specialized product ____
7 Competition from low-cost countries ____
8 Make other pieces ____

**2 🔊 15 Now listen to the interview and compare your answers.**

**3 Listen again with your eyes closed. Then listen a third time while you follow the script (page 157).**

**4 Discuss any interesting issues.**

## 6 An interview with a negotiator

### Exercises

**1 Answer the questions.**

1 The interviewer mentions six possible areas for negotiation: *price*, *specifications*, *quality*, *terms of payment*, *delivery* and *guarantees*. The negotiator says that four of these are either technical issues or standard in the company contract. Can you guess which four?
2 The negotiator says he tries to get more 'localization'. Put a tick ✓ next to the statements which you think he will make.
   a) Localization means local assembly in his country.
   b) Localization means transferring the whole manufacturing process to his country.
   c) Localization is a way to create jobs in his country.
   d) Localization is a way to transfer knowledge to his country.
3 The negotiator tries to get a lower PPM failure rate. What do you think the letters 'PPM' represent?

**2 🔊 16 Now listen to the interview and compare your answers.**

**3 Listen again with your eyes closed. Then listen a third time while you follow the script (page 157).**

**4 Discuss any interesting issues.**

## 7 An interview with a freight forwarder

### Exercises

**1 Answer the questions.**

1 A cargo is picked up at the factory gate in the UK on Monday morning and is ready for collection at Hong Kong airport on Friday morning. On which day do you think the following activities happen?
   a) Cargo arrives at the warehouse near Heathrow.
   b) Customs clearance and transport documents are arranged.
   c) Cargo leaves Heathrow.
   d) Cargo arrives in HK.
   e) Checking and customs procedures at HK airport.
2 The freight forwarder says 'it's very easy to scale up or scale down our work'. Do you think they a) have their own fleet of trucks, or b) rent trucks as needed?

**2 🔊 17 Now listen to the interview and check your answers.**

**3 Listen again with your eyes closed. Then listen a third time while you follow the script (page 158).**

**4 Discuss any interesting issues.**

## 8 An interview with an investment banker

### Exercises

**1 Answer the questions.**

1 The investment banker deals with *IPOs*, *M&A* and *raising funds*. Match each of these to the correct explanation below.
   a) helping a company to issue new shares or new bonds
   b) taking a private company to the stock market for the first time
   c) helping one company buy another
2 Match these terms to their explanation below: *underwriting*, *due diligence*.
   a) making a guarantee that the bank will find buyers for all the shares
   b) checking all the financial and legal background of a company
3 Write down one or two other professional groups or types of company that investment bankers work closely with.

**2 🔊 18 Now listen to the interview and check your answers.**

**3 Listen again with your eyes closed. Then listen a third time while you follow the script (page 159).**

**4 Discuss any interesting issues.**

## 9 An interview with a consultant working internationally

### Exercises

**1 Answer the questions.**

1 Guess which country is being discussed.
   a) politeness and harmony are important so no open disagreement in meetings
   b) family and government connections are important; many young business leaders educated in the States or Europe
   c) lots of talking and disagreeing in meetings; focus on the result, not on the process of doing business
   d) like queuing (standing in line); use understatement to say something is good
   e) logical, direct, serious, like technical details

2 The interviewee adds one more factor that affects business culture. Guess which one:
   a) family                 c) organization
   b) big cities             d) profession

**2 ⊙ 19 Now listen to the interview and compare your answers.**

**3 Listen again with your eyes closed. Then listen a third time while you follow the script (page 160).**

**4 Discuss any interesting issues.**

## 10 An interview with a sales director

### Exercises

**1 Answer the questions.**

1 This company has four channels to market: small retailers, large chain stores, hotels and restaurants, and vending machines. Can you guess the product?

2 Someone who owns a franchise is a franchis_ _. They license their product to a franchis_ _, who sells it to the end-user.

3 This particular company is a franchisee. Do you think they have responsibility for marketing?

4 The company already has vending machines on the street, in buildings, and in the metro (subway). Can you think of another public space where they could put their machines?

**2 ⊙ 20 Now listen to the interview and check your answers.**

**3 Listen again with your eyes closed. Then listen a third time while you follow the script (page 160).**

**4 Discuss any interesting issues.**

## 11 An interview with a takeover specialist

### Exercises

**1 This takeover specialist is an entrepreneur who buys failed companies, restructures them and then sells them. Underline the words in italics that you think describe his situation.**

1 He *likes / doesn't like* the CEO of the target company to have a vision for the company.

2 After a takeover he generally *keeps / doesn't keep* most of the old management in place.

3 His new instructions to the managers are: *cut costs / increase sales.*

4 One thing he nearly always finds in failing companies is *poor marketing / too many employees.*

5 He *feels sympathy / doesn't feel sympathy* for the people whose jobs are lost after the restructuring.

**2 ⊙ 21 Now listen to the interview and check your answers.**

**3 Listen again with your eyes closed. Then listen a third time while you follow the script (page 161).**

**4 Discuss any interesting issues.**

## 12 An interview with an exporter

### Exercises

**1 This exporter produces a food product for sale in supermarkets. Answer the questions.**

1 Different supermarket chains can sell this product at different prices. One reason is that the product may be on special offer. What is the other reason?

2 The exporter uses a merchandising company as its 'eyes' in the export market. Write down one or two things you think the merchandising company does.

3 The exporter is paid either by *letter of credit, open account* or *cash in advance*. Which one of these is a) used for customers who they trust; b) a guaranteed payment by the customer's bank; c) used only very rarely?

**2 ⊙ 22 Now listen to the interview and check your answers.**

**3 Listen again with your eyes closed. Then listen a third time while you follow the script (page 162).**

**4 Discuss any interesting issues.**

# Listening scripts

## Listen and repeat exercises

**Track 01 Exercise 31.5**
1 Hi, how's it going?
2 Not bad. And you?
3 I don't think we've met. My name's Jo.
4 Nice to meet you, Jo.
5 Simon, I want you to meet someone.
6 Simon, this is Julie, a colleague of mine.
7 Pleased to meet you.
8 Pleased to meet you, too.

**Track 02 Exercise 32.7**
1 Let me help you with your bags.
2 Did you have a good flight?
3 Is this your first time in Zurich?
4 It's good to see you again.
5 It's nice to finally meet you in person.
6 Would you like something to drink?
7 Sorry I'm late. Did you get my message?
8 My colleague is on her way.

**Track 03 Exercise 33.3**
1 Can I give you a hand?
2 It's OK. I can manage.
3 Do you mind if I open the window?
4 No, not at all. Go ahead.
5 Thanks very much for everything. I really appreciate it.
6 Don't mention it. It was my pleasure.
7 I'm sorry, I can't come with you.
8 Oh, that's a pity. Maybe next time.

**Track 04 Exercise 34.7**
1 So where are you from originally?
2 What do you do, by the way?
3 Who do you work for?
4 And where are you based?
5 Have you always worked in the auto industry?
6 Can I get you anything from the buffet?
7 Have you been to Marrakesh? What was it like?
8 A strange thing happened to me once.

**Track 05 Exercise 44.6**
1 Is that Linda? Hi! It's John here.
2 Good morning. This is Al Kent from ABC Limited.
3 Could you put me through to the Accounts Department, please?
4 I'm calling in connection with the email you sent me.
5 I'm returning your call from this morning.
6 ABC Limited, Linda speaking, how can I help you?
7 I'll try her number for you.
8 I'm sorry, she's not at her desk right now.

**Track 06 Exercise 45.8**
1 Is this a good time to talk?
2 There are three things we need to discuss.
3 It should take around 15 minutes. Do you have the time?
4 I need to make sure I understand everything.
5 I'll send you an email to confirm the details.
6 Thank you for taking the time to explain things.
7 I look forward to hearing from you.
8 Nice talking to you. Bye.

**Track 07 Exercise 46.7**
1 Shall I ask her to call you back?
2 Would you like to leave a message?
3 Can you spell that for me?
4 Can I read it back to you?
5 Which day would be best for you?
6 Shall we say ten o'clock?
7 The next week would suit me better.
8 Can you make Thursday instead?

**Track 08 Exercise 55.6**
1 OK, let's get down to business.
2 Really? Do you think so?
3 I'm not sure about that.
4 OK, shall we move on?
5 Can I just come in here?
6 Can I just finish my point?
7 Anyway, getting back to what I was saying.
8 That's as far as we can go today.

**Track 09 Exercise 56.5**
1 Sorry, I missed that.
2 I'm sorry, could you go over that again?
3 Sorry, I don't follow you.
4 Perhaps I didn't make myself clear.
5 Let me put it another way.
6 Can you be a little more specific?
7 Can you put a figure on that?
8 What kind of timescale are we talking about?

**Track 10 Exercise 60.5**
1 I'd like to thank the organizers for inviting me here today.
2 Can you hear me at the back of the room?
3 Please feel free to ask questions during my presentation.
4 I've divided my talk into three parts.
5 I'd like to stress one very important point.
6 Have a look at this next slide.
7 Before I finish, let me go over the main points again.
8 Does anyone have a question?

## Interviews with business people

🌐 Track 11

### 1 An interview with an accountant

**INTERVIEWER** *You're an accountant. My first question is this: how is an accountant different to a bookkeeper?*

**ACC** A bookkeeper records all the financial transactions in the company – it's a job that is done internally. You take the paperwork from sales and purchases – that means invoices, receipts, bills and payments – and enter the information in the correct place in a spreadsheet. In the old days it was a book.

**INTERVIEWER** *And what does an accountant do?*

**ACC** The accountant is an external person who takes this information, checks it, and then uses it to create the financial reports.

**INTERVIEWER** *The income statement, the balance sheet and the cash flow statement.*

**ACC** Yes. Those reports are filed with government agencies every year, and the accountant has to 'sign them off' – that means sign that they are correct.

**INTERVIEWER** *OK. Perhaps you could talk us through one of the reports.*

**ACC** Yes, I'll give you the example of the income statement – which many people call the profit and loss by the way. We start with revenue. This is the money that the company receives from its sales. Then from this revenue we take away the cost of making the goods, and that gives us the gross profit.

**INTERVIEWER** *Those costs of making the goods are called direct costs.*

**ACC** Yes. Things like raw materials, the wages of the factory workers – everything directly involved in making the product.

**INTERVIEWER** *OK.*

**ACC** From the gross profit we subtract the other costs, the indirect costs. These are things like marketing, administration, and so on. The figure we get at the end of that is the operating profit.

**INTERVIEWER** *OK.*

**ACC** Now we have to take away things like amortization, depreciation and tax.

**INTERVIEWER** *OK. Tax I understand. You make a profit so you pay tax. But what about amortization and depreciation?*

**ACC** They are very similar – in everyday language you can use either word. Only accountants need to know the difference! The basic idea is that you spread the cost of an asset like a computer or a vehicle over several years. Imagine that you buy a computer system for 5,000 euros. You don't enter all 5,000 in the accounts in one year. If you choose a five-year period, then you enter 1,000 euros each year.

**INTERVIEWER** *Right. So when you've subtracted tax and amortization, what's left?*

**ACC** The amount that is left is the net profit. It's like the final profit.

**INTERVIEWER** *Of course it could be a loss instead of a profit.*

**ACC** It certainly could!

**INTERVIEWER** *So this net profit – is that what people refer to when they use the phrase 'the bottom line'?*

**ACC** Yes, it is. The top line is revenue, and the bottom line is net profit. You might hear someone say: 'top line growth last year was 4%, but we improved the bottom line by 10%'.

**INTERVIEWER** *That means that income from sales grew by 4%. But they managed their costs very well and so they got a final profit of more than that, 10%.*

**ACC** Yes. The opposite situation is also very common – high top line growth but only a small net profit.

**INTERVIEWER** *In this case a lot of goods were sold, but they were sold cheaply.*

**ACC** Exactly.

**INTERVIEWER** *So is net profit the final line on the income statement?*

**ACC** No, because we still have to show any dividends paid to shareholders. The shareholders took a risk when they invested their money in the company, and so they expect to see a part of the profits returned to them.

**INTERVIEWER** *But they don't take all the profit.*

**ACC** No – the rest is reinvested in the company for future growth. That part is called the retained profit.

🌐 Track 12

### 2 An interview with a B2B commercial director

**INTERVIEWER** *Can we begin with your job title and a little about what you do?*

**CD** Yes. I'm a Commercial Director and I work for a large pharmaceutical company. Our customers are doctors and pharmacies, so it's a B2B business – we don't sell to the end-user.

**INTERVIEWER** *And you're responsible for sales in the whole country.*

**CD** Yes. Under me there are Area Managers who look after each region inside the country, and then below them are the Medical Reps who actually go round and visit the doctors.

**INTERVIEWER** *Good. I know that you have some ideas about sales management that have general interest.*

**CD** Yes – the first thing I want to say is that it's important to give your staff as much responsibility as possible. A commercial company has three main elements: products, internal processes, and people. And in my opinion people are the real critical success factor in modern business.

**INTERVIEWER** *OK. So how do you give your staff more responsibility?*

**CD** In my case I will talk about my Area Sales Managers, the level directly below me. My philosophy here is that I should be like a bank, holding resources in my hands, and they should be like entrepreneurs inside the company, coming to me with their ideas.

**INTERVIEWER** *What kind of ideas?*

**CD** Basically a business plan for their region. They propose an annual plan for how to develop sales, we discuss it, I give them a budget, and then they have responsibility for taking the plans forward. I don't constantly monitor them – I just let them get on with it. I give them freedom to act. I firmly believe that the biggest motivator when you come in to work in the morning is the feeling that you have responsibility.

**INTERVIEWER** *So it's the opposite of a hierarchical approach.*

**CD** Yes, I think in modern business you can't just give orders. Some of the best ideas come from the people closest to the customers, and a senior manager has to be open to listen to those ideas and take them on board.

**INTERVIEWER** *OK. Now what about your second idea?*

**CD** My second idea is about the role and function of the sales rep. The old idea is this: the rep presents to you the technical specifications of the product, leaves you with some leaflets, and calls you a few days later to try to get an order. My philosophy is different: the rep should have an ongoing relationship with the client, and be more like a consultant.

**INTERVIEWER** *Can you explain that in a little more detail?*

**CD** It means that the rep should focus more on the medical condition than on the product. So the pharmacist or doctor can call the rep at any time and ask questions – just to understand the illness. Nothing to do with placing an order for a product.

**INTERVIEWER** *Start with the problem and not with the product.*

**CD** Exactly. Because each area of medicine is too complicated for the pharmacist to know everything about, but the sales rep can know everything about a very small area.

**INTERVIEWER** *I understand this approach with a pharmacist, because a pharmacist has less training than a doctor. But a doctor is supposed to know everything – how can a doctor use your sales rep as a consultant without losing face?*

**CD** Well, let's be honest, a general practitioner cannot know everything. They can call my rep and discuss an illness and the effects of various drugs – it's like two professionals discussing together. There is no loss of face if the rep just provides information – then it's up to the doctor to recommend the specific treatment.

**INTERVIEWER** *Is there a problem of personalities here? If I think of a sales rep, I think of someone who is friendly, extrovert, with very good interpersonal skills. But if I think of a medical consultant I imagine someone who sits quietly reading and memorizing technical data. It's a different personality type.*

**CD** I think your idea of sales is based on B2C, not B2B. In business-to-business the rep is always more of a product specialist.

 Track 13

## 3 An interview with a bank manager

**INTERVIEWER** *In this interview we're going to discuss motivation. Is that right?*

**BM** Yes. I work in banking, and I want to tell you about something that happened when I first got a job as a Branch Manager. I was put in charge of a small, busy branch. I think we served around five or six hundred customers every day, and we handled cash operations, opening accounts for new clients, cross-selling to existing clients, and so on. We also had to provide reports to our Regional Managers and Head Office. The problem was we only had a few people working there – just eight people.

**INTERVIEWER** *So the employees had to work very hard.*

**BM** Yes. They worked hard, but at the same time they were demotivated and morale was very low. There was no sense of teamwork.

**INTERVIEWER** *So when you became manager you decided to do something about it.*

**BM** Yes. The first thing I did was suggest to my colleagues that every Tuesday we all had breakfast together at the branch.

**INTERVIEWER** *An unusual idea!*

**BM** Yes. There was no time during the day to have meetings. The only way to come together was in the early morning.

**INTERVIEWER** *How was it organized?*

**BM** The branch opened at nine o'clock, and we met there at half past seven. Each week a different person prepared the breakfast. I offered to go first. I bought some stuff from the supermarket, and also baked some special bread at home the evening before. It was all very informal – we laid the food out on a table and helped ourselves, and then we just chatted. Then in the last 20 minutes or so I gave a kind of weekly report. I mean a verbal report.

**INTERVIEWER** *What did you say in the report?*

**BM** I gave some figures. I talked about what our customers wanted, and any special problems we were having. But, very importantly, I also gave people praise. I mentioned individuals by name and said what they had done.

**INTERVIEWER** *Public thanks and recognition.*

**BM** Exactly.

**INTERVIEWER** *Very interesting – the breakfast idea was used both for team building and for the sharing of information.*

**BM** Yes. And apart from the breakfast, I did other things as well. There was already a system for reviewing employees' performance. Everyone would meet with their manager once a quarter, and they discussed targets, based on the person's job. For example with operational staff there were targets based on the number of customers served, customer satisfaction levels, and so on. For sales staff it was how many products they sold to the client.

**INTERVIEWER** *And people received a bonus on top of their basic salary if they reached their target.*

**BM** Yes. This was the existing system. The change that I introduced was to have team targets as well as individual targets. The whole staff group got an extra bonus depending on the level of income or profit reached by the branch.

**INTERVIEWER** *Did the performance meeting only discuss targets and bonuses?*

**BM** No, not at all. Another thing I did was to agree with Head Office that I could have a budget for training. That meant that I was able to offer people something in terms of career development. I could assess an employee's future potential within the organization, and then offer them training. I also offered opportunities for job rotation – for example giving someone a chance to move from operations to sales to develop their business experience.

**INTERVIEWER** *What about promotion?*

**BM** This is very important for motivation, and the process has to be transparent. If I saw that someone was hard-working, reliable and loyal to the bank, then I would promote them. Now the danger is that other colleagues will think: 'Ah, he's been saying nice things to the boss, or maybe he's the cousin of somebody.' So you have to promote the right people, based on their work, and everyone must see that the system is fair. It's a very important motivating factor – perhaps the most important one.

🌐 Track 14

## 4 An interview with an events organizer

**INTERVIEWER** *OK, so can you tell me what you do?*

**EO** Yes. I'm an Events Organizer. I work to promote products abroad, so I'm in charge of organizing exhibitions to help exporters.

**INTERVIEWER** *And how exactly do you do that?*

**EO** We have two teams, one in the home country, and one local team in the export market.

**INTERVIEWER** *OK, let's take them one at a time.*

**EO** So, first the team in the home country. To begin with we need regular contact with our big exporters, and also to think about firms who may want to export in the future. We need to explain to them why it's worth going to the exhibition and having a stand. Some of the biggest companies who exhibit regularly are also our sponsors – that means they pay more to attend the exhibition, but in return they have their logo on all the communication, on the brochure, inside the hall, etc. We also set up big video screens in places like the coffee area and these

sponsors have their promotional videos running all the time.

**INTERVIEWER** *So that's the exhibitors.*

**EO** Yes. The first and most important thing is to find exhibitors and persuade them that it's worth paying to have a stand. But after that there are other specific things to arrange, and we need to involve some outside partners. For example, we need a travel agency to arrange all the flights, and a freight agency to arrange the shipping of large items. For instance an engineering company might have a large working model to show on the stand. We also need to contact speakers, because at the exhibition there will be seminars and round-table discussions, and people are attracted to the event by the speakers as much as the stands.

**INTERVIEWER** *How do you choose the speakers?*

**EO** That's a good question. The speakers need to have a high visibility, and they have to be experts in their field. If we get someone from one particular company, then of course all the competitor companies complain that they don't have a speaker. Wherever possible we try to choose independent speakers.

**INTERVIEWER** *Right, so that's the work of the team in the home market. What about the team in the export market?*

**EO** The first thing is to find a good venue. Usually we use a big hotel, and it needs to have a large hall for us to set up all the stands, and then smaller rooms to hold seminars and talks. We have to negotiate about food and refreshments at the exhibition and many other things. Then we need local partners to carry out specific functions – the most important is a local communications agency to promote the event to potential customers. This agency needs to have good contacts, because the exhibition is only for decision makers and business people in the country, not for the general public. We need a lot of visitors otherwise it's pointless. The agency puts out a press release, organizes a press conference, makes a lot of calls to local companies, etc. We also need local suppliers who will build the stands inside the hall, and others who will decorate the hall with banners and so on.

**INTERVIEWER** *OK. So I can see that there are a lot of people involved. What exactly do you do in the middle of all this?*

**EO** I'm really a project manager. I coordinate everything. I need to know a little about communication, a little about logistics, a little about the world of travel and hotels, a little about everything. Basically, I am the point of contact for everyone, the link between everybody. And of course I also have responsibility for the budget. My boss gives me a budget, and I cannot overspend.

**INTERVIEWER** *Finally, can you give me an example of the kind of things that can go wrong at an exhibition?*

**EO** Lost baggage. Speakers with no audience. And then there's all the pressure of dealing with VIPs. Sometimes we have the ambassador, or even a government minister, to open the event. With people like that everything has to be perfect, and it's a lot of stress.

 Track 15

## 5 An interview with a specialized manufacturer

**INTERVIEWER**   *OK, I know that you make a specialized part for the automobile industry. Can you tell me a little bit more about your company?*

**MAN**   Yes, we are a small manufacturing company and we make just one part of the braking system for cars. Our part is inside the wheel of the car. And we really are very specialized because our part is only used by mechanics who repair and service cars. It's a replacement part; it's not used in new cars.

**INTERVIEWER**   *What is your channel to market?*

**MAN**   We sell to a distributor. This distributor carries a large amount of our product in stock, and they also sell other components of the braking system that come from other manufacturers.

**INTERVIEWER**   *Does your distributor only buy from you?*

**MAN**   They are free to buy from our competitors, and we are free to sell to other distributors, but in fact we have been working together for many years and the arrangement is exclusive on both sides.

**INTERVIEWER**   *And the distributor sells directly to the garages who repair and maintain the cars?*

**MAN**   Yes, to the garages, not the car manufacturers. Ours is a replacement part.

**INTERVIEWER**   *OK, I'd like to ask you to do a simple SWOT analysis of your business. So some internal strengths and weaknesses, and then some opportunities and threats in the market.*

**MAN**   OK.

**INTERVIEWER**   *Can you begin with your strengths?*

**MAN**   Yes, our first strength is that we have been in the market for over 30 years, and so we have a lot of experience. Second, the product itself is specialized – not many other firms make it. Third, the machines we use are also specialized – we use the very best German technology and the quality is very good.

**INTERVIEWER**   *OK, so those are the strengths. What about the weaknesses?*

**MAN**   Well, one weakness is that our employees are a bit demotivated. We are a small family firm in a small town and the workers have been there for many years. Everybody knows each other and nobody has ever been fired from the company. It's a safe job, but people don't work very hard.

**INTERVIEWER**   *And I guess there aren't many opportunities for promotion.*

**MAN**   That's right. We're a small company and we don't have a lot of layers.

**INTERVIEWER**   *OK. Any other weaknesses?*

**MAN**   Maybe the fact that in our situation we don't have any brand power. Only a very few people in the business know our company name. The distributor doesn't really want our brand name to be well known.

**INTERVIEWER**   *Why?*

**MAN**   It would give us more power to sell directly to the garages and mechanics, or just to go to other distributors.

**INTERVIEWER**   *OK, now what about the opportunities and the threats?*

**MAN**   The main opportunity is simply to grow and become larger. So we can try to find other distributors in other markets. Another opportunity is to make the other pieces of the braking system.

**INTERVIEWER**   *So instead of making a piece in a component, you could manufacture the whole component.*

**MAN**   That's right. It would be a big strategic decision because we would have to buy, or merge with, another company who produces the other parts. But I do think that some sectors of the market would prefer to buy the whole braking system, ready-made. It simplifies the installation for them.

**INTERVIEWER**   *So those are the opportunities. What about the threats?*

**MAN**   Well, an economic recession is always a threat. The auto industry is very sensitive to recessions.

**INTERVIEWER**   *And do you feel any threat from competitors in low-cost countries?*

**MAN**   Of course there is always this threat. But our quality is very good, and we sell to a local market where we have very good connections. We've been working with this distributor for years and there is a lot of trust on both sides. If they turn round and say: 'OK, we're going to start sourcing your product from China', then we can always say that we'll sell directly to the end-user and undercut them. We always have that option.

 Track 16

## 6 An interview with a negotiator

**INTERVIEWER**   *OK, we're going to talk about negotiating. Before we do that, can you give me a little background to your company?*

**NEG**   Yes, I'm Managing Director of a company that buys specialized parts and components from Germany, assembles them in my country, and then sells the finished pieces to one specific local industry in my country.

**INTERVIEWER**   *OK, in my mind when I hear the word 'negotiation' I think about price, specifications, quality, terms of payment, delivery and guarantees. Am I right?*

**NEG**   Let's go through your list. First price. Obviously that's important. Next is specifications and quality. Now these are technical issues, and the technical guys on both sides meet and talk. But they are not really negotiations in the sense that I think you mean – with bargaining and so on.

**INTERVIEWER**   *OK. What about terms of payment and delivery?*

**NEG**   These are standard things in our company contract. We do discuss them, but there isn't usually any serious disagreement. We call delivery 'terms of shipping' by the way.

**INTERVIEWER**   *OK, let's go back to price – we didn't get into any detail before.*

**NEG**   Yes. We have to pass on any price increase to our own customers, and so I have to know why the price is going up. I need a story to tell to my customers to explain it.

**INTERVIEWER**   *Do you try to resist the price increase?*

**NEG**   Yes, of course. But they have the power in the negotiation because they have specialized parts that are difficult to get from other sources. So instead I usually accept the price increase, but with certain conditions.

**INTERVIEWER**   *Such as?*

**NEG**   I say: 'OK, I'll agree to the new price, but in return you should allow me to localize more production in my country'.

**INTERVIEWER**   *What exactly does that mean?*

**NEG**   Localization means local assembly. The opposite is to import a finished, ready-made piece from Germany and resell it here. That's difficult and expensive: there are import taxes and all sorts of other obstacles. A second option, the one that we follow, is to import the individual parts and components and then assemble them here. That's localization. The parts are cheaper when they come un-assembled, and the import taxes are lower.

**INTERVIEWER**   *So in effect you transfer the assembly costs from Germany to here.*

**NEG**   Yes, our workers are cheaper. And the lower import tax is a very significant factor. It's a political issue – our government wants to encourage localization as a way to create jobs, so they make the tariffs much lower when the parts come in un-assembled.

**INTERVIEWER**   *Is there an issue here about knowledge transfer? If you do the assembly, then you are transferring knowledge from Germany to your country.*

**NEG**   This is relevant where they give us some know-how as part of localization. We have to sign that we will not transfer this know-how to third parties.

**INTERVIEWER**   *OK, have we covered all the areas for negotiation?*

**NEG**   You mentioned guarantees in your original list, and we haven't discussed it yet. For us this is very important. We're talking here about the failure rate that we are prepared to accept. We define this in terms of PPM – that means parts per million.

**INTERVIEWER**   *What would be a typical PPM failure rate?*

**NEG**   Let's say five. Of course it depends very much on the part – for electronic parts it's different to mechanical parts.

**INTERVIEWER**   *But you do negotiate about it.*

**NEG**   Very much so. We try to convince them to give us a better PPM. It's a key issue. If a part fails, that means that the whole finished piece fails. That means that the end-user who is using that piece has their own problems, and they complain to us. So we lose some goodwill in the market – our reputation suffers. It's not just about the simple replacement cost of the part.

🌐 **Track 17**

# 7 An interview with a freight forwarder

**INTERVIEWER**   *You're the manager of a large freight forwarding company, and I thought it would be interesting to know a little more about what you do.*

**FF**   It's very simple. We make world trade possible. Without freight forwarding you only have home production for home markets.

**INTERVIEWER**   *OK, so here is my understanding of freight forwarding. You are basically an international logistics company. You collect products from the place where they are made, you take them to a port or an airport, you ship them, and then you take them to their final destination.*

**FF**   Absolutely right. But let me add some details. First, you forgot about customs clearance and the paperwork side of things – that's a big part of our job. Second, you didn't mention the benefits we offer our clients. The main one is that clients can track the movement of their freight across the world. At any time they can go to the Internet, enter the consignment number, and know exactly where their shipment is.

**INTERVIEWER**   *OK.*

**FF**   And finally, you didn't mention the integration of our IT system with the IT system of our clients.

**INTERVIEWER**   *So tell me more about that.*

**FF**   With our major clients – consumer goods companies for example – our computers and their computers speak to each other. That means that we can directly manage their warehousing operations. It makes everything very quick.

**INTERVIEWER**   *Give me an example.*

**FF**   Let's take the example of sending goods from London to Hong Kong. We make this kind of movement ten or twelve times a day. We see on the computer that a cargo is going to be ready at the client's factory gate in the UK on Monday. We pick it up on Monday morning, and it arrives at the warehouse near Heathrow later that day. We do all the customs clearance and other transport documents on Tuesday, and Wednesday morning it's ready to go to the cargo section of British Airways or Lufthansa or Air China. It flies that day.

**INTERVIEWER**   *Wednesday.*

**FF**   Yes. It arrives in Hong Kong on Thursday morning. It's checked by the airport authorities there, and our operator in Hong Kong does all the customs procedures on that day. He should finish in one day. That means it's ready for collection at Hong Kong airport on Friday morning.

**INTERVIEWER** *And then you take it to its final destination.*

**FF** That's right.

**INTERVIEWER** *So from the factory gate in the UK on Monday to the final destination in Hong Kong on Friday.*

**FF** Exactly. Of course there can be a problem at any stage, but we – and the client – immediately see it on the computer and we can act to sort things out.

**INTERVIEWER** *Now obviously you work very closely with the airlines. What about trucking companies for road transport?*

**FF** We rent trucks as needed from the trucking companies. We don't own trucks – we don't want to get involved in maintenance, mechanics, garages, all that kind of thing. We own no physical assets – we just exist in an office with computers and phones.

**INTERVIEWER** *You have very few fixed costs in comparison to the size of your business.*

**FF** Yes, and this means it's very easy to scale up or scale down our work. In general our capacity is very easy to manage. One thing we do is fix the space we need in advance. We say to the airline or the carrier we will sign a contract for X tonnes a week or X containers a week over one year – and then they fix a price. Both sides know exactly where they stand.

**INTERVIEWER** *So you guarantee a certain level of business to the airline, and in return they give you a lower cost.*

**FF** That's right.

**INTERVIEWER** *And what happens if you don't use that capacity?*

**FF** Of course we pay. We pay for the empty space.

**INTERVIEWER** *So what is the advantage of doing it?*

**FF** We have guaranteed space on the flights and we can guarantee a service level to our clients. Our clients pay a little more, but they get quality and reliability.

🌐 Track 18

## 8 An interview with an investment banker

**INTERVIEWER** *You're an investment banker.*

**IB** That's right.

**INTERVIEWER** *In this interview I'd like to cover the three areas of investment banking: IPOs, M&A, and raising funds. I'd like you to explain a little bit about each one.*

**IB** OK.

**INTERVIEWER** *Let's begin with an IPO – initial public offering – where you take a private company to the stock market for the first time. Can you tell me the role of the investment bank in this process?*

**IB** Yes. First we have to find a promising company that is ready to go public. Often we are approached by whoever owns the company – usually a private equity firm. They come to us and say they have a company ready to go

public. Then it's our job to decide on the price that we will ask for the shares when they are listed on the stock market on Day One. And finally it's our responsibility to find buyers for those shares – large financial institutions.

**INTERVIEWER** *What about underwriting?*

**IB** Yes, underwriting is making a guarantee that we will sell all the shares. Of course we do the underwriting. If we can't sell all the shares, we have to buy them ourselves. But normally we know beforehand, and we ask the company to reduce the number of shares it will make available.

**INTERVIEWER** *Is there anything else that you do?*

**IB** Well, at the beginning a lot of time is spent doing due diligence. That means checking everything – the financial statements, the rules of the company, the background of the senior managers, and many other things. Everything has to be legal and correct before the regulatory body of that stock exchange will accept a public listing.

**INTERVIEWER** *OK. So that's the first area of an investment bank's work, IPOs. Let's move on to the second: mergers and acquisitions.*

**IB** OK. A company might come to us and say they are looking for another company to buy. Perhaps they want to expand, or to enter a new market.

**INTERVIEWER** *And then you look for a suitable target company.*

**IB** Yes. We approach the target company and see if the major shareholders want to sell. And if they do, we do due diligence on both companies.

**INTERVIEWER** *Who decides what changes there will be after the acquisition? For example which offices will close, who will lose their job, etc?*

**IB** Well, the senior management decides, but very often they bring in a consulting company to help them. We don't do that.

**INTERVIEWER** *OK. And now the final area of an investment bank's business is to raise funds for its clients, either through issuing new shares or through issuing bonds.*

**IB** Yes. Of course there is a third way to raise funds which is to ask for a bank loan, but that isn't our job.

**INTERVIEWER** *Right. So what happens?*

**IB** The company comes to us and says that they need to raise money, and we discuss with them which is the best way. A new share issue means the existing shareholders might not be very happy – their stake in the company is diluted, and their dividends are diluted. But if it's to raise money for expansion, then it might be OK. A bond issue is different – you are raising money with a loan. It means that the company takes on more debt, which has to be repaid.

**INTERVIEWER** *What is the advantage of raising money through debt?*

**IB** It costs less for the company. If the company has a good credit rating, it can issue bonds quite cheaply.

**INTERVIEWER**   *OK, so my final question is this: how does the investment bank get its income in each of the three cases?*

**IB**   Commission. In all cases. We get a commission for a successful IPO, a commission for a successful acquisition, and a commission for a successful share or bond issue.

**INTERVIEWER**   *And does anyone else get a commission?*

**IB**   Oh yes. Accountants and lawyers and consultants. There are always accountants and lawyers and consultants.

🔘 Track 19

## 9 An interview with a consultant working internationally

**INTERVIEWER**   *I know that you work for an international consulting company, and that you've lived and worked all over the world. I should also mention that you yourself come from an Asian country.*

**CON**   Yes, that's right.

**INTERVIEWER**   *So today we're going to talk about doing business in different cultures.*

**CON**   And please remember that anything I say is just my own personal opinion – it's not necessarily right or wrong.

**INTERVIEWER**   *OK. Let's start with Japan – I think you currently live there.*

**CON**   Yes, I do. Well everyone says that Japanese culture is quite indirect, and I think that's true.

**INTERVIEWER**   *Can you give me an example?*

**CON**   For example if a Japanese person says 'I'm not sure' or 'I'll think about it', it means 'no'. If an American says: 'I'll think about it', it means: 'I'll think about it'.

**INTERVIEWER**   *And the reason for the indirectness?*

**CON**   Politeness and harmony. Harmony is a very important part of Japanese culture – the idea is to avoid conflict, especially where teamwork is concerned.

**INTERVIEWER**   *So this makes open disagreement, in a meeting for example, impossible.*

**CON**   Oh yes. A disagreement causes conflict and discomfort. For this reason Japanese people tend to keep silent about their opinions, and just speak in a meeting to ask information questions. When I meet with Americans it's very different – lots of talking and disagreeing and asking other people difficult questions.

**INTERVIEWER**   *But doesn't decision-making always involve disagreement? There will always be more than one point of view, surely.*

**CON**   If you have another opinion, you speak to people privately, one-to-one, using very careful language. But only the top people really make the decisions anyway – Japanese organizations are quite top-down.

**INTERVIEWER**   *Are things changing?*

**CON**   Yes, I would say so. But there is a still a strong idea in all Asian cultures that you should not be disrespectful to the boss by disagreeing.

**INTERVIEWER**   *How would you compare Chinese and Japanese business culture?*

**CON**   There are many similarities – for example not using a lot of words to describe things. People sense the meaning – it's like reading between the lines. But there are differences too. In China connections are very important: family connections, government connections, all kinds. It's less true in Japan. But one thing you always have to remember is that a lot of younger Chinese business leaders were educated in the States or in a European country, so they carry that influence back home with them.

**INTERVIEWER**   *And what is the influence of American or European business culture?*

**CON**   In the US they focus on the result, not on the process of doing business. What you say matters, who you are doesn't. In Asian cultures it's different – you have to know the person first, to build trust. For example in China a contract might be made after a long meal, in Japan after a visit to a karaoke bar.

**INTERVIEWER**   *What about Europe – how is Europe different?*

**CON**   It's very difficult to talk about Europe as a whole – the countries are very different. I find that UK people are similar to Japanese in some ways – indirect, polite, and you both like queuing! And in both countries you hate boasting – you use understatement to say that something is good. In Germany people are logical and direct. I find them quite serious, and they like technical details. In Germany it's good to write everything down so there are no misunderstandings. Of course these are all generalizations, but there is some truth there somewhere.

**INTERVIEWER**   *Yes, we must never forget that every individual is different.*

**CON**   And big cities are different as well. If you go to London or Frankfurt or New York or Shanghai, you will find an international business culture that is different to the typical national culture where that city is.

🔘 Track 20

## 10 An interview with a sales director

**INTERVIEWER**   *Can you introduce yourself and your company?*

**SD**   Yes. I'm a Sales Director for a well-known soft drinks company.

**INTERVIEWER**   *To begin with I'd like you to describe your different channels to the market.*

**SD**   Yes, we have four channels. The first is small retailers who sell our drinks, the second is large chain stores, the third is hotels and restaurants where our drinks come out of a shotgun, not a bottle or can, and the fourth is vending machines.

**INTERVIEWER**   *And which channel has the most sales?*

**SD**   The vending machine channel is the most important for us. We have 70,000 vending machines in our city.

**INTERVIEWER**   *How many sales reps do you have?*

**SD**   Our company, which is a franchise by the way, has about 1,000 employees. Of those about 800 are sales and delivery people.

**INTERVIEWER**   *So what exactly do the sales and delivery people do?*

**SD**   The delivery people go round the city every day, in a van, restocking the machines and collecting the money. Also they clean and maintain the machines. And the sales people visit potential new customers – maybe restaurants that don't yet sell our product, or the owners of apartment blocks that don't have a vending machine.

**INTERVIEWER**   *And as Sales Director, what do you do?*

**SD**   I check the budget. I look at the planned sales, the actual sales, and the variance between the two. And I check that information every single day.

**INTERVIEWER**   *So you look at sales from the vending machines, the shops, the restaurants, the bars, the hotels, everything.*

**SD**   That's right. If it shows that in one shop the sales have suddenly gone down, then I ask the Sales Rep if they know the reason. After that, if they don't know, I send them to visit the shop to see what's going on.

**INTERVIEWER**   *OK. Now you mentioned earlier that your company is a franchise.*

**SD**   That's right. We have the license to bottle and sell the product.

**INTERVIEWER**   *And do you have the franchise for the whole country?*

**SD**   No – in my country there are about ten franchisees. We just have the franchise for the capital city.

**INTERVIEWER**   *Can you explain in basic terms the relationship between you and your Head Office? For example, who has the responsibility to pay for the advertising?*

**SD**   Our job is to make, distribute and sell the product, that's all. We pay the franchisor for the raw material, the syrup. From this money they run their operation, which includes all the marketing side such as product development and advertising.

**INTERVIEWER**   *So the ads we see on billboards, on TV, at the cinemas, you have nothing to do with this. This is all paid for by the franchisor.*

**SD**   That's right. It's completely separate.

**INTERVIEWER**   *OK, now with this business model how is it possible for your company to grow? There can't be space for many more vending machines!*

**SD**   It's a good point. But we can find a few new opportunities – for example in car parks. Next to the machine where you pay for your parking we can put a machine selling drinks.

**INTERVIEWER**   *And what do you do in the winter? I imagine your product is quite seasonal.*

**SD**   Yes, our business is very dependent on the weather. If it's hot, sales go up. But now we are trying to find a way to sell hot drinks in the winter as well. It's another possible area of growth for us.

 Track 21

# 11 An interview with a takeover specialist

**INTERVIEWER**   *You're an entrepreneur who buys failed companies, is that right?*

**TS**   Yes.

**INTERVIEWER**   *And what is the structure of your company?*

**TS**   I run my business as a holding company. I look for a takeover target, buy it, restructure it, and then sell it. I have no interest in running the target company, and the industry sector also doesn't matter.

**INTERVIEWER**   *We're talking about buying companies where the shares are held privately, right?*

**TS**   Yes.

**INTERVIEWER**   *And where for some reason the company isn't doing well, and some of the shareholders want to sell.*

**TS**   That's right. Usually there's some kind of a crisis situation and I can buy the shares very cheaply. I always negotiate confidentially – for example I don't buy all the shares in my own name. I don't want the other shareholders to know who is accumulating shares and how many because then they will increase their price to me.

**INTERVIEWER**   *When you buy a company, do you leave the original management in place, or do you put your own guys in there?*

**TS**   Let's start with the CEO. I keep the CEO if they have a finance background – because with me they are going to be focused on figures and profitability. I hate it when the CEO talks about dreams and vision – it was their vision that got the company into a mess in the first place.

**INTERVIEWER**   *And the other managers?*

**TS**   Remember that it's usually a hostile takeover – the senior management know nothing about the change of ownership. When they find out, they are always against us – they know that I'm going to shake up the company and some will lose their jobs. But in general I try to keep most of the management in place because they know how to run the business – even if they were doing it badly. Of course I give them new instructions.

**INTERVIEWER**   *Which are?*

**TS**   To cut costs.

**INTERVIEWER**   *So what are the typical cost-cutting measures that you would take? How do you cut costs without hitting sales?*

**TS**   I restructure the company. That means removing staff who are unnecessary or who are performing poorly. One thing you nearly always find in failing companies is too many employees – the boss doesn't have the courage to fire them because they have been there for a long time, or something like this. But I don't just fire people.

Restructuring means taking out layers of management, consolidating into one office work that was previously done in two, changing job descriptions, making unproductive people take on more work, and so on. So generally making the company more efficient in its use of resources.

**INTERVIEWER**   *And as an outsider you can make these radical changes much more easily.*

**TS**   Oh yes. Of course I am hated for it, but I do it. It's my business.

**INTERVIEWER**   *So now you've got a restructured company, and it's more profitable. Who do you sell it to?*

**TS**   To other private investors, such as private equity groups. We don't do an IPO with a stock market listing because the companies aren't big enough.

**INTERVIEWER**   *OK. One last question. Do you ever feel any sympathy for the people whose jobs will be lost because of the restructuring?*

**TS**   No, never. Cutting costs is a necessary thing, because without it the company would go out of business anyway. In a way I'm saving the company – saving the jobs that are still left.

🔘 Track 22

## 12 An interview with an exporter

**INTERVIEWER**   *We're going to talk about exporting. As background information, can you say a few words about your company?*

**EXP**   Yes, I work for a company in a small Latin American country that produces one particular kind of food. You find it on the shelves in supermarkets. We export to many other countries in Latin America, and also to the United States.

**INTERVIEWER**   *OK. Let's begin with how you first find your customers in the export market.*

**EXP**   Yes. It depends if you already have customers in that market, or if you're looking for the first one. If you have no presence in the market at all, then you have to do quite a lot of research. And not just about business opportunities, there may be certain packaging requirements, legal requirements, and so on. But if our products are already on sale in one supermarket chain, and they are selling well, then other chains will come to us – we don't have to go to them.

**INTERVIEWER**   *I imagine it's quite common for different chains to have your products on sale at different prices. Does that create a problem?*

**EXP**   Yes. That creates a problem. Sometimes we get a call from one chain asking us to reduce the cost price to them, because another chain has our products on the shelves much cheaper. We have to explain that maybe this other chain has our products on special offer, or something like that. Of course sometimes we really do sell at a different price to the other chain because they

take more product. It can be very difficult to have this kind of conversation.

**INTERVIEWER**   *And how do you know the retail price of your products in the different chains? They can vary from week to week.*

**EXP**   It's a good question. We work with a local merchandising company. It's their job to go round every supermarket and look at the competitors' products and prices, and also to see what price our products are selling for. They are our eyes in the export market.

**INTERVIEWER**   *Does the merchandising company do anything else?*

**EXP**   Yes, they check how our products are displayed on the shelves. For example, what length of shelf space is given to us as compared to the competitors, whether our products are at eye level or not. All these things we agreed with the supermarket chain at the beginning, but the merchandising company goes round and checks.

**INTERVIEWER**   *And apart from the merchandising company, which other third party companies do you work with?*

**EXP**   On the transport side of things we need a freight forwarder to arrange the shipping of our containers, and we need a logistics company to take the container to the dock.

**INTERVIEWER**   *OK, finally let's talk about payment. How are you paid?*

**EXP**   If it's a new client and we don't know anything about them, we always use a letter of credit. This is where the customer's bank guarantees the payment to us. There is no risk for us.

**INTERVIEWER**   *Do you get paid immediately?*

**EXP**   No, you can have for example a 30-day letter of credit. The bank pays you after 30 days. But remember it's the bank's job to get the money from the customer, not ours.

**INTERVIEWER**   *And for regular customers who you trust?*

**EXP**   Then the payment system is called open account. We supply the goods without any payment, and they pay us within a certain time period, depending on the terms of payment we negotiate. When it's time to pay, they pay us directly through an international bank transfer.

**INTERVIEWER**   *OK so that's letter of credit and open account. Do you use any other payment methods?*

**EXP**   Very rarely, with a small order, we might use cash in advance. In some situations it's actually better for the customer to do it this way because they don't have to pay the bank for the letter of credit. But then of course the risk passes to them – they have given us their money and we still haven't shipped the goods.

# Answer key

## 1 Company types and structures

### Exercise 1.1
1 self-employed  2 associates  3 shares  4 listed  5 state-owned enterprise  6 buying parts and raw materials  7 Customer Services  8 Human Resources  9 Research and Development  10 lawyers  11 run  12 responsible for  13 more senior people  14 a higher level  15 line manager  16 liaise  17 is part of  18 report directly

### Exercise 1.2
1 checks  2 arranges  3 answers  4 collects  5 deals  6 maintains

### Exercise 1.3
1 meet their needs  2 makes a profit  3 day-to-day basis  4 back-office functions  5 liaise closely  6 recruit  7 behind the scenes  8 step on someone's toes

### Exercise 1.4
1 estate-owned state-owned  2 cultural culture  3 bureaucracy bureaucratic  4 responsible responsibility  5 relegates delegates  6 bottom-down bottom-up  7 top-up top-down  8 innovation innovative

## 2 Start-up and growth

### Exercise 2.1
1 entrepreneur  2 capital  3 founder  4 premises  5 purchase  6 turnover  7 shares  8 acquisition  9 collateral  10 demand

### Exercise 2.2
1 start-up company  2 exit strategy  3 brand name  4 a going concern  5 private equity  6 a gap in the market  7 do some market research  8 employ staff  9 fail to get enough customers  10 make a profit  11 raise capital  12 rent premises

### Exercise 2.3
1 a going concern / do some market research  2 raise capital / private equity  3 a gap in the market / rent premises

### Exercise 2.4
1 lends you  2 borrow money  3 giving  4 taking  5 a loan

### Exercise 2.5
1 develop  2 distribution  3 promotion  4 employ  5 ownership  6 growth  7 expand  8 competitor / competition  9 failure  10 acquire

### Exercise 2.6
1 channels  2 up  3 growth  4 even  5 suppliers  6 known  7 profitable  8 public  9 out  10 flow

## 3 Individual company profile

### Exercise 3.1
1 c  2 a  3 g  4 f  5 h  6 d  7 e  8 b

### Exercise 3.2
1 1c/2a  2 7e  3 5h  4 8b  5 3g  6 4f

### Exercise 3.3
1 milestone  2 subsidiary  3 key factor

### Exercise 3.4
1 b  2 c  3 a

### Exercise 3.5
1 2c  2 1b  3 3a

### Exercise 3.6
1 sector  2 aimed  3 in  4 employs  5 Head Office  6 majority  7 manufactured  8 established  9 abroad  10 extensive  11 collaborations  12 a range  13 brand  14 competitors  15 sales  16 revenue  17 share  18 leader  19 in  20 lower  21 knowledge  22 products  23 efficient  24 policy  25 employees  26 damage

## 4 The manufacturing sector

### Exercise 4.1
1 supplier  2 warehouse  3 inventory  4 negotiating  5 waste  6 rework  7 200 batches  8 produce  9 supplies  10 distribute  11 control  12 replace

### Exercise 4.2
1 supplier  2 inventory  3 waste  4 rework  5 distribute  6 control

### Exercise 4.3
1 store products in a warehouse  2 eliminate waste  3 unload goods from trucks  4 add value for the customer  5 outsource production all over the world  6 coordinate the global supply chain  7 get things 'right first time'  8 be fit for purpose

### Exercise 4.4
1 fit for purpose  2 waste  3 supply chain

### Exercise 4.5
1 breaking / serviced  2 wrong lead / fit / device  3 funny / fixed / unplug / out-of-order  4 mains / socket / runs / batteries  5 properly / adjust / settings / panel  6 machine tools / production run

## 5 The service sector

### Exercise 5.1
1 modal model  2 customerize customize  3 in-the-house in-house  4 needings needs  5 in on  6 month monthly  7 basic basis  8 orientationed oriented

### Exercise 5.2
1 d  2 b  3 f  4 a  5 e  6 h  7 g  8 c

### Exercise 5.3
1 in  2 of  3 from / to  4 for  5 for  6 on  7 at  8 on  9 to  10 to

### Exercise 5.4
1 provide  2 charge  3 allow  4 differentiate  5 handle  6 customize  7 assess / advise / implement

### Exercise 5.5
1 handle your financial planning  2 meet your needs  3 offer the full range  4 take a long-term approach  5 charge an initial set-up fee  6 have immediate access

## 6 Markets and competitors

### Exercise 6.1
1 French  2 B2B  3 bull  4 niche  5 is worth  6 in  7 on  8 share  9 competitors  10 highly  11 with  12 face

### Exercise 6.2
1 domestic / home / foreign  2 existing / current / potential  3 free / open / protected  4 growing / expanding / declining  5 huge / enormous / small  6 niche / specialist / mass

### Exercise 6.3
1 huge  2 protected  3 domestic  4 mass  5 free

**Exercise 6.4**

1 competitive   2 competitiveness   3 competition   4 competitor

**Exercise 6.5**

1 research   2 trend   3 decline   4 entered   5 take over   6 price
7 position   8 withdraw from   9 leader   10 line

## 7 Marketing – the four Ps

**Exercise 7.1**

1 delivery   2 range   3 leaflet   4 offer   5 coupon   6 online
7 guaranteed   8 difference

**Exercise 7.2**

1 feature   2 benefit

**Exercise 7.3**

1 brand   2 segments   3 margin/mark-up   4 range   5 fee
6 charge   7 intermediaries   8 outlets   9 outdoor
10 word-of-mouth

**Exercise 7.4**

1 value proposition   2 price point   3 retail outlet   4 distribution
channel   5 channel partner   6 public relations   7 search engine
8 advertising campaign

**Exercise 7.5**

1 price point   2 advertising campaign   3 retail outlets   4 channel
partner   5 search engine

**Exercise 7.6**

1 set   2 charged   3 place   4 aim at   5 translate   6 attend
7 sponsor   8 handled

## 8 Marketing strategy and brands

**Exercise 8.1**

1 objective   2 target   3 research   4 allocate   5 endorse
6 sponsor   7 appeal to   8 well-known   9 competing   10 loyalty

**Exercise 8.2**

1 positioning   2 facelift   3 awareness   4 withdraw   5 forecast
6 slogan   7 identity   8 behaviour

**Exercise 8.3**

1 promotion   2 competition/competitor   3 distribution/distributor
4 advertisement/ad   5 sponsorship   6 target   7 recognition
8 loyalty

**Exercise 8.4**

1 strategy   2 packaging   3 range   4 budget   5 word-of-mouth
6 solutions   7 appeals   8 brand

## 9 Describing products

**Exercise 9.1**

1 d   2 a   3 e   4 c   5 b   6 h   7 f   8 i   9 j   10 g   11 o
12 k   13 n   14 l   15 m

**Exercise 9.2**

1 d   2 c   3 a   4 e   5 b

**Exercise 9.3**

1 energy-efficient/environmentally friendly/long-lasting
2 easy-to-clean/portable/well-built
3 fully automatic/high-performance/limited edition

**Exercise 9.4**

1 features   2 don't include   3 shape   4 size   5 long   6 length
7 weigh   8 weight

**Exercise 9.5**

1 length   2 width   3 high/height   4 deep/depth/in
5 weighs/weight   6 by/square   7 size/cubic   8 of/composite

**Exercise 9.6**

1 steel   2 moulded plastic   3 copper   4 leather   5 nanomaterials
6 reinforced concrete

## 10 Customers

**Exercise 10.1**

1 client   2 end-user   3 customer   4 consumer

**Exercise 10.2**

1 supplier/vendor   2 personalized/customized/tailor-made
3 satisfied/repeat purchase   4 requirements   5 package/specific

**Exercise 10.3**

1 meet   2 carry out   3 do   4 offer   5 have   6 reach   7 do
8 enter

**Exercise 10.4**

1 deal with it   2 give   3 ship it   4 satisfy their needs   5 ask the
questions

**Exercise 10.5**

1 follow it up   2 deal with it   3 provide it   4 place it   5 fill it in

**Exercise 10.6**

1 guarantee   2 warranty

**Exercise 10.7**

1 relationships   2 scheme   3 reward   4 coupon   5 placed
6 online   7 points   8 claimed

## 11 Orders, invoices and payment

**Exercise 11.1**

1 d   2 a   3 g   4 c   5 h   6 e   7 b   8 f

**Exercise 11.2**

1 c   2 f   3 h   4 a   5 b   6 e   7 d   8 g

**Exercise 11.3**

1 makes an enquiry   2 quotes a price   3 confirms the order
4 issues an invoice   5 tracks the shipment   6 sends a reminder

**Exercise 11.4**

1 a charge   2 an enquiry   3 letter of credit   4 placed   5 bills
6 up at the front   7 terms   8 overtime   9 deliver   10 install

**Exercise 11.5**

1 quote   2 deliver   3 enquiry   4 order   5 Delivery   6 contact
7 attached   8 terms   9 records   10 invoice   11 overdue
12 disregard

## 12 Money

**Exercise 12.1**

1 earned/from   2 lent/to   3 borrowed/from   4 invested/in
5 owed/to   6 won/on   7 saved up/for   8 lost/by   9 made/
from   10 cost/to   11 wasted/on   12 spent/on

**Exercise 12.2**

1 salary   2 account   3 withdraw   4 overdraft   5 savings
6 borrow   7 interest rate   8 loan   9 instalments   10 debt

**Exercise 12.3**

1 discount   2 sales   3 afford   4 worth   5 bargain   6 receipt
7 mortgage   8 change

**Exercise 12.4**

1 on   2 to   3 for   4 on   5 in   6 under   7 over   8 for

**Exercise 12.5**

A rip-out rip-off   B sell sale   A of off   B reduction reduced
A price money   B ford afford   A recipe receipt   B with by
A currents currency

## 13 Company finance

**Exercise 13.1**

1 turnover   2 earnings   3 gross   4 net   5 owns   6 owes
7 accounts payable   8 working capital

**Exercise 13.2**

1 cost of goods sold   2 operating costs   3 revenue   4 gross profit
5 operating profit   6 net profit after tax   7 dividends
8 depreciation   9 tax   10 retained profit

**Exercise 13.3**

1 Revenue   2 Gross profit   3 Operating profit   4 depreciation
5 Dividends

**Exercise 13.4**

1 record profit   2 healthy profit   3 reasonable profit   4 slight loss
5 significant loss   6 heavy loss

**Exercise 13.5**

1 T   2 T   3 F

## 14 The language of trends

**Exercise 14.1**

1 d   2 c   3 b   4 f   5 e   6 a

**Exercise 14.2**

1 went up   2 have gone up   3 rose   4 have risen   5 rise
6 has grown   7 grew   8 growth   9 has fallen   10 fell   11 fall
12 increase

**Exercise 14.3**

1 stayed   2 reached a peak   3 stable   4 increase   5 fell

**Exercise 14.4**

1 in   2 from/to/of   3 at   4 on   5 for

**Exercise 14.5**

1 significant increase   2 sharp drop   3 gradual rise   4 slight fall
5 steady growth

**Exercise 14.6**

1 percentage terms   2 20% down   3 advertising budget
4 increased significantly   5 within a range   6 final figure
7 sharp drop   8 starting to rise

## 15 Numbers

**Exercise 15.1**

1 c   2 e   3 a   4 e   5 b   6 d

**Exercise 15.2**

1 four hundred (and) sixty   2 one thousand, three hundred   3 six
thousand, nine hundred (and) fifty   4 eighty thousand, five hundred
5 seventy three thousand   6 four million, two hundred thousand

**Exercise 15.3**

1 thirty-seven minus five is (makes/equals) thirty-two
2 twelve times (multiplied by) three is (makes/equals) thirty-six
3 one hundred (and) forty-three plus sixty-eight is (makes/equals)
two hundred (and) eleven
4 four hundred and eighty divided by fifteen is (makes/equals) thirty-
two

**Exercise 15.4**

1 fifteen euros and fifty cents/fifteen euros fifty   2 four pounds and
sixty pence/four pounds sixty   3 fifty square centimetres
4 fifteen cubic centimetres

**Exercise 15.5**

1 f   2 c   3 h   4 b   5 e   6 a   7 d   8 g

**Exercise 15.6**

1 one third   2 nine point three   3 six point seven five
4 six to one   5 twelve point five per cent   6 one and three quarters
7 zero point zero two   8 thirteen out of forty

**Exercise 15.7**

1 to   2 over   3 of   4 out of   5 On   6 in/of   7 to   8 by

**Exercise 15.8**

1 ~~out~~ out of   2 ~~three by two~~ three to two   3 ~~for average~~ on
average   4 ~~Rough~~ Roughly   5 ~~percentage~~ per cent   6 ~~increase on~~
increase in   7 ~~Three quarters the people~~ Three quarters of the
people   8 ~~1,000 of euros~~ 1,000 euros

## 16 Time

**Exercise 16.1**

1 a short time ago   2 immediately   3 starting now   4 a long
time ago   5 for a short time   6 these days   7 recently   8 at the
present time   9 soon

**Exercise 16.2**

1 took   2 lasted   3 lasted   4 took   5 lasted   6 took

**Exercise 16.3**

1 over   2 at the latest   3 By the time   4 haven't spoken to my
boss yet   5 nowadays

**Exercise 16.4**

1 e   2 b   3 d   4 g   5 f   6 c   7 a   8 h

**Exercise 16.5**

1 on   2 behind   3 ahead of   4 into   5 for

**Exercise 16.6**

1 deadline   2 miss   3 on time   4 yet   5 go   6 behind schedule

## 17 Office equipment

**Exercise 17.1**

1 scissors   2 dry wipe board (whiteboard)/flipchart   3 staples
4 pad/pencil sharpener   5 drawing pins   6 packs/stationery
cupboard   7 shredder/waste bin (trash can)   8 box file/shelves
9 correction fluid   10 wall planner   11 hole punch   12 padded
envelope/bubble wrap   13 ring binder/filing cabinet   14 sticky
tape (sellotape)/packing tape   15 scales   16 sheet   17 document
wallet   18 cartridges/toner   19 tray   20 paper clip

**Exercise 17.2**

1 screen/monitors/devices/click/keyboard/type
2 battery/drive/capacity/operating/processor/wide/enabled/light
3 hard copy   4 turn/brightness down   5 switch/webcam off

## 18 Using the Internet and email

**Exercise 18.1**

1 S   2 D   3 S   4 D   5 S   6 D   7 D (usually you download it
first before installing it)   8 D   9 D (a file is in a folder)   10 S

**Exercise 18.2**

1 scroll   2 buttons   3 block   4 click   5 register   6 enter
7 preview   8 send   9 delete   10 attach

**Exercise 18.3**

1 search engine   2 default setting   3 video clip   4 drop-down
menu   5 social networking   6 browsing history   7 smart phone
app   8 drafts folder   9 mass mailing   10 subject line

**Exercise 18.4**

1 search engine   2 social networking   3 drop-down menu
4 default settings   5 drafts folder   6 subject line   7 mass mailing
8 smart phone apps

**Exercise 18.5**

1 to (or on)/at   2 down   3 into   4 on   5 in   6 into   7 up
8 on/off

**Exercise 18.6**

1 subject line   2 mobile device   3 remaining information
4 bullets   5 Reply to All   6 recipients   7 capital letters
8 forwarded

## 19 Working conditions

**Exercise 19.1**

1 spacious / equipped / plan   2 subsidized / canteen / break-out
3 claim / expenses   4 off / lieu   5 noisy / cramped / cubicle
6 entitled / overtime   7 priorities / communication / style
8 awareness / politics / along   9 unfairly / promotion / increase

**Exercise 19.2**

1 subsidized   2 claim   3 expenses   4 cubicle   5 be entitled to
6 awareness   7 office politics   8 promotion

**Exercise 19.3**

1 comply with regulations   2 be injured at work   3 sue the
company because of an injury   4 demand compensation
5 ensure that there are appropriate warning notices   6 issue
protective equipment   7 organize regular fire drills   8 fit smoke
alarms   9 keep floors free from hazards   10 train first-aiders

**Exercise 19.4**

1 regulations   2 injured   3 compensation   4 notices   5 issue
6 drills   7 hazards   8 first-aiders

**Exercise 19.5**

1 workplace   2 workstation   3 workload   4 gossip   5 gender
6 bullying

**Exercise 19.6**

1 clean and tidy   2 protective clothing   3 hard hat   4 waste
material   5 canteen   6 assembly point   7 sign in   8 unauthorized

**Exercise 19.7**

1 range   2 empathy   3 follow-up   4 going   5 fine   6 outcome
7 argue   8 dialogue

## 20 Your job

**Exercise 20.1**

1 hard   2 stressful   3 boring   4 challenging   5 varied
6 rewarding   7 secure   8 glamorous

**Exercise 20.2**

1A What do you do   1B a lawyer   2A kind of work   2B as a
scientist   3A for a living   3B in advertising   4A are you doing
4B on a project   5A full-time   5B on a short-term   6A deal with
6B face-to-face   7A in charge   7B responsible for   8A report to
8B line manager

**Exercise 20.3**

1 earn   2 title   3 for a living   4 on   5 as   6 job   7 short-term
8 a freelancer   9 spend   10 to support   11 responsible   12 of

**Exercise 20.4**

1 in charge of   2 responsible for   3 deals with   4 looks after
5 takes care of   6 handles

**Exercise 20.5**

Sales and Marketing: a, i, m
Production and Operations: d, e, h
Finance: f, k, n
Human Resources: j, l, o
Administration: b, c, g

## 21 Projects and teams

**Exercise 21.1**

1 be the team leader   2 be back on track   3 allocate resources
4 set a start date   5 make a rough estimate   6 be kept in the loop
7 fall behind schedule   8 finish ahead of schedule   9 delegate
tasks   10 keep within the budget   11 find common ground
12 brief team members   13 draw up a proposal   14 put work out
to tender   15 get on with our work

**Exercise 21.2**

1 be the team leader   2 make a rough estimate   3 be back
on track   4 allocate resources   5 fall behind schedule   6 be
kept in the loop   7 keep within the budget   8 finish ahead
of schedule   9 find common ground   10 get on with our
work   11 put work out to tender   12 brief team members

**Exercise 21.3**

1 teamwork   2 deadline   3 allocate   4 delegate   5 specifications
6 breakdown

**Exercise 21.4**

1 up   2 up   3 between   4 to / on   5 up   6 on   7 to   8 back

**Exercise 21.5**

1 loop   2 track   3 board   4 yet   5 running   6 Leave   7 where
8 tender   9 draw   10 rough

## 22 Plans and forecasts

**Exercise 22.1**

1 S   2 S   3 D   4 D   5 D   6 S   7 S   8 D   9 S   10 S

**Exercise 22.2**

1 succeed / ahead   2 reviewed / goals / unrealistic / ambitious / taking /
risks   3 set / chances / we'll   4 detailed / definitely / implementation
5 according / outcome / won't

**Exercise 22.3**

1 c   2 e   3 b   4 a   5 d

**Exercise 22.4**

1 hope   2 expect   3 hope   4 expect

**Exercise 22.5**

1 in detail   2 realistic objectives   3 implemented   4 taking risks
5 accept some risk   6 long term   7 the outcome was   8 go wrong
9 abandoned

**Exercise 22.6**

1 He developed a plan.   2 He put forward the plan.   3 They went
ahead with the plan.   4 They thought about modifying the plan.
5 They decided to stick to the plan, with some changes.
6 They dropped the plan.

## 23 Problems, problems

**Exercise 23.1**

1 with   2 around   3 with   4 out   5 into   6 on   7 on   8 up
9 up   10 back

**Exercise 23.2**

1 d   2 a   3 f   4 e   5 c   6 b

**Exercise 23.3**

1 1d   2 5c   3 2a   4 4e   5 3f   6 6b

**Exercise 23.4**

1 matter   2 wrong   3 tried   4 would   5 were   6 mention
7 better   8 fix

**Exercise 23.5**

1 placed the order   2 Leave it   3 missing items   4 Let me just
check   5 damaged on arrival   6 It sounds like   7 it's faulty
8 send a replacement   9 working properly   10 what's going on
11 make a claim   12 refund your money   13 the same fault
14 send me a sample

## 24 Strategy and leadership

**Exercise 24.1**

1 strategy = plan   2 opportunity = chance   3 threat = danger
4 factor = thing that influences a situation   5 substitution =
replacement   6 acquisition = takeover   7 purpose = reason
8 challenge = thing that tests your skill

**Exercise 24.2**

1 purpose   2 factors   3 acquisitions   4 challenge
5 opportunity / threat

**Exercise 24.3**

1 develop a long-term strategy   2 look at the big picture
3 analyze five factors   4 drive down prices   5 weaken
your position   6 start from scratch   7 have products in the
pipeline   8 focus on a few core areas   9 cut costs internally
10 be seen by the outside world

**Exercise 24.4**

1 develop a long-term strategy   2 weaken your position   3 look
at the big picture   4 start from scratch   5 be seen by the outside
world   6 have products in the pipeline

**Exercise 24.5**

1 effective = working well and producing results
2 coherent = clear, logical and consistent   3 broad = general, overall
4 dynamic = full of energy and ideas   5 outstanding = exceptional
6 develop = create over a period of time
7 implement = put into action   8 outline = give the main ideas
9 propose = suggest   10 involve = include (as a necessary part)

**Exercise 24.6**

1 broad   2 coherent   3 implement   4 outlined

**Exercise 24.7**

1 b   2 d   3 a   4 h   5 f

## 25 Hiring, firing and promotion

**Exercise 25.1**

1 S   2 S   3 D   4 S   5 D   6 D   7 D   8 S

**Exercise 25.2**

1 recruitment   2 laid off   3 redundancy   4 unemployment
5 retirement   6 promoted   7 applied   8 length

**Exercise 25.3**

1 on   2 off   3 in   4 from   5 on   6 out   7 over   8 to

**Exercise 25.4**

1 redundancy package   2 state pension   3 talent management
4 career ladder   5 salary scale   6 executive search

**Exercise 25.5**

1 talent management   2 executive search   3 salary scale
4 state pension

**Exercise 25.6**

1 a   2 c   3 b   4 e   5 f   6 d   7 g   8 j   9 k   10 h   11 i
12 l   13 m   14 o   15 r   16 q   17 p   18 n

**Exercise 25.7**

1 challenging   2 demanding   3 rewarding

## 26 Pay, benefits and motivation

**Exercise 26.1**

1 earn   2 employees   3 pay   4 overtime   5 commission
6 wage   7 gross   8 tax   9 take-home   10 benefits   11 scheme
12 sick   13 perks

**Exercise 26.2**

1 white-collar job   2 pay rise   3 end-of-year bonus   4 income tax
5 health insurance   6 company car   7 career development
8 non-financial rewards

**Exercise 26.3**

1 pay rise   2 income tax   3 non-financial rewards   4 career
development   5 health insurance

**Exercise 26.4**

1 leave   2 perk   3 achievement   4 recognition

**Exercise 26.5**

1 perks   2 recognition   3 leave   4 achievement

**Exercise 26.6**

1 lost   2 reach   3 motivate   4 improve   5 modify   6 fit
7 based   8 co-operate

## 27 Cross-cultural communication

**Exercise 27.1**

1 relationships   2 a pleasure   3 introduce   4 call me   5 lose face
6 are embarrassed   7 talk   8 put the other person at ease
9 misunderstood   10 shake hands

**Exercise 27.2**

1 maintaining harmony   2 working lunch   3 humour
4 punctuality   5 eye contact   6 titles

**Exercise 27.3**

1 informal   2 diplomatically   3 taboo   4 gestures

**Exercise 27.4**

a I wonder if you could help me for a moment?   b I'm not very
happy about that.   c Unfortunately we've had one or two little
problems   d Could you tell me where the restroom is?   e With
respect, wouldn't it be better to start next year?
1a   2c   3e   4b   5d

**Exercise 27.5**

1 iceberg / onion   2a behaviour   2b beliefs   2c values
2d attitudes

## 28 Business and the environment

**Exercise 28.1**

1 waste   2 depletion   3 habitat   4 recycled   5 sustainable
6 biodegradable

**Exercise 28.2**

1 biodegradable   2 depletion   3 sustainable

**Exercise 28.3**

1 industrial waste   2 climate change   3 natural resources   4 fossil
fuels   5 living standards   6 emerging economies   7 renewable
energy   8 carbon emissions   9 social responsibility   10 working
conditions

**Exercise 28.4**

1 climate change   2 fossil fuels (or natural resources)
3 living standards   4 renewable energy   5 social responsibility
6 working conditions

**Exercise 28.5**

1 environmental   2 environment   3 environmentally

**Exercise 28.6**

1 respond   2 blame   3 acts   4 reduce   5 pay   6 include

**Exercise 28.7**

1 stakeholders   2 equal opportunities   3 mainstreaming
4 governance

## 29 CV (resume) and cover letter

**Exercise 29.1**

1 skills   2 experience   3 applicant   4 candidate

**Exercise 29.2**

1 applicants / rejected   2 experience / entry-level   3 application
4 qualifications   5 rates   6 updated / closing date   7 apply / cover
letter   8 position / vacancy

**Exercise 29.3**

1 interviewing

**Exercise 29.4**

recruitment / selection

**Exercise 29.5**

1 search   2 apply for   3 fill in / out   4 register with / matches
5 replied to   6 call you for

**Exercise 29.6**

1 reference   2 background   3 running   4 attached   5 involved
6 high-pressure   7 interpersonal   8 candidate   9 challenges
10 notice

## 30 Job interview

**Exercise 30.1**

1 assessment   2 achievement   3 challenge   4 qualities

**Exercise 30.2**

1 b   2 d   3 c   4 a   5 h   6 g   7 f   8 e

## 31 Greetings and introductions

**Exercise 31.1**

1 d   2 b   3 f   4 a   5 e   6 c

**Exercise 31.2**

1 Excuse me   2 that's right   3 must be you   4 How was your
journey?   5 Can I help you   6 I'd appreciate it   7 follow me
8 How are you?   9 Fine, thanks   10 good weekend   11 at home
12 What about you?   13 Whereabouts   14 enjoyed it

**Exercise 31.3**

1 Is this seat free?   2 Can I introduce myself?   3 Where are you
from?   4 And what do you do?   5 What about you?   6 Who do
you work for?

**Exercise 31.4**

1 met Johan Nilsson before   2 so   3 introduce   4 want   5 this is
6 as   7 Nice to meet you too   8 do

## 32 Welcoming visitors

**Exercise 32.1**

1 to   2 regards   3 in   4 behalf / to   5 remind

**Exercise 32.2**

1 come in   2 drop you off at your hotel   3 get down to business
4 have an appointment   5 meet you in person   6 show you round
the plant   7 wear this badge at all times

**Exercise 32.3**

1 Come in   2 meet you in person   3 get down to business
4 drop you off at your hotel   5 show you round the plant

**Exercise 32.4**

1 Did you have a good flight?   2 Welcome to Switzerland   3 Is this
your first time in Zurich?   4 You can freshen up at the hotel, then
we'll have some lunch   5 Tim sends his regards, by the way   6 Let
me help you with your bags   7 Will you have time to look around
before you go?
1 a / c   2 f   3 e / i   4 h   5 d   6 b   7 g

**Exercise 32.5**

1 Where are you staying?   2 It's nice to finally meet you in person.
3 Would you like something to drink?   4 Did you find us OK?
5 Sorry I'm late. Did you get my message?   6 How long are you
here for?
1 b   2 e   3 a / g   4 d / i   5 h   6 c / f

**Exercise 32.6**

1 behalf   2 pleasure   3 run   4 tour   5 refreshments
6 opportunity   7 building   8 overview   9 belongings
10 responsibility   11 missing   12 safety   13 strictly
14 prohibited

## 33 Standard responses

**Exercise 33.1**

1 a   2 b   3 b   4 a   5 a   6 a   7 b   8 a   9 b   10 a   11 a
12 b   13 b   14 a   15 b   16 a   17 a   18 b   19 b   20 a
21 b   22 a   23 a   24 b

**Exercise 33.2**

1 give / hand / under / control
2 Would / helpful
3 let / know / Of course
4 everything / appreciate / mention / pleasure
5 like / join / kind / Another / time / maybe
6 by / mistake / These / things / happen
7 Make / yourself / home
8 by / any / chance / might / have / look
9 depressed / take / time
10 not / best / person / ask

## 34 Small talk

**Exercise 34.1**

1 Do   2 How   3 Is   4 How   5 What   6 Where   7 Have
8 Can   9 What   10 What   11 How   12 Have   13 Are   14 Do
15 Where   16 Have   17 Who   18 What   19 How / What
20 How   21 What   22 What

**Exercise 34.2**

1 a   2 g   3 j   4 c   5 f   6 k   7 l   8 i   9 d   10 e   11 b   12 h

**Exercise 34.3**

1 Whereabouts   2 buffet   3 talking shop   4 Really

**Exercise 34.4**

1 massive   2 crowded   3 fascinating   4 freezing   5 delicious

**Exercise 34.5**

1 registration / By the way   2 recommend   3 do / do   4 time / year
5 Try   6 mind / have / look   7 happened / once   8 work for
9 What / like   10 way / do   11 wonderful / must / looking forward to
12 Someone told   13 based   14 reminds me / time
15 heard / amazing   16 before

**Exercise 34.6**

Introducing yourself 1 / 6
Job 3 / 8 / 13 / 16
Food and drink 2 / 5 / 10
The weather 4
Talking shop 12
Travel – past 9 / 15
Travel – future 11
Telling a story 7 / 14

## 35 Likes, free time, interests

**Exercise 35.1**

1 love it   2 special   3 at all   4 I'd prefer   5 weight   6 on
7 into   8 boring   9 interested   10 the stage

**Exercise 35.2**

1 go   2 join   3 keep   4 do   5 play   6 have

**Exercise 35.3**

1 Me too   2 fancy going   3 meet up   4 can't stand
5 Me neither   6 much rather   7 bring her   8 join us
9 kind of   10 Shall we

**Exercise 35.4**

1 hiking   2 theatre   3 playing football   4 live music   5 yoga
6 watching a movie   7 gardening   8 looking round a gallery

**Exercise 35.5**

1 cast   2 shot   3 track   4 plot   5 portrait

## 36 Home, city, country

**Exercise 36.1**

1 parents   2 aunts/uncles   3 cousins   4 in-laws
5 relatives/relations

**Exercise 36.2**

1 was born   2 was brought up   3 grew up   4 got married
5 partner   6 like   7 at   8 from

**Exercise 36.3**

1 city centre   2 crime rate   3 cycle lanes   4 housing estate
5 leisure facilities   6 metro system   7 rush hour   8 summer
festival   9 surrounding area   10 tourist attraction

**Exercise 36.4**

1 city centre   2 rush hour   3 surrounding area   4 crime rate
5 leisure facilities   6 cycle lanes   7 tourist attraction
8 housing estates

**Exercise 36.5**

1 blocks   2 locals   3 property   4 commute   5 crowded   6 stuck
7 entertainment   8 hurry   9 community   10 lonely
11 opportunities   12 atmosphere

**Exercise 36.6**

1 interior/scenery/landscape   2 century/invaded/ruled/defeated/
battle/reunited/great moment/history

## 37 Food and drink

**Exercise 37.1**

Meat: beef/chicken/lamb/veal
Fish: haddock/salmon/trout/tuna
Vegetables: aubergine/cauliflower/lettuce/mushrooms
Fruit: cherry/grapes/pineapple/strawberry
Seafood: prawns/squid
Other: nuts/olive oil

**Exercise 37.2**

1 ham   2 sardines   3 broccoli   4 courgettes   5 satsumas
6 noodles   7 herbs

**Exercise 37.3**

1 meal   2 course   3 plate   4 dish   5 meals   6 course   7 plate
8 dish

**Exercise 37.4**

1c   2h   3a   4b   5e   6f   7g   8d

**Exercise 37.5**

1 bitter   2 grilled   3 steam   4 bland/mild   5 bake/roast   6 Still
or sparkling

**Exercise 37.6**

1 ~~pink~~   2 ~~fatty~~   3 ~~tap~~   4 ~~ripe~~

**Exercise 37.7**

1 starving   2 full   3 spoil/appetite   4 dressing/vinegar/mustard
5 recipe   6 pint/bitter/half/lager/draught

## 38 At the restaurant

**Exercise 38.1**

1 host/guest   2 chopsticks   3 napkin   4 jug   5 dessert
6 check   7 tip   8 receipt   9 vegetarian   10 allergic   11 healthy
12 hungry/thirsty   13 specials   14 speciality   15 order

**Exercise 38.2**

1 b   2 a   3 h   4 i   5 e   6 c   7 f   8 d   9 j   10 g

**Exercise 38.3**

1 a table for two   2 house red   3 local speciality   4 main course
5 service charge   6 side plate   7 soup bowl   8 wine list

**Exercise 38.4**

1 try/do   2 unusual/like   3 order/separately   4 hungry/portion
5 specials/board   6 ready/order   7 have/main   8 put/middle
9 Here's/project   10 Enjoy/meal   11 place/often   12 bring/bill

**Exercise 38.5**

1 This is very good. How's yours?
2 Could you pass the water, please?
3 Shall we have another bottle?
4 Would you like to see the dessert menu?
5 Let me pay.
6 I'll get this. You're my guest.
7 It was a fantastic meal.
8 Should we leave a tip?

**Exercise 38.6**

a Better not, I'm on a diet.
b Here you are.
c I'm glad you enjoyed it.
d There's no need. Service is included.
e No, this one's on me. You paid last time.
f I'm fine, but please go ahead.
g Thanks very much. I'll invite you when you come to my country.
h It's delicious.

**Exercise 38.7**

1 h   2 b   3 f   4 a   5 e   6 g   7 c   8 d

## 39 Leaving and saying goodbye

**Exercise 39.1**

1 Bye, Duncan. I'm off.
2 Don't forget to keep in touch.
3 Anyway, I'd better get on.
4 Have a good weekend.
5 It was nice meeting you.
6 I have to go now. I'll catch you later.
7 Thank you again for coming.
8 If you're ever in Lisbon, give me a call.

**Exercise 39.2**

1 a   2 e   3 c   4 d   5 g   6 h   7 b   8 f

**Exercise 39.3**

1 1a/4d   2 3c/6h   3 5g   4 2e/7b   5 8f

**Exercise 39.4**

1 It was great working with you.
2 I should get back to work now.
3 Give my regards to Monique.
4 I have a long day tomorrow.
5 Keep in touch!
6 Can we leave it until Monday?
7 I look forward to it.
8 It's time to make a move.
9 I really should be going.
10 Take care!

**Exercise 39.5**

1 safe journey   2 See you   3 some time   4 Take care   5 meet
again soon   6 Come back   7 luck   8 for now
The other person is going on a journey 1/4
The other person is moving to a new city/job/etc 7
You will meet again soon and the situation is informal 2/8
You are not sure if you will meet again 3/5/6

**Exercise 39.6**

a getting late/should be   b for everything   c long day   d your
help/really appreciate   e going now   f get home   g very much/
useful meeting   h How long   i meeting you/in touch   j at all
k so soon

**Exercise 39.7**

1 a  2 k  3 c  4 h  5 f  6 g  7 d  8 j  9 e  10 i  11 b

## 40 Social English: summary and review

**Exercise 40.1**

1 how  2 Good  3 going  4 bad  5 things  6 busy  7 met
8 Nice  9 this  10 too  11 should  12 soon  13 now  14 later
15 Have  16 You  17 really  18 always  19 touch  20 thanks

**Exercise 40.2**

1 where/based  2 flight  3 mind/join  4 seat  5 for  6 journey
7 in  8 in person  9 let's get down to  10 originally  11 By the
way  12 to  13 do/do  14 for

**Exercise 40.3**

1 meet up with/go out for  2 in a rush  3 grew up  4 commute/
stuck in traffic  5 single  6 main industries  7 crowded
8 a drink/night in  9 small town  10 leisure  11 north-south
12 countryside

**Exercise 40.4**

Free time 1/8
Family/Origins 3/5
City 2/4/7/9/10
Country 6/11/12

**Exercise 40.5**

1 Cheers everyone!
2 This one's on me.
3 Nice place. Do you come here often?
4 I'll get this. You're my guest.
5 I think I'll have the fish.
6 Enjoy your meal!
7 It all looks very good.
8 This is very good. How's yours?
9 Can we have the bill, please?
10 You should try the lamb.

**Exercise 40.6**

Discussing the menu 5/7/10
Start of the meal 1/6
During the meal 3/8
End of the meal 2/4/9

## 41 Flights and travel

**Exercise 41.1**

1 trip  2 journey  3 travel  4 journey  5 travel  6 trips

**Exercise 41.2**

1 journey  2 booked  3 an aisle  4 pass  5 by  6 call  7 took
off  8 sign  9 fare  10 change  11 a receipt  12 deal
13 missed  14 waiting for  15 departure  16 arrivals

**Exercise 41.3**

1 make a booking
2 be away on a trip
3 drop you off at Terminal 1
4 pick you up from Arrivals
5 go through security/passport control
6 walk around and do some shopping
7 board the plane
8 put your bag in the overhead locker
9 follow the signs for Baggage Reclaim
10 cut short the trip

**Exercise 41.4**

1 make a booking  2 pick you up from Arrivals  3 drop you off at
Terminal 1  4 put your bag in the overhead locker  5 cut short the
trip  6 board the plane

**Exercise 41.5**

a terminal building  b jet lag  c check-in machine  d boarding
pass  e hand luggage/overhead locker  f frequent flyer  g flight
attendants  h final call  i passport control

**Exercise 41.6**

1 a  2 c  3 f  4 d  5 h  6 e  7 g  8 i  9 b

## 42 Hotels

**Exercise 42.1**

1 lobby  2 sign  3 rate  4 loyalty  5 wake-up  6 laundry
7 complimentary  8 transfer  9 facilities  10 unsuitable

**Exercise 42.2**

1 view  2 quoted  3 lift  4 unpack/freshen  5 currency  6 iron/
ironing board  7 cleaned/sheets/towels  8 spare  9 smell
10 heater  11 pillow

**Exercise 42.3**

1 down/up/out  2 up  3 in

**Exercise 42.4**

1 Can I ~~to~~ have  2 How ~~distance~~ far  3 ~~would~~ should  4 ~~stop to~~
~~serve~~ stop serving  5 ~~I can~~ Can I  6 ~~so soon~~ as soon  7 tell ~~to~~ the
8 ~~possibility~~ possible

**Exercise 42.5**

1 I'd like to check in  2 That's right  3 Can I just ask you  4 Can
you get someone to help me  5 Can you give me  6 I'd be grateful
if you could  7 That's very kind of you  8 If you'd like to follow the
porter

## 43 Conferences and exhibitions

**Exercise 43.1**

1 ~~discourse~~  2 ~~talkshop~~  3 ~~is holding~~  4 ~~on the display~~
5 ~~exchange contacts~~  6 ~~assist~~  7 ~~papers~~  8 ~~trade expo~~  9 ~~last~~
10 ~~be convenient for you~~

**Exercise 43.2**

1 panel/experts/audience  2 auditorium  3 venue/event
4 Registration/pack  5 stand/booth  6 refreshments  7 handout
8 display  9 virtual  10 samples  11 available  12 Please feel free

**Exercise 43.3**

1 at  2 for  3 on  4 in  5 in  6 on

**Exercise 43.4**

1 name badge  2 thinking of changing  3 what is available
4 very advanced design  5 at this stage  6 key features
7 ideal solution  8 suit your needs  9 a sample
10 leave your details

## 44 Telephoning: getting connected

**Exercise 44.1**

1 dialled  2 get through  3 engaged  4 make  5 call me
6 Is that  7 hold  8 Stay on

**Exercise 44.2**

1 c  2 b  3 f  4 a  5 h  6 d  7 e  8 g

**Exercise 44.3**

1 1c 2b 3f 6d
2 4a 5h 7e 8g

**Exercise 44.4**

1 on  2 through  3 up  4 off  5 in/with  6 about
7 through to  8 back

**Exercise 44.5**

Mini-dialogue 1
phone ~~to~~ the printers
Mini-dialogue 2
~~make~~ give him a call

Mini-dialogue 3
~~I am~~ This is
Mini-dialogue 4
~~Can I please to have extension 253?~~ Can I have extension 253, please?
Mini-dialogue 5
~~get cut~~ get cut off
Mini-dialogue 6
~~Talking~~ Speaking
Mini-dialogue 7
~~take~~ leave a message
Mini-dialogue 8
~~put me through~~ put me through to
Mini-dialogue 9
~~I call~~ I'm calling
Mini-dialogue 10
~~Do you like~~ Would you like

## 45 Telephoning: start, middle and end
### Exercise 45.1
1 good time to talk
2 call back later
3 in the middle of something
4 over there in Stuttgart
5 sort things out over the phone
6 have anything you would like to add
7 Do you have the time now
8 go through the agenda

### Exercise 45.2
1 go through the agenda   2 over there in Stuttgart   3 Do you have the time now   4 good time to talk   5 sort things out over the phone   6 have anything you would like to add   7 call back later / in the middle of something

### Exercise 45.3
1 an email to confirm the details
2 let me know as soon as possible
3 Have I left out anything
4 Thank you for taking the time
5 look forward to hearing from you
6 the best time to call
7 give my regards to Sue
8 going to be a lot of fun

### Exercise 45.4
1 Thank you for taking the time   2 going to be a lot of fun   3 an email to confirm the details   4 look forward to hearing from you / the best time to call   5 Have I left out anything   6 give my regards to Sue   7 let me know as soon as possible

### Exercise 45.5
1 your reasons   2 exactly / issue   3 Instead of / why don't
4 What if / rather than

### Exercise 45.6
1 back   2 over   3 through / around   4 as / as   5 out   6 for
7 to   8 in

### Exercise 45.7
1 Right   2 going to   3 anything else   4 help   5 calling   6 look forward   7 give / regards   8 talking

## 46 Telephoning: common situations
### Exercise 46.1
1 call you back
2 Let me just repeat everything
3 the country code
4 leave a message
5 I'll make sure

6 can you spell your family name
7 what's it in connection with
8 read it back to you

### Exercise 46.2
1 call you back   2 leave a message   3 can you spell your family name   4 the country code   5 read it back to you   6 what's it in connection with   7 Let me just repeat everything   8 I'll make sure

### Exercise 46.3
1 Which day would be ... best for you? / the most convenient?
2 Actually I'm ... quite busy around then. / tied up all day.
3 Does Wednesday ... look OK? / suit you?
4 That sounds ... fine. / good.
a 1   b 3   c 2   d 4

### Exercise 46.4
1 Are you free anytime next week?
2 I'll be there Friday at nine.
3 Shall we say ten o'clock?
4 So, that's four o'clock at your office.
5 Can you make the week after?
6 How about meeting for lunch?
a 1 / 5   b 3 / 6   c 2 / 4

### Exercise 46.5
1 a   2 g   3 c   4 i   5 b   6 h   7 e   8 f   9 d   10 j

### Exercise 46.6
1 What seems to be the problem?
2 Could you give me the details?
3 I must apologize.
4 I'll sort this out right away.
5 I'll make sure this is put right immediately.
6 Thank you very much for bringing this to our attention.

## 47 Telephoning: conference calls
### Exercise 47.1
1 chairperson   2 ground rules   3 introduce   4 interrupt
5 minutes   6 timing   7 agenda   8 digress   9 summarize
10 tasks

### Exercise 47.2
1 I will begin by saying all your names.   2 I need to check that everyone can hear everyone else.   3 Michael will be taking the minutes.   4 I'd like to finish by four o'clock.   5 Before we begin I want to establish some ground rules.   6 Please introduce yourself before you speak.   7 Please try not to interrupt other people.   8 Petra, I think you are going to introduce the first item.

### Exercise 47.3
1 come back   2 slow down   3 speak up   4 come in
5 hand over

### Exercise 47.4
1 project update   2 behind schedule   3 control costs
4 did you mean   5 related issue   6 I was saying   7 repeat that
8 Any comments

## 48 Telephoning: summary and review
### Exercise 48.1
a in connection with   b put me through   c how can I help
d over there   e speaking   f call back later   g give my regards
h left out   i on the line   j taking the time   k Right   l get cut off
m How about   n Shall we   o Actually   p would suit me
q instead   r sounds fine

### Exercise 48.2
1 d   2 c / e   3 g / k   4 i / l   5 o   6 p / q

### Exercise 48.3
1 She's not at her desk right now.

2 Let me just get a pen.
3 Would you like to leave a message?
4 Shall I ask her to call you back?
5 I'll make sure she gets the message.
6 Can I read it back to you?
7 And what's it in connection with?
8 Can you spell that for me, please?

### Exercise 48.4

1 She's not at her desk right now   2 Shall I ask her to call you back
3 Would you like to leave a message   4 Let me just get a pen
5 Can you spell that for me, please   6 Can I read it back to you
7 And what's it in connection with   8 I'll make sure she gets the message

### Exercise 48.5

1 introduce yourself   2 come back / main point   3 item / agenda
4 covered / summarize

## 49 Emails: basics

### Exercise 49.1

1 are   2 good   3 let   4 understand   5 got back to you
6 information   7 talk   8 I'll give

### Exercise 49.2

a Please send me the sales figures.
b I need the sales figures asap.
c How about asking Pam to send us the figures?
d Could you do me a favour?
e Could you send me the sales figures?
f Re the sales figures, I've attached …
g I'll send you the figures when I get them.
h Shall I send you the sales figures?

### Exercise 49.3

1 a / b / e   2 f   3 d   4 h   5 g   6 c

### Exercise 49.4

1 pleased   2 Unfortunately   3 Further   4 clarify   5 appreciate
6 forward   7 attached   8 chase

### Exercise 49.5

1 about   2 back   3 to   4 on   5 for   6 into   7 up   8 in

### Exercise 49.6

1st email: 1 b   2 a   3 d   4 c
2nd email: 1 c   2 b   3 d   4 a
3rd email: 1 a   2 d   3 c   4 b

## 50 Emails: meetings, arrangements

### Exercise 50.1

1 Perhaps we can arrange a meeting to discuss things in more detail?
2 Yes, that sounds like a good idea.
3 OK. When would suit you?
4 How about Thursday 17th?
5 Sorry, but I can't make it on Thursday. Is Friday any good?
6 Yes, Friday's fine by me.
7 Good. Shall we say 12.30 at my office? I'll take you to lunch.
8 Perfect. I'll see you then. Bye.

### Exercise 50.2

1 Further ~~to~~ our call   2 ~~confirmation~~ confirm   3 ~~I see you~~
I'll see you   4 ~~quite~~ quiet   5 can ~~to~~ talk   6 ~~detached~~ attached
7 forward ~~to~~ seeing   8 ~~wishing~~ wishes

### Exercise 50.3

1 ~~I really~~ I'm really   2 ~~Unfortunate~~ Unfortunately   3 ~~need rearrange~~
need to rearrange   4 ~~wander~~ wonder   5 instead ~~of~~
6 ~~inconvenient~~ inconvenience

### Exercise 50.4

1 in more detail   2 suit you   3 can't make it   4 Shall we say
5 really sorry / change / plans   6 wonder / could / instead

### Exercise 50.5

1 launch   2 click   3 link   4 event   5 venue   6 refreshments
7 delighted   8 attend

### Exercise 50.6

1 c   2 e   3 a   4 d   5 b

## 51 Emails: commercial

### Exercise 51.1

1 It would be great to have an opportunity to show you some of our products.
2 Following our conversation earlier today, I am writing to give you more details of our services.
3 If you have any further questions, please do not hesitate to contact me.
4 There are one or two things I need to clarify before going ahead with a firm order.
5 We require a letter of credit or 50% of the total amount in advance.
6 We offer a 5% discount for orders over €10,000.
7 You can track the shipping details by clicking the link below.
8 I will look into the matter immediately and get back to you within 24 hours.
9 I apologize again for any inconvenience this has caused.
10 Apparently, there was a query on the invoice – that is why we haven't paid it yet.

### Exercise 51.2

1 further   2 clarify   3 require   4 track   5 look into
6 get back to   7 apologize   8 query

### Exercise 51.3

1 discount   2 IBAN and BIC   3 terms of payment   4 warranty
5 letter of credit   6 invoice

### Exercise 51.4

1 introduce myself   2 leading provider   3 you might be interested
4 price list   5 going ahead with a firm order   6 place a small order
7 Please accept my apologies   8 I can assure you

## 52 Emails: formal language

### Exercise 52.1

1 Dear   2 regards   3 Yours   4 well   5 would / could
6 appreciate it   7 Would   8 wonder   9 unable   10 you're saying
11 require   12 hearing

### Exercise 52.2

1 well   2 pleasure   3 replying   4 Further   5 appreciate
6 wonder   7 Unfortunately   8 hearing

### Exercise 52.3

1 How's it going   2 Thank you for your email   3 getting back to
you   4 writing with regard to   5 I'd be grateful   6 is that right
7 apologize for the poor service   8 I'll look into it   9 let me know
10 do not hesitate   11 at the conference   12 look forward to
meeting

### Exercise 52.4

1 Can you tell me what   2 Would you like to   3 Do you know if
they   4 Would it be possible for us to   5 Can you tell me what

### Exercise 52.5

Thank you for your email of September 30th and my apologies for not replying sooner.
I am writing with regard to the meeting next week where you are going to come to our offices to present your web design services to myself and some colleagues. Two points:
First, as requested, I attach a document with the names and job titles of everyone who will be present at the meeting. I am pleased to say that our Managing Director Ms Lena Holmberg will now be able to attend.

Second, I would be grateful if you could show us in the meeting a working example of website analytics. I feel that at the moment we are not analyzing our website traffic as effectively as we might, and we would like some professional guidance in this area.

If you require any further information, please do not hesitate to contact me again.

I look forward to seeing you next week.

Kind regards

Marta Lopez

## 53 Emails: summary and review

### Exercise 53.1
1 let/know  2 back/sooner  3 Re/here  4 do/favour
5 Please/attached  6 Sorry/fault  7 be/touch  8 give/call

### Exercise 53.2
1 When/make  2 Shall/say  3 change/plans  4 wonder/instead
5 event/place  6 refreshments/provided  7 able/attend
8 delighted/forward

### Exercise 53.3
1 exactly/include  2 available/sizes  3 discount/quantities
4 terms/payment  5 letter/credit  6 order/arrived
7 look/matter  8 apologize/inconvenience

### Exercise 53.4
Email 1
1 speak to you  2 you are well  3 sending send  4 I'd like
5 particularly particular
Email 2
1 here is it the website  2 get back to me  3 some a favour
4 aren't be there  5 appreciate it your help
Email 3
1 Thanks for this  2 Sorry but I haven't  3 spoken to the FD
4 we're going to  5 knowing know
Email 4
1 Let's put  2 I'll give  3 want it me  4 I'll chase  5 let you know

## 54 Meetings: an introduction

### Exercise 54.1
1 issues/topics/subjects  2 attend  3 miss  4 purpose/reason
5 outcome  6 moderator/facilitator  7 items/agenda
8 go round the table  9 agree/approve  10 housekeeping points
11 emphasize/stress  12 key/central

### Exercise 54.2
1 hold  2 attend  3 miss  4 set up  5 chair  6 draw up
7 postpone  8 call off  9 deal with  10 raise  11 set  12 close

### Exercise 54.3
1 proposal  2 suggestion

### Exercise 54.4
1 c  2 d  3 i  4 g  5 a  6 e  7 h  8 b  9 f

### Exercise 54.5
1 heated  2 brief  3 lengthy  4 productive  5 vital  6 informal
7 face-to-face  8 regular  9 monthly  10 preliminary  11 urgent
12 follow-up

### Exercise 54.6
1 into  2 for  3 with  4 in  5 at  6 over

## 55 Meetings: basic phrases

### Exercise 55.1
1 get started  2 get down to  3 purpose  4 reason  5 From
6 As far as I'm concerned  7 you're right  8 I agree  9 move on
to  10 come back to  11 as far as  12 way

### Exercise 55.2
1 Actually = As a matter of fact

2 Apparently = It seems that
3 Basically = The point is
4 Frankly = To be honest
5 Hopefully = With any luck
6 Obviously = Of course
7 Presumably = I imagine
8 Unfortunately = Sorry to say, but

### Exercise 55.3
1 Hopefully  2 The main thing is  3 Apparently  4 With any luck
5 Basically  6 It seems that

### Exercise 55.4
1 OK, let's get down to business
2 I can see what you're saying
3 So, what about
4 As far as I'm concerned
5 The purpose of this meeting is
6 I'm not sure about that
7 Anyway, as I was saying
8 Can I just say something
9 I'm going to recommend
10 I think that's as far as we can go
11 I think the best way forward
12 What would happen if

### Exercise 55.5
1 OK, let's get down to business  2 The purpose of this meeting is
3 As far as I'm concerned  4 I can see what you're saying
5 I'm not sure about that  6 So, what about  7 Anyway, as I was
saying  8 Can I just say something  9 What would happen if
10 I think that's as far as we can go  11 I think the best way
forward  12 I'm going to recommend

## 56 Meetings: checking, clarifying, active listening

### Exercise 56.1
Asking for repetition
1 Sorry, I didn't catch that.
2 Sorry, I missed that.
3 Can you say that again?
4 Can you go over that again?
Saying you don't understand
5 Sorry, I'm not with you.
6 Sorry, I don't follow you.
7 Sorry, I don't see what you mean.
Asking for more detailed information
8 Can you be more specific?
9 Can you say more about that?
10 Can you put a figure on that?

### Exercise 56.2
1 Can you just say that again?  2 Can you be a little more specific?
3 Sorry, I'm not quite with you.  4 Can you just go over that again?
5 Sorry, I didn't quite catch that.  6 Can you just say a bit more
about that?

### Exercise 56.3
1 What exactly do you mean by that  2 My mistake. I should have
said  3 Can you be a little more specific?  4 What kind of timescale
are we talking about?  5 Sorry, I missed that.  6 Are you saying
7 What I'm trying to say is  8 Can you put a figure on that

### Exercise 56.4
1 Jennifer! I haven't seen her for ages.  2 Did you? That's fantastic!
Well done!  3 20%? Oh dear. That's bad news.  4 Really? Was it?
I'm not surprised – it was very good.  5 I'm sorry to hear that. Never
mind. Another day.

## 57 Meetings: developing the discussion

### Exercise 57.1

1 On balance = At the end of the day
2 In general = On the whole
3 We should = What we should do is
4 On the subject of = In relation to
5 Basically = In short
6 In addition = Moreover
7 However = On the other hand
8 Therefore = As a result

### Exercise 57.2

1 However  2 on the subject of  3 In addition  4 Basically
5 In general  6 Therefore

### Exercise 57.3

1 And  2 But  3 So

### Exercise 57.4

1 Firstly / First of all  2 Last but not least  3 On the one hand, but on the other hand  4 To cut a long story short  5 As far as finance is concerned  6 Taking everything into consideration

### Exercise 57.5

1 What we need to do is / Here's what we need to do  2 What we'll do is / Here's what we'll do  3 What we can't do is / Here's what we can't do

### Exercise 57.6

1 should / could / about / doing  2 Couldn't / Let's  3 Shall  4 don't we / might be worth trying

### Exercise 57.7

1 First of all  2 pros and cons  3 sounds interesting  4 work in practice  5 too many unknowns  6 what would happen  7 it seems to me 8 the next steps

## 58 Meetings: summary and review

### Exercise 58.1

1 In fact  2 As well as that  3 It seems that  4 To be honest
5 On the whole  6 In terms of  7 Shall we  8 Of course
9 Because of this

### Exercise 58.2

1 Therefore / Because of this  2 Frankly / To be honest  3 In general / On the whole  4 Also / As well as that  5 Let's / Shall we
6 Actually / In fact  7 In relation to / In terms of  8 Apparently / It seems that

### Exercise 58.3

a Getting back to what I was saying  b So, in other words, ... Is that right?  c Can I just come in here?  d Can you be a little more specific?  e So what are the next steps?  f Sorry, I didn't catch that
g Sorry, I don't follow you  h What about you?

### Exercise 58.4

1 g  2 f  3 b  4 d  5 h  6 c  7 a  8 e

### Exercise 58.5

a prepare / action plan  b go over  c as far as  d down / business
e move on / discuss  f come back to  g everything / consideration / seems  h purpose / meeting

### Exercise 58.6

1 d  2 h  3 e  4 b  5 f  6 c  7 g  8 a

## 59 Presentations: an introduction

### Exercise 59.1

1 projector  2 handouts  3 stage  4 flipcharts  5 slide
6 extension lead  7 template  8 keywords

### Exercise 59.2

(no answer)

### Exercise 59.3

I want to ask you a <u>question</u> // what is the <u>difference</u> between <u>data</u> and <u>information</u> // I'll <u>tell</u> you the difference // <u>data</u> are <u>infinite</u> in number // they <u>cost</u> almost <u>nothing</u> // and are <u>worth</u> almost <u>nothing</u> // <u>information</u> on the other hand // is <u>meaningful data</u> // it is a <u>key ingredient</u> in decision making // and is <u>enormously useful</u> and <u>valuable</u> to managers // but <u>how exactly</u> do you <u>turn</u> data into information // the answer is with <u>business intelligence software</u> // and // ladies and gentlemen // <u>we</u> are one of the world's <u>leading providers</u> of that software.

### Exercise 59.4

ironic

## 60 Presentations: structure and key phrases

### Exercise 60.1

1 start  2 take  3 divided  4 affects  5 stress  6 digress
7 brings  8 Have  9 notice  10 show

### Exercise 60.2

1 Good morning everyone and thanks for coming.
2 I'd like to thank the organizers for inviting me here today.
3 Can you hear me at the back of the room?
4 Please feel free to ask questions during my presentation.
5 So what does this mean in terms of costs?
6 That's all I want to say about changes in the market.
7 Let me go over the main points again.
8 Thank you very much for listening and I hope you found it useful.

### Exercise 60.3

1 for  2 at / of  3 for  4 of / at / about  5 back  6 on  7 to
8 up

### Exercise 60.4

1 It's always a pleasure  2 Please feel free to ask questions  3 I'll give you an overview  4 I'll talk in a little more detail  5 And I'd like to stress  6 The figures clearly show that  7 I'd like to move on now  8 To give you an example  9 That brings me to the end

## 61 Word families: verbs and nouns

### Exercise 61.1

1 apologize  2 apply  3 arrive  4 compete  5 decide  6 deliver
7 explain  8 invest  9 perform  10 produce

### Exercise 61.2

1 arrive  2 decision  3 apply  4 delivery  5 apologize (or explain)

### Exercise 61.3

1 assist  2 communicate  3 guide  4 identify  5 measure
6 reduce  7 repay  8 require  9 vary  10 withdraw

### Exercise 61.4

1 repay  2 variation  3 identify  4 measure  5 requirement
6 withdraw

### Exercise 61.5

1 signature  2 choice  3 succeed  4 growth  5 advice
6 complain

### Exercise 61.6

1 successful  2 innovative  3 achievable  4 competitive
5 productive  6 analytical

### Exercise 61.7

1 economist  2 accountant  3 competitor  4 engineer  5 lawyer
6 electrician  7 consultant  8 advertiser  9 director  10 analyst
11 visitor  12 supplier  13 assistant  14 administrator
15 participant  16 applicants / interviewees  17 manufacturer / distributors / retailers / end-users  18 employees  19 franchisee
20 licensee

## 62 Word families: adjectives and nouns
**Exercise 62.1**
1 accidental  2 apologetic  3 awareness  4 effectiveness
5 enthusiastic  6 majority  7 necessity  8 optimistic
9 politeness  10 reliability  11 seasonal  12 trial

**Exercise 62.2**
1 season  2 trial  3 effective  4 majority  5 reliable
6 optimistic  7 apology  8 necessary

**Exercise 62.3**
1 confidence  2 efficiency  3 importance  4 creativity
5 frequency  6 similarity

**Exercise 62.4**
1 similar  2 confidence  3 creativity

**Exercise 62.5**
1 critical  2 weaknesses  3 economic  4 economics
5 economical  6 hundredth

**Exercise 62.6**
1 length  2 long  3 shorten  4 short  5 heighten  6 higher
7 deep  8 depth

## 63 Word families: more adjectives
**Exercise 63.1**
1 acceptable  2 competitive  3 expensive  4 numerous
5 productive  6 profitable  7 suspicious  8 valuable

**Exercise 63.2**
1 valuable  2 numerous  3 accept  4 expense  5 productive

**Exercise 63.3**
1 changeable  2 disruptive  3 famous  4 inventive  5 impressive
6 memorable  / mysterious  8 suitable

**Exercise 63.4**
1 disruptive  2 mystery  3 suitable  4 impress  5 changeable

**Exercise 63.5**
1 competitive  2 wealthy  3 dangerous  4 budgetary  5 effective
6 ambitious  7 sensible  8 sensitive

**Exercise 63.6**
1 careless careful  2 useful useless  3 grated grateful  4 powerless
powerful  5 endingless endless  6 pointful pointless

**Exercise 63.7**
1 yellowish  2 businesslike

## 64 Word families: prefixes
**Exercise 64.1**
1 combine  2 decentralized  3 anticlockwise  4 discontinued
5 subcontract  6 underestimate  7 confirm  8 misinterpret
9 preliminary  10 unload  11 intermediary  12 renegotiate
13 monopoly  14 multitasking

**Exercise 64.2**
1 confirm  2 renegotiate  3 preliminary  4 decentralized
5 multitasking  6 unload  7 discontinued  8 underestimate

**Exercise 64.3**
1 demit  2 comparate  3 missucceed  4 distake  5 undersleep
6 oversided  7 prefirm  8 unturn

**Exercise 64.4**
1 compromise  2 misjudged  3 discourage  4 underused
5 predict  6 unscrew

**Exercise 64.5**
1 unsuccessful  2 non-existent  3 inefficient  4 unpredictable
5 unpopular  6 non-essential

**Exercise 64.6**
1 B  2 C  3 D  4 B  5 A  6 D  7 A

## 65 Word families: revision / extension I
**Exercise 65.1**
1 ability  2 acceptance  3 achieve  4 achievement  5 activity
6 additional  7 advice  8 advisable  9 agreement  10 analysis
11 analyst  12 application  13 attract  14 unavailable
15 benefit  16 budget  17 budget  18 commercialize
19 competitive  20 Competition

**Exercise 65.2**
1 decision  2 delivery  3 differ  4 director  5 distribution
6 economics  7 economical  8 inefficient  9 efficiency
10 unemployed  11 employee  12 expenses  13 expense
14 explanatory  15 extent  16 extend  17 finance  18 growth

**Exercise 65.3**
1 record  2 record  3 transferred  4 transfer

## 66 Word families: revision / extension II
**Exercise 66.1**
1 impressive  2 impression  3 industrialization  4 industry
5 inflationary  6 misinformation  7 informative  8 Innovation
9 innovative  10 insure  11 insurance  12 introductory
13 knowledge  14 unknown  15 legality  16 legislation
17 manageable  18 non-negotiable  19 negotiator  20 offer /
offering

**Exercise 66.2**
1 operational  2 operating  3 optional  4 preference
5 production  6 productive  7 profit  8 profit  9 profitable
10 reliable  11 reliability  12 satisfied  13 unsatisfactory
14 share  15 share  16 sponsorship  17 strength  18 succeed
19 unsuccessful  20 supportive

## 67 Compound nouns
**Exercise 67.1**
1 advertising agency / advertising slogan  2 business deal /
business objectives  3 customer enquiries / customer service(s)
4 market leader / market share  5 product launch / product range
6 production capacity / production plant

**Exercise 67.2**
1 advertising slogan  2 market leader  3 production capacity
4 business deal  5 customer enquiries  6 product range

**Exercise 67.3**
1 business  2 price  3 business  4 market  5 production
6 product

**Exercise 67.4**
1 sales campaign  2 Production costs  3 market price  4 price
range  5 business relationship  6 sales target

**Exercise 67.5**
1 c  2 b  3 customer requirements  4 market survey
5 percentage  6 c  7 product design-product development-product
launch  8 a product features b  product specifications  9 b  10 b

## 68 Compound adjectives
**Exercise 68.1**
1 badly-made  2 duty-free  3 full-length  4 last-minute  5 off-
peak  6 short-term  7 so-called  8 upside-down  9 well-known

**Exercise 68.2**
1 well-known  2 short-term  3 last-minute  4 so-called
5 off-peak

## Exercise 68.3

1 one-way street   2 50-euro note   3 three-bedroom house
4 three-hour   5 20-minute walk   6 six-month project
7 half-finished report   8 two-year MBA

## Exercise 68.4

1 brand-new   2 high-speed   3 mass-produced   4 old-fashioned
5 second-hand   6 trouble-free   7 up-to-date   8 user-friendly

## Exercise 68.5

1 brand-new   2 old-fashioned   3 user-friendly   4 high-speed
5 trouble-free / up-to-date

## Exercise 68.6

1 top-of-the-range   2 down-market   3 upscale   4 low-end
5 value-for-money

## Exercise 68.7

1 well-maintained   2 hand-held   3 year-round   4 government-
funded / interest-free (or long- or short-term)   5 round-table (or high-
level) / worst case

# 69 Word partners (collocation) I

## Exercise 69.1

1 makes   2 set up   3 run   4 grew   5 take over   6 restructure
7 join   8 expand   9 leave   10 closed down

## Exercise 69.2

1 renegotiate   2 go over   3 amend   4 draw up   5 get out of
6 keep to

## Exercise 69.3

1 meet   2 absorb   3 figure out   4 spread   5 cover

## Exercise 69.4

1 ~~for~~ with   2 ~~of~~ from   3 ~~to~~ with   4 ~~from~~ of   5 ~~across~~ over
6 ~~from~~ of   7 ~~with~~ of   8 ~~by~~ to

## Exercise 69.5

1 costs   2 contract   3 company   4 customer

# 70 Word partners (collocation) II

## Exercise 70.1

1 come onto the market   2 customize a product   3 disrupt
production   4 employ staff   5 lay off staff   6 put in an order
7 sell out of a product   8 ship an order   9 start production
10 take over the market

## Exercise 70.2

1 lay off staff   2 come onto the market   3 start production
4 put in an order   5 customize a product

## Exercise 70.3

1 ~~export~~   2 ~~develop~~   3 ~~win~~   4 ~~employ~~   5 ~~distribute~~

## Exercise 70.4

1 flooding   2 processed   3 charge   4 roll out   5 hit

## Exercise 70.5

1 shrinking   2 dried up   3 went out   4 are tied to   5 rise
6 sold out   7 reached   8 account for

## Exercise 70.6

1 hire and fire   2 hold / speed

## Exercise 70.7

1 price   2 staff   3 order   4 product   5 market   6 production

# Interviews with business people

## 1 An interview with an accountant

1 income statement / balance sheet   2 an indirect cost
3 net profit   4 dividends / shareholders

## 2 An interview with a B2B commercial director

1 b / d   2 b   3 pharmacists

## 3 An interview with a bank manager

1 In the interview the bank manager says that he organized a weekly
breakfast for everyone where they chatted informally and he gave a
verbal report.
2 In the interview the bank manager says that in these meetings he
discussed individual and team bonuses, training, job rotation and
promotion.

## 4 An interview with an events organizer

1 T   2 T   3 F   4 T   5 F   6 F   7 F   8 F

## 5 An interview with a specialized manufacturer

1 S   2 W   3 T   4 O   5 W   6 S   7 T   8 O

## 6 An interview with a negotiator

1 specifications, quality, terms of payment, delivery   2 a / c
3 parts per million

## 7 An interview with a freight forwarder

1 a Monday   b Tuesday   c Wednesday   d Thursday   e Thursday
2 b

## 8 An interview with an investment banker

1 a raising funds   b IPO   c M&A
2 a underwriting   b due diligence
3 The investment banker mentions accountants, lawyers and
consultants.

## 9 An interview with a consultant working internationally

1 a Japan   b China   c United States   d UK   e Germany
2 b

## 10 An interview with a sales director

1 soft drinks   2 franchisor / franchisee   3 No, marketing is the
responsibility of the franchisor   4 car parks

## 11 An interview with a takeover specialist

1 doesn't like   2 keeps   3 cut costs   4 too many employees
5 doesn't feel sympathy

## 12 An interview with an exporter

1 Because they take more product from the exporter and so buy it at
a cheaper price.
2 check the competitor's products and prices; see what price their
own products are selling for; check how their products are displayed
on the shelves
3 a open account   b letter of credit   c cash in advance